Doing Diversity in Higher Education

Doing Diversity in Higher Education

Faculty Leaders Share Challenges and Strategies

EDITED BY

WINNIFRED R. BROWN-GLAUDE

RUTGERS UNIVERSITY PRESS

NEW BRUNSWICK, NEW JERSEY, AND LONDON

LIBRARY OF CONGRESS CATALOGING-IN-PUBLICATION DATA

Doing diversity in higher education: faculty leaders share challenges and strategies / edited by Winnifred R. Brown-Glaude.

    p. cm.

Includes bibliographical references and index.

ISBN 978-0-8135-4446-5 (hardcover : alk. paper)

ISBN 978-0-8135-4447-2 (pbk. : alk. paper)

1. Faculty integration—United States. 2. Multiculturalism—United States. 3. Universities and colleges—Faculty—United States. I. Brown-Glaude, Winnifred R., 1966–

LB2332.6.D65 2008

378.1'9829—dc22   2008013953

A British Cataloging-in-Publication record for this book is available from the British Library.

Visit our Web site: http://rutgerspress.rutgers.edu

Manufactured in the United States of America

CONTENTS

PART ONE
Diversity and/as Intellectual Leadership

PART FOUR
Administration–Faculty Collaborations for Diversity

FOREWORD

Faculty as Change Agents–Reflections on My Academic Life

CHERYL A. WALL

For most people in the 1970s, the image of a college professor was a bearded gray-haired white man in a corduroy blazer with patches at the elbow. I did not look the part. When I joined the English department of Douglass College, I was twenty-three years old, with a short Afro and two years of graduate study at Harvard under my belt. Alienated by the ostentatious elitism of Harvard—not to mention the sexism—I was on a mission to find out whether I wanted an academic career. I answered an ad in the New York Times, was interviewed on campus that summer, and started teaching in September. Although there was no official mentoring program, another black woman, Adrianne Baytop, took me under her wing. A specialist in the Renaissance, Adrianne was tenured. She gave me tips on teaching, monitored my progress toward my PhD, and introduced me to the culture of the institution. At the time, I took her presence for granted. But I soon learned how rare my experience was and is: I have never been the only woman or the only African American in my department.

At Douglass, a women's college, I did not have to defend the legitimacy of scholarship that focused on gender and race. To the contrary, I worked with a community of scholars who were defining the new field of women's studies. The faculty was small enough that people moved easily across departments. Whether in English, history, sociology, or classics, we were asking similar questions. We were eager to share and test our findings both in person and on the page. While the leading journals were not yet welcoming—one famous editor warned junior faculty in my department not to submit anything on women because the topic was just trendy—a bevy of new journals appeared, many with "women" and "feminist" or "black" or "Afro-American" in their titles. We had places to publish and peers to review our work. We were also figuring out what a feminist pedagogy would be. Arranging desks in a circle, encouraging students to start discussions, requiring them to keep journals, and commenting on each other's work reduced the hierarchy of the classroom. Of course, it was not difficult to cede authority that I did not yet possess. In addition to my youth, I was working in the young field of African American literary study. Everything was open for discussion.

Three decades later, fields such as Africana studies, Chicano studies, Ethnic studies, and Women's studies have transformed the curriculum in traditional disciplines. For example, not only are African American history and literature courses now regularly taught, but that teaching and research has raised theoretical questions and uncovered lost texts that compelled a reconceptualization of American history and literature. Some years ago I heard a lecture given by one of the leading scholars of American literature. He spoke about Ralph Waldo Emerson and the idea of "Representative Men." He mentioned that he had recently concluded that Frederick Douglass was the American who best met Emerson's definition. Graciously, he thanked the black graduate student who had helped him achieve this understanding. Those of us who had taught the graduate student in our black literature classes reacted ambivalently, but we were pleased for the student who received this public affirmation. Today, my younger colleagues who are Americanists take for granted the importance of Frederick Douglass and Harriet Jacobs to nineteenth-century American literature. In most cases, it was what they were taught. This example comes from my field, but it can be replicated across disciplines. The impact of new knowledge that begins on the margins, if you will, re-forms the center. Indeed, it reconfigures the relationship of margin to center.

Other things have also changed. The Douglass College faculty was disbanded in the 1980s. The twenty-member English department was incorporated into a New Brunswick–wide department that numbered over eighty. I became undergraduate director for the department; then in 1997 I was elected chair. By that time I taught graduate students regularly, served on scores of departmental and university committees, and had mentored several young colleagues, though none quite as young and "green" as I had been. In the process I had learned something about how students learn, how scholars develop, and how institutions work.

My experiences are not unusual. Consequently, I was disturbed by the absence of voices like mine in the conversations and debates around affirmative action. Especially during the months leading up to the 2003 University of Michigan case, many other voices spoke loud and clear: university presidents, university counsel, and students on all sides of the issue. Both supporters and opponents outside the university weighed in: from the amicus briefs filed by corporate and military leaders who spoke in favor of retaining race as a factor in admissions decisions and from representatives of groups with names, misleading names, such as the Center for Equal Opportunity and the Center for Individual Rights, that spoke against it. What I did not hear—or at least not nearly loudly enough—were the voices of faculty who should be in the best position to evaluate the difference diversity makes in the classroom and across the curriculum. Who knew better, moreover, how to attract and prepare young people for academic careers than those of us who had pursued them?

Many colleagues on my home campus had spent years developing programs that broadened access to the university and provided academic support for students after they were admitted. I knew colleagues who had single-handedly or in small alliances mentored undergraduate and graduate students in numbers that enhanced the diversity demographic in their fields. Most of these efforts took place "under the radar," as it were; they were invisible to the larger university community, not to mention to the larger world. Although I have come to understand and respect the reluctance of some truly noble individuals to have the spotlight turned on their programs, I believe that faculty across the nation, many of whom work in much more hostile environments than that at Rutgers, would learn much from examples that I know well and admire.

One of these illustrates for me both the great potential that we as individual faculty members have to become change agents and the high price that this work sometimes exacts. Diversity work is too often seen as "service" that is totally unrelated to the teaching and research that are at the core of the faculty role. This service is sometimes dismissed as "institutional housekeeping," a phrase that further diminishes work that is more often than not performed by women and people of color. The truth is that diversity work is intellectual work. It requires imaginative thought, critical analysis, and careful study. It has the potential to transform not only the institutions of higher learning in which we work but the society that these institutions serve. Unfortunately, the current system of rewards does not recognize its value. For that reason, the story that follows inspires caution as well as celebration.

Known by her admirers as the Indomitable Dr. E., Francine Essien, professor of biological sciences emerita, joined the faculty of Douglass College in 1971. As an assistant professor, she was assigned to teach general biology and other introductory courses. Almost immediately, Essien began setting up tutorial sessions for students who were having difficulty. She also began advising students who had done well on the curriculum they needed to follow in order to pursue medical careers. Trained in genetics at the Albert Einstein College of Medicine at Yeshiva University, Essien set up her first lab at Douglass, where she began the research that eventually identified genetic mutations in mice that she hoped would provide insight into human birth defects, spina bifida in particular. Soon after setting up her lab, she invited students to assist with her research. As she once explained to an interviewer, "I do my teaching with love, but it's in relation to my research. I'm very proud of the fact that students can come into my lab, take part in research, be independent, and express their ideas." Her students were often named as coauthors on the many research papers and abstracts she published in academic and scientific journals.

Essien's diversity work was first given institutional form in 1986, when the Office of Minority Science Programs was established; she was its director. Currently known as the Office for Diversity and Academic Success in the Sciences (ODASIS), its goals are to increase significantly the recruitment of students from underrepresented groups who are interested in pursuing careers in the sciences, technical, or allied health professions; to increase the retention rates for these students by providing a supportive learning environment; and to increase the rate of students entering graduate or professional schools.

Early on Essien struggled to identify supporters. Her program needed resources and respect. In several ways, the latter was more difficult to achieve. She had to persuade her colleagues that the program should exist. Why should special programs be created for minority students? Mainstream students had to be highly competitive in order to succeed. No special treatment should be accorded anyone. Again and again, Essien argued that unequal preparation disadvantaged minority students. What her program was doing was leveling the playing field. She secured funding from the administration, then partnered with various programs on campus in order to provide tutors for her students. Eventually, she garnered support from other universities, especially the University of Medicine and Dentistry of New Jersey, local public schools, corporations, and foundations. But early on Dr. E. relied mainly on herself.

Essien worked six and sometimes seven days a week. She held office hours in the evening in order to be more available to her students. She called them over Christmas vacations to express her confidence in them and to renew their confidence in themselves. When money ran out for books and stipends, Francine Essien was often "the anonymous donor" whose contributions arrived in the nick of time. Her story highlights for me both the enormous potential that individual faculty members have to effect change and the high price these efforts exact. Her contributions did not go unacknowledged: the Carnegie Foundation for the Advancement of Teaching selected Francine Essien from a field of 192 national candidates to be the 1994–95 U.S. Professor of the Year for Research and Doctoral Universities. But hers is a story of self-sacrifice that goes beyond what any institution should expect of its faculty. Many of her colleagues believe that Dr. E. worked herself into ill health and premature retirement. To be sure, the program that she created was larger than any individual—let alone an individual who was still very much committed to a regular program of teaching and research—could have sustained.

But there is much about the way Francine Essien went about her work that we might try to emulate. With appropriate support, her approach is the kind that produces significant and lasting change. For example, she recognized that to create the change she hoped for, she had to adopt a comprehensive approach. The core program is "Success in the Sciences," which enrolls students in their first year. It provides structured and intense tutoring, advising, mentoring, motivation, and enrichment. At the end of their undergraduate careers, these students are poised to pursue professional and graduate study. Undergraduates were only one target population. She sought funding for graduate fellowships and stipends on the one hand, and for high school programs on the other. The high school program serves students from New Brunswick and Plainfield, two urban school districts in New Jersey with predominantly poor African American and Latino populations. The goal is to pique students' interest in science. Initially, the focus was on eleventh- and twelfth-graders, but the intervention came too late for twelfth-graders, and the program was redesigned for tenth- and eleventh-graders. When it became clear that students who were encouraged by their parents succeeded at a higher rate, support sessions were scheduled for parents; in New Brunswick, these sessions are available in Spanish as well as English.

At the other end of the spectrum is ACCESS-MED, a program that ODASIS has administered since 1991. Offered by an institutional consortium that includes Rutgers University, Robert Wood Johnson Medical School, and Seton Hall University, ACCESS-MED serves underrepresented minority and economically disadvantaged undergraduate students. The program is organized into two phases. Juniors participating in Phase I may choose to apply to various medical schools or to Phase II of the program, in which they may gain early admission to Robert Wood Johnson Medical School in their senior year at Rutgers.

The program now serves one thousand students annually. In the decade from 1997 to 2007, 145 ODASIS graduates have earned their MDs, and 229 have gone on to become chiropractors, dentists, physician's assistants, podiatrists, doctors of osteopathy, or are pursuing other health-allied professions. These numbers reflect the intellectual capacity and hard work of these students and their teachers; they reflect the commitment of administrators and the support of institutions and corporations. But they are an eloquent testimony to one woman's vision.

The great value of this book is that it begins to document stories like that of Francine Essien. The book describes curriculum transformation projects, mentoring programs, K–12 outreach initiatives, partnerships between diverse institutions of higher learning, and efforts at institutional transformation. Some succeeded. Others did not. But all affirm the power of individuals to make a difference. They constitute a set of adaptable models and cautionary tales. Collectively, they raise a series of questions and challenges:

- How can we expand the definitions of intellectual work to include the initiatives undertaken by faculty to enhance diversity in their disciplines?

- How can we acknowledge and celebrate those faculty members who devote their time and talent to work that advances scholarship in their discipline and at the same time serves the citizenry at large?
- How can we encourage younger faculty members to consider diversity work as an extension of their teaching and scholarship rather than a distraction from them?
- What would it mean if individuals and the programs they initiate received institutional support proportional to the benefit they bring the institution?

If we believe that we are doing a good job of educating students to live and work in an increasingly diverse nation and in a world that grows smaller every day, it is time that we began saying so. *Doing Diversity in Higher Education* begins a conversation among faculty—as well as among administrators, students, and alumni—who are advocates and agents for change.

ACKNOWLEDGMENTS

This project is the result of a collaborative effort that grew out of a conversation in 2002 with Gertrude Fraser, who at that time was the program officer of the Education, Knowledge and Religion Unit at the Ford Foundation. Mary Hartman and Lisa Hetfield, director and associate director of the Institute for Women's Leadership (IWL), Rutgers University, had approached her with a different research project but left that meeting with great excitement about a new research idea—"Reaffirming Action: Designs for Diversity in Higher Education." I am grateful to Gertrude Fraser for her vision, and to the Ford Foundation, especially Irma McClaurin (program officer, 2005 to 2007), for helping the Institute for Women's Leadership to make this vision a reality.

I am grateful to all of our faculty teams from the twelve participating colleges and universities for their hard work in carefully uncovering and documenting the efforts of their colleagues as they try to create a more inclusive campus environment. I appreciate their painstaking writing and rewriting of their reports and chapters. I am particularly appreciative of the support of the administrators and university presidents of the twelve participating institutions who welcomed the "Reaffirming Action" project and graciously agreed to meet with me, the co-principal investigators, and the associate director of the IWL during our campus visits to talk frankly about diversity on their campuses.

I am thankful to the Rutgers University administration—particularly the Office of the President, Dr. Richard L. McCormick, for ongoing support. I appreciate, too, the encouragement for this project from Dr. Philip Furmanski, Senior Executive Vice President for Academic Affairs. I am especially grateful to the Office of Faculty Diversity Initiatives created by Dr. McCormick and directed by Dr. Karen Stubaus for taking steps toward implementing the vision of "Reaffirming Action" at Rutgers, as well as for logistical support.

The IWL Board of Directors has been an invaluable partner throughout the development of the "Reaffirming Action" project. Consisting of officers of the seven member units of the IWL consortium—the Center for American Women and Politics, the Center for Women and Work, the Center for

Women's Global Leadership, the Department of Women's and Gender Studies, Douglass Residential College, the Institute for Research on Women, and the Institute for Women and Art—this advisory group has been critical in shaping the project. I thank them all. I also thank Carolyn Kumah, Danielle Phillips, and Rhokeun Park, graduate students at Rutgers University, for their hard work on the project. I am grateful to Pat Dooley, office manager at the Institute for Women's Leadership, for her technical and administrative expertise throughout the years of this project and beyond.

I am indebted to Marlie Wasserman at Rutgers University Press for her patience and guidance throughout the years as this project took shape. I especially appreciate her enthusiasm regarding this project. I thank the project editor and copy editor at Rutgers University along with Dawn Potter for their meticulous work in bringing this book smoothly to publication.

Throughout this project the "Reaffirming Action" team at Rutgers has learned to work with colleagues across various campuses and disciplines. This has been a tremendous experience that I will always carry with me. I want to thank Mary Hartman and Cheryl Wall, co-principal investigators of the "Reaffirming Action" study. You have not only been supportive colleagues but also mentors. Thank you both for your leadership, wisdom, and expertise, which you display with incredible style. I also want to thank Lisa Hetfield, associate director of the IWL, for your vision and uncanny ability to ask tough and practical questions with a soft-spoken elegance. It has been my pleasure working with you all and I look forward to future collaborations.

Last, but certainly not least, I thank my family, Eddie and Langston Glaude, for their love and support. You are my rock.

Doing Diversity in Higher Education

Introduction

Listen to the Submerged Voices—Faculty Agency in a Challenging Climate

WINNIFRED R. BROWN-GLAUDE

On June 28, 2007, in a landmark decision destined to affect school districts across the country, the U.S. Supreme Court struck down two voluntary school-integration plans, one in Louisville, Kentucky, and the other in Seattle, Washington. The Court's ruling in these joined cases challenged voluntary integration policies in K–12 schools, maintaining that such policies discriminate on the basis of race. The Court's conservative majority found that the schools' methods for achieving racial diversity went too far. According to Justice John Roberts, the districts "failed to show that they considered methods other than explicit racial classifications to achieve their stated goals." Rejecting arguments for the use of race-based distinctions to remedy societal discrimination, he opined, "The way to stop discrimination on the basis of race is to stop discriminating on the basis of race" (Greenberg and de Vogue 2007).

In a concurring opinion, Justice Anthony Kennedy agreed that the Louisville and Seattle school integration plans went too far, but he disagreed with Roberts and other Court conservatives' view that race may almost never be considered as a factor in school integration efforts. Instead, Kennedy argued that race may be a component of school plans to achieve diversity, leaving the door slightly ajar to all school districts that are contemplating future options. Although these cases concerned K–12 schools, many educational leaders, civil rights attorneys, and higher education officials also kept a close eye on them, especially because they drew on the legal briefs from the 2003 *Grutter v. Bollinger* Supreme Court ruling involving the University of Michigan's Law School, which upheld the right of institutions in some circumstances to consider race in admissions. Many who defended that right feared that the Seattle and Louisville cases would give the Supreme Court an opportunity to attack the *Grutter* decision. They were relieved when that did not happen.

1

What the Louisville and Washington cases have exposed, nonetheless, is continuing, organized opposition to efforts to redress the effects of past discrimination and improve educational access for underrepresented groups. The cases showed once again that public discussion of these topics has increasingly been influenced by critics who claim that the goal of equality is being replaced by a system of racial preferences that runs counter to the American creed. In this narrative, whites are portrayed as victims of reverse discrimination in dramas designed to fuel resentment of any attempt to achieve greater racial balance in education. Meanwhile, public supporters of policies that take race into account are not focusing on the many arguments that support their views, including the demonstrable, universal benefits of diverse classrooms, curricula, and teachers. Instead, they have understandably felt obliged to devote their energies to rebutting the critics, reminding them of real, if polarizing, evidence that people of color everywhere in the United States continue to be regularly discriminated against, even in institutions of primary, secondary, and higher education.

These opposed stances, in various articulations, occupy center stage in ongoing public forums on affirmative action and diversity in education. While such forums may exemplify some of the best qualities of a democracy, such as an ability to engage divergent perspectives, it is striking and troubling that those most deeply involved in education "on the ground"—namely, K–12 teachers and college and university professors—are not playing a more central role in public debates on diversity. These individuals have firsthand experience with the effects of diverse classrooms and curricula (or the lack thereof) on their students' learning outcomes. Yet save for a small, vocal group of largely white male faculty, many of whom have migrated to think tanks supported by right-wing funders, the voices of a much larger group of classroom educators and research scholars—those who argue in favor of the positive effects of affirmative action and diversity—are rarely heard in public.

This book is part of a wider effort to change the debate by focusing on the transformative work of a group of largely unsung and overworked faculty members who are leading diversity initiatives in the academy. They turn out to be primarily older tenured women and faculty of color, joined by a hardy if smaller group of older tenured white male allies. As far as I am aware, no collective account of their activities has ever been published. The Ford Foundation generously gave the Institute for Women's Leadership at Rutgers University the opportunity to gather and present these stories, challenging us to identify faculty members in a variety of American institutions of higher learning who have taken the lead in creating and supporting diversity initiatives. Included here is a four-year research project (2004–2007) exploring the work of faculty teams at twelve colleges and universities who have invented and promoted new organizational structures, policies, practices, leadership networks, cultures, and programs that are contributing to successful and sustainable progress in gender and racial equity.

Aware that public discussion of affirmative action and diversity continues to focus chiefly on race, the Ford Foundation encouraged the Institute for Women's Leadership to explore more inclusive definitions and visions of diversity. It welcomed our proposal not only to broaden the representation of race and ethnicity beyond simplistic categories of black versus white but also to include gender, especially given that both women and persons of color remain relatively scarce among faculty and high-level administrators. Even among students, all women and students of color continue to be underrepresented within major fields such as mathematics, the sciences, and engineering; women are also grossly underrepresented among candidates for graduate degrees in these fields—despite the fact that female undergraduates now surpass the number of male undergraduates. While this book's central emphasis is on faculty members as change agents in leading and supporting a range of diversity initiatives, we also pay attention to the very different institutional contexts in which they operate: public and private institutions, women's colleges, historically black institutions, an Ivy League school, a midwestern state university, and more.

A Challenging Climate

The Louisville and Seattle court cases, and others like them, show that public discussions on affirmative action and diversity are greatly influenced by opponents' approaches to structuring the debates. Often race is the focal point, with opponents arguing that these policies and programs endorse a system of racial preferences while supporters declare that such policies are needed to remedy ongoing discrimination against people of color, particularly in jobs and education. But close interrogation of both sides of the debate reveals two problems. First, the debates emphasize the policies while overlooking the broader problems those policies are trying to address. Second, by focusing on race, they treat gender and class as marginal issues.

Policies versus Problems

Affirmative action is a redistributive measure to enhance the standard of living and quality of life for all Americans. In the educational system its policies are aimed at guaranteeing a quality education for all students, many of whom have been denied access because of racial segregation, gender, and class barriers. In their impassioned reactions to affirmative action policies, both opponents and proponents often overlook the persistence of structural inequalities that necessitate some form of governmental intervention.[1] Moreover, each side describes the underlying problems in fundamentally different ways. Although affirmative action policies have helped women and people of color make inroads into academe, inequalities persist. These policies have not been as intrusive as critics have charged or as effective as advocates have hoped. White men continue to dominate in institutions of higher learning (Rai and Critzer 2000). In 2007, for instance, African Americans made up 5 percent of full-time faculty in our nation's colleges and universities and less than 3 percent in the highest-ranking colleges and universities. According to the American Council on Education between 1993 and 2003, college enrollment of African American, Native American, and Hispanic students rose by 42.7, 38.7, and 68.8 percent respectively. Yet the study also showed that graduation rates for African American students (36.4 percent) and Hispanic students (42 percent) fell behind the rates for white students (58 percent) and Asian students (62.3 percent). When we examine the distribution of students who earn doctoral and professional degrees, African Americans, Hispanics, and Native Americans are poorly represented, especially in science, technology, engineering, and mathematics (the STEM disciplines) (Borden and Brown 2003).

Regarding women in the academy, current trends are somewhat more positive, yet they remain troublesome. The American Association of University Professors reported that, in school year 2005–2006, women accounted for 39 percent of full-time faculty while men accounted for 61 percent. When we examine rank, we find that only 31 percent of women held tenured positions in comparison to 69 percent of men; of those tenured women only 24 percent were ranked as full professors (West and Curtis 2006). Among all races, more women than men are attending colleges, and they are earning bachelor's degrees at higher rates than men. Yet men, particularly white men, continue to earn the majority of professional and doctoral degrees, especially in the STEM disciplines. These figures are significant given the importance of post-baccalaureate degrees for entry into the highest-paying jobs.

Our national class trends are just as troubling. According to a recent Century Foundation study, 74 percent of students attending top-tier schools come from families in the top quarter of the social and economic scale. Just 3 percent come from the bottom of the scale, and roughly 10 percent come from the working and lower classes (Carnevale and Rose 2003; Sacks 2003). This suggests that most working- and lower-class students are attending state colleges and universities as opposed to private and elite institutions. But most states have been cutting their funding for state universities, which has triggered annual tuition hikes to offset this loss. Students are left to absorb these hikes, which are rising faster than their family incomes and more sharply than state or federal grant aid. A 2003 report from the College Board demonstrated that, while total college charges at four-year public institutions represent 5 to 6 percent of the income of families from the highest income quintile, they represent 19 percent of family income for middle-income families and 71 percent for low-income families (College Board 2003).

Very few states have made serious efforts to assist students in need. In fact, some states, like Georgia, have moved away from need-based financial aid packages to ones that are merit-based, a trend that adversely affects working- and lower-class students (Mortenson 2000). The College Board's 2006 report on student aid shows that, from 1995 to 2006, financial aid in the form of grants has steadily declined. As a result, the rate of borrowing among students has increased exponentially: federal loans now constitute 51 percent of total aid (College Board 2006). This means that more students, especially those from the lower classes, are graduating from college and entering the labor market with substantial debt. All these factors exacerbate class differences among students, decrease college enrollment among students from the working and lower classes, and contribute to our society's widening economic gap.

Solving these deep-rooted structural inequities requires multiple strategies, including affirmative action policies and diversity programs. But public discussion on the topic is disturbingly subdued, tending to focus on the content of specific policies while obscuring actual problems of social inequality. So how do we revitalize these debates?

As we think about answers to this question, we must be careful not to conflate the history and structural effects of race with those of class. A pressing issue in the debates has been whether race-based affirmative action and diversity programs are still relevant today or if socioeconomic status is the principle barrier to a quality education. While it is difficult to overlook our country's growing economic inequalities, we must be careful not to ignore the continued significance of race, both as an issue in its own right and as it intertwines with class inequality. Indeed, while lower-class students of all races confront the challenges of affording a quality education, the combined effects of race and class compound the experiences of lower-class students of color.

In their classic study, *American Apartheid*, Douglass Massey and Nancy Denton have demonstrated that racial residential segregation is much higher among African Americans than among any other racial or ethnic group in the United States (Massey and Denton 1998). These patterns of segregation are the result, in large part, of racially discriminatory practices in the housing market, which lock most lower-class blacks into disadvantaged neighborhoods with poor-quality schools.[2] The hyperconcentration of racialized poverty among African Americans, especially in the inner cities, places them at a great disadvantage among the lower classes as a whole. The issue, then, is not simply helping lower-class students pay for a quality education but examining broader structural impediments to their K–12 preparation for college.

Emphasis on Race

In public debates, race is often simplified into binary categories: black versus white. The particular experiences of individual racial groups such as Asian Americans, Native Americans, and Hispanic Americans are either lumped with blacks into the broad minority category or they vanish from the discussion altogether. Thus, the impact of affirmative action policies on Native Americans, who are vastly underrepresented in higher education, is not debated, and the experiences of Asian Americans, whose reactions to affirmative action policies are mixed and ambiguous, are not adequately addressed (Potter 2003; Schmidt 2003). A narrowly defined conception of race also ignores the fact that white women are the primary beneficiaries of affirmative action policies. When discussions center on race, many white women remain ambivalent, inactive, or even opposed to policies from which they benefit, creating divisions among women and constraining social action.

Most troubling in these debates is the way in which whiteness has been redefined and re-presented. As a racial category, whiteness has historically signified privilege, but that privilege, like whiteness itself, has also been treated as invisible (McIntosh 1990). In discussions of affirmative action and diversity, however, whiteness has become politicized, it is now visible, but its privileges remain hidden so that whiteness can be redefined as a disadvantage (Winant 1997). Whites are often presented as victims of affirmative action policies, which are described as mechanisms of reverse racial discrimination. This argument's success is a tribute to the skillful ways in which neoconservative opponents have captured the civil rights movement's language of equality, reshaped it to promote their own agendas, and thus reversed the movement's goal of expanding resources and access to all citizens.

Global Implications of Structural Inequality

The purpose of higher education is not only to impart knowledge to students but also to prepare them to become productive workers. Yet the labor market has become more complex. Because advances in technology drive globalization, the new global worker must have sophisticated and adaptable technological skills as well as the ability to interact with a diverse citizenry, both locally and globally.

In debates on affirmative action and diversity in higher education, there is often tension between individual needs and qualifications versus institutional needs and obligations, and the realities of globalization complicate these tensions. Opponents of affirmative action tend to emphasize individual needs and qualifications, which they often articulate as arguments for merit. That viewpoint, however, does not take into account institutional obligations to all students.

Many economists, including Alan Greenspan, former chairman of the board of governors of the Federal Reserve, predict a shortage of skilled workers in North America, partly due to rapidly evolving technology and the inability of U.S. workers to keep up with global transformations (Greenspan 2001). The fact that white women and men and women of color are vastly underrepresented in STEM disciplines can only contribute to this labor shortage. Institutions of higher education, then, need to offer a larger and more diverse body of students the skills they need to flourish in our new economy.

In *Grutter v. Bollinger*, the U.S. Supreme Court agreed that colleges have a compelling interest in enrolling a racially diverse student body: not only does exposure to diverse ideas and perspectives broaden students' intellectual development but, as Justice O'Connor and others have noted, universities train large numbers of our nation's leaders. According to the Court, institutions of higher education must cultivate future leaders who will have legitimacy in the eyes of a diverse citizenry (Madden and Bigelow Leedom 2003). Diversity, in other words, is an obligation.

Learning from the Academy's Submerged Voices

Those of us who care about education and have been listening to the debates on affirmative action and diversity find it remarkable that the voices of our teachers and faculty members have not been heard. Most have thought deeply about the complexity of these issues, and many have developed creative ways to address the inequities they encounter daily in classrooms and on college campuses. Many have sophisticated understandings of race that expand binary categories and recognize the continued privileges of whiteness. Their experiences with and conceptualizations of diversity defy one-dimensional conceptions of inequality and difference and illuminate multiple and intersecting structures of power. Most important, they have worked relentlessly through curriculum development, institute building, mentoring, and research to transform their institutions into more equitable environments for themselves and their students.

This book shares the stories of faculty leaders who are committed to diversity and educational excellence. It describes how they conceptualize the complex challenges of diversity on their campuses and develop various strategies for change. As we read their narratives, we learn who these leaders are and why they work so hard to diversify their campuses. We learn about the outcomes of their efforts and what kinds of environments encourage and discourage faculty engagement. Most vitally, we learn about the important roles that faculty members continue to play in moving their institutions toward "inclusive excellence."[3]

This book is the result of a four-year study funded by the Ford Foundation. Titled "Reaffirming Action: Designs for Diversity in Higher Education," the project emphasized the role of faculty change agents in leading and supporting progress toward diversity, pinpointing specific strategies they used to initiate and support organizational structures, policies, practices, leadership, networks, cultures, and programs that work toward racial and gender equity. Twelve institutions participated in the study: Clark-Atlanta University, Columbia University, Rutgers University, Smith College, Spelman College, the University of Arizona, the University of California–Davis, the University of California–Santa Barbara, the University of Maryland, the University of Miami, the University of Missouri–Columbia, and the University of Vermont. The selection included women's colleges, historically black colleges, public and private institutions, Ivy League and Research I institutions, and those from regions with significant concentrations of certain populations (for example, Hispanic). This rich variety helped us examine the complex ways in which diversity is defined and practiced in higher education and provided a wide array of models for institutional change.

A key argument in "Reaffirming Action" was that barriers related to race and gender equality are embedded in institutions' organizational structures and practices. Consequently, systemic change has been difficult to achieve, as evidenced by the lagging rates of people of color and women who acquire advanced degrees and hold senior faculty posts or academic leadership positions. Yet while these barriers do exist, faculty members have managed in different ways to break them down, demonstrating time and time again various models of leadership for change.

The theoretical framework that guided this study was influenced by feminist scholarship, particularly the theory of gendered organizations, which demonstrates not only that gender is present in apparently neutral institutional processes, practices, and power structures but also that organizational practices play a central role in re-creating gender hierarchies, symbols, and identities (Acker 1990). Indeed, most organizations have "inequality regimes" that produce and maintain class, gender, and racial inequalities among their members; and as a result, social equality has been difficult to achieve (Acker 2006).

Drawing on this scholarship, the study asked, "If barriers to gender and racial equity are embedded in organizational structures and practices of higher education, what, if anything, are the people who are also embedded in these organizations doing to potentially transform them?" This question assumes that social structures are not all-determining, that human beings can act intentionally to bring about change. And as this book will show, faculty change agents have done exactly that.

As a complement to the study we've commissioned a survey hoping to learn more about themes that emerged in the case studies and to get answers to questions about faculty motivation for diversity work and differences in generational perspectives. Although we are still in the early phases of this portion of the "Reaffirming Action" study, preliminary analyses suggest a number of intriguing findings. We've learned that minority faculty are far more likely to be associated with diversity efforts than majority faculty, and a disproportionate number of faculty activists were women. Moreover, the faculty who gave their time and energy to diversity matters were not simply focused on diversity. These faculty members were engaged with their campus community in all kinds of ways that distinguish them from their nonactivist colleagues. They serve on more committees of every kind, more frequently take on administrative roles, and were more likely to have served as department chairs than their nonactivist colleagues. Many saw themselves as being effective in their various roles and also were more likely to believe that the contributions of faculty change agents were not well rewarded by their institutions. Although we are still learning more about the activities of faculty from these surveys, the preliminary data are quite promising. The data show that the faculty activists in these twelve case studies are not alone. To be sure, faculty across the nation who are committed to their students and their universities are working relentlessly to create a more inclusive learning environment for all.

Doing Diversity in Higher Education: Faculty Leaders Share Challenges and Strategies provides a comprehensive and complicated picture of diversity in higher education, showing that institutional change happens "on the ground." Notably, the contributors reject worn and simplistic conceptions of diversity as service work separate from and less important than academic excellence. Instead, they treat diversity as central to excellence. For many faculty change agents, diversity work is an intellectual project in which students and scholars ask questions about issues that often fall outside their intellectual canons and thus generate new knowledge that expands their individual fields. The contributors also resist a one-dimensional conception of diversity, focusing instead on diversity as a multilayered process—evidenced in one way at historically black institutions, in other ways at the intersection of race and gender, in still other ways as diversity interacts with religion and sexuality. In this fashion, the contributors disclose the complex ways in which power operates and is negotiated in institutions of higher learning.

Doing Diversity in Higher Education is organized around four themes that emerged out of the "Reaffirming Action" research project: (1) diversity and/as intellectual leadership, (2) dismantling or challenging hostile climates, (3) the challenges of incomplete institutionalization, and (4) administration-faculty collaborations for diversity. In part 1 of the book, we learn how faculty members created change at the University of Maryland, Spelman College, and the University of Missouri–Columbia. A common theme is a reconceptualization of diversity and diversity work as intellectual endeavors. The faculty leaders in these chapters do not think about diversity as separate from their own intellectual projects but transform their diversity scholarship into social action to improve the campus climate for themselves and their students. Chapter 1 discusses the ongoing transformation of the University of Maryland campus climate, tracing the life histories of three influential scholars who specialize in the study of intersectionality and have dedicated much of their academic lives to creating a just and democratic university community. Chapter 2 traces the development of "The African Diaspora and the World," a faculty-designed, two-semester, required course that disrupted notions of sameness at Spelman College, an all-black, all-female campus. In chapter 3, the authors present a series of case studies supporting the argument that, for many faculty members, diversity work is intellectual work and should be valued as such.

Part 2 examines campus cultures in which faculty engage in diversity work. Although the three campuses under study (Smith, Clark-Atlanta, and UC–Davis) are vastly different, all effectively illustrate the complex power relations that faculty have to negotiate as they develop strategies for change. Chapter 4 studies the revolving-door phenomenon at Smith College. The authors investigate campus microclimates such as departments, committees, and reading groups, arguing that these sites help explain why Smith's retention rate is declining. Chapter 5 considers gender-based discrimination practices challenging women STEM faculty at historically black colleges and universities. Through interviews with these women, the authors begin to develop a framework that explains their unique and overlooked experiences. Chapter 6 paints a vivid picture of faculty work outside a university system as a way to create change within it. It describes strategies devised by two faculty change agents to reverse the negative effects of the passage of California's Proposition 209 on the number of women faculty hires at the University of California–Davis.

Part 3 shows how faculty members at Rutgers University, the University of Arizona, and the University of Miami have tried to transform their campuses by developing institutes to attract diverse students and faculty and to use campus-wide committees to implement strategies for change. While these efforts have enjoyed some success, the chapters also emphasize the critical need for long-term institutional commitment to ensure sustainability. Chapter 7 documents the activism of women feminist faculty members at Rutgers University's New Brunswick campus, which has helped the university develop into an institution nationally recognized for its diverse student and faculty populations. Yet while the authors celebrate the successful outcomes of faculty activism, they also argue that lack of complete institutional support raises serious questions about the limits of self-help strategies. Chapter 8 examines how faculty members created the Millennium Project, modeled on a study launched at the School of Science at Massachusetts Institute of Technology, to measure acts of institutionalized discrimination on their campus. The authors evaluate the effectiveness of such strategies to diversify the campus and discuss the project's mixed results. Chapter 9 assesses the Caribbean Writers Summer Institute and the Caribbean Literary Studies Program. Created by faculty members at the University of Miami, these efforts have helped retain students and faculty of color at the institution by providing structural support. Yet the authors conclude that such diversity initiatives cannot survive without endowed funding and institutional recognition of the humanities as an academic field that can disseminate greater understanding of diversity.

Part 4 demonstrates how faculty at the University of California–Santa Barbara, the University of Vermont, and Columbia University developed successful strategies for change through collaboration with university administration. Chapter 10 examines how faculty members at Santa Barbara successfully negotiated the limits of Proposition 209. Chapter 11 documents the story of the Faculty Women's Caucus at the University of Vermont and assesses how the efforts of a small group of committed women faculty continues to provide essential services more than a decade after its founding. Finally, chapter 12 traces the successful implementation of a faculty-led diversity initiative at Columbia University. The authors argue that the initiative provides important lessons about how faculty mobilization can fuel campus-wide strategies to increase diversity and how faculty activism can be linked to administrative support.

Doing Diversity in Higher Education is multidisciplinary in organization and structure. You will hear the voices of professors of law, English, philosophy, women's studies, political science, biology, sociology, and history, to name just a few. Some readers may find this multidisciplinarity challenging: one chapter may be written in a sociological voice, the next in a literary one. But this variety speaks to our broad commitment to diversity. One of the triumphs of the "Reaffirming Action" study and hence this book has been getting faculty to speak to each other across disciplines and campuses. We've learned that despite our differences in disciplines many faculty members care about our universities and students and are willing to create a more inclusive environment for all. We hope that this book is only the first of many more cross-disciplinary conversations and collaborations.

NOTES

1. Proponents of affirmative action tend to do a better job at recognizing the persistence of structural inequalities, yet they tend to emphasize racial inequalities and marginalize gender and class.

2. These areas also suffer from poor-quality health care, heavy policing, limited employment opportunities, few retail spaces, high retail prices, fewer recreational facilities, fewer after-school programs, and other disadvantages.

3. "Inclusive excellence" is an expanded notion of excellence that centers on the infusion of diversity into the cultures, policies, and practices of academic institutions for the purpose of enriching learning and teaching experiences (Milem, Chang, and Antonio 2005).

REFERENCES

Acker, Joan. 1990. "Hierarchies, Jobs, Bodies: A Theory of Gendered Organizations." *Gender and Society* 4 (2): 139–158

——— 2006. "Inequality Regimes." *Gender and Society* 20 (4): 441–464.

"Black Faculty in Higher Education: Still Only a Drop in the Bucket." 2007. *Journal of Blacks in Higher Education* 55. http://www.jbhe.com/index.html.

Borden, Victor, and Pamela C. Brown. 2003. "Special Report: The Top 100 Degree Producers." *Black Issues in Higher Education*, 20 (8) and 20 (10).

Carnevale, Anthony P., and Stephen J. Rose. 2003 "Socioeconomic Status, Race/Ethnicity, and Selective College Admissions." A Century Foundation Paper. New York: The Century Foundation. Also available online at http://www.tcf.org/Publications/Education/carnrose.pdf.

College Board. "Trends in College Pricing." 2003. The College Board. http://www.collegeboard.com/prod_downloads/press/cost03/cb_trends_pricing_2003.pdf.

———. "Trends in Student Aid." 2006. The College Board. http://www.collegeboard.com/prod_downloads/press/cost06/trends_aid_06.pdf.

"Gender Equity in Higher Education: Are Male Students at a Disadvantage? Updated Tables and Figures, August 2003." *American Council on Education Center for Public Analysis.* http://www.acenet.edu/bookstore/pdf/2003_gender_equity_update.pdf.

Greenburg, Jan Crawford, and Ariane de Vogue. 2007. "Supreme Court Strikes at Affirmative Action." ABCnews.com, June 28. http://abcnews.go.com/TheLaw/Politics/story?id=3195825 (accessed September 18, 2007).

Greenspan, Alan. 2001. "International Trade." *Vital Speeches of the Day.* 67 (13): 36.

Madden, Michael, and Bennett Bigelow Leedom. 2003. "U.S. Supreme Court Decisions in University of Michigan Court Cases." NACUANOTE 1 (5). http://www.asu.edu/counsel/affirmnacua.doc (accessed July 24, 2007).

Massey, Douglass, and Nancy Denton. 1998. *American Apartheid: Segregation and the Making of the Underclass.* Cambridge, MA: Harvard University Press.

McIntosh, Peggy. 1990. "White Privilege: Unpacking the Invisible Knapsack." *Independent School* 49 (2): 31–36.

Milem, Jeffrey F., Mitchell J. Chang, and Anthony Lising Antonio. 2005. "Making Diversity Work on Campus: A Research-Based Perspective." Making Excellence Inclusive Initiative Series. Association of American Colleges and Universities. http://siher.stanford.edu/AntonioMilemChang_makingdiversitywork.pdf.

"Minorities in Higher Education: Twenty-second Annual Status Report." 2006. American Council on Education.

"Mixed Messages on Affirmative Action." 2007. *Inside Higher Ed.* June 29. http://www.insidehighered.com/news/2007/06/29/affirm.

Mortenson, Thomas C. 2000. "Poverty, Race and the Failure of Public Policy: The Crisis of Access in Higher Education." *Academe* 86 (November–December): 36.

Potter, Will. 2003. "American Indians Seek a Voice in Affirmative-Action Debate." *Chronicle of Higher Education* 49 (June 6): 39. http://chronicle.com/prm/weekly/v49/i39/30a02201.htm.

Rai, Kul, and John Critzer. 2000. *Affirmative Action and the University: Race, Ethnicity and Gender in Higher Education Employment.* Lincoln: University of Nebraska Press.

Sacks, Peter. 2003. "Class Rules: The Fiction of Egalitarian Higher Education." *Chronicle of Higher Education* 49 (1): 46. http://chronicle.com/free/v49/i46/46b00701.htm.

Schmidt, Peter. 2003. "For Asians, Affirmative Action Cuts Both Ways." *Chronicle of Higher Education* 49 (1): 39. http://chronicle.com/prm/weekly/v49/i39/30a02201.htm.

———. 2007. "Supreme Court Leaves Affirmative Action Precedents Intact in Striking Down School Integration Plans." *Chronicle of Higher Education.* June 29. http://chronicle.com/free/2007/06/2007062901n.htm.

West, Martha S., and John W. Curtis. 2006. "AAUP Faculty Gender Equity Indicators 2006." American Association of University Professors. http://www.aaup.org/NR/rdonlyres/63396944-44BE-4ABA-9815-5792D93856F1/0/AAUPGenderEquityIndicators2006.pdf.

Winant, Howard. 1997. "Behind Blue Eyes: Whiteness and Contemporary US Racial Politics." *New Left Review* 225 (September–October).

PART ONE

Diversity and/as Intellectual Leadership

1

Instituting a Legacy of Change

Transforming the Campus Climate at the University of Maryland through Intellectual Leadership

AMY MCLAUGHLIN, BONNIE THORNTON DILL,
SHARON HARLEY, AND DEBORAH ROSENFELT

This chapter examines the role of faculty agency and interdisciplinary collaboration in transforming the climate of diversity at the University of Maryland (UM). It suggests that faculty agency and collaboration have infused a deeper understanding of social inequality (including race, gender, ethnicity, and other dimensions of difference) into teaching, learning, and research in units across the university and beyond its walls. To illuminate these processes of intellectual, social, and institutional change, we draw from the experiences and collaboration histories of three faculty members: Bonnie Thornton Dill, director of the Consortium on Race, Gender, and Ethnicity and chair and professor of the women's studies department; Sharon Harley, chair and associate professor of the African American studies department; and Deborah Rosenfelt, professor of women's studies and director of the Curriculum Transformation Project, which often partners with the women's studies department. Working both independently and collectively, these faculty members have significantly influenced UM's diversity climate by leading campus institutions that promote social change, showing that teaching, research, mentoring, and faculty development can bring about institutional transformation.

Our collaborative project was suggested by Ford Foundation Program Officer Margaret Wilkerson, who, after hearing proposals from each entity, suggested that a coordinated approach would be a more effective intervention. Together, the three units designed and conducted a series of three projects which emphasized each program's unique expertise and their shared commitment to scholarship at the intersections of race, gender, ethnicity, and other areas of difference. Each of these projects was supported by Ford Foundation funding, the most recent of which is titled "Collaborative Transformations in the Academy: Re-Constructing the Study of Gender, Race, Ethnicity and Nation." Our collaboration was enabled by a happy confluence of intellectual engagement, political commitment, and temperament that gave us not only shared aspirations but also shared inclinations toward mutual support, not to be minimized in the university's current entrepreneurial and competitive environment. This chapter grows from a similar collaborative process. As a research project it has been shaped especially by Amy McLaughlin, who conducted both individual and group interviews with Dill, Harley, and Rosenfelt, transcribed the interviews, and drafted the first version. Both the interview transcripts and the chapter itself were subsequently revised by a series of substantive and editorial interventions on our (Dill, Harley, and Rosenfelt's) parts. In much of the chapter, however, we use the third person about ourselves as collaborators, respecting Amy McLaughlin's shaping voice.

The featured faculty members have used three important interventions: interdisciplinary and collaborative investments, mentorship of the next generation of scholars, and the fostering of institutional change. Through this work they have sought to give scholars the tools to integrate intersectionality—that is, a focus on race, gender, and other dimensions of social difference not only as connected but as mutually constitutive—into their scholarship and teaching. Intersectionality is an outgrowth of both feminist and critical race theory and asserts that people have multiple, layered identities and social locations, simultaneously experiencing both oppression and privilege. The roots of this scholarly approach lie in analyses of the lived experiences of women of color, whose intellectual and social justice work reveal how aspects of identity and social relations are shaped by the simultaneous operation of multiple systems of power. Intersectional scholarship is interdisciplinary, focusing on how structures of difference combine to create new and distinct social, cultural, and artistic forms as well as to constitute complex identities. It is intellectually transformative because it centers the experiences of people of color and locates its analysis within systems of ideological, political, and economic power as they are shaped by historical patterns of race, class, gender, sexuality, nation, ethnicity, and age. Moreover, it provides a platform for uniting analysis, theory, education, advocacy, and policy development in pursuit of social justice. (See Crenshaw 1991; Collins 1998; and Dill et al. in press for key works on intersectionality.)

Transformative change cannot occur without commitment from the top. Historically a segregated institution, UM enrolled its first black undergraduate in 1954, when *Brown v. Board of Education* compelled the University of Maryland Board of Regents to admit students to all state campuses without regard to race. But the university system remained segregated in fact if not in law for three decades. It was not until 1985 that the university finally presented an acceptable plan to the Office of Civil Rights for compliance with Title VI of the Civil Rights Act of 1964. Then-chancellor John Slaughter, himself African

American, made significant progress in recruiting African American faculty and students. His successor, William "Brit" Kirwan, insisted on the connection between excellence and diversity and broadened the term to include age, gender, disability, sexual orientation, religion, social class, national origin, and ethnicity.

Kirwan is widely recognized as the leader who, following Slaughter's initiative, transformed the campus climate by devoting significant resources to institutionalizing a commitment to diversity and by expressing his own commitment in public statements. Under Kirwan, a campus climate initiative was instituted to study and remediate a documented chilly climate for women and for racial ethnic minorities. The women's studies and African American studies departments were strengthened, and the Curriculum Transformation Project was initiated with generous university funding. A pivotal event was UM's ultimately unsuccessful defense of the Banneker Scholarship Program for African Americans, launched under Slaughter, which targeted incoming African American students. The Supreme Court's 1995 refusal to review a lower court's ruling that the program was unconstitutional effectively terminated it as a university recruitment tool. Yet the act of defending this program by publicly documenting the residual harm of UM's segregationist past to the state's African American population demonstrated the strength of the university's commitment to a higher education that would serve the needs and explore the experiences of a broad range of constituencies.

Another notable accomplishment during Kirwan's tenure was support for an activist Office of Human Relations Programs, which launched several initiatives designed to improve the campus climate for both students and staff as well as helping to coordinate diversity efforts across campus. One of its important undertakings was collaboration between the Office of Human Relations Programs, the Ford Foundation, and the Association of American Colleges and Universities to create *Diversity Blueprint: A Planning Manual for Colleges and Universities* (Brown 1998), which discusses the fundamentals of diversity at UM:

- *Accountability.* Who will ensure that programs meet their diversity goals?
- *Inclusiveness.* All dimensions of diversity should be represented campus-wide.
- *Shared responsibility.* All UM faculty, staff, and students must work toward our diversity goals.
- *Evaluation.* We need continuous feedback on the success of our efforts.
- *Institutionalization.* We must incorporate diversity efforts into the university structure.

These fundamentals shaped UM's diversity accountability implementation plan (DAIP), which involved identifying institutional leadership for diversity initiatives, decentralizing the ability to contribute, developing an evaluation structure to monitor progress, using existing organizational structures to facilitate accountability and evaluation goals, and ensuring adequate administrative support within each major university unit (college, school, or vice presidential area).

The manual was issued just as Kirwan left to become president of Ohio State University, to be succeeded as UM's president in 1998 by C. D. Mote Jr., UM's current president. As a concluding note to Kirwan's work at UM, the *Diversity Blueprint* marked his determination to institutionalize diversity. Unfortunately, because it is rarely referenced in current campus discussions, its usefulness as a resource and a consistent plan for change is questionable. Indeed, a 2000 panel on diversity convened by President Mote found that diversity work on campus had become fragmented and was rarely evaluated; the DAIPs, said the panel, "simply do not fulfill the function for which they are intended," since "there is no accountability for lack of progress in implementing diversity on our campus." Social change remains dependent on the commitment of leaders; support that is not institutionalized into the daily operations of university offices, departments, and programs can shift as leadership changes.

President Mote had been recruited to lead the university to national prominence. According to his Web site, "In 2005, the University was ranked 18th among public research universities, up from 30th in 1998. President Mote has emphasized broad access to the university's model enriched undergraduate curriculum programs and launched the Baltimore Incentive Awards Program to recruit and provide full support to high school students of outstanding potential who have overcome extraordinary adversity during their lives." (Office of the President Web site: www.president.umd.edu (accessed September 1, 2006)). Mote has also maintained various presidential commissions, including those on ethnic minority issues; disability issues; women's issues; and lesbian, gay, transsexual, and transgender issues. He has improved the level of recognized excellence on the campus, but although the grade point average of entering students, the amount of grant monies secured, and the success of special honors programs are indisputably higher, racial diversity still lags in some areas.

Thirty-four percent of the undergraduate student body is now racial-ethnic minority (down 2 percent from 2000), and the university ranks fifth nationally in the number of African American baccalaureates graduating from predominantly white institutions—figures to be proud of. Yet the UM faculty is more diverse racially at the assistant professor level than at the full professor level. More than fifty years after university desegregation, UM's percentage of African American and Hispanic faculty remains at 4 and 3 percent respectively, and scholars from these groups are least likely to be tenured. President Mote has appointed an associate vice president with a diversity and equity portfolio, but the university's administration remains largely white and male. Similarly, the university's percentage of graduate students of color does not fully reflect the diversity of the United States. As Mote himself has suggested, the university's progress on diversity is cause for satisfaction but hardly for complacency. Still, the university has remained supportive of individuals and programs committed to further research, teaching, mentoring, and curricular development, like those in our study, so long as they have also garnered external support as well.

How the Research Was Done

This essay is based on modified oral history accounts of the scholarship and life events that empowered each of the faculty members engaged in this study to create and/or support transformative organizations. We used a nontraditional collaborative approach; team members read and commented on all interviews, both individually and as a group, thus creating a dynamic and collective conversation throughout the process of gathering and analyzing data.

Oral histories are ideal for capturing the ideas, memories, and understandings of individuals at a particular time. In this case, these histories helped us reflect on projects currently in place as a way to effect change and accomplish goals. Amy McLaughlin conducted two-hour interviews with each of the other members of the team. She followed these with a two-hour group interview to investigate the connections between the founding and support of transformative institutions and the faculty who create and nurture them. After this first set of interviews, team members shared transcripts for commentary and reflection. A second group interview explored common points of connection, questions, and insights generated by this collaboration. Each semistructured interview was recorded and transcribed, and questions followed several major themes:

- Scholarship, activism, and personal history
- Administrative support and success
- Collaboration and lessons learned

The interviews were supported by our examination of additional documents, including grant applications, annual reports, related journal articles, and other intellectual products that contribute to knowledge about faculty engagement in diversity issues. Thus, we sought to capture an institutional history that parallels the personal ones. Throughout the analysis and descriptions below, illustrative quotes from the interviews are included to enhance and clarify the direct voices of the faculty leaders.

The faculty work under study has been intertwined with several key diversity initiatives on campus. Consequently, it has been a challenge to capture the true complexity of the work of "doing" diversity. We collected additional data from interviews with Christine Clark, director of the Office of Human Relations programs; Andrea Hill Levy, associate vice president of academic affairs; James Greenberg, founder of the Center for Teaching Excellence; and Angel David Nieves, assistant professor of historic preservation, who arrived on campus in 2004 and has engaged extensively with the Consortium on Race, Gender, and Ethnicity, the Curriculum Transformation Project, and other avenues of campus diversity work.

The Collaborative Project

The collaborative project known as Collaborative Transformations in the Academy: Re-Constructing the Study of Gender, Race, Ethnicity and Nation, developed and supported by team members Bonnie Thornton Dill, Sharon Harley, and Deborah Rosenfelt, has enhanced the combined resources of three separate entities at UM: the African American Studies department (AASD); the Curriculum Transformation Project (CTP); and the Consortium on Race, Gender, and Ethnicity (CRGE). This collaboration grew out of the interests, directions, and relationships that have characterized these units. The programs have contributed to a pattern of multiple diversity work, a term suggesting that work on diversity issues can take place in a number of different locations, each of which operates somewhat independently but with cumulative impact. The impact of multiple diversity work is best captured in the words of Deborah Rosenfelt: "The various diversity projects on campus that have worked together on the whole have created something that is larger than the sum of its parts." Central to the mission of AASD, CTP, and CRGE since their inception has been the interdisciplinary, national, and international examination of the intersections of gender, racial, and ethnic issues with other dimensions of difference and social inequality. The separate work of each unit is an essential element in the creation of the strands of this multiple diversity work.

The African American Studies Department

Under Harley's leadership, AASD emphasizes the interdisciplinary and intersectional study of the African American experience, focusing on race, gender, and class both nationally and internationally. The department has developed several projects since 1998 designed to intervene in campus climate issues. Harley describes her mission and the mission of AASD as "a commitment to academic excellence with a strong community outreach." A central concentration has been two interdisciplinary research seminars called "The Meanings and Representations of Work in Black Women's Lives" and "The Meanings and Representations of Work in the Lives of Women of Color," which bring women scholars together to focus on women's work.

In 2002, this first seminar in which Harley collaborated with English professor Mary Helen Washington and Dill, focused on black women and was composed of fifteen local scholars (professors, museum specialists, artists, and policy analysts). Members produced fourteen major research papers, an annotated bibliography published as a working paper, and the anthology *Sister Circle: Black Women and Work* (Rutgers University Press, 2002), edited by Sharon Harley and the Black Women and Work Collective. The current Women of Color project supports a multidisciplinary, multiracial, and multiethnic collective whose members study women of color and issues of gender, race, ethnicity, nationality and women's work. This national/international group of scholars meets less regularly and communicates via the Internet and video conferencing. Members have presented their research in national and international public forums and a book, *Women's Labor in the Global Economy: Speaking in Multiple Voices* (Rutgers University Press, 2007). The collective was awarded a Rockefeller grant, directed by Harley and women's studies professor Lynn Bolles, for a Bellagio conference, "The Meanings and Representations of Work in the Lives of Women of Color: A Comparative Study," at which selected members from the original seminar were joined by scholars from South Africa, Jamaica, Trinidad, Tobago, Ghana, Canada, and the United Kingdom to enhance thinking about women of color and work.

Of course, ambitious projects come with their share of challenges; in this case, moments of ruptured or contentious communication were treated as opportunities for expanding comprehension of different experiences and points of view. For instance, understanding the value and limits of reading visual culture formed a productive discussion among the group, as did the dawning awareness that nationality affected scholars' definitions of "work" and even "intersectionality." Fittingly, debates such as these helped to extend an understanding of the concept of intersectionality as itself contingent on contexts not only of race and gender but also of discipline and nation.

Harley is intensely interested in institutionalizing the mentoring component of the project: "I understand from the junior scholars who were added in the final phase of the project . . . that they have . . . articles based upon contacts we [have shared with them]; we've helped workshop their papers." This transfer of knowledge, contacts, and support among scholars has been integral to the entire project. Other future goals include building an AASD PhD program and establishing a center for the study of race, gender, and labor. Finding the funding and support, however, is an ongoing challenge.

The Curriculum Transformation Project

"The Greer Report" was UM's internal assessment of the campus's chilly climate for women. After the report was released, consultant Betty Schmitz founded the Curriculum Transformation Project with a focus on women and gender, and in 1989, at the end of the project's first year, Deborah Rosenfelt was appointed project director and professor of women's studies. She has overseen CTP throughout most of its long history of innovation and accomplishments. Under her leadership, the program has encouraged faculty to explore intersectional issues, placing women at the center of analysis but always examining ways in which race, sexuality, ethnicity, class, nation, and ability define, refine, and mutually constitute the concept and experiences of gender.

In 1989, under Schmitz's direction, CTP began hosting summer institutes for faculty. Rosenfelt continued the institutes after that, enlisting faculty across campus to participate in "Thinking about Women, Gender, and Race." Participating faculty read and discussed scholarship on race, gender, class, and other dimensions of difference, as well as debating the pedagogical issues that surface once these issues explicitly enter a classroom. Most participants revised and reconstructed their syllabi, taking scholarship on race, gender, class, and other dimensions of difference into account. In the mid-1990s, the project received a Ford Foundation grant to add gender issues to international studies and to internationalize women's studies, a response to increasing public emphasis on globalization and its impact on women (see Monk and Rosenfelt 2000; Rosenfelt and Bolles 2002; Rosenfelt 2002). When it became clear that "internationalizing" could go only so far without the full participation of scholars from abroad, CTP, with support from Ford, began offering three-week institutes to generate international and interdisciplinary dialogue among UM scholars and scholars from China, Korea, South Africa, the West Indies, Eastern Europe, and Israel, located at universities with graduate programs in women's studies.

CTP has worked closely with the department of women's studies to jointly become a primary catalyst in founding an international consortium in graduate women's studies, including international participants from the summer seminars as well as scholars from Uganda, which has a very active women's studies program. Members of the consortium have participated in cooperative research ventures, visiting consultancies and faculty exchanges, and transnational teaching. CTP has recently been exploring ways to bring feminist pedagogies to the Internet. In the summer of 2004, it hosted a ten-day intensive institute titled "Web-Based Pedagogies and Feminist Theory," with scholars from all the previously mentioned regions in attendance. Ultimately, five different course modules were developed that could be integrated into a course on feminist theory or extended into a course themselves. Out of this work, five consortium scholars at five different universities developed a course titled "Women's Health and Well-Being," which culminated in a one-day video conference featuring the work at four campus sites: UM in the United States, Bar Ilan University in Israel, Makerere University in Uganda, and University of the Western Cape in South Africa.

In the summer of 2006, CTP turned its attention again to the UM campus, offering three one-week seminars on integrating scholarship on lesbian, gay, bisexual, and transgender issues; integrating disability scholarship; and bringing intersectional understandings of religion into the curriculum. Its current initiative expands and deepens work on the intersections of technology and pedagogy, with faculty institutes focused on visual literacy and diversity. Over the years, over a hundred faculty members at UM alone have participated in the faculty development institutes, with approximately fifty additional participants from throughout the state and abroad. Many more have attended a range of conferences, panels, and other public events sponsored by the CTP.

The Consortium on Race, Gender, and Ethnicity

Intellectual collaboration is very much a central component of CRGE. CRGE's mission is the creation, promotion, and support of research, scholarship, and faculty development of theoretical, pedagogical, and methodological insights in intersectionality among units and individual faculty, and the training of the next generation of intersectional scholars. Finding this niche was a central feature of CRGE's development and one that was strategically chosen as the most intellectually compatible and effective approach to changing the campus climate.

Founded in 1998 and directed until 2006 by Bonnie Thornton Dill, CRGE now has an extensive array of research projects and mentoring programs. The consortium facilitates intersectional research by administering interdisciplinary research interest groups, which focus on issues related to race, poverty, material and visual culture, health of low-income women and children of color, and qualitative methodologies. Senior faculty in CRGE read grant applications and tenure materials and meet regularly with faculty of color interested in intersectionality. Dill and current CRGE director and womenís studies professor Ruth E. Zambrana have mentored many of the junior scholars of color in the humanities, behavioral and social sciences, and education on the campus who have since received tenure. Though none of them had a formal connection with womenís studies, the home departments of both Dill and Zambrana, developing a new generation of scholars who are committed to the work of institutional change and social justice is a priority of both scholars, and they have considered it important to donate their time to this activity, even though they receive little institutional recognition or reward for this work. Through CRGE there is a formal mentoring program for graduate students. Among its components is a monthly seminar designed to feature, promote, and foster intersectional scholarship across the campus. On average, twenty-five students from approximately fifteen departments attend the seminar monthly. These sessions help students find peers in other departments who share their interests in learning more about intersectional perspectives and how to understand some of the complex questions about class, culture, race, sexuality, and identity that they are examining. Additionally, it provides the students exposure to faculty who are engaged in this kind of work but dispersed across the campus. More than thirty UM faculty members have participated in the sessions either as presenters or attendees. The seminar has featured such topics as "What Is a Public Intellectual?," "Black and Latina Feminist Thought," "Intersectional Methodology," "Combining Research and Activism," and "How to Get Published."

In order to overcome the isolation experienced by scholars interested in intersectional work both as a scholarly practice and as a tool for social transformation and social justice, who all too often are alone or one of very few faculty with similar interests in their home department, CRGE has also been building an online community of scholars. Its Web site releases information about CRGE research products, programs, and symposia to the campus community and beyond. Its intersectional research database contains a wealth of annotated research by scholars in the social sciences, arts and humanities, law, medicine, and many other fields. CRGE also maintains the only UM web calendar devoted to all diversity-related events on campus.

The collaboration that developed among AASD, CTP, and CRGE has touched most of the faculty and staff on campus who are actively engaged in diversity work and institutional transformation around issues of diversity. Thus, while all of the people interviewed have a specific portfolio of diversity work with which they are engaged, all acknowledged that the ongoing support and encouragement generated in meetings and shared events sustain and enliven the work of individuals as well as the impact of each programmatic unit. All interviewed respondents have worked with these three programs and reiterated their belief that the collaboration plays a valuable role at UM. Christine Clark, director of the Office of Human Relations Program at the time of this study, says that academic work is often "not part of a collaborative activist academia," suggesting that there is usually a separation between academic scholarship and collaborative activism on university campuses. The collaboration among CRGE, AASD, and CTP is an antidote to the traditionally insular nature of scholarship. Assistant Professor Angel Nieves made a similar observation when he suggested that although coalition work often highlights fundamental misunderstandings of interdisciplinary work across the color line, CRGE has been able to overcome those differences and build coalitions by using intersectional scholarship as a basis for the work.

Since collaboration has not been acknowledged as a characteristic modus operandi within academia—especially outside the natural and physical sciences—the decision to use collaboration as a strategy for both intellectual engagement and institutional transformation is an interesting one and leads one to ask why the principle leaders of these units chose this strategic approach. The answer, in part, is found in each of their biographies.

The Collaborators

Each of the scholars under study took different avenues into higher education. Bonnie Thornton Dill found her way through direct service and public policy programs; political activism predated Sharon Harley's initial career as a high school social studies teacher and her enrollment into the PhD program in the department of history at Howard University; Deborah Rosenfelt went straight to graduate school, an experience increasingly marked by extensive activism. Each was motivated (in part by her activist bent) during her training to break with tradition and develop new knowledge. As Dill states, "We are . . . children of the '60s, of the civil rights movement, of the other movements that followed. . . . Like so many of our generation, we believed and saw that change was possible, that activism could make a difference." Engagement with the injustices and movements outside of academia gave these scholars both the tools and the conviction they needed to make a difference on campus.

Literature that examines who is likely to engage in diversity-related work on campus documents the motivating force of this conviction. According to research, faculty who believe that institutional change is possible are likely to commit time and energy to the task (Gonzalez and Padilla 1999), as are faculty who perceive both political and personal benefits (Baez 2000). Baez also found that diversity facilitates opportunities for interpersonal support and is pursued across all faculty roles in research, pedagogy, and service. Mayhew and Grunwald (2006) emphasize the crucial role that an institution plays in supporting faculty engagement. In addition, there is some evidence that a faculty member's race or ethnicity influences her likelihood of engaging in research on race or campus activism. Milem (2001) found that African American and Chicano/Latino faculty were more likely than white or Asian American faculty to have conducted research on race or ethnicity. Likewise, whites and Asians were less likely to attend racial or cultural awareness workshops. Milem also found that women, African American, American Indian, and Mexican/Chicano faculty were more likely to be involved in teaching and learning activities that supported a diverse student body.

Bonnie Thornton Dill

As Dill became involved in a New York City program aimed at getting low-income students into the citywide college system, she found herself thinking about her programmatic experiences within "a broader historical . . . and comparative context." Although she began her PhD in sociology as a part-time student with some skepticism about an academic career, she was soon deeply engaged in the work and received a fellowship that permitted her to become a full-time student. Noticing that her professors often knew little about her particular areas of interest—African American women and families—she sought to create a network of scholars with similar interests and expertise outside her institution with whom she could explore ideas:

> I started looking for other young, up-and-coming scholars who were doing similar kinds of work, who I could really talk to about my work. I really didn't feel there were people who could read it critically, because they didn't know the race literature. If they read something I'd written and said, "This is great!" I was pleased but I wasn't sure I was getting a critical and informed reading of the race/gender issues.

Dill's first effort at campus climate change took place at the University of Memphis, where she drew on her network to found the Center for Research on Women (Dill, Higginbotham, and Weber 1997).

> The motivating force was to legitimize and institutionalize the kind of scholarship that I was doing and a lot of other people were doing. . . . A research center could do that. It could publish, disseminate and promote this new work. [It was an] opportunity to take this work that was really critical about society . . . make it more widely available [and] change the discourse.

The center at Memphis was an important intervention in two ways: it developed a database on intersectional scholarship and on southern women, and it hosted summer research and teaching institutes for promising scholars from around the country, allowing them to present their work in a venue that offered both support and critical appraisal. In addition, the center created ties among participating scholars, reducing isolation and encouraging those who worked in nonsupportive environments.

When Dill came to the University of Maryland in 1993, she had no intention of founding another center. But on her arrival she discovered "a larger number of black women scholars engaged in research on black women than I had imagined . . . [and] I had this sense of the potential for developing a community of scholars and felt that this represented an unusual moment in time. I thought, 'Oh my God, this is incredible; there cannot be many places in history where there has been this kind of collection of black women scholars and others doing work on race, gender, and ethnicity.'"

UM offered her the unique opportunity to do two things at once: to participate in developing this community of scholars, building a reputation for expertise in intersectional scholarship; and at the same time, to create a new kind of intervention in the campus culture, one that put scholarship at the forefront of understanding inequality based on social difference.

The opportunity to found CRGE happened just as the AASD "Black Women and Work" project was expanding and as CTP was searching for more funds. Their collaborative grant application to the Ford Foundation formalized their relationship.

Sharon Harley

A product of the Washington, DC, school system, Harley began her academic journey by aspiring to occupations she saw were available to women: "The two primary professions for women college graduates in my neighborhood must have been teachers or principals. And because I loved my teachers, my high school teachers so much, especially my history teachers, I wanted to be a history teacher." She taught for a few years in DC, then decided to try graduate school at Howard University. (Like Dill, she started out as a part-time student.) After two years, she knew she wouldn't return to teaching high school; she had shifted her focus to college students and writing in a new field of academic scholarship—African American women's history.

As Harley became initiated into her chosen field, she had realizations about her work that were similar to Dill's: "We would go to these conferences and there was almost nothing about black women's history . . . [so] we decided to stop complaining about the errors of the scholarship and . . . do something about it." Lack of support for scholarship on African American women became a motivating force in Harley's career. She and her fellow graduate students wrote an anthology and, after contacting many different presses, managed to get it published by Kennikat Press. This text, *The Afro-American Woman: Struggles and Images* (1978), helped to establish Harley and her coeditor Rosalyn Terborg-Penn as pioneer scholars in this field of study.

After graduation, Harley spent a year as an adjunct professor and then came to the University of Maryland in 1981. She recalls the campus climate: "At that time there were not many women faculty; there weren't many women of color; there weren't many African American faculty who even had my same scholarly interests. . . . So I developed a community of scholars at the Library of Congress . . . and for eight years I had a research desk [there] with these wonderful scholars from all over the world."

Harley emphasizes that she was looking for an alternative community to replace UM's chilly climate: "[I thought] if I cannot get the community in this place, then I'm going to look in other places to have a community that best meets both my intellectual and personal needs." Only after Slaughter's and Kirwan's presidential mandates began to take hold did she see changes in the climate: "I think it helped me to shift back to College Park as my primary center of academic thinking about work as these two men developed a strong interest . . . in diversity and academic excellence." Noting how they prioritized hiring faculty of color and defended the Banneker Scholarship as pivotal strategies for change, she describes the impact of such changes: "For faculty of color and faculty who are committed to areas of diversity, it's such a welcoming and wonderful environment to be in because you feel, both as a researcher and a faculty member, . . . so valued, and it's so nice to be at a place that values diversity—which doesn't preclude one's commitment to academic excellence."

Harley's commitment to AASD and the "Women and Work" projects grew out of her longstanding commitment to collaboration and dissemination of knowledge: "I'm always thinking, sitting around the room in the Women and Work research seminars, 'Wow! These are bright people in a wonderful seminar; let's share this information with so many other people—other academics, junior scholars, librarians, museum patrons and the public-at-large.'"

Deborah Rosenfelt

Rosenfelt started graduate school in the late 1960s, and after graduation, won a teaching position in the English department at California State University at Long Beach. Already involved in leftist political movements, she began participating in demonstrations to bring a women's studies program to campus: "The students [and] . . . young professors, we really wanted a program, but there was a lot of hostility on campus. . . . It was really an education in the . . . strategies and tactics of organizing in academia, and we drew our strategies from . . . left-wing practices, and we had demonstrations, we did street theater, and . . . we paraded with a coffin that said 'Academic Freedom Is Dead.'"

Eventually achieving the goal of starting a women's studies program, Rosenfelt worked for a number of years as its coordinator. Then she took a position at San Francisco State University as director and associate professor of women's studies, at a time when such well-known writers and activists as Gloria Anzaldua, Angela Davis, bell hooks, Cherrie Moraga, and others taught part-time in the program. There she continued working on curricular issues, and on faculty development as well. "I got together with some of our faculty and also a lot of faculty working in ethnic studies, and we came up with this very complex and . . . pretty good proposal to take on issues of race as a sort of curriculum transformation project. . . . [It] came out of our own experience at [the university with] . . . major racial issues and seeing a huge disparity between what was going on in women's studies and ethnic studies and what was going on in more traditional departments."

Rosenfelt was inspired to come to the University of Maryland in 1989 because "it was one of the few jobs I had ever seen advertised that said half your time will be dedicated to curriculum transformation; and since I had done that work without really naming it as such, . . . UM seemed ideal because it had a growing autonomous women's studies program, and it was going to invest money in a very visible project."

The move to UM cemented her commitment not only to curriculum transformation but also to overall institutional change. She believes her dedication to fostering social change has enhanced her work in the academy: "I love writing about literature, but I don't think I found my voice . . . until I got involved in political work." She also recognizes that her work has grown from her political experiences, including her deep involvement in the women's liberation movement. "The women's movement was very powerful . . . [because] we talked and studied about the relationship between our own life histories and institutional forms of oppression." Recognizing also that her own life history was partly one of power and privilege, she was determined to ensure that CTP included multiple aspects of diversity: "I wanted to name it in a way that would make people know that we were not just about gender, or not just about nationality, but that we were willing to think about race *and* gender and sexuality and a range of other issues as well. . . . [T]his would be a project that would help faculty to become equipped to incorporate this new scholarship into their classroom."

Obvious parallels in their work have brought these faculty members together. Although each has a specific area of expertise, together (with their allies around campus) their programs are a concerted attempt to transform the campus climate. Their ability to shape collaboration across departmental and college lines is crucial. As Harley says,

> To have an African American studies department so committed to gender issues and women's leadership, and then, on the same campus, Women's Studies so committed to women of color: . . . this is a very rare situation that hopefully can be replicated elsewhere. This collaboration in the academy should be encouraged through funding that allows more face-to-face meetings and compensates already-taxed women for shouldering another responsibility. As a result, we could ideally serve as a role model for cross-college, cross-discipline, intersectional collaborative projects.

The Costs and Benefits of Collaboration

First and foremost, collaboration among these programs has helped support each director. Dill explains the benefits of practical support: "I think in many ways we have contributed to each other's projects with ideas and names of people, and sometimes we haven't always been physically present but we have been able to suggest people who might participate or be helpful. So we're in touch even though we're not there on an everyday basis."

In addition, emotional support has reduced isolation and burnout. Rosenfelt says, "I think the collaboration helped really to keep me going." And Dill adds, "We can call somebody else and say, 'You know I need your support on this' or we have a colleague to strategize with." This type of support is critical when difficult problems arise.

Collaboration also supports continued intellectual development among not only individuals and programs but for the campus as a whole. As Harley says, "Collaboration is . . . at the core of an interdisciplinary department, and that has mutual benefits [for both department and campus]. . . . We bring a . . . multidisciplinary understanding of race and the construction of race and race theory . . . [that] benefits the intellectual discourse." Rosenfelt explains how it pushes scholars: "What's been important both intellectually and politically for me in relation to the other collaborations has been really, really trying to understand race, gender, and other dimensions of difference both in terms of how they operate here and how they operate in other locations." And Dill says that it also brings about new ideas: "I think that collaboration becomes more and more challenging in the climate we are in. The funding pots are smaller. . . . [O]ne of the things that has come out of this collaboration . . . seems to be this joint minor in black women's studies. I think that we have encouraged one another and been encouraged in a lot of ways to think internationally as well as nationally, [to] think globally and locally."

But collaboration has not always been easy. In a campus environment that promotes entrepreneurship and uses external grants awarded as an important measure of departmental success, units are more often placed in competition with one another. "When we first began this collaboration, said Dill, the campus grant reporting system did not even have a way to credit all three programs represented equally. Getting equal recognition for the work bureaucratically was a challenge and very time consuming." Since that time, the campus has come to more fully recognize and even encourage collaborative work, particularly because collaboration can often save dollars. As Harley points out: "The campus administration began to open up the academic barriers to collaboration by encouraging collaboration, putting money behind jointly sponsored college and academic unit projects. . . . And of course, with limited resources, the way to get things done is to pool our resources."

Collaboration is a central component of all three programs. Rosenfelt says she thinks of the Curriculum Transformation Project as in some ways the pedagogical arm of the Consortium on Race, Gender, and Ethnicity. She and Harley have presented work at CRGE forums, and both Harley and Dill have presented their work at CTP summer institutes, which have also engaged faculty in reading papers drafted by participants in Dill's and Harley's projects. Dill has consulted at institutions abroad that are part of CTP's consortial network. All three faculty members planned the jointly administered undergraduate citation in black women's studies. They also share materials, finances, and staff to facilitate each other's projects and host joint seminars and symposia. Dill provided the names of a number of scholars in Harley's Women of Color research seminar and has consistently advised the Curriculum Transformation Project as a senior scholar.

Mentorship

The interviews highlighted the importance both of being mentored and of mentoring future generations of scholars. As the literature shows, junior faculty of color particularly benefit from mentoring. Mentoring includes offering critical feedback, introducing junior scholars to senior faculty and administrators, and acting as a resource. Faculty of color are more likely than white colleagues to feel undervalued and unwelcomed (Fong 2000; Johnsrud 1993; Alexander-Snow and Johnson 1999; Jarmon 2001; Garza 1993), and in general they have different experiences and therefore require different strategies to ensure their retention. The stresses that faculty of color experience often hinder their progress toward achieving tenure and reduce their potential to produce excellent scholarship and be effective professors. To avoid such outcomes, universities must be committed to providing extra support for the retention of ethnic minority faculty. Mentors should work to motivate protégés, socialize them to the environment by revealing its "hidden rules" (Jarmon 2001), provide emotional support, be aware of extra demands and the need to protect personal time, and ensure that faculty of color are rewarded for their accomplishments and considered for promotion and tenure. Additionally, the campus culture must be conducive to diversity (Thomas 2001). Angel Nieves notes that organizations such as CRGE are closely associated with prominent scholars of color, "but [there needs to be a] focus on helping the next generation of scholars progress through their PhD programs." Mentoring is particularly important, according to Roche (1979), because it perpetuates itself: faculty who have been mentored themselves are more likely to mentor others.

Dill, Harley, and Rosenfelt were all mentored in the beginning of their careers and are committed to mentoring junior scholars and graduate students. As Harley states, "The mentoring part is important to us because we want to produce the next generation of scholars." The drawback is that mentoring requires a significant investment of time with little institutional recognition. Research bears out faculty members' sense that mentoring increases demands on their time. Because Harley and Dill are African American women, students of color often seek them out. In addition, as faculty of color they are often sought after for considerable committee work, which reduces their time for their research and scholarship (Johnsrud 1993; Fong 2000; Garza 1993; Howard-Vital and Morgan 1993). Harley, Dill, and Rosenfelt all talked about how their engagement in the work of institutional change and social justice had taken more time than they anticipated, definitely impinging on their own research, scholarship, and publication.

Alexander-Snow and Johnson (1999) suggest that faculty of color experience "cultural taxation." And Banks (1984) says that "rather than being allowed—and indeed encouraged—to concentrate on their academic work, many are sucked into a plethora of activities often unrelated to their competence and interests" (327). Harley points out that "the campus is more likely to recognize somebody with a major or minor grant who's done absolutely nothing in the mentoring area than somebody who does the multiple things that we do." Yet she continues to make plans to "expand the mentoring component of [the "Women and Work" project] and bring in more people. I'd like to expand and replicate it around the country." The challenge is obtaining institutional support.

CRGE's Interdisciplinary Scholars Program (CrISP) has been central to the center's efforts to retain minority scholars. CrISP fellowships are awarded to incoming graduate students interested in intersectionality, who tend to be students of color. Because CRGE is not a degree-granting program and does not offer courses, students are nominated by their home departments. CRGE works to ensure that they continue making satisfactory progress toward their degrees. With the fellowship, they are also offered a half-time assistantship that allows them to work at CRGE for ten hours per week. (This qualifies them for university health insurance, an important addition to the standard fellowship package.) Students develop and hone research skills through seminars, presentations, and their work as faculty research assistants. As they help administer the research interest groups, they receive training in both intersectional research and running a research institute. As one student said, "Through the CrISP program, I have access to formal and informal mentorship, research training, and a foundation in intersectionality that is critical to my present and future work."

The CRGE faculty has trained more than a dozen CrISP students from five different departments. UM is aware of the benefits of mentorship, but institutionalizing a mentorship program is expensive; and for both junior and senior scholars, the time involved is a major investment. To continue funding for CrISP, CRGE has had to strategically market it as a departmental recruitment tool. In exchange, department "buy-in" has increased from an initial commitment to funding a student for two years after the CRGE fellowship to also supporting one year of the two-year CRGE fellowship.

At times, it was challenging to "mentor" some of the junior scholars added to the Women of Color seminar, Harley recalls. "Some in this very bright cohort of scholars did not appear to fully appreciate the level of sisterhood that defined the group nor the degree of struggle the more senior scholars had engaged in to both increase the knowledge base in the field and open up the academy for subsequent generations. While not seeking a deferential attitude toward the "senior" scholars in the WOC group, we were still taken aback by the moments of perceived entitlement."

Conclusion

Challenges

Faculty members face challenges to continuing their work to transform the campus climate:

1. *Funding.* The competition for resources is fierce both on and off campus. The funding climate has changed considerably in the past ten years and probably will not improve in the near future (Dill, McLaughlin, and Nieves, in press; Hollander and Saltmarsh 2002). As a result, centers and programs sometimes work against one another instead of together.

2. *Obstacles to pooling resources.* Collaborative work takes place across traditional boundaries at the university and can be difficult to coordinate. Because the university tracks individual achievement, collaborative activities can fall through the cracks. For example, initially, the Ford Foundation grant was mistakenly posted solely under Bonnie Dill's name. The time and energy invested in ensuring that everyone receives adequate credit is time and energy taken from the work itself.

3. *Long-term university support.* As UM's external climate changes, so do its funding priorities, particularly when the majority of funds come from the state. For social change efforts to succeed, the senior administration must support diversity efforts. One way of doing this, suggests Christine Clark, is by diversifying senior leadership on campus. Andrea Levy adds, "[We must] recognize that diversity has a positive impact on educational outcomes. We cannot separate diversity/inclusiveness from any other part of students' education."

Strategies

Our data show that climate change has thus far depended on the leadership of faculty whose life experiences and scholarship have motivated them to devote energy and time to improving the campus climate at significant personal cost and without adequate compensation or recognition. How can transformation continue under such circumstances? While we have no simple or perfect answer, we note several important strategies.

1. *Making scholarship central.* While there have been historic tensions between activism and the academy, scholarship remains at the heart of the research university's mission and has certainly constituted the heart of the programs and academic units that these scholars have built. Their work both reflects and furthers the remarkable proliferation of work in women's studies, African American studies, cultural studies, ethnic studies, and other interdisciplinary programs that embrace an intersectional approach to understanding inequality. Interventions based in such

scholarship simultaneously tap into and challenge existing systems of university power. Institutional rewards depend on scholarship; an intersectional approach allows faculty members to incorporate transformative work while meeting university expectations. Such scholarship explores the complex causes of inequality and historic underrepresentation and can help to devise strategies for change and to envision a just society.

2. *Producing and publicizing the fruits of your labor.* This means carving out time to create such products such as anthologies, working papers, and well-documented reports that will count in university systems of achievement and increase opportunities for funding. Campuswide events are also important tools for raising the visibility of units and awareness of relevant scholarship. Carving out a unique niche (for example, with intersectional scholarship, or with diversity-oriented faculty development) makes your location *the* source for a specific intervention.

3. *Changing existing university patterns of recognition and reward.* The university should acknowledge and credit all those involved in collaborative activities. Mentoring and teaching should be equally recognized, and the increased workloads of scholars of color should be acknowledged by compensation and promotion. Currently, those with the most resources direct the course of collaborative activities. By changing administrative accountability, the work itself will become more visible and, as it is rewarded, will attract more supporters.

Finally, of course, we trust that this chapter documents the importance and the possibilities of collaborative work among projects and programs that have similar intellectual and social commitments. Collaboration can seem like an additional burden at times, and it can be especially difficult when competition for resources for programmatic development (let alone survival) seems necessary. We would suggest, however, that it is precisely in such an environment that working with instead of against one another can be most fruitful in building an institutional presence that makes diversity work visible and in nurturing the most hopeful visions of change.

REFERENCES

Alexander-Snow, M., and B. Johnson. 1999. "Perspectives from Faculty of Color." In *Faculty in New Jobs: A Guide to Settling In, Becoming Established, and Building Institutional Support,* ed. R. J. Menges et al., 88–117. San Francisco: Jossey-Bass.

Baez, B. 2000. "Race-related Service and Faculty of Color: Conceptualizing Critical Agency in Academe." *Higher Education* 39:363–391.

Banks, W. 1984. "Afro-American Scholars in the University: Roles and Conflicts." *American Behavioral Scientist* 27 (3):325–338.

Brown, G., ed. 1998. *Diversity Blueprint: A Planning Manual for Colleges and Universities.* Created by the Office of Human Relations Programs in collaboration with associates at the University of Maryland, College Park, and the Association of American Colleges and Universities (AACU). Washington, DC: AACU.

Collins, Patricia Hill. 1998. "Intersections of Race, Class, Gender,, and Nation: Some Implications for Black Family Studies." *Journal of Comparative Family Studies* 29 (1):27–36.

Crenshaw, Kimberle Williams. 1991. "Mapping the Margins: Intersectionality, Identity Politics, and Violence against Women of Color." *Stanford Law Review* 43 (6):1241–1299.

Dill, B. T., A. McLaughlin, and A. D. Nieves. In press. "Future Directions of Feminist Research: Intersectionality." In *Handbook of Feminist Research: Theory and Praxis,* ed. S. N. Hesse-Biber. Thousand Oaks, CA: Sage Publications.

Dill, B. T., E. Higginbotham, and L. Weber. 1997. "Sisterhood as Collaboration: Building the Center for Research on Women at the University of Memphis." In *Feminist Sociology: Life Histories of a Movement,* ed. B. Laslett and B. Thorne, 229–256. New Brunswick, NJ: Rutgers University Press.

Fong, B. 2000. "Toto, I Think We're Still in Kansas." *Liberal Education* 86:4.

Garza, H. 1993. "Second-Class Academics: Chicano/Latino Faculty in U.S. Universities." In *Building a Diverse Faculty,* ed. J. Gainen and R. Boice, 33–41. San Francisco: Jossey-Bass.

Gonzalez, K. P., and R. V. Padilla. 1999. "Faculty Commitment and Engagement in Organizational Reform." Paper presented at the annual meeting of the Association for the Study of Higher Education, San Antonio.

Harley, S., ed. 2007. *Women's Labor in the Global Economy: Speaking in Multiple Voices.* New Brunswick, NJ: Rutgers University Press.

Harley, S., and Black Women and Work Collective, eds. 2002. *Sister Circle: Black Women and Work.* New Brunswick, NJ: Rutgers University Press.

Hollander, E. L., and J. Saltmarsh. 2000. "The Engaged University. *Academe* 86 (4). http://www.aaup.org/AAUP/pubsres/academe/2000/JA/Feat/holl.htm (accessed April 23, 2007).

Howard-Vital, M. R., and R. Morgan. 1993. *African American Women and Mentoring.* Washington, DC: U.S. Department of Education.

Jarmon, B. 2001. "Unwritten Rules of the Game." In *Sisters of the Academy: African American Women Scholars in Higher Education,* ed. R. O. Mabokela and A. L. Green, 175–182. Sterling, VA: Stylus.

Johnsrud, L. K. 1993. "Women and Minority Faculty Experiences: Defining and Responding to Diverse Realities." In *Building a Diverse Faculty,* ed. J. Gainen and R. Boice, 3–15. San Francisco: Jossey-Bass.

Mayhew, M., and H. Grunwald. 2006. "Factors Contributing to Faculty Incorporating Diversity Related Course Content." *Journal of Higher Education* 77:148–168.

Milem, J. P. 2001. "Increasing Diversity Benefits: How Campus Climate and Teaching Methods Affects Student Outcomes." In *Diversity Challenged: Evidence on the Impact of Affirmative Action,* ed. G. Orfield and M. Kurlaender, 233–249. Cambridge, MA: Harvard Education Publishing Group.

Monk, J., and D. S. Rosenfelt. 2000. "Introduction: Internationalizing the Study of Women and Gender." In *Women in the Curriculum,* ed. J. Monk and D. S. Rosenfelt, 1–53. Baltimore: Uptown.

Office of the President Web site: www.president.umd.edu (accessed September 1, 2006).

Roche, G. R. 1979. "Much Ado about Mentors." *Harvard Business Review* 57:14–28.

Rosenfelt, D. S. 2002. "Culturally Challenging Practices and Pedagogical Strategies." In *Encompassing Gender,* ed. M. M. Lay, J. Monk, and D. S. Rosenfelt, 456–458. New York: Feminist Press.

Rosenfelt, D. S., and L. A. Bolles. 2002. "Internationalizing and 'Engendering' the Curriculum at the University of Maryland." In *Encompassing Gender,* ed. M. M. Lay, J. Monk, and D. S. Rosenfelt, 424–429. New York: Feminist Press.

Thomas, D. A. 2001. "The Truth about Mentoring Minorities: Race Matters." *Harvard Business Review* 79 (4):99–107.

2

Discourses of Diversity at Spelman College

ALMA JEAN BILLINGSLEA-BROWN AND
GERTRUDE JAMES GONZALEZ DE ALLEN

I am often asked why I would choose to lead an institution as "homogenous" as Spelman College. Of course, the question is based on a flawed
assumption. Though 97 percent of our students are racially categorized
as "Black," the student body is quite diverse. Spelman students come
from all regions of the United States and many foreign countries, from
white suburban and rural communities as well as urban Black ones. All
parts of the African Diaspora are represented, and the variety of experience and perspectives among the women who attend the college creates
many opportunities for dialogue.

–Beverly Daniel Tatum

Founded as a seminary for newly emancipated slave women in 1881, Spelman
College traditionally educates African American women from the South. Given
this tradition, issues relating to diversity at Spelman have centered not on race
but on intraracial, ethnic, national, regional, socioeconomic, and cultural differences primarily within the African Diaspora. Among the central issues
regarding diversity, one has been finding ways to identify, acknowledge, and
celebrate difference within a population that historically has resisted incur-
sions from those of different racial and ethnic origins, especially since for
African Americans, racial unity and sameness served as a revolutionary strategy
for the struggle against racism and sexism in the United States. Within the last
two decades there have been several programs within the college that
addressed diversity issues: the Comparative Women's Studies program and the
Women's Resource Center, the Japanese Studies program, the Continuing Education program, the International Studies program, the Environmental Justice
program, and the African Diaspora and the World (ADW).

Beginning with the descriptions of institutional history and legacy, institutional settings and problems, as well as current diversity issues, this chapter describes and explains the unique manifestations and suppressions of diversity at Spelman College, an all-black, all-women's institution. We delineate the unique legacy and history of intraracial and ethnic diversity at Spelman. We also describe the process by which faculty change agents created and formalized the ADW course, the only two-semester required course in the curriculum and a course that was the result primarily of faculty activism. Given our definition of diversity as a network of values, policies, practices, traditions, resources, and sentiments used to promote equity and fairness as well as to dismantle structures of domination, ADW can be usefully described not only as a diversity discourse but also as a discourse of resistance. We interpret the ADW course as a countervailing mechanism to disrupt structures of sameness, silence, overconformism, and authoritarianism. These structures assumed a special importance at both black and white institutions in the post–civil rights era when integrationist objectives were perceived as having been achieved. Sameness, silence, and overconformism were promoted primarily to demonstrate that the era of segregation and Jim Crow had ended (Hale 2004, 11). One consequence was a denial and suppression of difference.

Diversity and Difference

Before beginning this study, we thought that diversity at Spelman would be manifested in terms of regional, national, and international differences as well as differences relating to class, socioeconomic status, ethnicity, and culture. What we have discovered, however, is that there is a theoretical dimension to diversity that has presented itself in two ways. One is that diversity discourse at Spelman helps to clarify the intersection of difference and domination. The other is our perception that where diversity has been actualized in policy, practice, and values, it has helped to mediate the ways in which difference supports structures of domination and has helped to create structures of equality and fairness. In order to present and clarify the theoretical foundations for these findings, we considered that it would be useful to make reference to some of the originary, poststructuralist discussions of "difference."

The discourse of diversity at Spelman is a discourse of difference, but not the same as Derrida's postmodern conversation about the limits of language. According to Derrida, part of the problem of understanding difference is that we cannot go beyond language. In his theorizing, written or oral signification creates difference that is insurmountable because the act of meaning organizes in space and time an entity, idea, or object into something other than itself. Derrida calls this problematic of communicating difference using language in space and time *différance* (Derrida 1998, 441–464).

Unlike Derrida, we see difference, in many cases, as produced, communicable, and enforced. For example, the constitutional clause in which African Americans were deemed legally to be "three fifths chattels" was a construction of racial difference produced, communicated, and enforced through, by, and for the system of plantation slavery. One may challenge Derrida in terms of whether we can or cannot communicate difference because of language. However, it is clear that differences like race, class, gender, and sexual orientation are identified, pointed to and given value in U.S. society (Appiah 1992).[1] And because these differences are designated and valorized in particular ways, they can be used to create inequities that discourses and practices of diversity can usefully challenge, mediate, and disrupt.

We understand the importance of situated knowledge regarding difference and see this situated knowledge production as affecting how diversity discourse occurs at Spelman College. Using Zora Neale Hurston's work as springboard, literary theorist Barbara Johnson writes, "What Hurston rigorously shows is that the question of difference and identity are always a function of a specific interlocutionary situation—and the answers, [are] matters of strategy rather than truth" (Johnson 1986, 324).[2]

We believe that Spelman College has a distinct "interlocutionary situation." Difference has had varying and more complex connotations for black women in the United States than Derrida's universal erasure of all subjects through language. First, as Hurston notes, difference has been used as a mechanism to hide sameness between racialized groups, such as "whites" and "blacks," and to justify structures of dominance and subordination. In the same context, difference has also been used to inspire fear of African Americans, which in turn has fueled animosity from other racial, class, and ethnic groups. The historic permutations of this intersection of difference and dominance account for the complexity of black identities that are often purposefully evasive and evolving. To disrupt structures of racial dominance and animosity, blacks developed strategies of evasion through which they could appear to accept what whites believed about them while simultaneously asserting their own sense of cultural legitimacy and human worth. They developed identities that permitted them, in the words of the African American writer Ralph Ellison, to "change the joke and slip the yoke." The historical root of this evasive and evolving identity complexity for African Americans, according to Hurston, was a resistance to their oppressor's questioning. An anecdote from the southern civil rights movement captures the essence of this complexity. When a black maid was questioned about her involvement with the economic boycotts during the Birmingham movement and pushed to actually respond about whether she supported them, the maid's pleasant and evasive reply was "No m'am, I don't support what they are doing at all. As a matter of fact, since that boycott started, I don't even go downtown." As Hurston explains,

"The Negro offers a feather-bed resistance. That is, we let the probe enter, but it never comes out. It gets smothered under a lot of laughter and pleasantries" (Johnson 1986).[3]

Difference as it relates to discourses of race, class, gender, and sexual orientation, as Patricia Hill Collins observed, has meant the establishment of an "Other"-objectified-entity discourse that operates in a binary system that privileges one identity over another (Hill Collins 1991, 68–70). The consequence has been an inscription of inequality in the United States. Finally, the production of difference has meant impediments to creative change. Regarding this, Audre Lorde writes, "Too often, we pour the energy needed for recognizing and exploring difference into pretending those differences are insurmountable barriers, or that they do not exist at all. This results in a voluntary isolation, or false and treacherous connections. Either way, we do not develop tools for using human difference as a springboard for creative change within our lives" (Lorde 1984, 114).

This chapter acknowledges the complex ways in which the term "difference" has been understood to affect black women's lives. The most important understanding of difference used is as an oppressive framework that leads to indifference, silence, and inequality.

We see difference and diversity as intimately linked. Differences that are socially produced, ignored, or seen as insurmountable barriers lead to inequality. Diversity discourse attempts to shed light on these problems of difference in hope of correcting communal silence, indifference and inequality. As Audre Lorde writes:

> Institutionalized rejection of difference is an absolute necessity in a profit economy which needs outsiders as surplus people. As members of such an economy, we have all been programmed to respond to the human differences between us with fear and loathing and to handle that difference in one of three ways: ignore it, and if that is not possible, copy it if we think it is dominant, or destroy it if we think it is subordinate. But we have no patterns for relating across our human differences as equals. As a result, those differences have been misnamed and misused in the service of separation and confusion. (Lorde 1984, 115).

We are interested in the ways in which differences are submerged, ignored, and silenced at Spelman College, and we have tried to discover how faculty change agents work against this subterfuge.

Although the dialogue of diversity has been situated around dialogues of difference in "majority" institutions, we see a parallel and at times intersecting dialogue in an all-black all-women's institution. These parallel and sometimes intersecting dialogues of difference at majority institutions of higher education are also applicable to Spelman, because even within the specific communal context of an all-black all-women's institution, there still remain social indifference, silence, and inequality surrounding difference. We theorize that the diversity dialogue at Spelman is also about an observation made by Patricia Hill Collins that "Black women have insisted on our right to define our reality, establish our own identities, and name our history" (Hill Collins 1991, 70). Those who deviate from norms relegated to this space also have unique struggles and resistances.

Given these distinctions between diversity and difference, we considered that diversity at Spelman College would also include sexual orientation and the performance of dimensions of gender, especially in relation to the construction of the image of the Spelman woman.[4] However, we discovered that the African Diaspora and the World course at Spelman functions as the best example of an academic and intellectual manifestation of diversity. ADW builds a sense of identity in a population of young black women who, despite their common racial and gender identities, learn to negotiate socioeconomic, regional, national, ability, and ethnic differences. As a corollary, these same structures of difference and diversity function to strengthen the social sensitivity and empathy of Spelman faculty and students as they struggle for social justice and work for positive social change. Finally, we conclude that in this setting there have been strategies by which structures of difference and diversity have been actualized to promote rigor and excellence as well as to create a harmonious, accepting, and productive institutional climate.

From our interviews and observations, however, we have also discerned instances of suppression and sublimation of difference among students and faculty at Spelman. For example, in 2003 Spelman was named the richest historically black college or university (HBCU) in the United States. This rhetoric of institutional wealth displaces socioeconomic differences among students, faculty, and administrators. In addition, the terms "sisterhood" and "success" have become important socionormative frameworks for the valorization of student's social mobility and the acquisition of material wealth. The norm of sisterhood, which at the college promotes a particular unity along race and gender lines, is thus also a way to silence questions of socioeconomic diversity. As one faculty member who was interviewed for this study remarked, "Promoting sameness is promoting silence." In addition, Spelman's legacy and history, especially in relation to its founding as an institution promoting Christian values, ideas, and racial unity, offers major rationalizations for sublimating religious differences. Finally, there is the observation in the interviews we conducted that there is some reluctance to reveal gay and lesbian identity, which speaks to the discrepancy between the rhetoric of diversity around sexual orientation and the realities of the social climate at the college.

Institutional History and Legacy

Addressing issues of excellence, fairness, and diversity has been an important part of the scholarship about historically black institutions of higher education. From the foundational debates by scholars like Booker T. Washington, W.E.B. Du Bois, Carter G. Woodson to later work by E. Franklin Frazier and others it can be stated that the early scholarship on historically black colleges was focused around the coordinates of race, history, aims, orientation, and the value and the place of liberal arts education.[5] The well-known debate between Du Bois and Booker T. Washington reflects the fundamental ideologies underlying the discourse on the value of technical institutions that would teach African Americans to join the working class. Both men, however, agreed on the critical importance of racial uplift and on the value of black institutions of higher education, whether liberal, mechanical, or technical, for gaining social equity and mobility. There were two important consequences of the emphasis on collective racial identity and on industrial, agricultural, and mechanical (A&M) education. One was the attraction of black transnationals, like Edward Blyden, Claude McKay, and Marcus Garvey, who associated themselves, in discrete moments, with the philosophy of Booker T. Washington toward black institutions in the United States. Another consequence, especially relating to collective identity and racial uplift, was a privileging of race over national, cultural, gender, sexual, and ethnic identities in black institutions. In most instances that meant that issues of nonracial and intraracial diversity were either ignored or suppressed.

Observing the necessity even now of making students aware of intraracial difference, one faculty member interviewed for this study explains that she works to bring speakers and lecturers who are Afro-Brazilian, Afro-Cuban, Afro-Mexican, and Afro-Russian to demystify and "even break down the idea that 'blackness' is one and the same." Another faculty member explains how she works to achieve diversity in terms of course development. Having observed a substantive number of students who were either from the Caribbean or of Caribbean ancestry, the professor became an advisor for a Caribbean American Student Association and also developed a course entitled "Women and Gender in Caribbean History."

The ways in which Spelman faculty have challenged and attempted to fill in the openings created by minimizing and suppressing dimensions of differences within a racially homogenous group constitute the critical gap in diversity studies that this chapter addresses. In other words, because diversity issues have been focused on majority institutions and the recruitment of women and minorities in faculty and student ranks, this chapter also attempts to address the complex issues of diversity at historically black institutions of higher education that mainstream diversity studies have ignored.

Carter G. Woodson was one of the first scholars to offer a book-length study on the complexities of African Americans in higher education, addressing specifically the issues of class and assimilation. In his second study, *The Mis-education of the Negro*, Woodson asserted that black institutions do not teach black students to critique hegemony, but to fit into it. He also argued that historically black institutions have seen political silence as a way to achieve class goals. Building on Woodson's work we have identified socioeconomic and class difference as a diversity issue at black institutions. We have also observed how this difference is sometimes silenced by the discourse of material and socioeconomic progress.

E. Franklin Frazier, in his discussion of late nineteenth century education and the black middle class, articulates a rationale for the emphasis on socioeconomic and material progress. After explaining how early missionary influence on black institutions promoted values of "piety, thrift and respectability," Frazier then asserts that the orientation and aim of higher education for African Americans shifted in the first decades of the twentieth century, in part because blacks assumed more administrative control of the institutions and in part because "[r]espectability became less a question of morals and manners and more a matter of the external marks of a higher standard of living" (Frazier 1966 81). Symbols of material progress and middle-class respectability became goals for educated African Americans for several reasons. One was to refute the negative images and assumptions about black inferiority by pointing to the ability of African Americans to assimilate Euro-American cultural values and standards. To promote an assimilationist agenda and minimize social, cultural, and economic differences from whites, black intellectuals and educators articulated ideologies of sameness.

These ideologies of sameness, which in various manifestations have been an important strategy for African American struggles for equality, go back at least to nineteenth-century African American intellectual history. As early as 1854, in a speech entitled "The Claims of the Negro Ethnologically Considered," Frederick Douglass argues that the humanity of African Americans is the same as that of Europeans. Asserting the critical proposition that the "Negro race, are part of the human family and are descended from a common ancestry, with the rest of mankind," Douglass articulates the central thesis undergirding the ideology to which he and other abolitionists and public intellectuals of the time subscribed. "The argument to-day, is the unity, as against . . . the diversity of human origin" (Foner 1999, 287).

Since the nineteenth century, especially in the post–civil rights era, the use and function of the rhetoric of racial unity has become more complex at HBCUs.[6] The transformation of this rhetoric may be related to the hopeful but, by some accounts, mistaken assumption that there is no longer a need to combat overt political, social, and economic discrimination. Given that many

African Americans believe that there is no longer a need to deploy strategies of unified racial uplift to combat external forms of oppression, we believe it is possible for HBCUs now to have a more fruitful dialogue about intraracial and transnational diversity. In addition to a greater and more fruitful diversity dialogue, HBCUs can begin to initiate and control their discourses about diversity, including the extent to which transnationalism impacts their discussion. For that reason, this study includes information about the origin and source of intraracial diversity at Spelman College and examines the ways in which ADW provides some foundation for transnational diversity work.

Institutional Setting and Problems

The historic beginnings of the institution, while extraordinary and compelling, set the stage for many of the problems, issues, and successes relating to diversity that have been a part of the institution since its founding. The construction of the "Spelman woman" as both an idea and an ideal has engendered both successes and difficulties. Soon after the institution produced its first graduates, Spelman women, known to be academically prepared, pious, and service-oriented, were able to move into certain social arenas where they represented the first and sometimes the only markers of racial difference. The notion of the Spelman woman as dignified, well-mannered, and willing to serve gave Spelman women nominally greater access to participation in the larger U.S. social and professional community. Many Spelman women were among the first black women to break social, economic, race, and gender barriers.[7]

Multidimensional and evolving, the construction of the Spelman woman also has had negative implications for diversity. One faculty member, for instance, described the construction this way: "[W]e say that she [the "Spelman woman"] is a leader and she serves and she is a critical thinker, high morals which means she does not have sex outside of marriage, at least not much, she's religious, not spiritual, and mostly Christian and she's heterosexual." In another interview, a different faculty member clarifies one problematic of this construction. Explaining how students "talk about it all the time" this interviewee concludes, "And it is a problematic conversation and discourse because its often conceptualized as an identifiable set of characteristics and ideals that gets in the way, very often, of diversity." Still yet another faculty member observes how the construction evolves and means one thing at one historical moment and a different thing at other moments: "Just yesterday in the faculty meeting, a faculty member was saying that Spelman students today are different from the Spelman students of the past. This comment referred to boundary issues and respect for elders, respect for faculty members. They were talking about boundary issues. Even though we have the mission of producing leaders and scholars some faculty are very concerned that our students don't understand decorum or don't have social skills that will serve them in the future." While this comment focuses on concerns about student behavior, the specific concern with social skills and decorum resonates with the historical construction of dignity, etiquette, and leadership as markers for the Spelman woman. And while those are useful and commendable traits, the problem is, as another faculty member discerns, "whenever you construct idealized ways to be you are also silencing individuals who, for whatever reasons, don't, can't, wish not to participate."

In a thinly veiled reference to Spelman as a "Negro College for girls especially favored by the Rockefeller philanthropies," E. Franklin Frazier presents, in his 1957 study, a description that, although problematic in some ways, nevertheless clarifies how the institutional setting historically was antithetical to issues of diversity. Citing a European professor who taught French at the college in the 1930s, Frazier first recounts the professor's observation of the close "surveillance over its hand-picked students" and a faculty consisting primarily of "righteous and straight-laced New England women" (Frazier 1966, 73). Frazier later concludes, "The chief aim of this college was Christianization and moral training. The academic standing of the students was determined largely by the extent to which they developed a "religious spirit" (73). From this description of the college in the 1930s, we can see that sameness was promoted first through strategies of exclusion and then by means of emphasis on religion and spirituality.

Displacing the emphasis on piety and religious spirit to gender, a recent description of Spelman still promotes sameness with the assertion that the college was founded as an institution "by and for women" (Guy-Sheftall and Stewart 2006, 3). However, two very important historic markers of difference have been left out of that description. One is that two white women, Sophia B. Packard and Harriet Giles, founded the institution for black women eighteen years after emancipation. Packard and Giles also founded the institution on the basis of what they understood to be their Christian mission.[8] The Christian ethos, which was so important to the founding and organization of the institution and, according to Frazier, was maintained throughout the first half of the twentieth century, still remains in the college's motto: "Our school for Christ." The Christian missionary foundations of the institution have engendered both benefits and problems for diversity. One benefit was the expansion of Spelman's missionary program at the end of the nineteenth century to Africa and Latin America, thereby bringing intraracial diversity to the student population. As part of the missionary training program in the late 1890s, fourteen students from West Africa and South and Central America were recruited to matriculate at Spelman. The limitations of the missionary and evangelical motivation were that it was based on a very specific religious vision that silenced non-Christian voices.[9] Until very recently, this has meant that religious diversity at Spelman was not only devalued but in some instances suppressed.[10]

Currently, Spelman College's administration is attempting to develop religious diversity through Beverly Daniel Tatum's diversity dialogues, the creation of the WISDOM (Women in Spiritual Discernment of Ministry) Center, which hosts interfaith dialogue, and the institutionalization of a revised religious studies major including faculty whose areas of academic and intellectual expertise include Islamic and global feminist perspectives. At the same time, there is still a notable tendency, especially among staff and students, to adhere to and practice Christian-based rituals. The Christian hegemony, which is in some ways legitimated because it was an intrinsic part of the founding of the college, is now beginning to be recognized as hegemonic. Some faculty have seen it as difficult to disrupt, however. While the study of world religions was until recently a part of the curriculum, commemorative rituals and practices, baccalaureate and commencement services, historically, have been Christian-based. As one faculty member has discerned, with regard to diversity in religion and otherwise, "Spelman's challenge is to find a way to honor diversity at the same time it honors tradition."

During the first half of the twentieth century, the diversity challenge included expanding the geographic base of Spelman's community of students. Historically, the college primarily served black women from the South, but by the 1960s Spelman began to recruit black women from around the country and in one instance during the early 1960s several white women matriculated at the college on an exchange program.[11] As the number of diverse regional student populations expanded, tensions among students began to emerge on the basis of class, regional, and sociocultural differences. Nevertheless, these differences were in some ways leveled out by an emphasis on "sisterhood" and racial and gender unity (Dill 1983, 131–150).

There have been other significant diversity initiatives at Spelman within the last two decades, in terms of both programs and the curriculum. Two of those initiatives were the creation of the comparative women's studies major, which very intentionally brought to the forefront issues of gender equity and sexual orientation, and the launching of one of the earliest and truly interdisciplinary programs focused on intraracial diversity, the African Diaspora and the World. In 1991 the Sumiko Takahara Japan Studies Program was established. In 2003, the WISDOM Center, which created a space for interfaith dialogue, was founded. While some of these diversity initiatives were administratively conceived and implemented, others emerged from the organization and mobilization of faculty and support of administrators.

Diversity and Faculty Activism: The ADW Story

Perhaps the most compelling story of faculty activism connected to issues of equity and diversity at Spelman College is the story of the African Diaspora and the World (ADW) program. Institutionalized in 1993 as a two-semester core curriculum course required of all students, and recognized recently by Diversity Innovations, a national resource center for higher education, ADW is a defining experience for Spelman students. Designed to situate Africa and its new world Diasporas in the context of world developments over time, the course reifies the college's mission and remains consonant with the historic construction of the "Spelman woman." More important, from the initial conception of a course that would address intraracial and gender issues in early 1990 until the course's institutionalization in 1993, the ADW story delineates the critical relationship between faculty organization and action, administrative goals and directives, environment, and positive outcomes for diversity.

The story of activism began in the fall of the 1989, when a newly tenured associate professor of history, in conversation with faculty members across several disciplines, identified two issues about which faculty at that time had serious concern: the teaching load was too heavy, and there was a huge core curriculum. At that time, the core included a significant number of required courses, and the teaching load was four courses per semester. The content of the core courses in humanities and social sciences was also a major problem. As was true for many historically black institutions in the late 1980s, traditional courses in western civilizations and literatures were still being taught despite the awareness that intellectual and scholarly work on issues of gender equity and racial diversity were being addressed in majority institutions. There was a fundamental complexity to that issue, however, for Spelman College. On one hand, there was the attitude that Spelman's curriculum needed to be "multicultural" and include the study of African, Native American, and Asian civilizations in its core courses. On the other, there was a reactionary attitude that a changed curriculum was an inferior curriculum, and that the classic and canonical were about to be abandoned for newly constructed and suspicious academic and scholarly areas. There was also the moderate position that the curriculum needed revision but that care must be taken to avoid the pitfalls of hastily organized black and ethnic studies programs. Ultimately, by way of faculty intellectual innovation and activism, the ADW discourse was linked to a specifically academic dimension of the historic construction of race and gender at the college. While it was generally acknowledged that one value of a traditional curriculum was that it provided roughly the same educational experience as majority institutions, there was also the recognition that emphasis on diversity and equity would more effectively address the historic and contemporary experience of black women in the United States.

Faculty members took positions based on their areas of intellectual and academic interest, on their historic connection to the institution (as either alumnae or long-term faculty), and on their perception of whether the ADW program would ever succeed and be institutionalized. Despite a number of fringe ideological stances, three major groups emerged. These groups were named and described by one of the early faculty organizers of the course as "progressive," "traditional," and "reactionary." The small, core group of "progressive" faculty, negotiating the conflicts and contradictions of the other two groups, began early on to intensify their efforts to recruit and organize support from other faculty for the ADW project. One-on-one conversations over lunch, small group socials, and telephone communication constituted the informal recruitment strategies. At the same time, careful attention was paid to new and vacant faculty lines across departments, how positions were identified and advertised, and who would serve on search committees. One major outcome of monitoring new faculty lines and searches was that within a few semesters, black scholars from Trinidad, Jamaica, the Bahamas, Sierra Leone, and the Gambia were recruited to Spelman's faculty. Other scholars from Mozambique, India, and Algeria increased the ethnic diversity. Ultimately, these faculty members became crucial as change agents not only because they brought important scholarly resources and expertise but also because they became committed supporters of the project. Several of them subsequently taught sections of ADW.

Because other groups were working against the ADW project, ostensibly to support a broader "multicultural" initiative, one important factor in ADW's eventual success was communication with, information from, and ultimately tacit support from three key administrators at the college: a program director, an academic dean, and the new president. Soon after her arrival on campus, Dr. Johnnetta Betsch Cole, the first African American woman president of Spelman College, asked the faculty to identify its most immediate need. The nearly unanimous response was a reduction in the teaching load. Explaining early on that the college could not afford enough new hires to achieve the goal, Dr. Cole encouraged the faculty to explore alternative strategies to reduce teaching loads and suggested that interdisciplinarity would constitute a viable direction. What several faculty members recollect from that time is that the ADW cohort, discerning broad institutional directives and a particular administrative need, began to strategize ways to align the proposed course with those directives and not only to meet the need but also to emphasize values consonant with institutional goals and stated mission. The ADW was finally focused on, and promoted as, an interdisciplinary, gender-informed course that would reduce a five-course core to two and would broadly support the mission of the institution. Teaching loads were subsequently reduced and the administration was able to honor its commitment to faculty.

With a workshop to train faculty members who were selected to teach the course, the final stages of team building and construction of the syllabus were completed in summer of 1992. After an extensive review of the syllabus, which was regarded in some instances as too rigorous, the full faculty voted to adopt the African Diaspora and the World as a two-semester course that would be required of all students matriculating at Spelman College. In the spring of 1993, the first three sections of the course were piloted. One was taught by the departmental chairperson for history, the faculty member who had been at the forefront of the initial activism, another by an associate professor of art history, and a third by an assistant professor of English. By the autumn of 1993, roughly twenty faculty members from six departments had been recruited. Again by means of a summer workshop, the faculty members developed ways to become proficient enough in other disciplines to teach the course. Spelman faculty members used several strategies to both develop and implement this course, addressing issues of intraracial and gender equity as well as promoting a certain kind of rigor.

The course itself was a two-semester sequence that was required of all incoming and transfer students. Structures of difference and diversity informed the creation of ADW, because the two-semester sequence was both interdisciplinary and gender-informed. With issues of gender constituting a primary lens by which texts and themes are examined, ADW from its inception engaged the values and concepts central to Spelman's mission: leadership, sensitivity to cultural differences, the use of diverse methods of scholarly investigation, and the association between learning and social change. In making the African Diaspora the analytical center of inquiry, the course seeks to develop an understanding of the Diaspora in relation to other cultures and to major historical, philosophical, artistic, and scientific developments over time.

Using gender as a lens for the analysis of the African Diaspora in relation to world developments over time makes possible the examination of key issues affecting black womanhood and thus informs the construction of the Spelman woman. Beginning with an article written by a faculty member specifically for the course, ADW situates gender as an analytic category in the first semester and begins the process of the disrupting the masculinist orientations of African diasporic social and intellectual history to which most students have been exposed. In a similar way, a seminal text by the Brazilian intellectual and theorist Paolo Freire disrupts Eurocentric pedagogies and knowledge constructions to posit a "pedagogy of the oppressed" that offers yet another lens through which students are able to discern and disrupt structures of sameness and homogeneity to explore and exploit difference.

Because ADW had to combine and collapse core courses in history, literature, and fine art in order to reduce teaching loads, interdisciplinarity was fundamental to its organization. While the course proceeds in rough chronological fashion, texts and themes are examined through the conceptual frameworks of several disciplines. For the analysis of the Harlem Renaissance, for instance, the philosophies and opinions of Marcus Garvey and W.E.B. Du Bois are coupled with fiction of Nella Larsen and Gwendolyn Bennett, the drama of

Zora Neale Hurston, and the drawings of Aaron Douglas and Bruce Nugent. In the same way, when earlier permutations of the syllabus included *The Tempest*, Shakespeare's drama was also taught as a narrative of colonization and in the context of the several appropriations of the Caliban figure by Caribbean writers, critics, and theorists.[12]

The first semester of the course, ADW III, considers the political, scientific, and economic forces that led to the formation of the Africa's new world Diaspora. Attention is given to Old World provenance through the examination of African and Native American societies prior to the Atlantic slave trade. European imperialism, the Enlightenment, and a theoretical examination of the nature of slavery and its intellectual apology constitute the next units. This semester concludes with discussion of forms of resistance and cultural developments in the United States, the Caribbean, and Latin America with particular attention to cultural continuities, retentions, and transformations. ADW 112, the second semester of the course, considers the aftermath of slavery from sociopolitical and economic perspectives. Marxism and the revolutionary ideology of Franz Fanon inform the discussion of citizenship and nation after emancipation and decolonization. The course then examines the ways in which cultural expression, politics, and multiple forms of representation interact in the formation of diasporic identities and diasporic consciousness. The semester concludes with analysis of liberation movements and series of questions regarding current diasporic challenges and connections in the context of twenty-first century globalization.

The faculty activism around ADW has had ramifications at Spelman far beyond the creation of a core curriculum course. By means of common presentations, interdisciplinary discussions, and international and transnational scholarship, the faculty activism that began with ADW has helped to create a climate in which intraracial diversity and transnational discourse are not only accepted but have become commonplace. Before ADW, academic and scholarly discussion about Africa and its diasporas was limited at best. One example of the long-range effects was the global conference that took place in September 2006, called "Sisters of African Descent: Connecting Spirituality Religion and Vocation." Among the more than two hundred women in attendance were black women scholars, religionists, and theologians from Ghana, Zimbabwe, Kenya, Jamaica, Israel, and Scotland. Since ADW, conferences organized from a global perspective are no longer unique at Spelman. In May 2006, the conference of the Leadership Center included leaders from Liberia and Ghana. In 2003, the ADW program organized an Afro-Latin conference with black activists and leaders from Chile, Venezuela, Colombia, and Ecuador. The Women's Resource Center has hosted conferences at regular intervals looking at women's leadership in the United States and Southern Africa, issues in black women's health, especially regarding HIV AIDS, as well as a discussion about black women in the sciences and black women's studies across the disciplines.

In addition to these African Diaspora–related conferences and colloquia at the college, there has been another important outcome of the ADW diversity initiative at Spelman. The Association for the Study of the Worldwide African Diaspora (ASWAD) is an international academic constituency that "seeks to share the most recent research about the African Diaspora both within and across disciplinary and other conventional boundaries" (ASWAD). At the ASWAD third biennial conference held in Rio de Janeiro in 2005, there was a connection between the activism and intellectual conversation about intraracial diversity begun at Spelman more than twelve years ago. The presence of former and current faculty members from the college showed how diversity work goes beyond the boundaries of the institution and links to intellectual movements and academic constituencies focused on similar issues not only within the United States but also around the world.

Faculty members, some of whom helped develop the ADW program and some who currently teach it, gave presentations that showed transnational, transmodern, and intraracial dimensions. Conversations during the panel discussions focused not only on the transnational and intra-ethnic linkages to identity, history, and culture but also addressed strategies for effective pedagogy when dealing with issues affecting the African Diaspora. Among the most sensitive and complex subjects were the sources of data collection; interpretation of data and theoretical frameworks; linking activist communities with intellectual communities; communicating ideas across national boundaries with language barriers; how to continue the work of the intellectuals and activists who are now retiring, ill, or deceased; and how to support young students across continents interested in related issues. Most apparent was the continuation of a commitment to creating an intellectual community that carries out dialogues beyond the borders of the United States. Based on this evidence, we hypothesize that the impact of the intraracial diversity work begun with the ADW program goes beyond its gates and even beyond the country in which it resides. We can also hypothesize that ASWAD, both the association itself and its first international conference, may be seen as a most encouraging example of what can happen when an institution promotes serious research and curricula innovation on minority-focused issues.

Implications: Recent Diversity Initiatives by Faculty

While there have always been manifestations of diversity at Spelman, recent faculty initiatives include attention not only to myriad forms of difference but also to the ways in which diversity is linked to equity, excellence, fairness, and social justice. In spring 2007, a faculty member who participated in our study engaged in research and gave a talk on female suicide bombers in the Middle East. Later this faculty member also discussed the complexities of the choices made by all suicide bombers through a film presentation and discussion. The idea behind the events was to highlight the complexity of the contemporary social and political struggles in the Middle East and to link class, ethnic, cultural, religious, and ideological difference with questions of equity, fairness, and justice.

In the article "Queer Christian Confessions: Spiritual Autobiographies of Gay Christians," co-written by a Spelman faculty member who participated in this study, a link is made between a budding new genre—autobiographies of gay Christians who use the book-length story form to explore their spiritual journeys and other forms of life writing, like slave narratives and conversion testimonies. This little-explored autobiographical genre is seen as a unique manifestation of attempts at exploring the relationship between Christianity and gay identity. Although not an activist text, "Queer Christian Confessions" is representative of the ways in which Spelman faculty members address unique manifestations of difference and create interesting discursive engagements with these unique manifestations. Scholarly innovations such as this one also lead to interesting discussions with other students and faculty at Spelman both in and outside the classroom. Collaboration with other faculty members and engagement with students about the unique manifestations of the discourse of difference, then, are some examples of current diversity strategies by Spelman faculty.

A recently retired Spelman faculty member discusses her long-term effort to include nontraditional students, such as adults starting or returning to college, as a manifestation of difference at Spelman. This faculty member became an advocate for more than seventy adult students who had enrolled at Spelman since 1982. The challenge for this population was not only transitioning from home or work into an academic environment but also negotiating an environment where they "felt on the fringes or unwelcomed." The unwelcoming atmosphere was created, in part, by the scarcity of classes to fit within a working adult student's schedule, by the paucity of online and evening classes, and even lack of diversity in curricular offerings and pedagogical strategies. This faculty member clearly recognizes that diversity is at the heart of justice and fairness, but overall she thought that her efforts to actualize diversity in terms of nontraditional students were not as effective as she had hoped they would be. Despite the fact that Spelman historically served older women, current pressures to emulate other well-known liberal arts colleges around the country are not in tune with the reality that many black women are returning to receive a college education later in life.

Engaging in non-Christian-based practices with the college community at Spelman events is important to one faculty participant who sees the lack of true religious diversity as more problematic than class differences. Because the Spelman motto remains "Our whole school for Christ," this Spelman faculty member points to the expectation of a primarily Christian student and faculty body. Within this context, non-Christian-based spiritual practices were described by this faculty person as "tolerated" rather than fully embraced by the college community. Since Christian-based religious practices are deeply engrained in the college's traditions, hosting meditation sessions and non-Christian prayers during college ceremonies involving prayer is seen by this faculty member as an essential diversity initiative that is much needed to challenge Christian hegemony. Other faculty members have questioned the heavy emphasis on prayer at public events in a secular liberal arts college setting. In this environment, no attention is given to atheism among students.

With great awareness of ethnic differences within the student population, linguistic differences are also taught by faculty members who take students on study abroad trips. Special attention is paid not only to the host country and culture but also to the ways in which the African Diaspora operates within that cultural milieu. Some students do not have an idea that there are African descendants in other countries such as Brazil or the Dominican Republic. Witnessing this helps to form a lasting impression and understanding regarding the diverse nature of difference among black people.

Similarly, it is important to some faculty members that students be exposed to nonwhite and nonblack peoples. Faculty who participated in this study also have initiated international programs that engage students in race, ethnic, and cultural dialogues that are outside the U.S. black/white dichotomy. Along with this are summer seminars abroad to Asian countries such as Japan, a Japanese student exchange program, encouragement of the development of new courses featuring Asian studies, conferences that extend the dialogue to the Atlanta University Center, and yearly festivals such as the Cherry Blossom festival, which introduce the campus to Japanese foods, music, and crafts not ordinarily available on campus. In addition, faculty members encourage students to participate in activities involving Asian studies around Atlanta. A faculty member who participated in this study believed that student presence in diverse activities off campus demonstrates the students' and the college's active and continued involvement with diversity issues.

Offering safe spaces to discuss issues regarding difference is essential to some faculty members in our study. This entails creating a classroom environment where even male faculty members can openly discuss issues pertaining to gender and sexual orientation with a predominantly female class. It might also mean diverging from the syllabus to give students the opportunity to discuss current issues in their lives that are caused by the difficulties of difference at the college or outside the college. Finally, it means creating a friendly relationship with students so that they feel comfortable addressing the difficulties of difference on campus within office hours through advising and mentoring. This faculty member points to the idea that, because of pre-conceived notions about the students, some faculty members fail to encourage students when they are attempting to pursue difficult research projects. The problem of lack of appreciation of student intellectual curiosity was described as deriving, in part, from difficulties between some white faculty members and the students. Most distressing to this faculty member was a lack of awareness by some white faculty members and administrators of the dynamics and negative effects these white faculty members have on some students. For this reason, in addition to encouraging students during office hours, paying close attention to who gets hired was described as an essential strategy for promoting an atmosphere of difference. The faculty member we interviewed was clear in pointing to the fact that there are white faculty members at Spelman who are sensitive to the population they serve. For this reason, instead of just hiring the best and the brightest faculty without regard to student mentoring needs, participating faculty search committees need to ensure that faculty are hired who "can relate to the students and not judge them" is an important faculty strategy for diversity discourse.

Initiating new programs that are interdisciplinary in nature and allow students to solve problems such as environmental issues is a lasting diversity initiative. In addressing questions of the environment, questions of gender, race, class, and culture emerge, especially how these concern questions of power, fairness, and equity. Spelman faculty members believe that when students engage an environmental problem, they are able to see firsthand the effects of diversity or lack thereof and the importance of equity and fairness to social justice. Development of innovative courses that merge disciplines, especially in the sciences, is key to success in this effort.

Conclusions

Based on the results of the study, we have drawn several conclusions. First, because so many of the assumptions and presuppositions in the current diversity conversation are based on the experiences of minority populations in majority settings, the contemporary discourse is limited and incomplete. Second, we conclude, as a corollary, that looking at diversity in minority settings offers a useful lens through which a number of complexities can be discerned. One such complexity is how the expectation of conformity to race, class, gender, and sexual orientation standards at black institutions not only suppresses difference but also creates structures of authority and silence that can stifle the rigor and excellence associated with diversity. The third conclusion is that at its core diversity is about how the self can be fully manifested in community. The struggle for diversity is not simply about tolerance of "Others," groups outside a powerful majority. Diversity is also about individual selves seeking the freedom of choice to reveal the most basic and fundamental aspects of who they are. Finally, there is also evidence that the reality of intraracial, socioeconomic, religious, and ethnic diversity at HBCUs means that students, faculty, and administrators learn to negotiate the unique and sometimes difficult terrain of these institutions while recognizing their unique benefits.

Using this study, the Spelman College WISDOM Center, and President Tatum's "Diversity Dialogues" as indicators, we can also conclude that some progress has been made in creating a more positive and difference-affirming institutional atmosphere at the C\college. This means that the Spelman community is closer to acknowledging, actualizing, and affirming diversity in its midst and realizing its power and benefits. From the example of faculty activism and the ADW course at Spelman, we also realized that there is power and benefit in the language of action and activism, of social change, and naming faculty as change agents. We therefore theorize that such language should be intentionally put forth for faculty members to recognize and celebrate diversity efforts.

One of the interesting results of the interviews we conducted was that several faculty members who have been part of significant change at Spelman do not necessarily see themselves as change agents.[13] Rather, they see themselves as deeply committed to issues of social justice. This commitment is not only manifest in their academic and political alignments but in their scholarship and teaching as well. We also discovered that many faculty members at Spelman were innovators within and beyond the classroom in service learning programs, mentoring programs, the black women's health network, African Diaspora study abroad programs, and continuing education. They were also creators and facilitators of civic, political, and academic networks.

While faculty change agents at Spelman do not acknowledge themselves, our study also revealed that their activism has had far reaching implications. For example, the Sumiko Takahara Japan Studies Program that began in 1991 has reached beyond the walls at Spelman. In October 2006 students, faculty, and staff in the Atlanta University Center along with other institutions came together for a symposium to discuss viable strategies for strengthening and sustaining Asian studies at HBCUs.

From the encouraging response by the faculty interviewed in this study as well as some administrative support, we also conclude that the discourse of diversity begun at Spelman can be usefully extended to other black institutions. A workshop on diversity at the Atlanta UNCF Mellon-Mays conference held in October 2006 had at its focus the particular way in which diversity is manifested on black campuses. This discussion lends support to our thinking that there is some eagerness particularly among Spelman faculty to continue the discourse on intraracial diversity and take it to other spaces.

NOTES

I. In the book *In My Father's House,* Anthony Appiah discusses this very notion of social production of knowledge of differences, especially as it relates to science and its role in the production of racial, ethnic, cultural, and social difference.

2. Johnson makes extensive use of Hurston's work on in this essay, so subsequent references in this chapter to Hurston are cited from Johnson's work.

3. These assertions are derived from Barbara Johnson's discussion of Hurston in the essay "Thresholds of Difference."

4. Written sources and taped faculty interviews indicate an awareness of a particular orientation toward black womanhood at the college—one that has evolved over time. What we theorize is that the construction of the Spelman woman means that students learn to perform certain dimensions of black womanhood and to suppress others.

5. See, for example, W.E.B. Du Bois, "Talented Tenth"; Booker T. Washington, "Atlanta Exposition Address"; Carter G. Woodson, *Mis-education of the Negro;* Thomas Sowell, *Black Education: Myths and Tragedies*; E. Franklin Frazier, *Black Bourgeoisie: The Rise of the Middle Class.*

6. What we theorize in this regard is that before the civil rights era, racial unity was important for creating alliances to combat institutional racism. Although racism continued to be manifest after the social and political gains won by the civil rights movement, the rhetoric of racial unity was used not so much to combat racial discrimination as to achieve social mobility and material prosperity. Cultural theorist Kobena Mercer's assertion that the movement of Diasporic Africans from citizen to consumer supports this theory in some ways. See Mercer's "The Diaspora Was Not Made in a Day: African Aesthetics through Time," which was presented at the Howard University conference on the Black British in April 2007. Mercer's presentation also suggests that the preoccupation with social mobility and material prosperity is Diasporic and not just a United States phenomena. In this regard it is useful to note that in 2006 Spelman College was ranked first in social mobility by Washington Monthly (www.spelman.edu/about_us/glance/glance_rankings.shtml).

7. Examples are Nora Gordon, who was the first Spelman student to go to Africa, and Clara Howard, who was the first Spelman graduate to become a missionary to Africa. In the 1960s, Marion Wright Edelman became the first black woman to be admitted to the Mississippi bar.

8. Packard and Giles's vision was realized in great part by a gift from John D. Rockefeller.

9. While the study of world religions has always been a part of the curriculum, commemorative rituals and practices such as baccalaureate and commencement historically have been Christian-based.

IO. Dr. Beverly D. Tatum and the WISDOM (Women in Spiritual Discernment of Ministry) Center have begun to address this issue.

II. A photograph of five white exchange students appears in Guy-Sheftall and Stewart, *Spelman: A Centennial Celebration.* The women and the years of their exchange are not identified, however.

I2. A useful and more extensive description of the African Diaspora and the World course at Spelman is in Colby et al., *Educating Citizens.*

I3. More extensive and detailed review of the interviews with faculty indicates some complexity regarding this statement as it appeared in our earlier report. While some faculty members did not see themselves as "change agents for diversity," other faculty members indicated that they believed the work done on course development, advising student groups, and creating programs as work that engendered change at the institution. They saw this work as part of a commitment to social justice and social change.

REFERENCES

Appiah, Kwame Anthony. 1992. *In My Father's House: Africa in the Philosophy of Culture.* New York: Oxford University Press.

Association for the Study of the Worldwide African Diaspora (ASWAD). http://www.aswadiaspora.org/index.html.

Colby, Anne, et al. 2003. *Educating Citizens: Preparing Americaís Undergraduates for Lives of Moral and Civic Responsibility.* San Fransisco: Jossey-Bass.

Derrida, Jacques. 1981. *Dissemination.* Trans. Barbara Johnson. Chicago: University of Chicago Press.

———. 1998. "Différance." In *The Continental Philosophy Reader,* ed. Richard Kearney and Mara Rainwater, 441–464. New York: Routledge.

Douglas, Frederick. 1854/1999. "The Claims of the Negro Ethnologically Considered." *Frederick Douglas: Selected Speeches and Writing.* edited by Philip S. Foner. Chicago: Lawrence Hill Books.

Dill, Bonnie Thornton. 1983. "Race, Class, and Gender: Prospects for an All Inclusive Sisterhood." *Feminist Studies* 9(1):131–150.

Du Bois, W.E.B. 2002. "The Talented Tenth." In *African American Philosophy: Selected Readings,* ed. Tommy L. Lott. Upper Saddle River, NJ: Prentice Hall.

Falconer, Etta Z., et al. 1995. "A History of Minority Participation in the Southeastern Section." A supplement to *Threescore and Ten: A History of the Southeastern Section of the Mathematical Association of America* 1922–1992. A publication of the Southeastern Mathematical Association of America.

Frazier, E. Franklin. 1966. *Black Bourgeoisie: The Rise of a New Middle Class.* New York: The Free Press.

Freire, Paolo. 2000. *Pedagogy of the Oppressed.* 30th anniversary edition. Continuum International Publishing Group.

Guy-Sheftall, Beverly, and Jo Moore Stewart. 1981. *Spelman: A Centennial Celebration* 1881–1981. Charlotte, NC: Delmar.

Hale, Frank W. Jr., ed. 2004. *What Makes Diversity Work in Higher Education: Academic Leaders Present Successful Strategies and Policies.* Sterling, VA: Stylus.

Hill Collins, Patricia. 1991. *Black Feminist Thought: Knowledge, Consciousness, and the Politics of Empowerment, Perspectives on Gender.* Vol. 2. New York: Routledge.

Ibeanusi, Victor, Donna Phinney, and Anne Michelle "Thompson. 2003."Removal and Recovery of Metals from a Coal Pile Run-off." *Environmental Monitoring and Assessment* 84:35–44.

Johnson, Barbara. 1986."Thresholds of Difference: Structures of Address in Zora Neale Hurston." In *"Race," Writing, and Difference,* ed. Henry Louis Gates Jr., 317–328. Chicago: University of Chicago Press.

Lefever, Harry G. 2005. *Undaunted By the Fight: Spelman College and the Civil Rights Movement 1957–1967.* Macon, GA: Mercer University Press.

Lorde, Audre. 1984. *Sister Outsider: Essays and Speeches.* Feminist Series. Freedom, CA: Crossing Press.

Mercer, Kobena. 2007. "The Diaspora Was Not Made In A Day: African Aesthetics Through Time." Paper presented at the Howard University conference on the Black British, Washington, DC, April.

Palmer, Parker J. 2004. *A Hidden Wholeness: The Journey Toward an Undivided Life*. New York: Jossey-Bass.

Phillips-Lewis, Kathleen. "European Stereotypes and the Position of Women in the Caribbean: An Historical Overview." In *Crosswords of Empire: The Europe Caribbean Connection* 1492–1992, ed. Alan Cobley. Jamaica: University of the West Indies Press.

Read, Florence. 1961. *Story of Spelman College*. Princeton, NJ: Princeton University Press.

Sowell, Thomas. 1972. *Black Education: Myths and Tragedies*. New York: David McKay.

Tatum, Beverly Daniel. 2004. "Family Life and School Experience: Factors in the Racial Identity Development of Black Youth in White Communities." *Journal of Social Issues* 60 (1): 117–135.

———. 2005. 50 Years After Brown: Why Historically Black Colleges and Universities Remain Relevant. *eJournal USA* (November).

Tibbitts, Felisa, and Michael Kuelker. 2005. "Howard Zinn: A Conversation about Howard Zinn, Activism and Education." *Amnesty International USA* 15 (1).

Washington, Booker T. 1901/2002. "Atlanta Exposition Address." In *African American Philosophy Selected Readings*, ed. Tommy L. Lott. Upper Saddle River, NJ: Prentice Hall.

White, Daryl, and O. Kendall White Jr. 2004. "Queer Christian Confessions Spiritual Autobiographies of Gay Christians." *Culture and Religion* 5 (2):203–217.

Woodson, Carter G. 1933/2005. *The Mis-Education of the Negro*. VA: Khalifa's Booksellers & Associates.

———. 1919. *The Education of the Negro Prior to 1861: A History of the Education of the Colored People of the United States from the Beginning of Slavery to the Civil War*. Washington, DC: Association Publishers.

Diversity Web. 2006. "Diversity Innovations: Curriculum Change." http://www.diversityweb.org/diversity_innovations/ June 7, 2006.

3

Institutional Diversity Work as Intellectual Work at the University of Missouri–Columbia

JENI HART, MARGARET GROGAN, JACKIE LITT,
AND ROGER WORTHINGTON

The University of Missouri–Columbia (MU) is the flagship institution of the four-campus University of Missouri System. Located between Kansas City and St. Louis, it is the home of more than 1,200 ranked, full-time, tenure-track faculty members who serve more than 28,000 undergraduate, graduate, and professional students. A Carnegie research university, MU maintains international collaborations with institutions in South Africa, China, North and South Korea, and elsewhere and is home to one of ten European Union centers. Although students come from all fifty states as well as ninety-eight nations, most are from Missouri and reflect regional demographics. The greatest numbers come from St. Louis and Kansas City, but a large proportion also come from relatively insulated, homogeneous rural areas and suburban communities with a strong evangelical bent. About 25 percent of MU's undergraduates participate in fraternities and sororities with a tradition of nurturing future state leaders.

The university was established in 1839 as a whites-only men's institution. Women were admitted thirty years later, initially only in the Normal School (today's College of Education). In 1936, the first African American applicant to the university was denied admission, sparking a three-year legal battle that went to the U.S. Supreme Court, which ruled against MU in 1939. Still, the university did not admit African American students until 1950. More recently, however, MU has made strides toward building a more inclusive and welcoming campus among both students and faculty. Recent administrative initiatives have encouraged the recruitment and retention of minority faculty and students; provided diversity training for faculty, staff, and students; and explored institutional changes to promote equity and inclusiveness. To better understand how such initiatives fit within faculty responsibility, we provide a conceptual framework to help guide the remainder of the study.

Conceptual Framework

"Teaching," "scholarship," and "service" are terms embedded in the professoriate. At research universities such as ours, "service" work is considered the least valuable of the three roles. Diversity work is more often than not considered in the category of service and ultimately devalued. However, placing service in a category separate from other faculty roles (such as scholarship and teaching) creates false dichotomies. When faculty use their expertise, time, and energies to become involved in efforts to increase institutional and educational opportunities for marginalized students and faculty, they are connecting the different roles they undertake in academe. They are using the scholarly skills of identifying problems worthy of study, using their critical capacities to understand how the problem has (or could be framed), engaging in a presentation of evidence, and eliciting critical feedback (Glassick, Huber, and Maeroff 1997, cited in Ward 2003). Ward argues further that any work viewed as intellectual and tied to faculty expertise should be considered as scholarship. The knowledge that emerges from such work is most likely incorporated into the faculty member's teaching and research projects. Boyer (1990) used the term "scholarship of engagement" to refer to the idea of weaving together the scholarships of discovery, integration, teaching, and application, especially in the interest of addressing the most important social and civic problems.

"Scholarship of engagement" suggests that the faculty member is working on projects aimed at increasing the common or public good (Checkoway 2002). There is an emphasis on new research methods, education for democracy, and institutional change both from the bottom up and the top down. Diversity service work that is evidence-based and embedded in research findings can be recast as an intellectual enterprise—a professional activity that is approached with the same "depth, rigor, and curiosity as any other research or pedagogical project" (Ward 2003, 114). Clearly, instead of being seen as an add-on to the central faculty roles and responsibilities, this kind of service work should be regarded as integral to the core.

Women and racial minorities generally perform more institutional service work (including, but not limited to, diversity work) than other faculty members; this often constitutes a dual burden (Baez 2000; Glazer-Raymo 1999; Turner 2002). Women and members of racial and ethnic minority groups are disadvantaged by being placed on committees in order to ensure representation (see, for example, Baez 2000; Fields 1996; Glazer-Raymo 1999; Hernández and Morales 1999; Moody 2004; Tierney and Bensimon, 1996).

As such, the disproportionate weight of institutional service rests on the shoulders of the marginalized members of the academy, particularly when one factors in the "invisible service" like conducting independent studies and informal advising. Moreover, ensuring representation of faculty members on institutional committees along the lines of race, ethnicity, and gender also creates a dimension of responsibility among the underrepresented faculty to serve on committees and to advocate for other underrepresented groups (Moody 2004; Tierney and Bensimon 1996; Turner 2002). As a result, increased expectations of institutional service without reward may lead to higher levels of dissatisfaction and attrition from the institution (Fields 1996; Patitu and Hinton 2003). This further perpetuates the cycle of leaving more work to distribute among fewer women and racial/ethnic minority members.

Other studies, however, showed that this role of advocate is not always considered a burden, nor is service always viewed as compulsory. Baez (2000) demonstrated alternative reasons faculty members may choose to participate in institutional service. While other works focus on the responsibilities of women and racial/ethnic minority faculty members as a task resulting from cultural taxation (Tierney and Bensimon 1996), Baez (2000) showed that faculty of color have motivation for institutional service. Included were a "sense of obligation to advance the interests of traditionally-subordinated social groups; using service as a means of de-isolating one's self within the academy and networking with others; and seeking validation for experiences endured within the institution" (Baez 2000, 380). Thus, women and faculty of color often consider institutional service in these areas as central to their professional identity and success (Baez 2000; Bird et al. 2005). Cultural taxation of underrepresented faculty—the idea that one's cultural identity can lead to increased expectations to serve on committees, be the "voice of that culture," and always be available to represent that cultural identity for other staff, faculty, and students (Padilla, 1994)—should not be disregarded, these findings suggested that service could assist retention if the promotion and tenure processes acknowledged the commitment required to complete the service responsibilities of the academy (Baez 2000; Bird et al. 2005). The remainder of this chapter presents faculty narratives that empirically demonstrate how institutional diversity work produces knowledge and is intellectual work—the very work that the academy should reward in various ways, including promotion and tenure processes.

About the Research

Using a phenomenological approach, our team of researchers examined the impact of some of MU's diversity initiatives, considering how diversity work is done, sustained, and understood. Subsequent case study analysis helped us tease out the varied ways in which diversity work related to curricular and pedagogical initiatives and allowed us to give voice to the individuals involved.

To begin, we identified three initiatives currently active at MU, all focused on enhancing diversity through curriculum and teaching, all originally faculty-driven. Because two members of our research team were participants in two different initiatives, we chose uninvolved members as primary researchers for data gathering and analysis. It was also an asset, however, to have participant-researchers who could provide nuanced understandings of the cases that emerged. To identify individual faculty members involved in the initiatives, we used purposive and snowball sampling techniques. This is to say, that we intentionally invited members of each group who were known throughout the institution and by the research team. In addition, we asked each participant if there were additional people with whom we should speak about our study and subsequently invited them to participate. Through these processes, initiative leaders were invited to participate in a semistructured interview about their diversity work. We then asked these point people, and all subsequent interviewees, to suggest the names of other involved faculty members. In all, we interviewed fifteen faculty members. (One agreed to participate in two interviews because she was involved in two initiatives.) Interviews were tape-recorded with permission and transcribed verbatim. After a discussion of how we analyzed our data, we report who participated from each initiative under investigation. The nature of each initiative is detailed in the Findings section of this chapter.

For this case study, we analyzed transcripts and field notes from interviews (Merriam 1998). Three members of our team selected one case to analyze using a constant comparative approach (Strauss and Corbin 1990). For each case, patterns and themes emerged through open coding, and we analyzed this data for divergence and convergence using axial coding techniques (Merriam 1998). Peer review ensured trustworthiness of the findings and saturation of categories (Merriam 1998; Patton 1990; Lincoln and Guba 1986). We also used these techniques to compare and contrast themes among cases.

Women's and Gender Studies

Nine participants were connected to the Women's and Gender Studies (WGST) initiative. All were women; two self-identified as women of color and one as a lesbian. Three were full professors, and five were associate professors. One had been involved in the university for more than thirty years in a nontenure-track capacity. Because WGST was not a department at the time of this research, none had a full appointment in the program; however, two had joint WGST appointments. The others identified as program affiliates, and all had tenure homes in the College of Arts and Sciences. Although we invited fourteen people to participate, five opted out because of other commitments, including a sabbatical. One, a faculty member of color, said she was burned out and did not want to reflect on her diversity work because of her extensive involvement in this sort of work over the years, which unfortunately reflects one of the challenges related to diversity work on college campuses.

Theatre of the Oppressed

Four faculty members involved with the Theatre of the Oppressed (TOP) initiative agreed to participate. All were tenured women faculty members. Two were full professors and two were associate professors. One was a woman of color.

Unity

Three faculty members, all people of color, agreed to participate. One was a full professor; the other two were associate professors. One was male— the only male participant in the study. (Although Unity and TOP have involved other male faculty, both initiatives are dominated by women.) We invited four other faculty members to participate, but they either failed to respond or declined.

Findings

Women's and Gender Studies

The first women's studies course was taught at MU in 1971, but the program did not achieve official status until 1980. Affiliated faculty members taught courses in their home departments but cross-listed them with the program so that undergraduates could declare an interdisciplinary major with an emphasis in women's studies. Some graduate courses were also offered, and students could pursue a minor. In 1988, the first faculty member was hired with an appointment split between the women's studies program and a home department. In 2002 the program became known as women's and gender studies.

WGST is led by a director who works closely with an advisory board of faculty, staff, and students chaired by a faculty member who is not the director. For several years, the board had discussed the possibility of working toward acquiring departmental status. Then a new program director was hired in 2004. With the support of both the WGST search committee and the advisory board, she was charged with investigating that possibility. During the summer of 2005, interested board members formed subcommittees to recommend a departmental structure for a new department. This is the work that our research team has studied.

The primary goal was to turn the program into a university department, but those engaged in the initiative also identified corollary goals. According to participants in our study, departmental status meant legitimacy. The academic community would see WGST as a sanctioned field of study, which would elevate the status of its faculty and students. Amy said:

> I think legitimacy is a goal. I don't think it is a main goal. I think it affirms for our students that the choice that they are making is a good choice and that it is equal to a choice of majoring in English.

Susan echoed the need for legitimacy but cautioned that it was important to push beyond the normative model of institutional success:

> I feel like it is really important that, as we move toward a certain type of legitimacy, that we don't define success in the most narrow . . . measurable ways. I think that success has to be increasing the opportunities for women, minorities, lesbians, queer students to have the best possible educational experience they can and to get the skills that they want. It is real easy to succumb to the pressure of an institution, which I feel is becoming more and more standardized.

Departmental status would also help WGST secure an institutional location and autonomy. As a program, it has had to rely on the good will of other departments when hiring a jointly appointed faculty member. Celia described those frustrations in hiring, frustrations that would be alleviated if WGST became a department:

> I think we all agreed that there are so many hitches when you always have to find a tenure home and have to plead with other departments to hire. . . . Some departments are more open and willing, and others are not. Therefore, what happens is that you get all bunched up in one area.

Kathy agreed when she said:

> We tried to do a search for tenured faculty. We had permission to hire senior faculty; the problem is that we can't be the tenure home. What we found is that the applicants who are most interested in us because their work is very exciting and very interdisciplinary and funky had largely departed from the mainstream of their home disciplines. For that very reason, they were interested in us and we couldn't hire them because their tenure homes were suspicious at best. That is when it really came home to me that there is good reason even if there are some obvious risks . . . to become a department.

Participants saw the work related to this initiative as both intellectual and scholarly. Making demands for institutional autonomy reflected a new vision of academic knowledge, and those involved were savvy about how to proceed.

Yet several participants also described "flying under the radar" as critical to success in a university and a state that have historically been at best indifferent and at worst hostile to gender issues. Susan called the strategy "the stealth department."

In the spring of 2006, the provost approved the WGST program as a department, yet the planning process was itself was also a successful outcome. Amy shared:

> I think it has been successful because it has worked out a curriculum and given some sense of where we want to go, and I think a year ago we probably did not know that we had to hire somebody in popular culture whereas now people do because that has been recognized as a weakness.

Intellectual advantages were identified as another successful outcome. For example, Gail observed:

> [It gave us] some kind of space to talk about feminism or women's and gender studies issues in the classroom. What does it mean to . . . to teach these issues? What does it mean to identify yourself in the classroom from that location?

And these discussions brought diverse voices to the table, as Amy stated:

> I think the program . . . gives some different points of view that were absent before. I think those are all successes and I think especially [the director] is trying to reach out to other women on campus who might want to affiliate in some way.

Participants saw a need for more diversity, however. Several, including Gail, lamented that more faculty of color need to be recruited and retained and invited to the WGST table.

> I came away last year with a sense that we do need a U.S.-born woman of color on our faculty. We need that location; we need that voice desperately.

Throughout the process, certain administrators proved to be allies, and their support was crucial to success. Instead of taking administrative backing for granted, the director and others fostered those relationships.

Many faculty members involved in the initiative joined because of supportive colleagues who were also involved or aware of WGST. Often a single invitation from a trusted source was enough encouragement. Many interested parties began by attending a meeting for WGST affiliates or a brown-bag discussion. There they found a community of scholars with an intellectual passion for WGST.

Some participants believed the initiative helped connect them to students and helped students think about diverse issues, as Amy commented:

> I do it because I am committed to helping students grow. . . . Probably the most important thing for me is trying to . . . help our students develop into people who are sensitive around these issues and are more respectful of people who are different.

Leadership within the initiative was also central to sustaining faculty involvement, particularly the work of the director and the advisory board chair. In addition, the director's success as a scholar positioned her well for leadership. Sylvia stated:

> We have [the director's] leadership. That is cool. She . . . has done a lot of research and has a lot of background. She is very good about involving everybody and listening to everybody and making a cohesive statement about what all of the various points are to bring everybody to a certain point.

For faculty with joint WGST appointments, participation in the initiative included a mechanism of formal rewards related to job expectations, yet many, like Kathy, said they would have done the work anyway.

> I am lucky to have a joint appointment in WGST, and all of that stuff does count. I see faculty who are stuck in these positions where they desperately want to do more than they are able to do because these things don't count as far as their department is concerned. Luckily here, that is not true for me. I would do it anyway, but the fact of the matter is I *have* to do it anyway.

Unfortunately, many faculty members, even some with joint appointments, were not encouraged or rewarded for their participation. Gail and Amy declared:

> I think [involvement is] threatened in particular by our core faculty who are joint appointments . . . [because a home] department may be somewhat hostile because [it doesn't] recognize the service, and essentially they're ending up having to do full service. So the department's exploiting their joint appointment by getting full service out of them. (Gail)

> [In the reward structure, diversity] matters in some ways, but it is not clear what that means. A commitment to diversity? Does it mean that you have graduate students of color in your lab? . . . I don't think it matters in the tenure process, and I don't think there is any thought about that. I don't think it is rewarded, and I think the majority of faculty on this campus don't know what diversity means. (Amy)

Participating in diversity work may also be considered radical, which can be problematic at MU, although some participants believe that stereotype can be tempered:

> You get a reputation of being radical often and crazy [but] I think this has been overcome with a lot of serious research. People do publish; these books do get recognized. (Emily)

Yet many, as Amy described, sense that MU discourages involvement in diversity work:

> [The] whole institution seems to exist with this old boy's network which is not necessarily all white and . . . necessarily all boys either, but it is the culture . . . and it is really frustrating sometimes to work in and it feels oppressive.

Some respondents believed that women's issues and diversity were a low administrative priority. For example, Kathy said:

> In 2006 we are still saying we need to hire more women—let's not even raise the question about women of color. And the provost is saying that we need affirmative action for men!

Within the past three years, the university has hired a new chancellor, a provost, a deputy provost, a dean of the College of Education, and a dean of the College of Arts and Science. With changing leadership comes ambiguity about issues, which discourages involvement in diversity work.

Finally, participants mentioned Missouri's politically conservative state legislature as a block to their involvement in this initiative. Although faculty members always carefully considered how the political infrastructure might react, they did not shy away from potential backlash, a strategy that seemed to work since the program ultimately achieved departmental status.

Theatre of the Oppressed

In 2000 a member of the Theatre Department gathered a group of interested faculty members from theater, education, religion, and other disciplines who were excited about using theater techniques to address diversity in the classroom. The resulting initiative, known as Theatre of the Oppressed (TOP), combines the pedagogy of interactive theater with the work of raising awareness of oppression in higher education.

Under the auspices of TOP, paid student actors present short sketches in teaching assistant (TA) training sessions, faculty development workshops, and meetings with residence hall learning communities. Sketches deal with aspects of religion, ethnicity, gender, class, and homophobia; the audience includes faculty, TAs, and undergraduates. After performing a sketch, the actors remain in character so that the audience can ask them to clarify their feelings, motives, and other information that might shed light on the characters' behavior. Then audience members are invited to join the sketch as instructors or student leaders. The purpose is to provide a safe environment in which the audience can observe and, if brave enough, practice dealing with such situations.

The driving force behind this initiative is the theater professor, whose aims are to raise awareness of and stimulate discussion about multicultural issues in teaching and learning and to highlight the pedagogical potential of interactive theater. She has negotiated with her department to teach one fewer course annually so that she can manage the student actors, train facilitators, and schedule performances. She serves unofficially as project director. A department colleague who is also engaged in multicultural work directs the sketches on a volunteer basis.

Two College of Education faculty members collaborated on an early part of the project, which was to bring theater students into their undergraduate course on multicultural issues in education to offer lessons using theater techniques. Subsequently, they conducted a self-study, collecting data about how their students were responding and their own teaching was changing. Sylvia described:

> We had been trying to unlock this mystery of why teacher preparation and students are so resistant to multicultural theory . . . so this gave us a good opportunity to take a look, not only at the students but also at our own instruction.

Early on, Dorothy, a faculty member from the College of Arts and Science, joined the project as cochair of the initiative. She had also experienced student resistance to the notion of oppression in her classes:

> How do you work with people whose entire social milieu, from their churches to their schools, to what they get in the popular media, is telling them oppression doesn't exist? And those are the authorities they believe.

All three professors wanted to deal productively with the fear and anger that conservative students expressed in their classrooms, but their main motivation to remain involved with TOP has been their own development and growth as educators. All have used the project in their research agendas, and all have published papers relating to it.

Other faculty members have also been involved at various points, and two campus administrators have provided invaluable assistance. Importantly, the administrators have drawn attention to the initiative by their presence at events and by including it on the agenda of the Chancellor's Diversity Initiative.

Thus, small amounts of funds have become available—for instance, money for hiring a graduate assistant assigned to the theater professor. Faculty members have also received small internal grants to pay student actors and provide assistance with research projects. They recently obtained a large grant from the Ford Foundation to conduct research on difficult dialogues around religious intolerance and a grant from the National Science Foundation's ADVANCE program, involving one of the TOP faculty, to improve the status of women in science and engineering.

Faculty members see this work as central to their professional and personal lives.

> [The initiatives] have become the focus of my work. . . . It's why I am here as a professor. . . . If these initiatives completely disappeared, I'd look for another university. (Dorothy)

> There's a common political commitment among [us] . . . to work on social change in the academy. . . . We enjoy working together, and we enjoy the writing of it. (Joan)

> It is truly my life . . . , finding a voice and finding opportunities for [marginalized people]. (Sylvia)

Interactive theater taps into the emotions and prompts reflection that can change participants' attitudes. The TOP team has created a research project around these performances with both qualitative and quantitative components. Results show that the experience is meaningful, especially for instructors who have been seeking ways to deal with diversity, but that a brief sketch alone will not change certain people's attitudes or competencies. Terri explained:

> I think our experiences have given us the idea that, yes, [TOP] . . . does stimulate reflection, it stimulates awareness, it gets people thinking, but that there's another piece that we need too.

She is referring to other kinds of interventions. For instance, members of the initiative are excited because a new Ford Foundation grant will allow them to work with law school faculty, with the goal of learning to add conflict resolution and deliberative dialogue techniques to the sketches.

Although faculty members receive no recognition per se for doing this work, it does fit the general values and beliefs of the College of Education, which may not be the case for other colleges. And there is always the possibility, in a conservative state such as Missouri, that initiatives like TOP that expose racism, sexism, homophobia, and religious intolerance will become targets. Terri said:

> I mean this is a liberal cause, if you will, and the whole conservative political backlash out there could pose a threat.

Faculty members, like Sylvia, also worry about institutional commitment to diversity.

> I don't see that there is institutional commitment—a place of promi-
> nence in institutional dialogue. That's totally absent. . . . We have Black
> History Month, Women's History; as soon as it's over, it's gone and for-
> gotten. There is no real recognition. I don't think it's on anyone's radar
> that this community is a diverse community. That's certainly stated
> when it's appropriate and when it's in the best interest of the institu-
> tion to do so. [But] there's no attempt that I can see to meld this insti-
> tution into a diverse community.

Unity

Unity was formed in May 2004. According to the former director of the university's Program for the Excellence in Teaching (PET), the initiative began
after she received an e-mail from several African American faculty members
who shared concerns about the classroom climate. Many taught courses
focusing on race, ethnicity, or gender and often confronted resistance and
disrespect. These hostile experiences made teaching and career progression
difficult.

PET's response was to invite a visiting speaker, Lester Monts, to give a talk
about the challenges faced by faculty of color. The event was funded by the
Office of Minority Affairs, International Programs, Faculty Development, and
the associate provost's office; it was the first official Unity program.

After Monts's visit, faculty members met to decide on a direction for the
initiative. One faction suggested bringing in more speakers; another wanted
to design a faculty support discussion group for women of color. Because
Unity had no funds, it followed the second route and became a discussion and
support group, and the associate provost hosted a formal celebration in its
honor.

Soon group members decided that two facilitators should organize and
direct the initiative. As Sylvia shared, they searched "for those who are
respected for their scholarship and roles at MU, who aren't radical, who'll look
toward building rather than complaining." At the same time, they secured
permission to receive a list of minority women faculty members. After the new
facilitators met with the group, Unity decided to expand membership to
include male faculty members of color. Invitations were sent to all colleagues
of color, and in January 2005 about forty faculty members attended a reception for the newly configured initiative.

To assist Unity, the deputy chancellor's office designated a graduate student staff member to execute its activities. Thus far, the group has organized
several programs, with varied attendance. Sessions on classroom and

department dynamics had only three to six participants, but those on promotion and tenure and on teaching renewal were better attended, and the promotion and tenure session was offered again during the next academic year. Participants shared the observation that faculty of color often face being an "outsider within" (Hill Collins 1990):

> Being inside the institution by virtue of having a role. Being outside the institution by not being invited in or not understanding the rules and norms and how things work. Mentoring, in this context, is showing you the ropes . . . and then you are invited in. (Sylvia)

> Part of the design [of Unity] is that we are going to mentor junior faculty and give them a place to go to air concerns and to get support, mentorship, and guidance. (William)

The goals of Unity are to provide a space on campus where minority faculty members can be mentored and supported, where their intellectual perspectives can be nurtured and legitimated, where they can get tips for succeeding in a relatively hostile environment, and where they can take collective action. The initiative is new, however, and the organization and its members are still finding their way.

William felt that his own legitimacy and credibility as a scholar and professor are considered suspect by some of his colleagues and students. He is generally optimistic about the effects of the diversity work and the potential of Unity on campus; however, he adds a depressing caveat:

> I [meet] every single day . . . with students who are extremely resistant and very conservative, and sometimes even graduate school students can be very demeaning. It can be in small things. It can be in big things. I mean, I think of it in terms of those micro-aggressions that occur in everybody's life on a day-to-day basis. That is something that I feel . . . constantly in my life as a professor, . . . and they come from everywhere. They come from students, and they come from other faculty.

Yet those participating in Unity steer their diversity work toward intellectual work. All believe that mentoring, support, and community building serve the broader goal of expanding the canon of academic knowledge and legitimating the diverse intellectual perspectives and academic excellence generated by the faculty's racial diversity. Linda reflects:

> I think [Unity] is very important for a consequential segment of the MU population . . . constituted by minority faculty of color . . . and all of the people who engage in that type of scholarship, . . . [which] relates very well to present-day societal problems. I don't think the university is so much that ivory tower where there is no connection to the real world.

And I think [our] issues are . . . real-world concerns, like talking about
HIV in Africa and talking about women raped or women abused, and
this is not academic. It is out there. I think that is very important.

All participants believe that Unity sessions have helped individual faculty
members. For example, Linda said:

The [promotion and tenure] panels were successful because . . . from
the standpoint of the faculty, this business of tenure and promotion
is the single most important aspect of their career and their life. . . .
Faculty of color tend to do research in things that pertain to color, ethnicity, minority, and so on. . . . [I tell them to think about] where to
publish, and how they can document [a journal's] credibility and . . .
prestige.

Some group members disagree over whether Unity should continue to support individual faculty or target institutional change. Sylvia, for instance, said
that her involvement in the initiative "gives me a sense of satisfaction" yet has
not ushered in "any real change" on the institutional level:

It has been my observation that individuals don't [create change] but
[the] collective does. . . . If you want to effect change, I think you have
to catch the attention of an institution or the organization.

Rather than see it as an activist group, it became clear to William that it was
going to be more of support and mentoring group:

I thought it was going to be a precursor for an activist group, . . . a
group of people who came together and said that we need to do something about issues related to diversity on campus that affect faculty,
whether that means increasing faculty diversity itself or addressing, for
example, curricular or student issues that affect faculty of color or
women faculty or [lesbian, gay, bisexual] faculty. It seemed to start out
that way.

William contrasted his experience with Unity, in which he felt somewhat marginal, to another campus initiative on diversity in which he had become
deeply invested.

I could see actually the impact occurring at each stage of the
process. . . . Suddenly I [saw] particular issues being raised in particular ways that maybe [came] out of the work that we were doing. . . .
Because the interest was there and because those folks were responding to our data; and when we made those presentations [to adminis-
trators], I felt like we were having an impact and we were raising
awareness and increasing the dialogue.

But other participants see Unity as service work.

I think some could say that is some form of activism. I see it as some form of contribution. People who came to the last [panel where] we had various assistant professors . . . found it very useful. I also had a discussion with faculty of color . . . about the nitty-gritty things, and they found it very, very, useful. Do you call it activism? You can call it whatever you want. I call it more like pragmatism, and that is the reality of it because . . . [I want] everyone to be successful. And if I can contribute in any little way to make you successful, then I want to do that. (Linda)

If you are a good citizen of your profession, then you have to be directive and give some of yourself to areas that may not benefit you directly. Being a good colleague may mean from time to time teaching a class that nobody wants to teach or teaching in a time slot that is not really desirable. (Sylvia)

Service work, as it is valued at MU, can have negative effects. William stated that his "research has stagnated" because of the diversity work he does on campus. Clearly, like participants in other diversity initiatives, those involved in Unity dealt with challenges and barriers.

Shapes and Substances of Faculty Initiatives

As we analyzed the data from this study, one of the most interesting findings was that faculty diversity initiatives encompass a wide sphere of activities and range of purposes. The three initiatives described in this study share enough similarities that they can all be described as faculty initiatives. For instance, they all met the criterion of being faculty initiated and faculty led. They all involved faculty time and effort that was somehow "outside" their institutionally defined workloads. That work was most often described as service, although we define it as intellectual work as well as scholarship and knowledge production. All of the participants were engaged in activities that were designed to affect some kind of change, yet not all of the activities were geared primarily toward institutional change. Almost all the participants who were active in these initiatives were women—several were women of color. Most of the participants were on the tenure track and most already had tenure; of those who specifically participated in the interviews, all were tenured. Few were full professors, however. All the initiatives were fueled by a passion for the institutional benefits of expanding the canon of academic knowledge and legitimating the diverse intellectual perspectives and academic excellence generated by racial and other diversity characteristics among faculty and students.

However, each initiative took on a different shape and form. The WGST initiative was framed by the goal of institutional legitimization and the creation of academic autonomy. Although the ultimate aim of department status was, for most of the group, the goal that helped to sustain the initiative, it was not perhaps the most satisfying aspect in the end. The participants talked about how worthwhile the process was. For many of the participants, it was the process of meeting and discussing the advantages and disadvantages of departmental status that sustained them. The question of how best to attain departmental status within the constraints of a conservative institutional and state political climate drove their efforts. In and of itself, that work became a means of legitimizing, even furthering, their scholarship and research. It situated them within the academy and provided a space for them to plan curriculum and identify the future intellectual direction of the department. The WGST initiative provided opportunities for the participants to form a community of scholars who shared similar intellectual goals, including creating a more supportive and comfortable community than they found in their departments. They met, strategized, and argued, but there was a strong sense of purpose that held them together.

Offering a similarly clear focus for the participants, the TOP initiative brought together a group of people who were excited about a promising pedagogical technique. The ultimate goal for those involved was to keep TOP alive in some shape or form on the MU campus. And like those who participated in the WGST initiative, the TOP participants were driven by a commitment to diversity work. This initiative included a strong teaching and faculty development component as well as the goal of improving the classroom climate. Given the commitment to issues of diversity and social justice for all those engaged in diversity work, it is not surprising that two of the participants of the TOP initiative were also active members of the Women's and Gender Studies program at some point over the years.

The TOP initiative was in some ways quite unlike the WGST initiative, however. First, there was less focus on institutionalization and changing institutional structures in the TOP initiative. Individuals stood to gain more by the opportunities of this initiative to enhance their own teaching and research. Further, the director wanted the material and human resources to continue her work, but other faculty members involved were less invested in resource issues. Others believed in the value of the work and were willing to offer their time and energy to ensure that the project continued, but they also enjoyed the academic opportunities that emerged from the project. One could argue that if the project is sustained over time, there will be direct institutional benefits in the improvement of faculty and teaching assistant instructional skills and techniques.

Unity presents a picture of quite a different kind of initiative than the two previously described. There have been several activities associated with Unity over the past two years, but it is not very clear who considers herself or himself a member of Unity. A purpose for these activities can be clearly identified, however—offering support and mentoring for faculty members of color involved in the promotion and tenure process and in dealing with a hostile classroom climates.

One interesting aspect of the Unity initiative is that, early on, there was administrative support for it. The administrator who ran the PET and the deputy chancellor were involved in one way or another, but neither provided leadership for the initiative, nor was there any provision of substantial resources beyond offering meeting space and sponsoring a visiting speaker. Still, the need for a group such as Unity to mentor and provide support to faculty members of color was acknowledged by certain members of the administration. So although a faculty member initiated the first discussions and helped to articulate the need for a support group, Unity was more closely associated with the administration than the other initiatives were. We wonder what effect this may have had on the way members of the group took leadership and perceived their roles in the project.

When faculty members did come together around the issue of support for women faculty members of color (initially there was a race and gender focus), no clear leader emerged, unlike the case of the two other initiatives; instead, two facilitators, with relatively undefined responsibilities, were identified. Moreover, the political climate surrounding the emergence of this initiative was quite different from the other two, despite the fact that all three initiatives are centered on diversity. Many faculty members agreed on the purpose of creating a support group, but there was not strong agreement about who would do the work or how it was to be done. The nature of the initiative is much more amorphous. Currently, the group seems to be suffering from, as William noted, "an identity crisis." It is no longer even clear that the purpose is to support exclusively faculty members of color, given that invitations to recent events were sent to all faculty members.

Nevertheless, as the WGST initiative has done for feminist faculty, Unity has provided a space for those who share a passion for supporting faculty members of color so that they can survive the alienating institutional environment long enough to contribute much-needed intellectual diversity. Both initiatives offer "homes" for faculty to confront the structures and attitudes that marginalize diverse individuals and prevent them from helping to invigorate and strengthen the institution's academic capacity. Members of all three initiatives emphasized the value of the space they created in terms of place and time. But participants in the first two mentioned the notion of community more than the participants in Unity did. This is perhaps because the work of Unity can be conducted on a one-on-one basis through individual mentoring, but without a core of committed faculty members who organize activities and let junior faculty know of the existence of the group, sustaining the work of Unity may become difficult.

Scholarly Service

The findings of this study contribute to the emerging literature about how faculty become involved and stay involved in faculty-led initiatives around diversity (see Hart 2005 for a summary of the extant literature about faculty activism). Perhaps the most significant contribution of the current study is a broader understanding of service. We believe that this study challenges the existing literature, specifically about faculty diversity work that is considered service in the tripartite faculty responsibilities of teaching, research, and service. In fact, the patterns and themes that emerged demonstrate that intellectual work undergirds the efforts even in initiatives with differing goals, histories, and futures. Boyer (1990) made a distinction between institutional service and professional service, with professional service being embedded in intellectual work, and thus worthy of reward in the tenure and promotion systems in higher education. The study that underlies this chapter argues that institutional service is also embedded in intellectual work, and should be understood and rewarded as such. Hogan (2005) theorizes about service as intellectual work and knowledge production. This study grounds her theory in evidence that shows that diversity work can be scholarly service, service that builds upon existing knowledge and creates new knowledge—in ways that match the goals of research and scholarship more generally.

All three initiatives allowed opportunities for faculty to engage in intellectual work. For example, the WGST initiative demanded intellectual engagement and awareness of the state of research and teaching in the field and offered the intellectual stimulation necessary for the new collaboration. Several TOP faculty members were able to conduct research and publish directly as a result of their commitment to the project. Faculty members involved in Unity powerfully articulated the importance of promoting and supporting new knowledge and creating a community where such knowledge can be created without interference. Moreover, in all three initiatives, disciplinary boundaries were stretched by the collaboration of faculty from throughout campus. Through this work, traditional methods of curriculum, pedagogy, research, and service were challenged—all fundamental components of intellectual work and knowledge production. Ultimately, the academic demands and benefits related to being involved in these initiatives were important features and motivators for faculty to remain engaged in the work. The faculty members involved in WGST, TOP, and Unity drew from interdisciplinary backgrounds to come together to improve the academy. They focused on intellectual work and knowledge production—for example, creating syllabi, giving lectures, conducing research outcomes studies, developing governance structures, socializing other faculty to the academic culture, and writing reports. They organized to support these intellectual agendas. These examples are scholarly work, much like the "professionalized activism" described by Hart (2005), and deserving of merit and reward in a university. We do not deny that some service activities may lack a certain degree of knowledge production; activities like the initiatives central to this study, however, are not among them.

A diversity initiative can emerge and develop in several different ways. Individual personalities play a part, as do timing, coincidence, and serendipity. What seems most evident is that involved faculty members must find a way to nurture and protect their own passions and energies. Their commitment to diversity work inspires them to continue to engage in it despite constraining institutional environments. It is important that they see diversity work as scholarly service—the very type of service that Boyer (1990), Ward (2003), and Hogan (2005) have challenged higher education to recognize and reward.

REFERENCES

Baez, B. 2000. "Race-related Service and Faculty of Color: Conceptualizing Critical Agency in Academe." *Higher Education* 39:363–391.

Bird, S., J. Litt, and Y. Wang. 2004. "Creating Status of Women Reports: Institutional Housekeeping as 'Women's Work.'" *NWSA Journal* 16(1):194–107.

Boyer, E. L. 1990. *Scholarship Reconsidered: Priorities of the Professoriate.* Princeton, N.J.: Carnegie Foundation for the Advancement of Teaching.

Checkoway, B. 2002. "Creating the Engaged Campus." Paper presented at the annual meeting of the American Association for Higher Education, Faculty Roles and Rewards Conference, Phoenix, AZ.

Fields, C. D. 1996. "A Morale Dilemma." *Black Issues in Higher Education* 13(17):22–28.

Glazer-Raymo, J. 1999. *Shattering the Myths: Women in Academe.* Baltimore: Johns Hopkins University Press.

Hart, J. 2005. "Activism Among Feminist Academics: Professionalized Activism and Activist Professionals." *Advancing Women in Leadership* (Summer). http://www.advancing-women.com/awl/social_justice1/Hart.html (accessed June 7, 2005).

Hernández, T. J., and N. E. Morales. 1999. "Career, Culture, and Compromise: Career Development Experiences of Latinas Working in Higher Education." *Career Development Quarterly* 48:45–58.

Hill Collins, P. 1990. *Black Feminist Thought: Knowledge, Consciousness, and the Politics of Empowerment.* Boston: Unwin Hyman.

Hogan, K. 2005. "Superserviceable Feminism." *Minnesota Review* 63–64:112–128.

Lincoln, Y. S., and E. Guba. 1986. *Naturalistic Inquiry.* Newbury Park, CA: Sage.

Merriam, S. B. 1998. *Qualitative Research and Case Study Application in Education.* San Francisco: Jossey-Bass.

Moody, J. 2004. *Faculty Diversity: Problems and Solutions.* New York: RoutledgeFalmer.

Padilla, A. M. 1994. "Ethnic Minority Scholars, Research, and Mentoring: Current and Future Issues." *Educational Researcher* 23 (4):24–27.

Patitu, C. L., and K. G. Hinton. 2003. "The Experiences of African American Women Faculty and Administrators in Higher Education: Has Anything Changed?" *New Directions for Student Services* 104:79–93.

Patton, M. Q. 1990. *Qualitative Evaluation and Research Methods.* Newbury Park, CA: Sage.

Strauss, A., and J. Corbin. 1990. *Basics of Qualitative Research: Grounded Theory Procedures and Techniques.* Newbury Park, CA: Sage.

Tierney, W. G., and E. M. Bensimon 1996. *Promotion and Tenure: Community and Socialization in Academe.* Albany: State University of New York Press.

Turner, C. S. V. 2002. "Women of Color in Academe: Living with Multiple Marginality." *Journal of Higher Education* 73 (1):74–93.

Ward, K. 2003. *Faculty Service Roles and the Scholarship of Engagement.* San Francisco: Wiley.

PART TWO

Dismantling/Challenging Hostile Micro/Macroclimates

4

Faculty Microclimate Change
at Smith College

MARTHA ACKELSBERG, JENI HART, NAOMI J. MILLER,
KATE QUEENEY, AND SUSAN VAN DYNE

The phenomenon of a "revolving door" for women and minority faculty members has been implicated as one factor hindering efforts to diversify the professoriate (Moreno et al. 2006). Recognizing that understanding the institutional factors that promote this phenomenon is the first step toward eliminating it, we undertook the study described in this chapter. Our work examines the role of microclimates in faculty retention and engagement at one private women's liberal arts college, Smith College. While aspects of the study are no doubt specific to Smith or to other colleges with similar purpose and makeup, it is both our sense and our hope that many of the findings are, in fact, quite universal to the faculty experience regardless of institution type. Ideally, then, this chapter will provide a starting point for faculty and administrators committed to microclimate transformation within their own particular college or university.

Our work at Smith was inspired by a group of senior women faculty members who had been concerned since the 1980s with a perceived revolving door for women and minority faculty members, particularly in certain departments. Smith has instituted a variety of programs to recruit and hire women and minority faculty, but some departments, although they did well at hiring women and/or minority candidates, did not retain them as faculty members. Too many disappeared from campus before the tenure decision, either because they were not rehired or because they left "voluntarily." College administrators typically viewed each loss as idiosyncratic, rather than as reflecting a problem at the college or in the particular department. Those who did acknowledge a problem often claimed there was little they could do to address it because of the value placed on "departmental autonomy" at Smith.

Over time, we began to realize that overall efforts to change the culture at the college might be undermined by microclimates—the ways the climate of a particular department might affect a faculty member's willingness and/or ability not just to remain at the college but to thrive. Faculty members inhabit a world that is often quite circumscribed, and almost totally defined by their departmental colleagues. Where those colleagues are welcoming and support-ive, such limits may not be problematic, but where colleagues are not open to different modes or fields of research, different priorities for the structuring of lives outside of the college, or different self-presentations or lifestyles, the departmental climate can be devastating. Daily behaviors at the level of the department can effectively undercut virtually any collegewide initiative.

At the same time, we were aware that some departments that had difficulty retaining women and/or minority faculty members in the past had changed rather dramatically, and others seemed to be in the process of doing so. We used the opportunity provided by the research funding from the Ford Foundation Reaffirming Action project to seek answers to questions we had puzzled over for years: why have some left and others stayed? What factors contributed to a faculty member's decision to leave? What factors enabled others to stay—despite difficult obstacles? Further, since becoming a change agent on campus requires investing in the institution, potentially despite, or even because of, one's own experience with marginalization, we also wanted to explore what enables a faculty member to make such an investment, to engage productively (whatever her or his race, sexuality, or ethnicity) with others in realizing goals of diversity in the larger campus community. How might we facilitate such engagement?

One of our goals in this study was to understand the functioning of both dominant and alternative microclimates. We use the term "microclimate" to refer to a small, relatively self-contained environment within which a faculty member operates. It could be a department, a committee, an interdisciplinary program, a reading group, or a purely social configuration. Our research sug-gests that alternative microclimates[1] are critical for the retention of faculty: if they do not have alternative microclimates available to them, faculty mem-bers in chilly or actively hostile environments are more likely to disengage from the institution, or to leave it completely.[2]

The Local Context

Smith College is a private, residential liberal arts college for women, with an average enrollment of 2,600 undergraduate students. The faculty is currently composed of 285 members in 37 departments and programs. Smith has an increasingly diverse student body in terms of both race/ethnicity and socio-economic status: in 2006, 32 percent of the incoming class of first-year students were students of color who were also U.S. citizens, and 22 percent of the incoming class were first-generation college students. Although Smith shares many traits of the broader class of private liberal arts colleges, it is worth noting that the socioeconomic profile of its students is rather distinct within this institutional class. Specifically, in 2004–05 Smith had the second-highest percentage—25.9 percent—of Pell Grant–eligible students among all private liberal arts colleges in the country, a figure more than twice as high as the percentages at most of its self-identified peer institutions (see "At Smith College" 2005).

The issue of diversity within the faculty ranks at Smith has been addressed periodically by internal study. For example, in 1985, an ad hoc committee issued a report on "Recruitment and Retention of Minority Faculty" (de Villiers et al. 1985). This committee's work was spurred by the realization that, in the period from 1960 to 1985, of 67 regular faculty appointees who were underrepresented minorities (URM), 17 (25 percent) had resigned before tenure, and 27 (40 percent) were terminated by the college.

Our analysis of recent data found that recruitment and retention of both minority and female faculty has improved by quantitative measures. Specifically, during the most recent decade, marked by overall expansion of the tenure-track faculty, both women and underrepresented minorities increased both in absolute numbers and as a percentage of the total tenure-track ranks: women from 45.7 percent in 1995 to 52.5 percent in 2006, and faculty of color from 6.9 percent to 13.6 percent. Nonetheless, assessing success in retention must include an analysis of turnover rates among underrepresented groups. We applied the quantitative analysis developed by Moreno et al. (2006) to examine turnover patterns in hiring at Smith. We found that turnover rates for URM faculty (42 percent) and for women in all race/ethnicity categories (52 percent) were, in fact, lower than for the faculty as a whole. Closer analysis of the URM data, however, suggests different patterns for different racial/ethnic groups, with black faculty, in particular, subject to a noticeably higher turnover rate.

While these data may in fact reflect a revolving door pattern within at least some URM subgroups, the sample sizes for any one racial/ethnic category are simply too small at an institution the size of Smith to allow us to draw any definitive conclusion from the numerical data alone. Hence, our belief in the importance of qualitative as well as quantitative data for understanding trends in hiring and retention.

About the Research

To gain a better understanding of how individual faculty members experience their professional lives, we applied a phenomenological version of qualitative inquiry (Merriam 1998). One member of the research team, external to Smith but familiar with the college, conducted individual interviews with faculty from three different departments, selected both to provide divisional representation and to exemplify microclimates that seemed to have undergone recent changes in climate related to race, ethnicity, and gender.

We selected participants characterized by diverse voices in relation to gender, race/ethnicity, academic rank, assumed involvement in other microclimates at the college, and length of employment at the college. Within each department three cohorts of faculty members were identified as potential participants: "leavers"—those who had left the department (by choice, in retirement, or for other reasons); "stayers"—those who had been departmental members for ten years or longer; and "new faculty"—those who had been at the college for less than ten years. Twenty faculty members were interviewed, seven from each of two departments and six from the third. Four "leavers" were included among these twenty. Eight of the participants were men and twelve were women. Since those interviewed were not asked formally to identify their racial or ethnic status, separate data are not included in the study, but invited participants did include members of minority racial-ethnic groups.

The external researcher interviewed participants using a semistructured protocol designed by the research team and approved by the Smith College Institutional Review Board. She worked closely with the Smith researchers to identify the most powerful patterns and themes. Strikingly, there was relatively little difference among the comments of leavers, stayers, and new faculty, and little divergence in the salient themes among the three departments studied. The quotes that appear in this chapter are therefore identified only by gender and tenure status. Quotations from leavers reflect the faculty member's rank at the time of departure.

Findings and Analysis: A Close-up Look at Microclimates

A prevailing microclimate may be fairly homogenous in terms of gender, or it may be relatively unified in age. Members may have made relatively similar choices about whether and when to become parents. Department members may share a loose consensus about accepted or most important fields of research or methods and may share a preference for certain teaching strategies. The department may be made up almost entirely of tenured members. By contrast the new hire may differ from the departmental norm by gender, race, ethnicity, and/or sexuality. Quite often, particularly in the social sciences and humanities, the new colleague may have been hired in a field in which the research questions, methods, and validity of the field itself may be perceived as ideologically or politically charged.

The departments we chose for this study had experienced imbalances along these vectors of difference. Their continued failures either to hire effectively or to retain those whom they did hire suggested problems of recruitment and retention that deserved attention. Yet these departments also appeared to be in transition toward more productive microclimates for new members, providing a unique opportunity to learn what factors had facilitated and contributed to those changes.

Tolstoy wrote, "All happy families are alike; each unhappy family is unhappy in its own way" (Tolstoy [1873] 2000, 1). That generalization may not be any more true of families than of departmental microclimates: while there were certainly similarities in the reported characteristics of "happy" microclimates, there were also significant commonalities in the negative behaviors reported by those who experienced "unhappy" departments.

Negative Microclimates: What Practices Limit Faculty Members' Investment?

Perhaps the most striking finding of our study was the number of our colleagues who reported bullying behavior on the part of senior colleagues, both within the department and on the campus more generally. Bullying behavior was reported across the divisions, and it took a variety of forms.

When senior members bully or attack untenured members—and, especially, if no one comes to the defense of the person attacked—the behavior creates a toxic atmosphere that colleagues may well strive to avoid whenever possible. Unfortunately, the bullying behavior often cannot be escaped: faculty members are effectively required to attend department meetings; senior members are required to make class visits and review the teaching and scholarship of untenured colleagues; and most departments expect that members will serve on a variety of departmental committees. When bullying behavior takes place in any of these contexts, collegial "citizenship" becomes a chore at best, a dreaded commitment at worst. Further, bullying behavior can create a hostile microclimate that serves to discourage a faculty member from engaging with the institution as a whole.

It is worth noting that, in several of the reported instances, the bullies were male and those most intimidated were female, a not unexpected pattern when men still outnumber women at the senior ranks. One tenured male noted, "There is a woman in my department who could tell you things about how she was treated here for years. It was just outrageous. There is a guy in my department who had it in for her. I don't think he would have done what he did to a man. He tried to do that to me and I basically threatened to knock his block off, and he was one of those guys who would back right down when he got a response."

Of course, this quote speaks fairly explicitly to mechanisms for effective neutralization of a bully, but it also serves to illustrate how transparent the gender imbalances in bullying can be to other faculty members. An exacerbating factor at an all-women's college like Smith may be the habit of seeing women in a student role, which may make treating women faculty members as professional equals unfamiliar or even threatening. Gendered power imbalances remain salient in the professoriate as a whole and even at Smith, although the ratio of female to male new hires overall has improved over time and has resulted in an overall faculty that is majority female.

Participants in our study described many types of bullying and harassing behavior. While many of these reported behaviors were public and visible, some were more subtle. A tenured male observed, "He was a very dominant and bullying type of person . . . and he exerted control over things that went on in many devious ways. . . . One thing that characterized him, and I have never seen anyone else really do this, but he used the telephone as a weapon. He would call people up and he would just talk at you until he wore you down and he would not hesitate to call people in the middle of the night."

Speaking openly about such behaviors can have a noticeable impact. In most cases it seems that bullies do not limit their intimidation to one faculty member; so the ability of the bullied to share their experiences is a first step toward limiting the bully's power. Just as on the playground, then, one of the best defenses against bullying may be the power of collective action within a microclimate. Conversely, bullying behavior in a departmental microclimate can prevent departments from acting collectively in productive ways within the larger institutional setting. Bullying can be seen as but one specific way in which microclimates become factionalized. The factionalized department emerged as another theme in descriptions of hostile microclimates. In its simplest and perhaps most insidious form, the factionalized department seems divided along both professional and personal lines. A tenured male reported, "My department is not a collegial department and it is not clear why that is the case. For some of us, that has to do with geography because we are spread all over the place. [All members of the department are not housed in the same building.] The outside review committee was shocked at that [thinking that] if they put us all in the same box it would be wonderful. Some of my colleagues' responses were 'Geez, I would not want to be in the same box as her or him for all of the tea in China.'"

Perhaps a more serious form of departmental factionalization occurs when faculty members are split along lines related to real or perceived divisions within their discipline. This type of split is especially troubling from the perspective of faculty diversity, since new research areas and methods are often embodied in candidates who are differently trained or who come from different ethnic or national backgrounds. One tenured female faculty member summed up the situation in her department by saying, "I can still say even now that anyone who does queer theory or who does Marxist theory would not be very welcome. They would be regarded as very suspicious." Even when experienced faculty attempt to "help" their newer colleagues navigate such divisions, they may unwittingly further marginalize their colleagues. An untenured male observed, "When I first came to Smith, the first thing that people who were trying to help me did was to take me to coffee or lunch and to tell me exactly how the department is divided. Some people think of it as a divided department in terms of conservative or forward thinking. The stereotype that was passed on to me was that half of the department did not want anyone in my field because it is not a real field and it is identity politics."

Even in cases where department members are not necessarily hostile toward each other or split into obvious factions, the absence of shared goals can create a climate that is not supportive of its members. One of the prime characteristics of an unhealthy environment is the sense that members share no consensus about departmental goals or priorities and do not feel themselves accountable to each other as professionals engaged in a common enterprise.

Several respondents spoke specifically of a commitment to teaching as the shared enterprise that they hoped would unite their departments. Many faculty members described a sense of disappointment that this was not the case. Sometimes this sense communicated explicitly: "When I came, my chair sat me down and said to me that, 'I hope you know your ability to get tenure at this institution has nothing to do with how well you get along with the rest of your colleagues or your teaching, but it has everything to do with your research," said an untenured female. While such a message may be standard fare at a research university, it was disappointing to this faculty member, who came to Smith *because* of her commitment to teaching at a liberal arts college. Further, when faculty members feel that teaching is devalued at the broader institutional level in ways they did not expect, the weighting of scholarship can strengthen, rather than break down, divisions based on other vectors of difference.

In many ways the forms of factionalization described can lead to a sense of isolation for some faculty members, most often, perhaps, the newer members of a department. This isolation can be exacerbated when the department serves as the sole microclimate a faculty member experiences, a situation that also tends to amplify negative characteristics (for example, bullying or contentious factions) within the department. One extreme form of isolation is associated with departments that function like traditional families, where everyone is expected to put departmental needs (usually as defined by senior members) above individual needs. Members might be expected to be available for committee meetings at any time, to meet with students or other faculty members in the evenings or on weekends, or to make the department the center of their social lives. Such expectations can be particularly problematic for faculty with familial or other obligations beyond the college. But they also constrain members who are (apparently) single: "I do certainly feel that . . . the college asks a lot of us at different times of the year, on weekends, and at nights, and I think that falls disproportionately on people without children because the rest of us have a ready excuse why we can't do it," said a tenured female.

When a faculty member finds the departmental microclimate to be factionalized or otherwise hostile, to whom can s/he turn for support or assistance? On many campuses the department chair is expected to take this sort of leadership role and can effectively shape the departmental microclimate. Smith, however, operates with what faculty members term a "weak chair" system[3] that does not seem to support this form of leadership. A tenured male explained, "We have no budgetary control over salaries or even recommendations over salaries, so chairs have no control over their faculty, [but] they are responsible for their faculty. So they are responsible without having the power to do anything. It is a very peculiar situation. I think it is an odd position they put chairs in here: powerless but responsible." Thus, chairs may not feel empowered to enforce good behavior within their departments.

A more subtle effect of this system and how faculty perceive it is that it discourages chairs from seeing their role as an opportunity for leadership in a more positive (as opposed to punitive) sense. New faculty members may in turn be disappointed when the chair does not intervene or take the lead in a difficult situation, thereby making a hostile environment even more demoralizing.

A heavily tenured department can also leave untenured members feeling cut off and pessimistic about investing in the institution, not least because the prospect of any significant change seems far off. "At this point we are heavily tenured. We have only one who is an untenured tenure-track person. It is a real senior, top-heavy department, which is a problem," a tenured female said.

The role of faculty hiring both in faculty diversity more generally and in microclimate transformation more specifically is clear. Recruitment is the first step in this process. When a departmental microclimate suffers from negative influences, hiring new faculty is one obvious way to change it. But the hiring process itself can have a negative impact on faculty microclimates. And faculty reactions to hiring can reflect how members evaluate current colleagues. When one's faculty colleagues dismiss a candidate or even more broadly an entire scholarly field, it can reinforce the marginalization already felt by faculty members whose work diverges from the more "traditional" work of colleagues, especially senior colleagues.

Coupled with respondents' experiences with hiring that deliberately devalued some forms of diversity as it is reflected in scholarship was a pervasive sense that the framework for hiring in their departments was built explicitly on the notion of "hiring the best candidate." While the goal is laudable, the language of an objective "best candidate" often serves as a proxy for hiring a candidate whose personal and professional choices most resemble those who are already faculty members, particularly senior faculty. As one tenured male respondent noted, "That ['hiring the most qualified person'] was the principle that all of the argument was based upon. 'The most qualified person,' as this senior colleague defined it, was never a woman."

Of course, Smith's small size may heighten the perceived risk of transformative hires. In a small department each faculty member's impact on the microclimate as a whole is magnified, and an awareness of this may make faculty less likely to gamble on a new hire whose work or identity seems somehow foreign. A tenured female noted, "When we were first hiring, we had to fill up the department and people were really concerned with people who they were really sure would get tenure. So, you were looking at people from the same graduate programs; you were looking for the standard person and when you do that you often don't end up with a very diverse faculty."

Positive Microclimates

What factors contribute to faculty satisfaction and retention? To a considerable degree, and not surprisingly, the characteristics of productive microclimates represent the flip side of the unproductive ones. Supportive microclimates are characterized by collegiality and a shared vision for their work. Many have changed over time to make their members feel less isolated. At its most basic level a positive microclimate is one in which faculty members get along with each other (Fogg 2006). While personal idiosyncrasies are certainly present, in supportive microclimates faculty members have learned to deal with their differences in a collegial manner. "We don't all agree with [one another on] matters of curriculum or matters of policy but most people are really content to make it work and eager to work together as colleagues," noted a tenured female.

How can such an atmosphere be fostered when it does not arise organically? Respondents indicated that social functions may provide one venue for transforming a department. A tenured male reported, "At a certain point one of my predecessors started having a department party and it was [just] one party but it was something that people do each year now . . . people see each other more outside." Practices that encourage collegiality may be quite spontaneous, even serendipitous. And they may take forms quite different from formally expected or mandated behaviors.

When new members do not experience a microclimate as collegial, or when a department is simply so large that it can feel overwhelming to new hires, some members find support in smaller cohorts of their peers, even with those outside their department: "One faculty member in particular, an untenured male and his wife, were very, very supportive of me and there were also other women my age or a little bit older in another department who had just arrived. One . . . was my next door neighbor and she and I got to know each other quite well because we were neighbors even though we were in different departments," recounted an untenured female. At its best a cohort within a department can embolden its members to act to encourage microclimate transformation. An untenured female reported, "[Having a critical mass] made it [the department] more open. More issues were brought up. . . . since there were three women and if we saw something, it was not one person speaking out and everyone looking at you like an idiot. There were three and if we all agreed that something was wrong, then we felt like we could speak out."

Given the links in some of the comments between departmental collegiality and interactions outside the workplace, it should come as no surprise that one aspect of a positive microclimate is its ability to support a faculty member's life outside the college. Both male and female faculty members spoke of the need to balance personal and professional obligations, and of the ways positive microclimates support that balance. An issue for a large number of faculty members is the juggling of children with their careers: "Having day care that we have access to, that is close to campus, that is really high quality day care is a huge deal because I don't feel bad about our child being there. . . . So that is a big thing and it also helps in my department that several of the junior faculty have small children so you don't always feel like you are the one reminding people that we can't actually have a meeting then or I have to miss a meeting because my child is sick," said a tenured female.

Faculty also recognize the two-way relationship of work/life balance to departmental microclimate. Sometimes the microclimate—specifically, the presence within the department of a cohort with similar concerns—supports that balance. At other times, work/life balance may also influence the microclimate itself: "People have busy full lives and there is not as much time for internal [negative departmental] stuff. I think it has made the mood better. Because you see people with their children, you have a sense of them as human beings that you might not see in the department meetings. I think it has probably helped that each of the chairs since this baby boom started has been a parent. . . . It has been a good thing," observed a tenured male.

Whereas collegiality in all its forms is concerned with a more general description of the interpersonal interactions within a microclimate, more specific relationships between individuals can have similar impact on a faculty member's experience of his or her microclimate. Mentoring is a common strategy for generating supportive microclimates. We define mentors as those who take an active interest in a particular younger scholar; the mentor's support enables the mentee to be productive, to feel valued, and to thrive. A successful mentoring relationship can allow faculty members to thrive even when their microclimate is not hospitable to all its members: "I have all kinds of help. I am not sure everybody feels the help that I have felt over this time. I am sure there are junior faculty members who have left that did not feel this kind of support that I have had," said an untenured male. Significantly, when the senior faculty are predominantly male and white, as is most often the case nationally, it is important to consider whether it is as easy for women and faculty of color to establish mentoring relationships through the types of informal interactions that this and other statements seem to reference.

Both research and faculty opinion suggest that good mentor matches are somewhat serendipitous and that they cannot be structured or arranged. At the same time, additional recent research suggests that good mentors can work cross-racially and across disciplinary specialties. The critical element is that the relationship combine mutual respect and openness to mutual learning (see Stanley and Lincoln 2005). Success may also depend in part on the mentee's willingness to identify specific instances where a mentor can help. One tenured female recalled, "I was assigned an official mentor like everyone at Smith, and she was great . . . she is on my hallway and I always knew if I had a question I could go see her . . . When I was preparing my tenure dossier and I saw her at the printer she said 'can I do anything for you' and I said 'actually yeah . . . can you read my personal statement?' It was fabulous. You can't expect that one person is going to give you the climate and the advice you need—you really have to look a lot of places for it." Further, the creation of a truly supportive microclimate requires a culture where mentoring is seen as an ongoing process, not something that ends at milestones such as reappointment or tenure.

For a microclimate to undergo positive transformation, faculty members may need to institute mentoring when no such local model is in place. One tenured female respondent said, quite simply, "I made a promise that I would offer the junior people the mentorship that I did not get when I was here. I think that has paid enormously." An untenured female reported, "I don't know that I personally experienced discrimination, but some of my colleagues sure did, and I kind of became part of the group trying to lend support to them." Faculty members within a given microclimate are generally best positioned to identify problems there; when they are willing to act, they can do so efficiently and effectively.

Faculty need not be senior to act as mentors. Indeed, it can be empowering for junior faculty to act as mentors to each other: "We actually have an informal group, Junior Faculty in Sciences and Engineering . . . that meets pretty much every month for lunch," said a tenured female. Mentoring interactions of this type could equally be described as the development of an alternative microclimate, a phenomenon that many respondents cited as a positive influence on their experience at Smith.

"Alternative microclimates" can be any one of a number of contexts in which colleagues come together outside formal departmental structures. These might include participation in college committee service, engagement with interdisciplinary programs, or membership in informal social/collegial networks. Indeed, participation in such alternative climates seems to have been the largest single positive factor affecting those who have persisted and thrived at the college over the years. As one tenured female faculty member described it, "I think the most important things have been support and connections outside of the department. When I first got here I was involved right away in some writing workshops and some teaching workshops and that helped me meet some people. Being involved in [the program] has been really important to my sanity frankly." Alternative spaces can also offer unique opportunities for leadership: "We were a collective; it was a very, very powerful place to bring together women of color and to give them real intellectual leadership," noted a tenured female. From the point of view of senior, more established, faculty, they also provide additional contexts in which to serve as mentors and/or advocates.

These additional venues can provide a microclimate that is an alternative to the department not only intellectually, for example in the case of interdisciplinary programs, but also in the types of personal interactions they generate: "The academic unit is intimate for several reasons. We eat together very often and we co-teach all of the time. I have co-taught every year that I have been here . . . and co-teaching really builds bonds. Eating together really builds bonds and we do that all the time. After every lecture in our lecture series we always go out for drinks," said an untenured male. It is interesting to note in the preceding quote that some of the support this faculty member derives from the alternative microclimate relates to the shared purpose centered around teaching, something that was often missing in less successful microclimates.

Alternative microclimates can be most effective when they are viewed as complementary to, rather than competitive with, the departmental microclimates to which most faculty belong. In fact, acceptance of these alternative microclimates is in itself one mark of a supportive department. A tenured male reflected, "I think people now, people in my generation . . . are more comfortable with the idea of faculty members having several allegiances and of [interdisciplinary] programs having some say in what they teach. There is not quite the same territoriality and suspicion that there was when I first got here." This type of acceptance is particularly important when considering newer areas of scholarship themselves, many of which are interdisciplinary by nature.

It is perhaps somewhat counterintuitive that respondents in our study spoke favorably of college service as an alternative microclimate that enhanced their experience at Smith. Like any alternative microclimate, a committee can simply connect a faculty member with colleagues who are supportive. As the following tenured female respondent notes, though, part of the positive aspect of this work is, again, a sense of shared purpose: "[Committee service] does not sound like an obvious way to support my role as a faculty member, but it makes you feel like you are part of the college and you get to know people in other departments, particularly when [my] department was somewhat an acrimonious and unharmonious place and sometimes claustrophobic." An untenured male faculty member described how such service work complements other positive aspects of his work as a faculty member: "It is that balance of being happy and a trouble maker that drives me to do the work I do in all areas. It drives me to be on committees."

What makes comments like these somewhat surprising is their juxtaposition with a number of comments from faculty who do not believe such work is highly valued, particularly for junior faculty. "The college makes pretty clear that service does not really count at all toward tenure. So there is generally a sense among junior faculty that you only need to have some sort of token thing to put on your record or on your tenure dossier because it does not really count," said a tenured female.

There is a disconnect among our respondents, then, between the value that individual faculty members place on their service work and the value they feel it is accorded by those they feel have the power to validate it. Finding ways to bridge that gap may therefore be one relatively simple strategy for enhancing faculty microclimates.

Many respondents spoke about the special role of teaching as a central aspect of Smith's distinctive mission. As described earlier, a number of faculty members found their microclimates to be compromised by the lack of a clear message about the centrality of teaching to faculty work. Those who identify teaching as one positive aspect of their experience at Smith have often been able to find a microclimate that supports this work. One tenured female respondent stated, "I do believe in the mission of a liberal arts college. . . . I think it is important to feel that we are part of that, and one does feel that." It is notable, however, that in some cases when faculty spoke of their positive experiences with teaching, their comments reflected a more solitary commitment to this work: "I know I am an undergraduate teacher. . . . I am on dissertation committees at [list of research universities], but it is not what I think of as college teaching. I have spent my whole life teaching in women's colleges and that is what I want to do," said a tenured male.

From responses like these it seems that there is an opportunity at Smith—and perhaps elsewhere—to draw on what many faculty members seem to see as a very individual commitment to and passion for teaching as one mechanism for strengthening microclimates of all sorts.

Many faculty members also share a sense of purpose that is unique to Smith and to other women's colleges: the commitment to education for women. "This is a perfect combination of research and teaching and it is a women's college and it is not so uppity or laid back. It is modern and it is the perfect school. That is what has kept me going through the hard times and all of the stuff and saying that well, I could get up and leave and go someplace else, but I really learned and I really appreciate that this is still historically a women's college in the mission of it," reported a tenured female.

While Smith's mission is somewhat unusual, the idea that faculty can be sustained by their commitment to such a mission is a more general one. It suggests that a clear message to faculty about the mission of their institution can itself be a factor in generating positive microclimates, when the mission is one that faculty members support and when faculty members feel their work toward that mission is supported in turn.

Factors That Contribute to Improving Microclimates

What makes change? Throughout our study it is often impossible to separate the positive and negative characteristics of microclimates from the mechanisms used to transform them. Many of the faculty spoke explicitly of ways in which their microclimates were changed for the better, even as the respondents focused on particular static characteristics of their departments. In this final section we highlight some of the factors that emerged as most likely to generate positive changes that support and enhance the lives of a diverse faculty. While our analysis has led us to propose and enact specific measures at Smith, the discussion here focuses on general strategies that could be adapted for a range of institutions.

It is important to note that our study was focused from the outset on the issue of faculty diversity. Our examination of microclimates and how they transform was aimed at understanding how to enable faculty members who are "different" from the perceived majority of Smith (or any) faculty—in race, ethnicity, gender, sexuality, or nontraditional research and teaching field—to feel ownership in the institution and to feel recognized as contributing to the college's larger goals. The consistency of our findings provides strong evidence that the lessons we derive from this work will, in fact, improve the working lives of all members of the faculty. While there is no doubt that the vectors of difference outlined earlier can play a profound role in how different faculty members experience their institution, it is heartening to see that faculty aligned in diverse ways along those vectors share to a large extent a vision of what makes a supportive microclimate.

We begin by summarizing some of the mechanisms for change that emerge directly from the quotes and analysis in the preceding two sections. Arguably the most important theme that emerges is the idea of a sense of shared purpose in faculty work. The presence of such a purpose defines a positive microclimate, and its lack is felt as a negative. Finding ways for the institution to communicate its mission to departments consistently and effectively can help members come together in their contribution to that mission. At Smith the faculty interviewed overwhelmingly find (or wish to find) that shared mission in undergraduate teaching; the shared purpose will certainly be different for different types of institutions.

A finding that we did not expect was the extent to which faculty value college-level service as an expression of their shared purpose. This finding has prompted us to suggest to departments that they rethink their traditional model of emphasizing department- rather than college-level service as a way for junior faculty to satisfy their service "requirement" during the probationary period. The alignment of service responsibilities with expectations for tenure and promotion is no doubt a complicated dance at many types of institutions, but we are confident that by simply adjusting to some extent the type rather than the amount of service expected from junior faculty members, colleges and universities might provide an untapped source of support for their junior faculty. The ways colleges and universities reward and otherwise demonstrate their appreciation of service at all levels also plays an important role in the engagement of faculty and the likelihood of their acting as agents of change.

In general colleges and universities would do well to enact structures and policies that encourage the development of positive microclimate characteristics and discourage the negative ones. Since these two categories are largely mirror images of each other, it is not difficult to see the types of measures that are needed. For example, isolation is a negative, and cohorts are a positive. To the extent that cohorts can be created, either by hiring in groups (a strategy that is perhaps more practical at larger institutions) or by measures that bring together faculty who may be physically separated within different departmental microclimates, our study suggests that faculty will feel more supported and engaged. The specific ways that cohort formation can be encouraged and implemented will vary with the culture of different institutions, but from this study it appears that faculty themselves are a rich source of ideas for how cohorts and alternative microclimates can be created and sustained. Continual assessment of institutional practices, whether the practices are formal or informal, is essential to ensuring that these practices meet the needs of current faculty.

In the remaining discussion we highlight some ideas about effective mechanisms for microclimate transformation that came directly from faculty respondents. One theme that emerged repeatedly—despite the prevailing rhetoric about the virtual "sanctity" of departmental autonomy—was the importance of administrative pressure in encouraging a department to make changes to improve its climate and to integrate attention to diversity into departmental decision making. Thus, as one untenured male faculty member put it, "Sometimes decisions come on high and cause us to think in new ways. If we can't change it, then maybe we can make the best of it." A tenured male faculty member noted, "We thought we had a better chance of getting that position . . . if we did it in that field instead of a more traditional field." These two examples demonstrate that administrative pressure can be applied quite effectively in hiring; it is only fair to note, though, that administrative attempts to influence hiring can have negative as well as positive outcomes: "I would say that the department was rather lukewarm and they did not seem to be committed. They seemed to be more strong-armed into a position [by the administration] where they were supposed to tenure a woman," observed a tenured female. The fact that this type of pressure can be difficult to apply successfully is not reason enough to assume that it will not work. Since some faculty members—both the hired and the hirers—report positive experiences when the administration helps focus departments on diversity in hiring and retention, there are models for how to make such pressures work.

From the faculty responses to our study it seems that administrative pressure and/or leadership for effecting microclimate change outside of hiring has been less successfully applied. A tenured female respondent reported about a negative microclimate, "I think they [the administration] could have intervened earlier. They knew it was toxic. . . . but when the climate continued to be terrible they kept hoping that it would heal itself." Another tenured female faculty member spoke more explicitly about how the administration could exert pressure in ways that were likely to engender positive outcomes: "The administration can help by reminding chairs and departments that it is important for promotion to occur in a timely fashion. Also, the administration can help by creating conditions to allow departments to behave autonomously and still meet the college's goals. I think empowering individuals and departments are clear initiatives that can work hand-in-hand with administration. It cannot be covert or forced." Her comment echoes in a way the theme of shared purpose with the mention of meeting "the college's goals." For the college to have any influence over microclimates, there must be a shared understanding among faculty that autonomy is not orthogonal to a shared vision for the institution as a whole.

Another aspect of the preceding comment that merits emphasis is the respondent's singling out of promotion as an important facet of faculty satisfaction. Several faculty members spoke of the transition to full professor (along with receiving tenure) as defining moments in their engagement with the institution. As one tenured female faculty member said of tenure, "It was very good as a reward and acceptance into the community. I actually did not own a part of Smith, but now I belong in a different kind of way." The importance of promotion in empowering faculty to become agents of change is described by another tenured female faculty member: "Once people are full [professors], it frees them in ways tenure doesn't. There is a certain amount of self-censorship in place, so increasing the speed and encouraging departments to think about promotion more aggressively is great." Again the notion of administration involvement ("encouraging departments") is present. The issue of promotion and how it affects microclimates is inextricably linked to faculty demographics;

even at Smith, where women now make up the majority of the faculty, they are underrepresented at the senior ranks.

While action by the administration was cited in several instances as a way to foster microclimate change, it became clear through this study that a fairly common "strategy," if it can be called that, is simply to wait for death and/or retirement to allow the transformation of a department. In some cases these events are simply the only way a department can hire new, more diverse faculty: "What I think happened was that we had a bunch of new hires about six or seven years ago because we had a lot of retirements and a death. Because the number of [female] graduates coming out of graduate schools [has] increased, there were a lot of good women candidates. So they ended up getting hired," said a tenured male. Even when there is no apparent change in the diversity of a department with turnover, there is often a sense that personnel changes create a more positive microclimate.

While there is no doubt that a changing of the guard provides an unparalleled opportunity for departments to reinvent themselves, there is a negative side to this phenomenon. In many situations, faculty perceived turnover in a department as the only effective way to deal with department members who bullied or otherwise contributed to a negative microclimate. As one tenured male respondent said in reference to a particularly recalcitrant former colleague, "I told her [a senior administrator] my biggest worry was that this man was going to find a way not to retire and that it was absolutely essential for our department to get rid of him and we could get nowhere when he was there." In such cases, the resiliency of those who remained did pay off as the departments eventually became less hostile and uncomfortable. Many of those who persisted made use of the strategies outlined earlier in the chapter, such as alternative microclimates, to sustain themselves and their work through the hard times. It is clear, though, from the many anecdotes about the behavior of these colleagues and its impact on the department microclimate that, while some faculty survived the experience, there were numerous casualties along the way.

Because bullying behavior was such a common experience for faculty members who participated in this study, it seems critical to identify solutions to this problem other than faculty turnover. In fact, some effective strategies are suggested by faculty voices captured earlier in this chapter. For example, the faculty member who spoke of the power of a critical mass described rather explicitly how a group felt more able to face its perceived adversaries than she did as an individual, saying, "Especially since there were three women and if we saw something, it was not one person speaking out and everyone looking at you like an idiot."

We end this discussion of factors that foster change by recalling a faculty member's description of a bully's "outrageous" treatment of a female colleague, noting that, "He tried to do that to me and I basically threatened to knock his block off, and he was one of those guys who would back right down when he got a response." One wonders what could have happened if this respondent had acted similarly on behalf of the female faculty member. More generally what this idea describes is an *advocate* who will work publicly to support a less powerful colleague. The work of an advocate, while potentially quite effective in neutralizing bullies, is not limited solely to this kind of one-on-one interaction and can in fact be affirming rather than contentious. Advocates might be senior faculty members who provide public forums for work on race, gender, sexuality, and their intersections to be presented, validated, and constructively critiqued. They might work for issues of special urgency to untenured faculty members. They might represent the integration of diversity issues in visible committee service. In short, an advocate takes on some of the hard, visible work of microclimate transformation in exchange for the benefits that are accrued by all when the transformation occurs.

In ecology, a microclimate is defined as "the atmospheric conditions affecting an individual or a small group of organisms, esp. when they differ from the climate of the rest of the community; or the entire environment of an individual or small group of organisms" (*Collins English Dictionary*, 987). In the context of the academy it becomes particularly important to examine microclimate change in order to understand how faculty members from underrepresented groups, including women, people of color, and people from often simultaneously "marginal" and/or "cutting-edge" specialties in their disciplines, may experience different conditions than the majority faculty in any given institution.

Transforming microclimates isn't easy, and indeed isn't always "safe," whether in the natural world or in the academy. Transformative change is a natural part of the process of learning, however, and it is imperative for any academic community to attend not only to the macroclimate but also to the diverse range of microclimates that constitute the intellectual health of the academy. A recent study of feminist academics observes that "as agents for change, feminist academics frequent a territory in which micro and macro processes are analytically related" (Morley and Walsh 1995, 1), a truth to which this research project on faculty microclimate change clearly attests. As agents of change, we believe that faculty members have both the responsibility and the agency to transform the academy and we offer our study, grounded in faculty voices and experiences, as one map-in-process for the journey.

NOTES

We wish to acknowledge Susan Bourque, provost, and Carol Christ, president, of Smith College for their support of this project and their commitment to acting on its findings. Cynthia DiGeronimo in the Office of the Provost and Cate Rowen, director of institutional research, helped enormously with data collection and analysis. Nancy Young, college archivist, unearthed earlier reports on various aspects of diversity at Smith. We are especially grateful to those colleagues—both current and former members of the Smith faculty—who gave generously of their time to participate in the interviews that form the core of this project.

1. On the nature and importance of alternative "spaces" or microclimates see Hill Collins's discussion (1991) of "safe spaces," Fraser (1992) on "subaltern counterpublics," and Davis (1999) on the "kitchen legacy."

2. On hostile or "chilly" climate issues see, for example, American Psychological Association 2004 and 2006; Anonymous and Anonymous 1999; Avalos, 1999; Committee on the Status of Women in the Economics Profession, 2001; Committee on the Status of Women in the Profession 1999 and 2001; Cress and Hart 2005; Fox 2000; Freyd and Johnson; Geiger and Travis 1999; Ginther 2003; Jacobs et al. 2002; Tokarczyk and Fay 1993

3. Department chairs at Smith are typically elected by their departments to three-year terms.

REFERENCES

American Psychological Association, Women's Programs Office. 2006. *Women in the American Psychological Association. available at* www2.apa.org/pi/wpo/womeninpsych 2006.pdf.

American Psychological Association. 2004. *Surviving and Thriving in Academia: A Guide for Women and Minorities.* APA Women's Programs Office. www.apa.org/pi/oema/surviving.

Anonymous and Anonymous. 1999. "Tenure in a Chilly Climate," *PS : Political Science and Politics* 32 (1):91–99.

"At Smith College, a Mission to Serve the Underserved." 2005. *Chronicle of Higher Education,* May 12. http://chronicle.com/weekly/v52/i36/36a01401.htm.

Avalos, Manuel. 1999. "The Status of Latinos in the Profession: Problems in Recruitment and Retention." *PS Online* (September). www.apsanet.org/PS/dec00/latino.cfm.

Collins English Dictionary (Aylesbury, UK: HarperCollins, 1994).

Committee on the Status of Women in the Economics Profession. 2001. *2001 Annual Report.* www.cswep.org/CSWEO_nsltrWinter_2002=2.pdf.

Committee on the Status of Women in the Profession. 1999. "Improving the Status of Women in Political Science: A Report with Recommendations." *PS Online* (September). www.apsanet.org/PS/sept92/csw.cfm.

Committee on the Status of Women in the Profession. 2001. "The Status of Women in Political Science," *PS: Political Science and Politics* 34 (December): 319–326

Cress, C., and Jeni Hart. 2005. "The Hue and Cry of Campus Climate: Faculty of Color and White Faculty Views on Creating Equitable Environments." *To Improve the Academy* 23; 111–129.

Davis, Olga. I. 1999. "In the Kitchen: Transforming the Academy Through Safe Spaces of Resistance." *Western Journal of Communication* 63 (3):364–381.

de Villiers, Jill, Elizabeth Ivey, Carolyn Jacobs, and Donna Nagata. 1985. "Report of the ad hoc Committee to Study the Recruitment and Retention of Minority Faculty at Smith College." October.

Fogg, Piper. 2006. "Young PhD's Say Collegiality Matters More Than Salary." *Chronicle of Higher Education,* September 26. http://chronicle.com/weekly/v53/i06/06a00101.htm.

Fox, Mary Frank. 2000. "Organizational Environments and Doctoral Degrees Awarded to Women in Science and Engineering Departments." *Women's Studies Quarterly* 28:47–61.

Fraser, Nancy. 1992. "Rethinking the Public Sphere: A Contribution to the Critique of Actually Existing Democracy." In *Habermas and the Public Sphere,* ed. Craig Calhoun (Cambridge: MIT Press).

Freyd, Jennifer, and J. Q. Johnson. "References on Chilly Climate for Women Faculty in Academe." http://dynamic.uoregon.edu/~jjf/chillyclimate.html (last accessed May 4, 2008).

Geiger, Shirley Tolliver, and Toni-Michelle Travis. 1999. "The Status of African American Faculty in Political Science Departments in the Southern Region." *PS Online* (September). www.apsanet.org/PS/june97/spsa.cfm.

Ginther, Donna. 2003. "Is MIT the Exception? Gender Pay Differentials in Academic Science, 1973–1997." *Bulletin of Science, Technology and Society* 23 (1):21–26.

Hill Collins, Patricia. 1991. *Black Feminist Thought : Knowledge Consciousness, and the Politics of Empowerment.* New York: Routledge.

Jacobs, L., J. Cintrón, and C. E. Canton, eds. 2002. *The Politics of Survival in Academia: Narratives of Inequity, Resilience, and Success.* Lanham, MD: Rowman and Littlefield.

Merriam, S. B. 1998. *Qualitative Research and Case Study Applications in Education.* San Francisco: Jossey-Bass.

Moreno, José F., Daryl G. Smith, Alma Clayton-Pedersen, Sharon Parker, and Daniel Hiroyuki Teraguchi. 2006. "The Revolving Door for Underrepresented Minority Faculty in Higher Education." Research brief from the James Irvine Foundation, Campus Diversity Initiative Evaluation Project. ww.irvine.org/assets/pdf/pubs/education/insight_Revolving_Door.pdf.

Morley, Louise, and Val Walsh, eds. 1995. *Feminist Academics: Creative Agents for Change.* London: Taylor Francis.

Riger, Stephanie. n.d. "Chilly Climate Studies Regarding Women Faculty." www.mith2.umd.edu/WomensStudies/GenderIssues/ChillyClimate/list-of-reports.

Stanley, Christine A., and Yvonna S. Lincoln. 2005. "Cross-Race Faculty Mentoring." *Change* 37 (March): 44ff.

Tolstoy, Leo. 1873/2000. *Anna Karenina.* Trans Richard Pevear and Larissa Volokhonsky, with a preface by John Bayley. London: Allen Lane Penguin Press.

Tokarczyk, M. M., and E.A. Fay, eds. 1993. *Working-class Women in the Academy: Laborers in the Knowledge Factory.* Amherst: University of Massachusetts Press.

5

We, They, and Us

Stories of Women STEM Faculty at
Historically Black Colleges and Universities

JOSEPHINE BRADLEY, DEBORAH COOK,
DEIDRE MCDONALD, AND SARAH NORTH

In this chapter we consider the oral histories, or her-stories, of women faculty members in the fields of science, technology, engineering, and mathematics (STEM) at four historically black colleges and universities (HBCUs) in Georgia. Our study addresses the absence of these women's experiences from larger discussions of diversity and equity in higher education. Because of the history of HBCUs and the populations they serve, there is often a presumption that diversity is not an issue there. Our research shows, however, that diversity and equity are critical issues for women STEM faculty at HBCUs and that we need a new framework to explain women's unique experiences.

A panel convened by the National Academy of Sciences (NAS) reports that "women in science and engineering are hindered not by lack of ability but by bias and outmoded institutional structures. . . . Women from minority groups are virtually absent" (Dean 2006). Maggie Fox (2006) reports that the under representation of women and minorities in STEM faculties arises from issues firmly rooted in our society's traditions and cultures. She states, "Compared with men, women faculty members are generally paid less and promoted more slowly, receive fewer honors and fewer leadership positions. These discrepancies do not appear to be based on their productivity, the significance of their work, or any other performance measures" (Fox 2006). Moreover, no biological differences hinder women's ability to excel in science, mathematics, or engineering.

These findings require a closer examination of both the academy and the shortage of women STEM faculty. Feminist scholars have taken the initiative, calling for changes in the way that institutions deal with issues of diversity. This feminist thrust has initiated numerous debates regarding acceptable research methodologies for studying women's roles in the academy, especially in STEM fields. Research in these fields has been rooted in the male-centered natural, physical, and social sciences, where accepted paradigms have been grounded in a positivist epistemological approach centered on objectivity. This masculine construction of scientific knowledge is shaped by and reinforces modes of power that are central features of social life—for example, patriarchy, elitism, heterosexism, and racism (Hesse-Biber and Yaiser 2004, 11).

In contrast, "research conducted within a feminist framework is attentive to issues of difference, the questioning of social power, resistance to scientific oppression, and a commitment to political activism and social justice" (Hesse-Biber and Yaiser 2004, 11). A feminist model recognizes that women have often been omitted from the scientific dialogue and are "outsiders within" the STEM academic structure (Collins 1999, 127). At times, these faculty members even move from the margins of their departments to the center and then return to the margins (hooks 1987, 57).

Yet while a feminist model effectively critiques the masculine model of objectivity in scientific research and attends to gender inequality in the sciences, it often assumes that the experiences of all women STEM faculty at various institutions are similar. Consequently, a model of diversity and transformative strategies has emerged in the academy that views women faculty collectively, identifying challenges, developing activist approaches, and engaging in dialogue with administrators and faculty to achieve gender or racial equity. This paradigm advances the notion that women STEM faculty are potential change agents who can transform their institutions.

As examples of this paradigm, consider the women STEM faculty at the Massachusetts Institute of Technology (MIT) and the California Institute of Technology (Caltech). In the summer of 1994, three women at MIT initiated action based on the fact that the six departments of the School of Science had only 15 tenured women faculty members compared to 194 men (MIT Faculty Newsletter 1999). While junior women STEM faculty members reported departmental support and did not perceive gender as an issue for career advancement, these same women believed that family-work conflicts might affect their careers differently from those of their male colleagues. MIT senior women faculty members reported a level of marginalization and exclusion from significant roles in their departments, and "that marginalization was often accompanied by differences in salary, space, awards, resources and response to outside offers between men and women faculty with women receiving less despite professional accomplishments equal to those of their male colleague" (MIT Faculty Newsletter 1999). In response, MIT instituted affirmative action initiatives to ensure equity for women faculty members in all schools, improve the quality of life for junior faculty, and expand the number of minority faculty.

A study at Caltech in 2001 revealed comparable findings, indicating that, of 280 faculty members of varying rank, only 31 (11 percent) were women. Women were also paid less and had lower job satisfaction than did their male peers, especially in relation to the tenure and promotion process. As a result of the study, Caltech, like MIT, increased the ranks of female faculty to one woman for every ten men. Academic divisions adopted formal mentoring processes to help both males and females negotiate the tenure process; they have also asked division chairs to outline strategies for more effective recruitment and retention of female faculty and initiated a family-friendly committee to plan for child-care concerns (K. Brown 2002, 22).

These two cases highlight transformative-activist-diversity strategies that have worked in predominantly white institutions (PWIs). But are they pertinent to the challenges of women STEM faculty at HBCUs? One might argue that HBCUs are absent from broader discussions of diversity and equity primarily because of preconceptions about the nature and purposes of these institutions and the populations they serve and employ. Yet these very preconceptions explain why we need a paradigm shift from the strategies used at PWIs. For instance, one common assumption about HBCUs is that the majority of faculty members are African American. Another is that HBCUs serve a student population that is primarily African American, thereby creating a one-dimensional environment that does not prepare students to work and function in the "real" world that is dominated by those of majority groups. Finally, many assume that diversity and equity are not challenges for HBCUs because they primarily serve and employ African Americans. Clearly, there has been limited recognition that HBCUs are distinct entities with distinct challenges relating to diversity. While our research on women STEM faculty at these institutions does not necessarily conflict with the power dynamics of their colleagues at PWIs, it has expanded our definitions of activism and social-change strategies at all American institutions.

A Brief History of HBCUs

The first black colleges and universities (originally called normal institutes or seminaries) were founded shortly after the Emancipation Proclamation. Missionaries played a large role in setting up educational facilities in the South for newly freed people, and over time education came to represent a path to freedom and upward mobility for African Americans.

> Perhaps one of the greatest struggles faced by blacks in the United States has been the struggle to be educated. This struggle has been guided by the philosophies of black scholars who believed that without struggle there was not progress; black revolutionists who believed

education was the passport to the future; and black clergy who sermo-
nized that without vision the people would perish. Education is now,
and always has been, a vital weapon in the black arsenal. Essentially,
black Americans used education as their primary source of ammuni-
tion in the fight against a segregated society, racism, illiteracy, and
poverty. The steadfast desire of the black population to be educated
influenced the development of HBCUs, and HBCUs have likewise
contributed much to the advancement of the black population.
(Coaxum)

Although the 105 HCBUs in the United States make up just 3 percent of all
of the nation's colleges and universities, they are responsible for educating 28
percent of all African American students in higher education and administer
40 percent of all doctorates and first professional degrees earned by African
Americans (National Science Foundation 2002). In 2003, African Americans
accounted for 57.9 percent of full-time faculty at HBCUs, compared to 4 percent of full-time faculty at other institutions (National Center for Education
Statistics 2004). HBCUs were responsible for graduating more than 40 percent
of black students who received degrees in the physical sciences, environmental sciences, and mathematics (National Science Foundation 2002). According
to Steve Suitts they "are playing a critical role today in helping America overcome a looming shortage of scientists and engineers who are vital to the
nation's future economic growth and competitiveness." Nonetheless, they are
less likely than other institutions to receive significant institutional grants to
sustain their efforts (2003, 205).

In a comprehensive study of black students at PWIs and HBCUs, Walter
Allen reported that black students who attend HBCUs have better academic
performance, greater social involvement, and higher occupational aspirations
than do those at PWIs. "On black college campuses, students emphasized feelings of engagement, extensive support, acceptance, encouragement, and connection. Further, HBCUs communicate to black students that it is safe to take
the risks associated with intellectual growth and development" (Allen 1992, 27).

About the Research

There is limited published research on how HBCU women STEM faculty members perceive diversity, equity, and activism in their academic climates. We
note two important exceptions: *Black Women Scientists in the United States*
by Wini Warren (1999) and *Sisters in Science* by Diann Jordan (2007). Compared
to the top fifty PWIs, HBCUs have more women STEM faculty (Cook 2006). Yet
"HBCUs have been conspicuously absent, with few exceptions, in the national
debates about diversity. A number of questions which are usually absent from

diversity projects are crucial at HBCUs" (Guy-Sheftall 1997). But if HBCUs are absent from discussions about diversity and equity, the women who teach and conduct research at HBCUs are also absent. We wanted our research to ensure their inclusion.

The ADVANCE Study

We began our research with a National Science Foundation ADVANCE leadership award, which allowed us to sponsor a conference focused on the concerns of women STEM faculty at HBCUs. The conference focused primarily on the challenges of recruitment, tenure, promotion, and retention. The ADVANCE research was based on an agenda set by National Science Foundation (NSF) that was concerned with investigating challenges identified by women STEM faculty across the nation as priority agenda items: salary, space, recruitment, tenure, promotion, and retention. However, a primary focus for the Clark Atlanta University's ADVANCE grant was STEM women faculty at HBCUs. We selected this group because of the limited research available on women STEM faculty at HBCUs; the institutional location, environment, and academic climate and the relevance of each to recruitment, tenure, promotion; and retention of STEM women faculty; the uniqueness of HBCUs in the higher educational structure in the United States; and the need for a database on women STEM faculty at HBCUs. Not only had we noted the absence of HBCUs in broader discussions of diversity in the sciences, but we were also aware that they have been found lacking in institutional commitment, initiative in dealing with the issues of women STEM faculty, objectives and strategies for recruiting underrepresented minorities and women into academic science departments, programs and activities that affirm and validate the presence of women in the STEM fields, and financing to maintain programs and faculties at the level of those offered by PWIs (Pollard 2000, 5).

In preparation for the conference, we held several meetings with women STEM faculty members from four of the six institutions that make up the Atlanta University Center: Morris Brown College, Clark Atlanta University, Spelman College, and Morehouse College. All four are private institutions. The meetings were well attended, and the women seemed eager to participate in the conference as workshop leaders. We decided to invite women from PWIs as featured presenters. Most had been principal investigators on studies funded by the transformation grants, which at the time required matching funds (20 percent) of recipient colleges and universities, as well as a principal investigator who could foster institutional change. HBCUs are not often financially able to provide matching funds for various grants and as a result could not qualify as recipients.

Overall, the STEM women faculty who attended the conference were attentive and responsive to presenters' strategies for activism and transformation.

But when we reviewed the conference evaluations, we noted that the women representatives of HBCUs had some unexpected reactions to topics and presentations. Although they were receptive to issues related to gender inequality, they felt they had not been able to share experiences and concerns that specifically related to HBCUs. Our preliminary study thus confirmed the need for further research on women STEM faculty at these institutions. We needed to tell the stories behind the numbers.

Telling Our Stories

Georgia is home to ten HBCUs, two of which grant specific professional degrees. Four institutions (two private, two public) agreed to participate in our study, although we are keeping their identities anonymous. We interviewed fifteen women working in the STEM fields, using questions from our academic climate survey (formulated during the ADVANCE grant stage) and specific additional questions pertinent to each particular campus. Our study focused on two central issues: What affects equity and diversity among women STEM faculty at HBCUs? How are women STEM faculty and administrators engaged in transforming their campuses?

In addition to conducting individual interviews, we collected data from four focus groups that met on each of the four campuses (Wilkinson 2004). The groups varied in size from three to eight people per session, and each session was audiotaped and later transcribed and analyzed. Our primary objective in the focus groups was to listen to the women's experiences as STEM faculty. We also found that the groups gave participants a place to celebrate their differences while making "collective sense of them" (Morgan and Spanish 1984, 253).

Our data revealed some unexpected results. First, the women at HBCUs deconstructed our initial concerns—recruitment, tenure, promotion, and retention—and added others that were specific to their experiences. Among these issues were formalized mentoring programs in which persons in a parallel or complementary STEM field serve as mentors; competitive salaries for recruiting and retaining women faculty; decreased course and laboratory loads when faculty are expected to engage in meaningful research; more funds for equipment, conferences, and student assistants; increased institutional support for STEM fields (especially those situated in liberal arts institutions); and more female STEM administrators.

A second unexpected finding involved the composition of existing faculties. At none of the four HBCUs under study were the majority of STEM faculty members, either men or women, African American. Rather, a significant number of faculty members were from other racial-ethnic and international groups. In most instances, women STEM faculty members were in the minority. Faculty composition can affect the manner in which diversity, equity, activist, and transformative strategies are conceptualized and addressed. In the HBCU context, the racial and ethnic composition of STEM faculty gives rise to the question of what "diversity" means for faculty, administrators, and, most importantly, for students in an environment that superficially appears to be diverse. The experiences of black women STEM faculty members reveal that patriarchy is not their only concern. They also worry that their race, ethnicity, or gender may lead to the marginalization and silencing of their particular voices and experiences. In most instances, these black women were outnumbered by the "other," both male and female. Indeed, these women were minorities among minorities.

After considering the data we turned our attention back to the conference we had organized under the ADVANCE grant. While participants had responded positively, we now realized that it had omitted the specific voices of African American women STEM faculty. We had worked under the assumption that all the women present shared the agenda identified by the transformative grant presenters and the women at MIT and Caltech. Our interviews and focus groups, however, revealed that African American women STEM faculty members were identifying other unrecognized and unacknowledged epistemological approaches as well as psychological, cultural, and political issues that required attention.

A Paradigm Shift

Our preliminary research revealed that activism on the four HBCU campuses under study has four identifiable stages. In the course of more research, more stages may emerge. In the following explication, we detail each stage using the voices of the fifteen women we interviewed.

STAGE 1: RECOGNITION OF DIVERSITY. Diversity is the "recognition of differences in outlooks, attributes, and experiences among people based on race, ethnicity, gender, class, religion and access to power and resources. . . . The goal in diversity efforts is to dismantle inequality based on these differences and to build a greater democracy through the acceptance, respect, and coalition building across them" (Brown-Glaude 2005). HBCUs have the reputation of being academic exemplars of diversity, especially as it pertains to differences that are unique to each group in the multicultural community (Jones 2004, 126). As discussed earlier in this chapter, the STEM departments at HBCUs are not predominantly composed of African American faculty members. Rather, they are a composite of Africans, Indians and other Asians, and European Americans. Yet systems of oppression exist under this apparent diversity, especially for people of color and women. One participant commented, "The department was majority white. . . . So that was an unusual situation there . . . [and] took some getting use to for a couple of reasons. One was that some of the people there were my teachers . . . and most of them were white. And it was really interesting going back because . . . as a student you do not think about all the politics involved at that level. . . . I learned a lot of things, like it is hard to keep black people in that department" (2006).

Oppression is "socially constructed, historically rooted, based on unequal distribution of power and supported by ideology. It is at once pervasive, invisible and dynamic" (Demos et al. 2007, 557). One respondent observed, "The white faculty, if there were issues we voted on or conflicts, they would band together, very strongly, to get their agenda through. They would forget about all the others in fighting for what they might have. . . . Then it would be white against black" (2006).

The dynamics of oppression within diversity influence the kinds of transformative activism in which women of color engage. If our participants were not tenured, most were reluctant to engage in overt transformative activist strategies. One respondent captured the attitude of many women of color: "We're more sensitive about jobs that we do, and it shows whether the administrator or male faculty appreciates it or not. It really is not my concern anymore because I have learned to just move forward with whatever . . . I have to. I create my own domain. . . . I clear the energies around me, everywhere I walk, and I'm hoping my energy [will] move forward with me" (2006).

The tenuous position of black women faculty in these spaces and their exposure to subtle ways in which power operates have led many to do whatever work is necessary, in spite of job expectations, to help their departments move forward. These female faculty members took on the extra tasks necessary for the smooth operation of the departments.

STAGE 2: MANEUVERING CULTURAL SPACE. Women use a kind of advocacy to negotiate the oppressive space in which they work on a daily basis. Their responses may look like a form of withdrawal or resignation but are really a declaration of their social space and location. Their actions reflect their need for well-being and self-respect.

HBCUs, by their very nature, present challenges of space and location. Both require reassessment if women are to bring about any critical and meaningful campus transformation as it relates to gender oppression. The STEM departments are particularly challenging and resistant to change because of their diverse yet strongly male populations. Moreover, attention to HBCUs' unique attributes of cultural space and location helps us recognize the many levels of meaning imposed on these spaces. For instance, cultural space involves the various work-related cultural intangibles that confront women STEM faculty, including race and gender oppression, women's personal experiences, and male attitudes toward women's intellectual performance.

Another challenge for women faculty at HBCUs is their struggle against stereotypes that circulate about black institutions, which are often wrongly perceived as spaces that provide a second-class education. Compounding this stereotype, especially for the four HBCUs included in our study, is spatial location—the South, a region often perceived as a confining place for African Americans.

Space also includes attitude, "a predisposition to respond in a characteristic manner to some situation, values, idea, object, person, or group of persons" (Asante and Karenga 2006, 334). Male STEM faculty members tend to evince a certain attitude toward women colleagues. For example, the chair of one STEM department told a European American woman that the grant for which she was applying was too much for her and that she should just concentrate on her undergraduate teaching. This woman professor, however, had a history of extramural research funding. One might read the chair's comments as cultural misunderstanding: he was from a country in which the role of women is defined differently from the way it is in the United States. Nonetheless, for the women STEM faculty members we interviewed, maneuvering cultural space included negotiating such externally imposed stereotypes about the spaces in which they work and attitudes related to gender roles and norms within these spaces. These challenges required various activities and responses.

At the HBCUs under investigation, women often appeared to engage in activities that evinced resignation to the situation. Yet in reality their actions advocated for the pedagogical methods of their choice—a subtle form of activism. What appeared to be resignation was in reality cultural resistance. They were both engaging the cultural responses of their male colleagues (who are mostly from India, Pakistan, Africa, and Japan) and struggling against the cultural response of infrastructures dominated by men who did not acknowledge the institutional oppression of women faculty.

One factor that influenced a woman's choice of strategy in the HBCU space was the male-female relationships within a particular STEM department. A participant described the relationships in her space: "We have a friendly relationship in terms of interpersonal relationships. And then you have an exclusion relationship in terms of decision-making. Many women have been excluded from the decision-making process in the department. All of our coordinators are male, and they head up most of the committees, and [women] get the fallout from them" (2006).

Given the attitudes of male colleagues and their institutions' lack of responsiveness, some women expressed doubt about being able to bring about change. According to Tray Ore, "Beginning the work of transforming systems of oppression and privilege is often difficult. When we first become aware of systems of inequality, many of us are overwhelmed and do not have a clear idea of where to begin to bring about social change" (Ore 2003, 17). As one participant told us, "I would want to help the students and faculty, because I've been a student and I know the struggles. I'm now faculty, so I know the struggle. . . . I would try to be an advocate for the people. But it's too political [and] you can't really. . . . I don't know what happens if people just give up or forget, but I don't think I could do that. So I say, "Well, how else can I direct my energies?" . . . I choose research and students" (2006).

There are similarities between the experiences of women STEM faculty at both HBCUs and PWIs. "Not unlike their counterparts throughout the academic community, women STEM faculty at HBCUs are marginalized in the areas of salary, status, space, awards, resources, hiring policies and promotion practices" (Hale 2004, 17). Yet responses to our academic climate survey as well as data from our focus groups and interviews revealed that diversity and equity activism at HBCUs does not parallel the process at PWIs. One reason is that there is less collaboration among women STEM faculty at HBCUs.

On each of the four campuses under study, transformative diversity activism was impeded by institutional practices: undesignated financial resources, lack of federal funding to HBCUs, and lack of women's leadership. In addition, despite shared experiences with gender discrimination, African American women and European American women did not engage in transformative collaborative activism. We have not yet determined the reasons for this collaborative disconnect, but factors seem to include an overload of work responsibilities, lack of resources necessary for fulfilling teaching responsibilities, and lack of women's leadership in guiding efforts for social change within the context of professional growth and development.

The women we interviewed avoided confrontations with male colleagues and the administration, instead directing their energies toward teaching, research, and students. Nonetheless, as one participant commented, "Women in the STEM disciplines have to maintain a steadfast attitude while developing a backbone and nerves of steel" (2006). Another said, "In a male-dominated environment, it has been always challenging to . . . work from a different angle or a different way to show performance to others" (2006). This approach to the oppressive environment is a form of activism because it adopts a survivalist mentality in order to move outside the departmental norm.

In general, women junior faculty members are reluctant to participate in transformative activities. Thus, in locations at which women do not constitute a critical mass, overt activism does not arise as a transformative act. At HBCUs, then, both African American women and other women faculty find themselves at a crossroads. In some ways the behavior of African American women mimics the behavior of African American faculty members at MIT, where black administrators and faculty organized to deal with their concerns. Yet the group eventually lost momentum and failed to engage in any transformative activism for social change and equity (Williams 1999, 77). At both PWIs and HBCUs, African American women and other minorities acknowledge that institutional attitudes toward diversity, recruitment, promotion, tenure, retention, and inclusion are related to gender oppression. All of the women we interviewed saw themselves as recipients of some form of oppression, whether based on gender alone or on a combination of gender and race. Overall, they found themselves marginalized by those in power—male STEM faculty members from diverse backgrounds. One participant said, "Even though you are a part of the university, you are disconnected: you're in your unit, you're in your particular department, and you may not even know what to do. And what works in one area may not be the thing that works in another area" (2006).

STAGE 3: COMPROMISE AND EMPOWERMENT THROUGH ACTIVISM. "Compromise is adjusting aspirations to accommodate an external reality" (Brown and Brooks 1996, 179). Once women STEM faculty at the HBCUs under study recognized that collaborative transformative activism was not an option, they sought alternative approaches that provided meaning and significance to their cultural identity, enhanced their perception of feeling valued and respected as colleagues equal to the men on the STEM faculty, and improved the quality of intergroup relations. These outcomes affected the relationship between cultural identity and work-group functioning and provided guidelines for cooperation between African American women and other women in the STEM fields.

Positioning African American women STEM faculty members within this academic space requires a paradigm shift. The reality of their experiences is different from both traditional masculine and feminist approaches and takes into account the multiple ways in which women are defined at HBCUs. There is the African American women's agenda ("we"), the other women's agenda ("they"), and the combined agenda of both ("us"). Combining this cluster is the diversity challenge: "[These] multiple perspectives . . . differ on certain dimensions but . . . share as a goal, the generation of knowledge, which contributes to emancipation, empowerment and change" (Berman et al. 1998, 3). Women as "us" engage in activism at a different level. Although they are more individualistic in their approach to social change, teamwork and encouragement are helpful strategies.

In the past, the "we" and "they" groups of women STEM faculty at HBCUs have sometimes consulted with each other or provided emotional support when negotiating the political and social rigors of being a gender minority seeking equity in salary, hiring, tenure, promotion, and retention. One respondent, who had served as an administrator for more than a decade, said that she had fought for the right of professors to carry fewer classes when engaged in research. Another participant said she was better able to handle work and motherhood because her department chair, who was a woman, understood those conflicting challenges. Another respondent, who had been an administrator, taught classes in order to help women faculty find more time to engage in research. Over time, women by force carved their own identity into the male-dominated STEM fields at these HBCUs, becoming both visible and audible. Their actions were activist-transformative ones that changed the manner in which women were able to transcend their academic environment.

STAGE 4: ETHICS OF CARING. According to Patricia Hill Collins, engaging in an ethics of caring is a form of activism because it "suggests that personal expressiveness, emotions, and empathy are central to the knowledge validation process" (Collins 2000, 215). Women STEM faculties at HBCUs engage in a reconceptualization of women's activism that includes embracing the activist behaviors of women STEM faculty in general. This urge does not overlook the institutions' unique issues related to interlocking components of race, class, gender, and inclusiveness; but it does mean that the women accept their social responsibility for social change.

African American women STEM faculty members embrace the meaning of activism from an Afro centric standpoint (Keto 1995). They are enabled by efforts to overcome barriers, both individually and collectively, and create their own brand of black women's activism (Yee 1992, 11). Simultaneously, however, African American women and other women employed by HBCUs share some critical recognition. First, they recognize that problems in the relationship between "we" and "they" are due to women's dislocation, especially among African American women, who are marginalized as the "outsider within" the cultural space that was created for them and who, in general, share the expressed gender oppression of women STEM faculty. Second, differences in power constrain women's ability to connect with one another even when they are engaged in dialogue across differences. Third, coalitions emerge around a common cause, such as ensuring that women STEM faculty are mentored, encouraged to seek doctorate degrees if needed, assisted with tenure requirements, and supported in efforts to improve working relationships with their male colleagues. Fourth, African American women inherit concepts of individual activism for change in the academic and black communities. Yet the unspoken actions that occur between African American and European American women STEM faculty increase connectivity, not fragmentation, and push forward the agenda of transformative activism. Notions of cultural grounding, academic excellence, and social responsibility have relevance for black-white activism (Asante and Karenga 2006, 408), and European American women can participate in this approach.

The women activists who participated in our study emphasized the importance of educational opportunities and of serving as role models for undergraduates. All the women interviewed said that teaching and dedication to their students' progress and development were their goals. One participant is employed at the college from which she received her undergraduate degree. After receiving her master's degree, she was recruited by her alma mater. Her female chair provided the needed mentoring that encouraged her to pursue a doctorate. In many ways, her pathway to academia supports W. E. B. DuBois's notion of the talented tenth who receive their education and return to help others. As one respondent said, "I just love my people. . . . So my whole passion is to let [African American women] students know that they can successfully pursue a career in the sciences" (2006). Thus, women STEM faculty members spend considerable time in creating learning opportunities for students. Another faculty member described the challenge of ensuring that students learn to dissect animals. She was discouraged from adding dissection to the curriculum even though the college had a record of sending large numbers of students to medical school: "In my opinion, we were doing a disservice, and I ordered stuff, and I said, 'I want pigs, I want frogs, and I want turtles'" (2006).

Other activist strategies pertain to students and their success in the STEM disciplines. One woman department chair indicated that, if she wanted students to receive effective advising, she assigned them to women STEM faculty. In addition, some faculty members have written grants and received multiyear funding in order to increase the number of minorities entering STEM fields. They have become involved in federally funded student training and research programs from such agencies as the National Institutes of Health (NIH), National Science Foundation, National Aeronautics and Space Administration (NASA), Department of Energy (DOE), and United States Department of Agriculture (USDA). Some of these efforts involve precollege programs designed to provide academic and other support services to students who will major in STEM fields. An African American woman STEM faculty member who has served in various government positions felt that HBCUs were overlooked by many funding categories and encouraged them to provide funding opportunities to HBCUs. It is important to note that most of such activism is the work of tenured women STEM faculty members. Therefore, women STEM faculty members at HBCUs are less assertive in their activism because so few of them are tenured.

Conclusions

The narratives of the women we interviewed for this study reveal the importance of inventing a new paradigm for assessing the diversity, transformation, and activism of women STEM faculty at HBCUs. Regardless of race and ethnicity, these women share common political and sociocultural issues that form an agenda for combating their marginalization. There is room at HBCUs for future transformative collaborative undertakings, even though the institutions' financial resources may not be as sustaining as those of PWIs. At present, the women STEM faculty members we interviewed do not clearly voice a common agenda even though they engage, it seems, in similar forms of cultural resistance in responding to the HBCU cultural space. They find ways to circumvent the objections of their chairs and other male colleagues who are not supportive of their career goals. Similarities exist among these women because they experience the same challenges related to salary, space allocation for laboratories, recruitment, tenure, promotion, and retention. As our interviews show, HBCUs do not seem to allow women to speak openly or to contribute freely to needed changes in the cultural space in which they work. Yet while they deal individually and often subtly with these challenges, their behaviors are nonetheless a form of cultural resistance to oppression and marginalization.

Resolutions against gender oppression require coalition politics that foster women's ability to act as a group for transformation. Restructuring a system embraces women's determination to transform their experiences at a particular location into sustainable entities of equity. From all indications, our ADVANCE work set into motion the leadership that women STEM faculty members at HBCUs need. Clark Atlanta University's necessary leadership role became apparent during the planning stages for a conference at which approximately twenty-five women from Spelman, Morehouse, and Morris Brown colleges were willing participants. University faculty planners met the triple challenges of "cultural grounding, academic excellence and social responsibility" advocated by women STEM faculty (Asante and Karenga 2006, 440). Our goal continues to be to help women STEM faculty at HBCUs "to learn to speak in a unique and authentic voice, [to] 'jump outside' the frames and systems authorities provide and create their own frames" (Belenky et al. 1996, 134). As an interdisciplinary faculty research team our participation in the ADVANCE Leadership award and the Designs for Diversity project were, in and of themselves, activist and transformative acts in the HBCU environment.

REFERENCES

Allen, W. R. 1992. "The Color of Success: African-American Student Outcomes at Predominantly White and Historically Black Colleges." *Harvard Educational Review* (Spring):26–44.

Asante, M., and M. Karenga, eds. 2006. *Handbook of Black Studies.* Thousand Oaks, CA: Sage.

Belenky, M., N. Goldberger, and J. Tarule. 1996. *Women's Ways of Knowing: The Development of Self, Voice and Mind.* New York: HarperCollins.

Berman, H., M. Ford-Gilboe, and J. Campbell. 1998. "Combining Stories and Numbers: A Methodological Approach for A Critical Nursing Science." *Advances in Nursing Science* 21:1–15.

Brown, D., and L. Brooks, eds. 1996. *Career Choice and Development.* San Francisco: Jossey-Bass.

Brown, K. 2002. Accomplished Women. *HHMI Bulletin* 15:20–25.

Brown-Glaude, Winnifred. 2005. "Reaffirming Action: Designs for Diversity in Higher Education." Rutgers University: Institute for Women's Leadership. http://iwl.rutgers.edu/news-fall2005.pdf.

Coaxum, J. "Historically Black Colleges and Universities, The Development of HBCUs and Social Experience at HBCUs." http://education.stateuniversity.com/pages/2046/Historically-Black-Colleges-Universities.

Cook, D. A. 2006. "An Accounting of Women Science and Engineering Faculty at Historically Black Colleges and Universities." Manuscript in progress.

Dean, C. 2006. "Panel Says Institutions Hinder Female Academicians." *New York Times,* September 18.

Demos, V., A. J. Lemelle, and S. Gashaw. 2007. "Systems of Oppression: Ten Principles." In *Intersections of Gender, Race, and Class,* ed. M. T. Segal and T. Martinez, 557–564. Los Angeles: Roxbury.

Ely, R. J., and D. A. Thomas. 2007. "The Effects of Organizational Demographics and Social Identity on Relationships among Professional Women." In *The Sociology of Organizations: An Anthology of Contemporary Theory and Research,* ed. A. S. Wharton, 294–346. Los Angeles: Roxbury.

Fox, M. 2006. "Report Finds Bias Keeping Women Out Of Science Jobs: Academics Urged to Tackle Gap in Faculty Numbers." http://www.boston.com/news/nation/washington/articles/2006/09/19/report.

Guy-Sheftall, B. 2005. "Faculty Involvement: Teaching Diversity at a Historically Black College." *Diversity Digest* 1, no. 2. http://www.diversityweb.org/Digest/w97/HBCU.html.

Hale, F. W. Jr. 2004. *What Makes Racial Diversity in Higher Education?* Sterling, VA: Stylus.

Hesse-Biber, S., and M. Yaiser. 2004. *Feminist Perspectives in Social Research: An Interdisciplinary Reader.* New York: Oxford University Press.

Hill Collins, P. 1999. "Learning from the Outsider Within: The Sociological Significance of Black Feminism. In *Feminist Approaches to Theory And Methodology: An Interdisciplinary Reader,* ed. S. Hesse-Biber, C. Gilmartin, and R. Lydenberg, 127. New York: Oxford University Press.

———. 2000. *Black Feminist Thought: Knowledge, Consciousness, and the Politics of Empowerment.* New York: Routledge.

hooks, b. 1987. *Talking Back: Thinking Feminist, Thinking Black.* Boston: South End.

Jones, L., 2004. "The Development of a Multicultural Student Services Office and Retention Strategy for Minority Students: Still Miles to Go!" In *What Makes Racial Diversity in Higher Education?,* ed. F. W. Hale Jr., 125–145. Sterling, VA: Stylus.

Jordan, D. 2007. *Sisters in Science.* Lafayette, IN: Purdue University Press.

Keto, T. 1995. *Vision, Identity, and Time: The Afrocentric Paradigm and the Study of the Past.* Dubuque, IA: Kendall/Hunt.

MIT Faculty Newsletter. 1999. http://web.mit.edu/fnl/women/women.html.

Morgan, D. L., and M. T. Spanish. 1984. Focus Groups: A New Tool for Qualitative Research. *Qualitative Sociology* 7:253–270.

National Center for Education Statistics. 2004. "Enrollment in Postsecondary Institutions." http://www.nces.

National Science Foundation. 2002. "Science and Engineering Degrees, 1966–2000." Table 46, NSF Document no. 02–327. Arlington, VA: National Science Foundation.

National Science Foundation. 2007. "Integrated Science and Engineering Resources Data System." http://webcaspar.nsf.gov. See also http://www.nsf.gov/statistics.

Ore, T. 2003. *The Construction of Difference and Inequality: Race, Class, Gender, and Sexuality.* Boston: McGraw-Hill.

Pollard, L. N. 2000. *Embracing Diversity.* Hagerstown, MD: River and Herald.

Suitts, S. 2003. "Fueling Education Reform: Historically Black Colleges and Meeting a National Science Imperative." *Cell Biology Education* 2:205–206.

Warren, W. 1999. *Black Women Scientists in the United States.* Bloomington: Indiana University Press.

Wilkinson, S. 2004. "Focus Groups: A Feminist Method." In *Feminist Perspectives in Social Research: An Interdisciplinary Reader,* ed. S. Hesse-Biber and M. Yaiser, 271–295. New York: Oxford University Press.

Williams, C. G. 1999. "The MIT Experience: Personal Perspectives on Race in a Predominantly White University." In *What Makes Racial Diversity In Higher Education?,* ed. F. W. Hale Jr., 74–93. Sterling, VA: Stylus.

Yee, S. J. 1992. *Black Women Abolitionists: A Study in Activism,* 1828–1860. Knoxville: University of Tennessee Press.

6

Unprecedented Urgency

Gender Discrimination in Faculty Hiring at the University of California

MARTHA S. WEST

This is a story about a controversial approach to seeking change within higher education—tapping into political power off campus.[1] The key players, Professors Gyöngy Laky and Martha West, faculty members at the University of California Davis (UC–Davis), had reluctantly come to realize, after many years of struggle, that significant, meaningful change at the University of California (UC) would not take place by continuing to work within the UC system. Their cause: gender equity in faculty hiring. In one year the percentage of women among new faculty hires at their campus, UC–Davis, had dropped 22 points: from 35 percent in 1997–98 to only 13 percent in 1998–99. Although Davis was only one campus among the nine-campus system, the hiring of women faculty—both tenured and tenure-track faculty—had been declining at all the campuses. Rather than just complain or take it up with the university one more time, West and Laky decided to go outside the system. They managed to get the attention of a state senator, the state auditor, and the state legislature. Only by creating outside pressure on the UC system were they finally successful in catching the ear of UC President Richard Atkinson, which, in turn, caused him to take steps to effect change.

These faculty members focused their efforts on calling attention to issues of sex discrimination—current and continuing discrimination against women in the UC faculty hiring process. In their view, outside pressure was needed to encourage faculty to stop discriminating against women candidates in the hiring process and hire women at rates reflecting women's availability among the primary category of qualified candidates—recent U.S. PhD recipients. Both federal law, Title VII of the 1964 Civil Rights Act, and state law prohibit employers from discriminating on the basis of gender in hiring. In 1998, 48 percent of recent U.S. PhD recipients were women, but only 13 percent of UC Davis faculty hires were women. Within the UC system as a whole, only 25 percent of faculty hires were women in 1999–2000. This was strong evidence of sex discrimination, particularly in the absence of alternative explanations for this large gap between the qualified labor pool and actual hires.

West and Laky were not interested in the use of affirmative action policies to hire faculty. The term "affirmative action" refers to a policy or practice where race or gender are taken into account in making a decision in order to redress historic underrepresentation of protected groups. It was most commonly used in university admissions policies, giving a plus or a few extra points in the admissions process to students of color who were historically underrepresented on campus, compared to their presence among high school graduates. Affirmative action as a viable public policy or political strategy had already died in California. In 1995 the UC Regents adopted Resolutions SP-1 and SP-2, abolishing affirmative action as university policy in both admissions and employment. In 1996, California voters passed Proposition 209, amending the California constitution to forbid any state entity from giving "preferences" based on race, ethnicity, or sex in employment, contracting, or providing state benefits. It was ironic, however, that this political abolition of affirmative action, in fact, led to increased discrimination against women at UC. The end of affirmative action served as a signal to many faculty decision makers that it was again acceptable to go back to traditional practices, practices that had long denied women equal access to university faculties. In essence, Proposition 209 brought an end to more equitable treatment of women and encouraged historical "preferences" for white men in faculty hiring. With hopes that California's experience is not duplicated elsewhere, the story of what happened in the UC system following passage of Proposition 209 is particularly instructive for those in other states where attacks on affirmative action policies continue to take place.

The issue of discrimination in faculty hiring is particularly difficult because the decision makers are faculty members themselves. The decision of whom to hire as a faculty member is made by faculty at the department level, a highly decentralized process within the UC system. A senior campus administrator can veto a proposed hire but cannot make an actual decision to hire someone. Thus, it is a daunting challenge to sensitize faculty to issues of sex, race, or ethnic discrimination in order to bring about change among such a wide group of decision makers.

The Problem and the Players

Throughout the 1980s, on a national level, women were obtaining PhDs at unprecedented rates: in 1981–82, women accounted for 35 percent of PhD recipients among U.S. citizens; by 1991–92, women's percentage had increased to 44 percent. Reflecting the movement of more women into PhD programs, more women faculty were being hired throughout the UC system. Professor West, an expert in employment law at the UC–Davis Law School, had been monitoring the progress of women among faculty hires at UC since the mid 1980s. In 1984–85, women obtained 25 percent of these UC faculty positions (77 women among 314 hires systemwide). By 1990–91, women accounted for 29 percent of faculty hires (153 women among 530 hires). Women reached a peak in 1993–94, obtaining 37 percent of new positions (108 women among 292 hires). Although the percentage of women among faculty hires was always below the percentage of women in the "qualified labor pool" of recent PhD recipients, the upward trend in women's percentage of hires paralleled the upward trend in women's participation in graduate education.

This positive picture began to change in 1995–96, immediately after UC Regent Ward Connerly convinced the other UC Regents to abolish affirmative action as university policy. The Regents' primary target was student admissions policies, but the Regents' resolutions included employment practices as well. After his success at UC, Regent Connerly and his friends then placed Proposition 209 on the statewide ballot, and it passed in November 1996. Even though the Regents' resolutions and Proposition 209 purported to eliminate "preferences" based on race, sex, and ethnicity, they both contained clauses permitting UC and other state entities to continue to follow federal affirmative action employment requirements in order to preserve the receipt of federal funds. Federal Executive Order 11246, which covers any entity employing at least 50 employees and receiving $50,000 or more in federal funds, requires universities to follow federal affirmative action policies in hiring employees. Because each UC campus receives considerably more than $50,000 in federal funds, neither the Regents' 1995 resolutions nor the adoption of Proposition 209 in 1996 should have affected university employment practices, including faculty hiring. Unfortunately, however, the political message sent to faculty by the statewide abolition of affirmative action was much more powerful than the continuing federal employment requirements, about which the university was silent. Instead of giving candidates from underrepresented groups a plus in the hiring process, faculty at the department level returned to old patterns of discrimination, preferring candidates most like themselves— mostly men.

In 1995–96, 36 percent of new UC faculty hires were women (140 out of 391). By 1996–97, women's percentage had fallen 10 points, to 26 percent (99 out of 376 hires). The lowest point was reached in 1999–2000, when women represented only 25 percent of new faculty hires (92 of 369 hires). This was the lowest percentage of women among faculty hires in twelve years, since 1987–88. Meanwhile, women's percentage among U.S. citizen PhD recipients continued to climb, reaching 48 percent in 1999. No longer were UC hires of women paralleling women's increasing percentage of the national PhD pool.

The situation at the UC–Davis campus was even worse than the systemwide picture. Davis had been hiring women at a higher rate than at the system-wide level. In 1994–95, a whopping 52 percent of faculty hires were women (22 out of 42 hires). By 1998–99, however, only 13 percent of the new hires were women (7 of 46 hires). In Professor West's opinion, these numbers indicated a serious problem of discrimination. Under employment discrimination theory, if the "qualified labor pool" is 48 percent women, but the hires from that pool are only 13 percent women, a prima facie case of systemic discrimination is indicated. Plus, as a recipient of federal funds, UC was theoretically still required under its affirmative action plans to make "good faith efforts" to eliminate gender, racial, and ethnic under-representation on its faculty. The data both at the systemwide level and at Davis demonstrated that not only had affirmative action efforts on behalf of women ceased, but the faculty decision makers at the department level had switched back to traditional discriminatory hiring practices.

West discussed the situation with Professor Gyöngy Laky. At that time, Laky was professor of environmental design in the College of Agriculture and Environmental Sciences. West and Laky had worked closely together on faculty hiring issues since 1984, when they first met while serving on the UC–Davis Academic Senate Affirmative Action Committee. They had both later chaired that committee and Laky had gone on to chair the senate's systemwide Affirmative Action Committee. Laky had also served on the Davis senate's Committee on Academic Personnel. West had been on numerous campus task forces in the 1980s and 1990s, focusing on the need to diversify the Davis faculty. In addition, West had served as associate dean of the Law School from 1988 to 1992. She then chaired the UCD elected faculty senate committee that appointed the Academic Senate's faculty officers and members of all other faculty committees. Both West and Laky knew the campus and systemwide academic organizations very well and had worked for years to encourage faculty and administrators to take seriously issues of race and gender discrimination among faculty on campus.

In the fall of 1999, West and Laky learned that internal Davis statistics showed that faculty hires for that year, 1999–2000, based on decisions made the previous year, would include only 18 percent women hires. Now, with two years of data, they knew this dramatic downturn was not just a fluke. At the same time that fewer women were being hired, the UC system was projecting a significant increase in faculty hiring—UC expected to hire approximately 7,500 new faculty statewide over the next ten years, more than the total 6,400 UC faculty then employed. Because faculty tend to remain at their institutions for long careers, this tremendous hiring surge would shape the makeup of the UC faculty for the next half century. Massive faculty turnover from retirements and expansive new hires, combined with the alarming decline in hiring women, made the need for change urgent.

Laky and West considered the possibility of getting someone in the state legislature to champion their cause and be their voice. They knew they would have much stronger support for gender equity issues among members of the state legislature than they had among UC administrators or Regents. They also knew time was of the essence and the slow pace of bureaucratic change within the UC system made internal action hopeless. Laky mentioned their concern to an old friend, Phyllis Friedman, a prominent UC–Berkeley alum and financial supporter. Without hesitation, Friedman said she knew just the right person: State Senator Jackie Speier.[2] The next day Friedman contacted Speier, who was clearly interested.

In December 1999, Professors Laky and West, along with Phyllis Friedman and Professor Jessica Utts from Davis's statistics department, met with Senator Speier. After discussing the dramatic decline in women faculty hires and the many obstacles Professors Laky, West, and Utts had faced on campus, Speier suggested a state audit of UC's hiring practices. This would give them a baseline from which to work. Before she requested an audit, however, Speier wanted to meet with faculty from other UC campuses to understand the problem more broadly. Consequently, in July 2000 Senator Speier met with a group of thirteen senior UC faculty women representing five campuses. The women were unanimous in detailing the need for an investigation of UC's hiring practices. One woman after another described the difficulties she had encountered in bringing the serious underrepresentation of women among the ladder rank faculty to the attention of campus officials. After Proposition 209, neither the UC Office of the President (UCOP) nor campus administrations seemed concerned that the hiring data indicated increasing gender discrimination. At the meeting, Speier agreed to seek approval from the legislature for an audit of UC's hiring practices.

On August 22, 2000, the Joint Legislative Audit Committee approved Speier's request, and $250,000 was appropriated to fund the audit. UCOP representatives present at the committee's meeting were supportive, publicly acknowledging that there appeared to be a "problem." During the autumn of 2000, word spread among UC faculty and staff that an audit of gender issues in faculty hiring was occurring. Once the audit was underway, Senator Speier's office began preparations for the Select Committee on Government Oversight to hold a hearing in January 2001. Professor Laky took the lead in finding tenured faculty, both women and men, from each campus to testify.

The Three Hearings—January 2001, March 2002, February 2003

Hearing 1

The first of what would become three one-day hearings was held on January 31, 2001.[3] Seventeen faculty members from throughout UC testified.

Two national experts, Professor Nancy Hopkins, from the Massachusetts Institute of Technology, and Professor Elaine Shoben, from the University of Illinois College of Law, offered a national perspective on the difficulties women faculty faced. Professor Hopkins had been responsible for organizing women faculty members at MIT and generating a report in 1999 describing the difficulties women faculty in science had faced at MIT. Hopkins commented that women and men who testify are brave because there is always the fear, and sometimes the reality, of retaliation. She herself had experienced alienation from many MIT faculty members because of her actions. She also testified that women faculty members without children experienced the same problems of isolation and hostility from some male faculty members as women faculty members with children, so that women's family choices could not be blamed for the disparities women faced in academia. Professor Shoben commented on the UC hiring statistics, agreeing that the steep decline in hiring women at UC since 1996 was an anomaly. In her opinion, the hiring system at UC needed to be changed.

Professor Laky, the first UC faculty member to testify, pointed out that in the UC system, Proposition 209 had become an "affirmative action" program for men: men were being given "preference" by being hired at rates 30 percent above their availability in the PhD pool. Furthermore, national data showed that women were, in fact, more interested than men in academic employment: in 2000, 56 percent of women receiving PhDs chose to apply for academic jobs, as opposed to only 44 percent of men earning PhDs.

Professor West testified that after Proposition 209 passed, it appeared the faculty (80 percent male) "relaxed," thinking affirmative action was gone and that everything was back to "normal," meaning hiring people most like themselves. In the absence of pressure from UC administrators to hire diverse candidates, faculty reverted to their traditional hiring practices of finding the "best" graduate students, primarily men, recommended by their mostly male colleagues at other schools. Professor West offered a second explanation for the relatively low percentage of women among UC faculty hires: UC hires over 40 percent of its new faculty at the tenured ranks of associate or full professor. When hiring at the tenured level, UC is hiring from a pool of faculty already teaching at research universities, a pool that includes only 20 percent women. When hiring at the entry-level assistant professor rank, the "qualified labor pool" expands to include 48 percent women—recent PhD recipients. Ten years of UC–Davis data from 1988 to 1998 showed that among faculty hired with tenure, only 25 percent of the hires were women, whereas among faculty hired at the entry level without tenure, 37 percent of the hires were women. Based on this data, West and other faculty members had been able to convince the Davis administration in 2000 to adopt a policy that hires at the higher tenured levels be limited to 20 percent of hires in any given year.

Professor West recommended that if UC truly wanted to increase the hires of women, it should severely limit the number of hires at the tenured ranks.

Boalt Hall Law Professor Marge Schultz testified that the picture was particularly bleak at the UC–Berkeley School of Law: between 1997 and 2000, the Law School had made ten offers to men and no offers to women, during a time when women made up 46 percent of law school graduates. At Boalt Hall itself, 64 percent of the entering class were women.

UCLA Law Professor Carole Goldberg pointed out that according to UCLA's own analysis, women should have represented 35 percent of UCLA's faculty in 2000, instead of its current 23 percent. She testified that a narrow focus on specialization, plus continuing favoritism and cronyism among senior faculty at feeder schools, encouraged faculty to hire people most like themselves. She discussed recent research on cognitive biases, shared by both men and women, which lead decision makers to overvalue the accomplishments of men and undervalue the accomplishments of women. Thus, for women to get hired, they have to be significantly better qualified than men. In her view, no one in the UC system was holding departments accountable for their failure to hire women at rates commensurate with their presence in the available pool of PhD recipients.

The UC Office of the President was represented at the first hearing by Chancellor M. R. C. Greenwood, head of the UC–Santa Cruz campus. She pointed out that the UC system was doing better in its overall percentage of women faculty (23.5 percent) than other elite institutions, such as MIT (14.5 percent), Harvard (12.9 percent), or Stanford (17 percent). She testified that having a PhD was no longer sufficient for most faculty positions. Some teaching experience, publication in an outstanding journal, or independent research funding was often required, making the pool of recent PhD recipients an inadequate measure of qualified candidates. Nevertheless, prompted by the state audit then underway and by Senator Speier's request for testimony from the Office of the President, Chancellor Greenwood announced eight new "action" items that UCOP would pursue during the coming year to increase the hires of women. These action items included setting new campus goals, analyzing candidate pools, providing new resources, and holding chancellors accountable for making progress on their campuses.

In response to Senator Speier's request for suggestions on how to improve the situation, Professor Andrew Dickson, from UC–San Diego's Scripps Institute of Oceanography, testified that progress in hiring women was made when faculty were hired at the entry level as assistant professors, instead of hiring at the tenured level of associate or full professor. By focusing on assistant professor hires, Scripps had gone from 10 percent women hires to 50 percent, hiring four women out of eight new hires during the past year.

Professor William Bielby, an expert on the manifestations of racial and gender bias in organizations from the sociology department at UC–Santa

Barbara, testified that hiring decisions are vulnerable to bias when they are based on arbitrary, idiosyncratic, and subjective criteria for evaluating the qualifications and "fit" of candidates. This is particularly true when the job context is one in which there has long been severe underrepresentation of women and persons of color, such as on university faculties. To minimize bias, campuses need to develop well-defined, systematic processes to evaluate strictly job-relevant information about faculty candidates. Professor Bielby suggested that campuswide monitoring of hiring statistics and of departments' practices could help identify weaknesses and increase the integrity of decision making.

Senator Speier was strong and articulate at the conclusion of the hearing in summarizing the difficulties women faced in obtaining UC faculty positions. Professors Laky and West were pleased with the impact of the first hearing. The room was crowded and many UC administrators were there, both from the UC Office of the President and UC—Davis. The press coverage in northern California was excellent, particularly because the hearing took place two days after an historic meeting at MIT where Professor Nancy Hopkins and the MIT president had gathered leaders from nine of the top science and engineering research universities, including UC—Berkeley, to discuss steps they could take to increase the hires of faculty women. Senator Speier's hearing was also covered in the *Chronicle of Higher Education,* reaching a national audience.

The state audit of UC's hiring practices was completed in May 2001. The audit found that "UC's hiring data for the past 5 years show that a significant disparity appears to exist" between the proportion of women faculty hired by UC and the proportion of women receiving doctorates nation-wide. To address this underrepresentation of women, the audit made several recommendations:

- Avoid all-male search committees.
- Direct deans and department chairs to more fully consider the rank at which hires are made.
- Require written search plans and incorporate the data on the underrepresentation of women into the plans.
- Collect hiring data on a systemwide basis and set benchmarks for departments to meet.

Many of these suggestions had, in fact, been required by federal affirmative action guidelines since 1978, but, obviously, neither the university nor the federal government had been enforcing the federal requirements. The release of the state audit in May 2001 and UC's official response to the audit in the fall provided the basis for Senator Speier's second hearing in 2002.

Hearing 2

State Auditor Elaine Howle opened Senator Speier's second hearing on March 11, 2002. She was pleased to report that, in response to the audit, UCOP had issued its new "Affirmative Action Guidelines on Recruitment and Retention of Faculty" in January 2002, reminding the campuses that they were still required under federal law to make "good faith" efforts to end the under-representation of women and minorities. Although the UC Office of the President had issued these new guidelines, Auditor Howle was unsure how the UC system was actually going to implement them. She requested that the UC President's Office ask each campus to respond to the problems identified by the audit and detail how they would comply with the new UCOP guidelines.

Following Auditor Howle's testimony, Provost Virginia Hinshaw from UC–Davis, representing the UC president, reported that the hires of women faculty at UC had increased from 25 percent in 1999–2000 to 30 percent in 2000–01. The improvement was even greater among faculty hires at the assistant professor level, increasing from 27 percent in 1999–2000 to 37 percent in 2000–01. Provost Hinshaw also reported that President Atkinson had allocated $6 million to support hiring faculty engaged in research that advances the understanding of issues of race, gender, and ethnicity as they intersect with traditional academic fields.

At the close of Provost Hinshaw's testimony, there was a lively dialogue among Senator Speier, Auditor Howle, and Provost Hinshaw about what UC was actively doing to remedy the problem of gender disparity in faculty hiring. Senator Speier had numerous questions and recommendations that she asked Provost Hinshaw to deliver personally to UC President Atkinson. Speier announced that she had spoken with President Atkinson before the hearing and obtained his promise that he would personally appear at a third hearing the following year.

Similar to the first hearing, a panel of nine faculty members from the majority of UC campuses testified at the second hearing. Professor West noted that the state audit found that only 20 percent of the applicants for faculty jobs were women. This was surprising in light of the fact that by 2001, women were earning 50 percent of PhDs among U.S. citizens, and 44 percent of all PhDs. She urged UC to examine why women were not applying for faculty jobs at the rates one would expect. She also urged UC to formalize how departments were keeping track of who the actual "applicants" were. Professor Goldberg from UCLA noted that the state audit had generated significant activity at UCLA; the College of Letters and Science was putting a new electronic method in place to monitor searches, identify the gender and ethnicity of applicants, and track how they fare in the search process. Also, UCLA had created a new position: of associate vice chancellor of faculty diversity.

Professors Angelica Stacy and Deborah Nolan from Berkeley testified that although Berkeley hired 27 percent women in 2000–01, nine years earlier in 1993, 35 percent of the UC–Berkeley hires had been women. If the 1993 hire rate had continued, 90 more women faculty would have been hired at

Berkeley. Professor Stacy, recently appointed as Berkeley's associate vice provost for faculty equity, testified that all seventeen of the deans and senior administrators who approve faculty hires were men. Among the sixty-three department chairs, only fifteen were women. In her words, "the vast majority of [UC Berkeley] faculty are reviewed by an entirely male administration."

In addition to the faculty testimonies, Dr. Carol Mandell testified about her experience in applying for a faculty position at the UC–Davis School of Veterinary Medicine. As a board-certified veterinary clinical pathologist and a PhD research scientist, Mandell had received a three-year NIH grant and had authored numerous publications in peer-reviewed journals before she applied for a faculty position in 1998. During the final phase of the search process, five candidates were interviewed: four women and one man. Three of the women, including Mandell, had not only received PhDs but had also received competitive federal grants. The male candidate was the only one who had not yet received his PhD; he had yet to take his PhD oral qualifying exams. Nonetheless, the faculty awarded the position to the man. Mandell had been told during the search by a department faculty member that the man was being groomed for the job. Furthermore, one member of the search committee was the male candidate's PhD advisor and close personal friend. Mandell subsequently sued UC Davis for sex and age discrimination. [We learned after the hearing that the local superior court dismissed her case at the summary judgment stage, but the appellate court reversed and remanded her case for trial. The case eventually settled, but Dr. Mandell never obtained a faculty position at UC–Davis.]

At the end of the second hearing, the faculty members who testified were unanimous in their recommendation to Senator Speier that she continue the hearings for another year. In their opinion, whatever progress was occurring on their campuses was a result of the interest and political pressure generated by the hearings and the state audit.

In November 2002, between the second and third hearings, UC President Atkinson convened his own President's Summit on Faculty Gender Equity. He invited approximately forty senior faculty women from all the campuses to meet for one and a half days in Oakland to develop recommendations. Senator Speier gave the keynote address and several of the women who had testified at the hearings participated in the Summit. Among the summit's numerous recommendations, the participants stressed the need for each campus chancellor to provide visible leadership on the faculty hiring issue. Although President Atkinson promised to convene a second summit the following year to monitor progress, he had resigned by the fall of 2003, and none was held.

Hearing 3

Senator Speier's third hearing was held on February 19, 2003. The data on the previous year's hires, 2001–02, had just been released by UC. It showed a disappointing increase of only 1 percent over the prior year: 31 percent of faculty hires were women (154 of 493 hires). More disturbing, at the assistant professor level, women's percentage had actually declined, from 37 percent in 2000–01 to 34.5 percent in 2001–02. President Atkinson testified, acknowledging that UC still had a ways to go to reach the 37 percent women hires made in 1993–94, before Proposition 209 passed. Senator Speier responded that "disappointment is an understatement. . . . Gentle persuasion has had limited results. We need less talk, less lip service, and more action."

The fourteen UC faculty members who testified continued the same themes from the previous hearings. Professor West pointed out that the gap between the percentage of women in the PhD pool and the percentage hired had doubled: in 1994 women were 46 percent of the PhD pool and 37 percent of the hires, a 9 point gap; eight years later, in 2002, women were over 49 percent of the PhD pool but only 31 percent of the hires, an 18-point gap. Berkeley had made more progress than the rest of the system, increasing its percentage of women hires to 34 percent, according to Professor Angelica Stacy. On the other hand, in the Berkeley math department, one of the largest producers of female math PhDs in the nation, not a single woman had been hired over the past ten years—the department had hired twenty-eight men, with no intervention by the campus. The dean of UC Berkeley's Graduate Division, Mary Ann Mason, presented data showing that women with babies are 33 percent less likely than others to land a tenure-track position; she focused her presentation on the need for UC to develop more "family friendly" personnel policies.

Professor Martha McCartney from the chemical engineering department at UC–Irvine was distressed that the percentage of women faculty hired at Irvine had declined from 31 percent in 1999 to 28 percent in 2002, even though UC Irvine had received an ADVANCE grant from the National Science Foundation in 2000–01 to increase the number of women faculty in science and engineering. Professor Michael Bernstein, chair of history at UC–San Diego, testified that the "majority of male faculty members [do] want to see the hiring of women improve." In his view, however, the goals of the search process itself privilege white men. Departments are asked by UC to increase their academic excellence and gain academic visibility. They do this primarily by hiring prestigious faculty from other institutions, who are overwhelmingly white men. When this happens, departments are rewarded by additional resources from central campus funds. In his view, only if departments are forced to recruit at the assistant professor level will the percentage of women among new hires increase.

In contrast to Berkeley, UCLA's hires of women fell significantly during the past year, from 33 percent in 2000–01 to 20 percent in 2001–02. Professor Susan Prager, former dean of the UCLA Law School, was particularly concerned about the steep decline in women hires at the assistant professor level: the percentage fell from 45 percent to only 20 percent women. She believed this data indicated serious discrimination against women when one compares these entry-level hires to the PhD candidate pools. In her words, faculty and administrators "may well be overlooking the overarching legal framework, . . . namely, the anti-discrimination principle itself." Finally, Professor Christine Gailey, chair of women's studies at UC–Riverside, testified that research demonstrates that women as a whole must be at least one-third more productive than men to get equal treatment. Furthermore, women of color must be twice as productive, twice as well qualified as men to get equal treatment in hiring.

Senator Speier's three hearings produced a variety of recommendations for UC:

- Disseminate widely the past year's hiring data and relevant PhD pool information by gender, race, and ethnicity.
- Issue a UC directive to expand the percentage of faculty hired at the entry level of assistant professor to 80 percent of new hires, instead of the current 60 percent.
- Set up uniform procedures to monitor faculty searches.
- Reward departments and department chairs who are making effective progress in diverse hiring.
- Appoint more women to administrative leadership positions.
- Review the performance of deans on hiring issues on an annual basis.
- Provide stronger leadership at the campus and system-wide levels to address gender equity issues affecting women faculty.

As a result of this legislative activity and the hard work of many faculty members on each campus, the percentage of women among new faculty hires did gradually increase at UC. During the 2000–01 academic year, while the state audit was occurring and the first hearing was held, women's percentage among new hires rose from 25 percent to 30 percent. At the end of the 2001–02 academic year, based on data UC released just before the third hearing in 2003, women's percentage of hires stood at a disappointing 31 percent. By the end of the 2002–03 academic year, however, after the third hearing, women's percentage rose to 36 percent, where it has remained through the 2005–06 academic year.

On another important measure—the hiring of nontenured assistant professors—the hearings generated some improvement. According to the 2003–04 hiring data, the percentage of women among assistant professor hires increased from 38 percent in 2002–03 to 41 percent in 2003–04. This was, however, only a temporary improvement, with hires falling back to 39 percent women in 2004–05 and 2005–06. The hiring of women as assistant professors lags significantly behind the percentage of women available among

PhDs recipients for the past ten years. As Senator Speier said during the three years of hearings, "We need less talk, less lip service, and more aggressive action attracting women. UC is underutilizing a valuable resource by not hiring more women. When women are shut out it not only affects the type of research conducted, it also limits the questions pursued." As UC slowly adds more women to its faculty, women continue to expand their participation in graduate education, obtaining a majority of the PhDs earning by U.S. citizens every year since 2002.

Evaluation of the Use of Political Pressure to Create Change on Campus

Certainly there were short-term improvements in the rates of women faculty hires during and immediately after the hearings. The rate of hires probably would have improved somewhat without the hearings, but the cumulative effect of the state audit, the three hearings, and the organizing that took place on the campuses no doubt had an impact on the hiring environment. By increasing the percentage of women hires from 25 percent in 1999–2000 to 36 percent in 2002–03, approximately 210 more women faculty were hired between 2002 and 2006 than might otherwise have obtained UC faculty positions. As predicted in 1999, UC hired a record number of new faculty in recent years: 2,095 new tenured or tenure-track faculty joined UC between 2002 and 2006 (519 in 2002–03, 591 in 2003–04, 542 in 2004–05, declining to 442 in 2005–06). In the absence of the California senate hearings, it is likely the percentage of women among new hires would have hovered around the 30 percent or 31 percent reached in 2000 and 2001. (Only 28 percent of faculty hires during the previous four-year period. 1996–2000. were women.) By calling attention to the problem and generating activity at both the state level and at the various campuses, the impact of the hearings can be seen in the increase from the 31 percent of hires in 2001 to the 36 percent reached by the 2002–03 academic year. This 5 percent increase resulted in 105 more women faculty being hired between 2002 and 2006 than if the percentage of women hired had remained at 31 percent. This is the most tangible result of the involved faculty members' political activity from 1999 through 2003.

The impact of the faculty members' political activity is also reflected in a negative way by the failure of the women's hire rate to move up further after the hearings ended. Women's hire rate has remained at 36 percent since 2003, dropping to 35 percent in 2004–05. Is this a consequence of the fact that no more hearings have been held? With no hearings, UC has made no progress in increasing its rate of hiring women faculty, despite the fact that women's percentage among U.S. citizen PhDs rose to 51 percent in 2002, where it remained through 2005, according to the latest data available.

The use of political pressure worked temporarily for these UC faculty members in California because members of the legislature, and in particular Senator Jackie Speier, were very supportive of equality for women and were much more attuned to the changing demographics of California than were the UC Regents and the UC administration. In other states, faculty members might not find greater concern in a state legislature than on campus to work on gender equity issues.

One major limitation on seeking political support outside of campus is the transient nature of politics. California enacted term limits several years ago, so political leaders cannot remain in the legislature for more than two or three terms. Senator Speier reached her term limit in 2006 and has now retired from the legislature. Although there are other legislative leaders who would be supportive, it would involve serious effort on the faculty members' part to bring another set of legislative staff members up to speed on all the data and UC history that Senator Speier and her excellent staff mastered during the four years of intensive work on this issue.

Perhaps even more difficult is the amount of work expended to organize even a few faculty members on each of the nine UC campuses to testify at the hearings and generate pressure for change on their campus. As a way to prepare for the hearings, Professors Laky and West organized an informal faculty advocacy group, California Academics for Equity (CAFÉ). Most of the organizing was done by e-mail; by the end of three years, Professor Laky had more than three hundred names from the nine campuses on her CAFÉ mailing list. Professor Laky sent newsletters to interested faculty two or three times a year, keeping everyone informed about the planning for each hearing and reporting afterward on the hearings' proceedings. Some faculty members, in turn, forwarded Laky's e-mails to their campus networks. Keeping this network current took a great deal of time. In 2006, Professor Laky retired from the university. Just as state legislators turn over from time to time, so do faculty. It will take another crisis in the university before someone else steps up to take Professor Laky's place as an active faculty organizer.

The other major center of turnover has been the UC Office of the President. Just as President Atkinson committed himself to take leadership on the issue of faculty gender equity, he retired. He was replaced by President Robert Dynes in the fall of 2003. President Dynes was distracted in 2005 and 2006 by a host of problems, among them continuing criticisms of extravagant financial perks for high-level administrators during a period of significant student fee increases. He has not made any statements, to the author's knowledge, about the importance of increasing the numbers of women hired as faculty members. His staff members have done significant work on expanding family-friendly policies for UC faculty in recent years, which help support faculty women after hire, particularly those raising young children. He has not, however, focused on the need to hire more women faculty as a starting point to achieve gender equity.

Without vocal leadership at the top, it is very difficult to bring the message to faculty at the department level that they must diversify both their hiring methods and their results to reflect the current composition of the PhD recipients in their academic fields. If faculty hirers do not feel the pressure to do things differently, they won't—they will just continue to hire those candidates their friends recommend and with whom they feel most comfortable. Although the composition of the UC faculty has changed slowly over the last ten years, it is still overwhelmingly male: 73 percent in 2005. Ten years earlier, in 1995, 77 percent of the faculty were men.

To make outside political pressure work, there must be a strong organizing campaign taking place on the campus as well. Faculty members can be successful organizers, but only for short periods of time. It is very difficult to maintain faculty networks on the basis of volunteer faculty efforts. With no paid staff support, faculty cannot maintain organizing efforts over long periods of time while simultaneously meeting their classes and maintaining their scholarship productivity. A tremendous effort was required to generate the level of political involvement that sustained these legislative hearings and the state audit over four years. The only hope for a longer-term commitment to gender equity issues in faculty hiring is to find leaders for the UC system who will take this challenge upon themselves, who have access to campus leaders, deans, department chairs, and faculty, and the necessary administrative support to carry this message to each campus on a yearly basis. Faculty are able to do the right thing, but only if they are reminded and strongly encouraged to do so. UC faculty need leadership to bring the University of California into the twenty-first century, or they will suffer the consequences when the legislature gradually changes to reflect the current demographics of the California population and abandons UC in the budget process because so few of their constituents have benefited from a UC education. Women are like the canaries in the mines—if the university is unable to hire women in an equitable fashion, reflecting their presence in the qualified labor pool, how will the university ever be successful in integrating the large numbers of people of color, now a majority of the school-age population in California, into its student body and its faculty? Time is of the essence in helping the university adapt to what UC–Berkeley Chancellor Robert Birgeneau refers to as "the majestic tapestry of California." It is to be hoped that new faculty change agents will emerge to meet the challenges of the future.

NOTES

1. This chapter is derived from a seventy-four-page report, "Unprecedented Urgency: Gender Discrimination in Faculty Hiring at the University of California," authored by

Martha S. West, Gyöngy Laky, Kari Lokke, Kyaw Tha Paw U, and Sarah Ham, published on the University of California–Davis Law School Web site in May, 2005 at http://www.law.ucdavis.edu/faculty/west_pub.shtml and.http://www.law.ucdavis.edu/faculty/westpdf/marthat percent20west.pdf. The report was funded by the Ford Foundation through the Institute for Women's Leadership at Rutgers University. Martha West, professor of law, is deeply indebted to her colleagues at UC–Davis: Gyöngy Laky, professor emeritus of design in textiles and clothing, Kari Lokke, professor in comparative literature, and Kyaw Tha Paw U, professor of atmospheric science in land, air, and water resources. She also acknowledges with great appreciation the work of Sarah Ham, research assistant, UC–Davis School of Law, JD 2004.

2. State Senator Jackie Speier was and is a courageous woman. About thirty years ago, as a young person on Congressman Leo Ryan's staff, Speier almost lost her life in the attempt to uncover the facts about the Reverend Jim Jones and his People's Temple. More than nine hundred people died on November 18, 1978, in the incident that has come to be known as the Jonestown Massacre. Jackie Speier was shot five times on the airport tarmac in Guyana and left for dead. Thankfully, Speier survived, and went on to serve in the California legislature for twenty years, from 1986 through 2006. She has strong ties to UC as an alum of both UC–Davis and the Hastings College of Law. Speier was then chair of the state senate's Select Committee on Government Oversight and had a strong record on women's issues.

3. Transcripts of all three hearings are located at http://www.senate.ca.gov/htbin/testbin/http://wwwseninfo_dated?sen.committee.select.goover.transcript.

PART THREE

The Challenges
of Incomplete
Institutionalization

7

Feminist Interventions

Creating New Institutional Spaces for
Women at Rutgers

MARY HAWKESWORTH, LISA HETFIELD, BARBARA BALLIET,
AND JENNIFER MORGAN

Rutgers, the State University of New Jersey, has a national reputation as a leader in diversity. During the last two decades of the twentieth century, Rutgers ranked among the top ten public Association of American Universities (AAU) institutions in percentages of women faculty and faculty of color. Rutgers-Newark is routinely ranked by *U.S. News and World Report* as one of the most diverse campuses in North America in terms of student composition. Moreover, as the home of Douglass College, the only women's college in the United States located within a major public research university, one of the top women's and gender studies departments in the world, and five major research centers and institutes on women, Rutgers University enjoys a reputation for gender diversity that is unparalleled.

This chapter explores the invisible labor of faculty and administrators—predominantly women—who worked over the course of the twentieth century to transform an all-male institution into a coeducational institution, featuring unique intellectual spaces for women and innovative academic programs, research centers, and institutes. Tracing a series of feminist interventions into the standard operating practices of the university, the chapter documents how entrepreneurial faculty and administrators have used their ingenuity to create and sustain spaces that undermine race and gender hierarchies within and outside the university. Through the creation of new academic spaces, interdisciplinary networks of scholars have developed the expertise to address pressing problems concerning inequities grounded in race, gender, and sexuality, generating innovative research and transformative policy proposals. Linking their scholarly investigations to teaching, advocacy work, and public programming, faculty have devised new curriculum and cocurricular opportunities for undergraduate and graduate students and new community, state, national, and transnational social justice initiatives. In and through these various initiatives, they have forged a diverse and inclusive community within the larger university.

Beyond illuminating the arduous invisible labor of faculty to sustain these initiatives, the chapter identifies a recurrent pattern of incomplete institutionalization. Despite decades of successful grant writing and fund-raising, each of these units experiences a paradoxical combination of strength, derived from national and international renown, and fragility, stemming from insufficient university resources and recognition. While the "self-help" tactics of entrepreneurial faculty and administrators have made the creation of new institutional spaces for women possible, more complete institutionalization requires enhanced support from the university.

Institutional Context

Rutgers has a unique history as a colonial college, a land-grant institution, and a state university. Chartered in 1766 as Queen's College, the eighth institution of higher learning to be founded in the colonies, the school opened its doors in New Brunswick to male students in 1771. In 1825, the name of the college was changed to honor a former trustee and Revolutionary War veteran, Colonel Henry Rutgers. Rutgers College became the land-grant college of New Jersey in 1864, resulting in the creation of the Rutgers Scientific School, with departments of agriculture, engineering, and chemistry. Further expansion in the sciences came with the founding of the New Jersey Agricultural Experiment Station in 1880, the College of Pharmacy (now the Ernest Mario School of Pharmacy) in 1892, the College of Engineering (now the School of Engineering) in 1914, and the College of Agriculture (now the School of Environmental and Biological Sciences) in 1921. Despite the impressive growth over the course of the nineteenth century, Rutgers remained an all-male institution.

Women in the state of New Jersey had no access to higher education, public or private, until the early decades of the twentieth century. During a period of intensive suffrage and women's rights activism, a number of influential women mobilized to demand access to educational opportunities and to create women's colleges. The New Jersey Federation of Women's Clubs launched a campaign to create a liberal arts college for women that would be nondenominational and affordable. Under the leadership of Mabel Smith Douglass, a committee of the Federation of Women's Clubs mobilized school superintendents and principals to support higher education for women. Lobbying wives of members of the Rutgers Board of Trustees, Douglass persuaded the president and the board to allocate land and a building for the new college. Tapping the political and economic resources of women across the state, Douglass initiated a "one-dollar women's subscription" to raise $150,000 to support the college. She succeeded in founding a college that would offer women "a cultural broadening in connection with specific training so that women may go out into the world fitted not only for positions on the lower rung of the ladder of opportunity but for leadership as well in the economic, political, and intellectual life of this nation" (Douglass 1929). The New Jersey College for Women (renamed Douglass College in 1954 to honor its founder) opened its doors in 1918, admitting the first women to what would later become Rutgers University.

In 1924 Rutgers College assumed university status and expanded significantly with the founding of an evening division—University College—in 1934, and the addition of the University of Newark (now Rutgers-Newark) in 1946, and the College of South Jersey at Camden (now Rutgers-Camden) in 1950. Legislative acts in 1945 and 1956 designated Rutgers as "the State University of New Jersey." Currently, the university encompasses twenty-nine degree-granting divisions; twelve undergraduate colleges, eleven graduate schools, and three schools offering both undergraduate and graduate degrees. The university enrolls more than fifty-one thousand students, including more than thirty-eight thousand undergraduates and thirteen thousand graduate students.

For the better part of its history, Rutgers operated as a collection of fairly autonomous confederated undergraduate colleges and graduate schools. In the early 1980s, however, President Edward J. Bloustein (1971–1989) restructured the New Brunswick campus as part of a long-term plan to become a "Research I Institution" under the Carnegie classification of colleges and universities and a member of the elite Association of American Universities. In the process, the formerly autonomous faculties of the undergraduate colleges in New Brunswick were merged into discipline-based departments, mostly within a new Faculty of Arts and Sciences (FAS). This reorganization created impressive strength in traditional disciplines while profoundly changing the working environment for individual faculty members, hiring priorities and practices, and student enrollment.

Demographics

Race and gender are present not only in the demographic makeup of an institution but also in institutional processes, practices, images, ideologies, and distributions of power. Embedded in organizational routines, race and sex segregation in the institution's workforce, recruitment practices that replicate raced and gendered employment and student enrollment patterns, and marginalizing practices that keep historically underrepresented groups on the periphery of decision making can be particularly difficult to change (Acker 1992; Duerst-Lahti and Kelly 1995). Analysis of thirty years of demographic data at Rutgers demonstrates how difficult it is to diversify a university and challenges optimistic assumptions that affirmative action produces gains for all historically underrepresented groups.[1]

Students

GENDER. In 1970 men constituted 68 percent and women 32 percent of the students at Rutgers University. Women students were concentrated in Douglass College and the Schools of Education, Nursing, and Social Work. While the number of male students has remained fairly constant over the past thirty-five years (hovering between 23,000 and 24,000), the number of women students has increased 2.5 times (growing from 11,300 to 28,000), as the total student enrollment grew from 35,256 to a high of 51,480 students in 2002. Thus, women students have been prime beneficiaries of affirmative action. It is interesting to note, however, that in absolute numbers, male students have not lost significant ground. While the number of male students has remained fairly constant, total student enrollment has expanded to admit more women. Women now constitute 54.6 percent and men 45.4 percent of the student population, but, male students have held their own in sheer numbers. It is important to note, too, that the men and women students are not uniformly represented across university units: the student population of the College of Nursing, for example, remains 90.6 percent female, while 81.7 percent of the students in the College of Engineering are male.

RACE/ETHNICITY. The racial composition of the student population was not officially recorded prior to 1976, when the federal government began requiring enrollment data by race and ethnicity. Fluctuations in number and percentage of minority students are related to enrollment management as well as recruitment patterns. To trace diversity trends, the following analysis compares the demographics of the university's student population with the changing demographics of the state of New Jersey.

- *Asian Americans.* Enrollment of Asian American students increased dramatically from 960 in 1976 to 8,503 in 2003, as their percentage of the student population increased from 2 percent to 16.6 percent. In 2004, Asian American students constituted 20 percent of the Rutgers student population. According to the U.S. Census, the Asian American population of New Jersey increased from 1.5 percent in 1970 to 5.7 percent in 2003.

- *Latino/as.* The number of Latino students more than tripled, from 1,296 in 1976 to 4,218 in 2003, as their proportion in the student body increased from 2.7 percent to 8.2 percent. While in the abstract this increase might appear impressive, the growth of Latino/a students has not kept up with the growth of New Jersey's Latino/a population. During the last three decades, the Latino/a population of the state doubled, growing from

6.7 percent of the state population in 1970 to 13.3 percent in 2003. In comparison to the demographics of the New Jersey population, then, Latino
students were significantly underrepresented in the student population
in the 1970s and remain significantly underrepresented in the Rutgers
student population in 2004.

- *African Americans.* In 1976 the proportion of African American students (11
  percent) at Rutgers approximated the proportion of African Americans
  (10.7 percent) in the New Jersey population, but this proportionality was
  not preserved during the subsequent thirty years. Indeed, African Americans lost significant ground. In the last half of the 1970s, the number of
  African American students increased on campus from 5,103 or 11 percent
  of the student population in 1976 to a high of 5,683 (11.5 percent) in 1979,
  the year in which the U.S. Supreme Court signaled its initial retreat from
  the principles of affirmative action in the *Bakke* decision. This high point
  in enrollment did not quite keep pace with the increase in the African
  American population in New Jersey, however, which reached 12.6 percent
  in 1980, as black student enrollment began to decline, falling to 4,392
  (9.2 percent) in 1987. As the black population grew to 13.6 percent of the
  New Jersey population in 2003, the proportion of black students at
  Rutgers stagnated in the 9.2 percent to 9.9 percent range. Like Latino/a
  students, African American students remain significantly underrepresented among Rutgers students, yet this commonality masks a critical difference. While the number of Latino/a students at Rutgers has increased
  from 1,296 to 4,218 during the past thirty years, the number of African
  American students on campus decreased from 5,103 in 1976 to 5,080 in
  2003, during a period in which total student enrollment increased from
  46,491 to 51,268. In absolute numbers and as a percentage of the total
  student population, African Americans were more underrepresented in
  2004 than they had been in 1976.

As in the case of gender, the racial and ethnic composition of the student population at Rutgers varies from one campus to another and from one school to
another. The Rutgers-Newark campus, which *U.S. News and World Report* has
ranked top in the nation for diversity for eight consecutive years, has a higher
percentage of students of color than other Rutgers campuses. In 2004, for
example, 22.9 percent of the students at Rutgers-Newark were Asian American,
19.6 percent African American; 17.3 percent Latino/a, and 35.7 percent white.
By contrast, in 2004, 21.2 percent of the students at Rutgers-New Brunswick
were Asian American, 7.9 percent African American, 7.4 percent Latino/a,
and 54.8 percent white; while at Rutgers-Camden, only 8.4 percent of the
students were Asian American, 12.2 percent African American, 5.5 percent
Latino/a, and 66.9 percent were white.

Faculty

GENDER. In 1976 women constituted 27 percent of the tenured/tenure-track faculty at Rutgers University, mirroring the average percentage of women employed in postsecondary institutions in the United States at that time. At Rutgers University, however, women faculty members were concentrated in a few units: 43 percent of the women faculty were employed at Douglass College. By 1986, women constituted 29 percent of the tenured/tenure- track faculty at the university, a level at which they remained until 1992–1993. During the decade from 1994 to 2004, the percentage of women faculty rose from 29.3 percent to 34.6 percent, half a percentage point per year. While the average proportion of women faculty at AAU institutions grew by 60 percent between 1990 and 2002 (Hornig 2003), the proportion of women faculty at Rutgers increased only 16 percent.

On the Rutgers-New Brunswick campus, where the Institute for Women's Leadership (IWL) is located, the numbers are also telling. In 1978 (the first year for which Institutional Research has campus-specific data), 573 women were members of the faculty, a number that declined steadily to a low of 510 in 1991–1992, then began a very gradual ascent. The number of women faculty on the New Brunswick campus surpassed the 1978 level only in academic year 2001–2002, when new hires brought the number of women to 586. The declining numbers of women faculty between 1978 and 1992 are masked by statistics that show the percentage of women faculty gradually increasing from 27 percent in 1978 to 28 percent in 1990, 30 percent in 1995, 31.8 percent in 2000, and 33.3 percent in 2003. The difference between women faculty's declining numbers and their increase as a proportion of the faculty results from the shrinking size of the total New Brunswick faculty, which fell from a high of 2,049 in 1978 to 1,842 in 2000, then rose to 1,913 in 2003–2004.

RACE/ETHNICITY. Rather than increasing the racial and ethnic diversity of faculty over the past three decades, Rutgers has lost significant ground with respect to two protected categories, African American and Latino/a faculty.

- *African Americans.* In 1976, African American scholars constituted 6.8 percent of the full-time faculty at Rutgers. That percentage has declined steadily over the past thirty years, falling to 5 percent in 1990–1991 and to 4 percent in 2003–2004. In absolute numbers: there were 175 African American scholars teaching at Rutgers in 1976; 128 in 1990–91; and 97 in 2003–2004.
- *Latino/as.* Latino/a faculty constituted 2.1 percent of the faculty in 1976 and 2 percent of the faculty in 2003–2004. As in the case of African American scholars, there were more Latino/a faculty teaching at Rutgers

in 1976, when 54 were employed there, than there were in 2003–2004. Rutgers currently employs only 50 Latino/a faculty, down from an all-time high of 63 in 1998–99.

- *Asian Americans.* Asian American representation has grown from 2.5 percent of the faculty in 1976 to 9 percent of the faculty in 2003–2004, as their numbers increased from 64 to 231.
- *"Whites."* Although aggregate statistics make it appear that the proportion of white faculty decreased from 88.7 percent in 1975–76 to 75 percent in 2003–2004, the apparent magnitude of this change is due largely to a change in record-keeping practices. According to official university data, from 1975–76 to 1995–96, the percentage of "whites" declined from 88.7 percent to 84 percent of the faculty. During this period, Rutgers did not list international ("foreign") faculty as a separate demographic category. Beginning in 1997, Rutgers classified international scholars as a separate demographic group. There is a very close parallel between the number and percentage of scholars in the new "foreign" category and the drop in number and percentage of scholars classified as "white." Since 1997, it appears that whites have decreased from 84 percent of the faculty to 75 percent of the faculty, as their numbers seem to have dropped by 212. During the same period, however, 242 faculty were reclassified as "foreign," making up 9 percent of the total faculty.

Campus Climate

The metaphor of a "chilly climate" for women has been used to characterize universities in North America (Hall and Sandler 1982, 1984, and 1986; Sandler 1992). Interview data gathered for a study of gender equity in the Faculty of Arts and Sciences (2001) at Rutgers-New Brunswick, as well as data from interviews conducted for this project, reveal that some women and minority faculty at Rutgers use starker metaphors, such as "arctic blast" and "toxic environment" to portray the climate in their departments, a climate that has changed little over the past three decades.

In 1971 in the College of Arts and Sciences at Rutgers-Newark, a small group of tenured women faculty filed a class-action sex-discrimination complaint with the Department of Health, Education, and Welfare (DHEW). Constituting themselves as the Committee on the Status of Women, they collected data to demonstrate multiple dimensions of sex discrimination on campus, with particular attention to serious pay inequities. Salary data showed that women faculty were paid less than their male counterparts in every discipline at every level. Women instructors were paid on average $400 less per course than their male counterparts; women full professors earned on average $4,000 less than their male colleagues at a time when average male salaries were $20,000. One African American woman faculty member hired by the psychology department was given a full-time teaching load but paid only part-time wages. Women were significantly underrepresented across all departments, and where they were present they were concentrated at lower faculty ranks, especially at the nontenurable ranks of instructor, assistant instructor, and lecturer. Only eight of the fifty-four women then teaching at Rutgers-Newark were tenured despite long years of service. Investigation of promotion practices revealed that the average time from PhD to professor for male faculty in one department was eight years, while it took eighteen years for the lone tenured woman to reach that rank. Men were awarded tenure with full support from their departments and college committees, while women with better credentials were routinely denied tenure and had to fight through long and difficult grievance mechanisms to have those decisions reversed. Analysis of workload practices demonstrated that women faculty carried far heavier teaching and service loads. Men were promoted to full professor with fewer publications than women whose promotion efforts were turned down. Males awarded graduate fellowships were given research assignments; women fellows were assigned secretarial duties such as typing faculty papers and answering correspondence. Moreover, women faculty members were subjected to marginalization, "condescension, and slurs that men are unlikely to experience" (Memorandum on the Status of Faculty Women at Rutgers, Newark, 1971, 3).

On the New Brunswick campus, women faculty members' experiences varied from one college to another. Women at Rutgers College and Cook College encountered far more difficulties than women at Douglass College or Livingston College. In 1972, for example, there were only five tenured women on the faculty at Rutgers College. When one newly recruited associate professor developed an affirmative action plan, at the dean's request, to assist with the implementation of coeducation at Rutgers College, the department chairs, an all-male enclave, refused to support the plan. Moreover, the woman faculty member who authored the plan was fired by her department chair, who retroactively claimed that her appointment as associate professor did not include tenure. She too filed sex-discrimination complaints with the Equal Opportunities Commission and the Civil Rights Division of DHEW.

The DHEW investigations into these cases corroborated the claims of women faculty members concerning multiple forms of sex discrimination at Rutgers. Acting on behalf of the university, Vice President John Martin approached DHEW and the Equal Employment Opportunity Commission (EEOC) to settle the complaints informally. The university pledged to introduce a variety of changes, including redress of specific grievances lodged by individual complainants, salary adjustments for women faculty on all campuses, and the development of a systematic affirmative action plan for the university as a whole. This informal settlement also imposed a nondisclosure agreement upon the parties who had lodged the official complaints. According to principals in these cases, the most egregious problems on some Rutgers campuses were not resolved, despite the salary increases and the development of the affirmative action plan. Women continued to experience discrimination in hiring, tenure and promotions.

Leading a coalition of women from Newark and New Brunswick campuses, Professor Nadine Taub, founder of the Women's Rights Litigation Clinic at Rutgers School of Law-Newark, pressured the university administration to take stronger measures to redress discrimination on campus. She identified multiple deficiencies in the affirmative action plan that President Bloustein developed for the university including: inadequate funding for redress of pay inequities; use of "merit" funds for pay equity adjustments, which would predictably foster resentment of male colleagues "deprived" of annual merit increases; allowing administrators responsible for existing gender-based pay inequities to control rectification efforts; and failure to hire sufficient staff to monitor affirmative action efforts. The legitimacy of these concerns was confirmed by reports of the university's newly created affirmative action office (Office of Affirmative Action and Employment Research1982), which documented declining numbers of women and minority faculty during the 1980s. Rather than acting to redress this problem, the university proposed to gather more data.

The 1989 report of the Office of Affirmative Action and Employment Research once again documented losses of African American and Latino faculty, along with increases in Asian Americans. While women faculty and faculty of color throughout the 1990s continued to monitor the reports of the Office of Affirmative Action and send letters to the president, provosts, deans, and board of governors seeking "systemic remedies," they remained underrepresented among university administrators and shut out of key decision-making committees, many of which restricted membership to faculty at the Professor II rank, the rank in which women and minority faculty were least represented.[2] In 1982, shortly after the rank was created, women constituted 7.6 percent of PII faculty; in 2000, they constituted 9 percent of the PII faculty.

The underrepresentation of women in the most senior faculty ranks was linked to an initiative introduced by President Bloustein in conjunction with his effort to transform Rutgers into a Research I institution. With a special allocation from the state legislature requested by Governor Thomas Kean, Rutgers began recruiting a cohort of "world-class scholars" to enhance its research profile. Authorization to recruit such scholars was restricted to departments ranked among the top 5 percent of graduate programs in the United States. Affirmative action guidelines requiring open searches were suspended under this program. Most hires were awarded to science departments, and all of the initial recruits were men. Calling attention to the gender inequities exacerbated by this program, a group of feminist administrators formed an ad hoc committee to identify world-class women scholars and pressure the administration to hire them. As a result of their intervention, three top women scholars were hired.

Although budget cuts in the early 1990s slowed the recruitment of world-class scholars, the precedent of hiring senior white male scholars without a national search or even an advertised position was set under this program. The language of "target of opportunity" hiring, deployed by the Office of Federal Contract Compliance (OFCC) and the EEOC as part of affirmative action efforts to increase representation of historically disadvantaged groups, was appropriated by some Rutgers departments to legitimate the hiring of white men. The suspension of affirmative action requirements that all positions be advertised and that women and scholars of color be allowed to compete for all open positions redounded to the benefit of white men, even as the number of scholars of color employed at Rutgers continued to decline.

During the tenure of President Francis L. Lawrence (1990–2003), the university continued its push to achieve top-tier status as a research institution. Increasing diversity was also among Lawrence's stated priorities, and publicity materials touted Rutgers in that area. Rather than comparing its current diversity record with earlier years, the university began comparing itself with its peer institutions in the AAU. Since that group had the lowest percentages of women and minorities on their student and faculty bodies, Rutgers' diversity record looked impressive. Rutgers was first among the twenty-nine public AAU schools in total minority enrollment, first in African American enrollment, third in Latino enrollment, and third in Asian-Pacific Islander enrollment. Rutgers also ranked among the top three AAU institutions in percentage of women on faculty and among the top ten for percentage of minority faculty. Under Lawrence, the affirmative action office was significantly downgraded. New faculty hires did not reflect the pool of available women candidates, especially in the natural sciences and the social sciences. In addition, intense negative publicity focused on President Lawrence in the aftermath of a speech to faculty in 1994, suggesting that "genetic differences" were responsible for the gap in African American achievement.

Women and minority faculty members continued to report hostile-climate issues throughout the 1990s and into the twenty-first century. A survey of women in the Faculty of Arts and Sciences-New Brunswick in 2001 revealed a "widespread sense of condescension, disrespect, marginalization, isolation, tokenism, exploitation, and institutional sexism." Nearly two-thirds of respondents reported that female faculty were more likely than their male counterparts to feel personal and professional isolation; over half did not believe female faculty were promoted at rates equal to male colleagues at similar stages of professional development; 43 percent said that they were not as central a player as they wished to be in their department's informal decision making; 33 percent stated that they had not found a supportive environment for their academic work; and 33 percent reported that they had experienced sexual harassment (Faculty of Arts and Sciences Gender Equity Committee 2001, 38). Women of color reported egregious examples of disrespect from students as well as faculty colleagues.

Even at the most senior ranks, eminent women scholars reported that only halfhearted efforts were made to retain them when they received outside offers from universities more prestigious than Rutgers; male faculty with comparable outside offers were given research appointments, summer salary supplements, large research accounts, and opportunities to create research institutions with FAS funds in the effort to retain them. Not surprisingly, then, outstanding women faculty continued to leave Rutgers. The FAS Gender Equity Report documented that 50 percent of the women who left Rutgers between 1995 and 2000, for example, did so to accept positions at other universities, compared to 14 percent of the men. For the vast majority of male faculty (76 percent), retirement was the reason for their "departure" from the university, suggesting that the university supports their career objectives and values their service over time. By contrast, only 41 percent of the departures for women faculty were due to retirement.

In 2003 when he became president, Richard L. McCormick launched several initiatives to address diversity issues on campus, among them a request to deans to assess faculty diversity efforts and, most recently, the establishment of an Office of Faculty Diversity reporting to the Office of the President. Other diversity initiatives have since been introduced. Still, the longer-term "chilly climate" experienced by many women faculty at Rutgers, persistent exclusion from decision-making circles, and dwindling numbers of women and minority faculty members helps to explain decisions to create new institutional spaces as a social-change strategy. By carving out autonomous spaces within the university, women faculty members and administrators created networks to provide solidarity and mutual support while also devising their own agendas to promote diversity and intellectual innovation. Through such autonomous organizing, feminist faculty members created an unparalleled set of academic programs, research centers, and institutes dedicated to the elimination of entrenched gender and racial hierarchies within and beyond the university.

Creating New Institutional Spaces for Women

Douglass College

When Rutgers College admitted its first women students in 1970 (two hundred women in a student population of three thousand men), considerable pressure was brought to bear on Douglass College to become a coeducational institution. Under the leadership of faculty members Elaine Showalter and Mary Howard, Douglass faculty resisted the pressure and articulated a commitment to pursue "a bold experiment in feminist education." They developed courses in women's history, status, and achievements; cultivated women's excellence in the arts, writing, mathematics, and science; sponsored research on women; initiated community outreach programs for women; fought for campus day-care centers; argued for a more racially and ethnically diverse student population; and promoted students' commitments to justice and social change (Showalter 1993). Identifying women's empowerment and women's leadership as core objectives, Douglass College became a fertile ground for feminist activism, advocacy, and scholarship as well as a significant site of diversity.

Douglass College also became a site for model programs to advance women and to transform women's education, including the Douglass Project for Rutgers Women in Math, Science and Engineering; the Douglass Science Institute, which offers science enrichment programs for high school students; and the Bunting-Cobb Math, Science, and Engineering Residence Hall (the first of its kind in the nation), which provides mentoring and cocurricular programs to create a supportive community for undergraduate women pursuing science and math majors. Project SUPER (Science for Undergraduates: A Program for Excellence in Research) fosters research collaboration between faculty and undergraduate students during the academic year and in the summer break. In partnership with the W. M. Keck Center for Neuroscience, the Douglass Project launched RUWINS (Rutgers University Women in Neuroscience), a series of seminars featuring prominent women in neuroscience who share their academic research and career experiences with students and faculty.

Having lost the power to hire its own faculty in the 1980 reorganization, Douglass nonetheless continues to be an invaluable resource for feminist faculty at Rutgers. The Douglass deans provided space—one of the university's most precious and limited resources—for feminist initiatives, assistance with lecture funds to bring distinguished feminist scholars and activists to campus, and innovative educational opportunities to groom Douglass students for leadership positions. The college has also been at the forefront in creating living-learning communities such as the Global Village, the Human Rights House, and the Middle East House, which foster international awareness and global activism.

Despite Douglass's laudable record, however, in 2005 a university task force on undergraduate education recommended the abolition of the undergraduate colleges, proposing a merger of Douglass, Rutgers, Livingston, and University colleges to create a new School of Arts and Sciences. This plan met with intense opposition from many women students, faculty members, staff, and alumnae. After a year of intensive contestation over the proposal, President Richard McCormick approved a proposal that preserved Douglass as a residential college within this larger school while eliminating the other colleges.

Women's Studies

If Douglass represents the creation of autonomous spaces for women's education, feminist interventions to create interdisciplinary women's studies involve systematic efforts to transform knowledge production, challenging generalizations based on the experiences of less than half the population, contesting methodologies that mask race and gender specificities and differences, correcting omissions and distortions entrenched in traditional scholarship, and devising new research questions grounded in the complex intersections of race, gender, ethnicity, sexuality, and nationality. Grounded in individual faculty control over course content protected by academic freedom, the first courses in women's studies emerged at multiple sites on campus. The shift from individual courses to program development, however, requires institutional support to authorize certificate programs, undergraduate minors and majors, faculty hiring, and allocation of office space and adminis-trative support. Feminist faculty members had varying levels of success and confronted different obstacles in their efforts to create interdisciplinary women's studies programs within the undergraduate colleges. Among the first institutions in the country to offer courses in women's studies, Douglass College by 1973 had a program, a concentration, fifty affiliated faculty and administrators, nineteen women students enrolled in the certificate program, and national recognition as a site for the development of women's studies.

Founded in 1969 with an explicit social justice mission, "Strength Through Diversity," and an explicit agenda to recruit a more diverse student body and faculty, feminist faculty at Livingston developed women's studies as a collective that featured student participation in decision making and curricu-lar planning, a focus on activism in conjunction with courses in humanities and the social sciences, and hiring of interdisciplinary program faculty. With few women on the tenured faculty at Rutgers College and considerable oppo-sition from many senior male faculty members from the formerly elite men's college, feminist faculty had limited success in program development until 1980. By training graduate students in feminist analysis, however, they helped expand the teaching pool for women's studies courses, guaranteeing that courses could be offered regularly and contributing to the development of interdisciplinary women's studies across the university's campuses.

Reorganization in the early 1980s was not friendly to women's studies. Faculty hired on women's studies lines were forced into discipline-based departments as part of the consolidation of the college faculties. The newly combined discipline-based departments were often dominated, simply because there were more of them, by the more conservative faculty from Rutgers College, who could determine the outcome of departmental votes when they chose to vote as a bloc. Of the interdisciplinary women's studies faculty members who were transferred into discipline-based departments, several failed to be awarded tenure—contributing to a brain drain for women's studies, as well as career trauma for the individual scholars.

Women's studies lost not only faculty but also space during restructuring. Consolidated at Douglass as a single New Brunswick-wide program in 1981, women's studies had to re-create itself without a departmental structure or tenured faculty lines. In meeting student demand, the program was dependent on the goodwill of chairs of discipline-based departments and a willingness to allow courses of feminist faculty to be cross-listed with women's studies. The program was dependent on adjuncts or part-time lecturers hired to teach core interdisciplinary courses not cross-listed with a department. The newly consolidated program received no administrative support from 1981 until 1985, and consolidation also delayed the approval of the proposed undergraduate major until 1984.

From 1985 to 1990, in space provided by Douglass College, women's studies was sustained by the activism of departmentalized feminist faculty members who continued to develop curricula and build new institutions that brought them together. Although faculty members convinced the administration to commit a non-tenure-track line for an assistant director and an administrative assistant, budget cutbacks were making it more difficult to get departments to loan their faculty to the program, and the development of strong gender programs in the disciplines, particularly history, political science, sociology, and English, placed heavier demands on feminist faculty members, making it harder for them to contribute to the voluntarism that was sustaining women's studies.

In 1990, several senior women faculty convinced then dean of FAS, Richard McCormick, to authorize interdisciplinary women's studies faculty to search for a new director for the program. With the hiring of eminent historian Alice Kessler-Harris, women's studies began the quest for more complete institutionalization, seeking to build faculty strength by allowing current women's studies faculty members to shift a portion of their line to women's studies and by hiring new faculty on joint appointments. The transfer of faculty lines encountered obstacles, however, when departments demanded "compensation" for the "loss" of partial lines to women's studies. In 1994, after three years of negotiations, then Richard Foley, then dean of FAS, agreed to create four new joint appointments between women's studies and discipline-based departments including history, political science, sociology, and English. These joint appointments required that tenure be granted in discipline-based departments, which effectively lodged hiring power with the tenuring department. Difficulties in collaborating on these joint searches delayed hiring an additional four years.

Frustrated in its efforts to strengthen the faculty through hiring, women's studies turned to curricular innovation, securing two major grants from the Ford Foundation to globalize the curriculum, which generated a proposal for an MA program focusing on transnational activism, new courses on comparative feminisms, and a revised text for the introductory course with a global focus. An external review, mandated by the university in 1994, was highly favorable, ranking the women's studies program as one of the top three programs in the United States. Despite this recognition, the university's Committee on Standards and Priorities in Academic Development (CSPAD), made up of PII faculty who reported directly to the president on the allocation of resources and space for programs and departments, refused to approve increased funding for the program, denying it legitimacy and resources. CSPAD's assessment revealed a failure to understand both the intellectual content of this area of study and the nontraditional structure of the women's studies faculty. Organized as a program and lacking full-time tenured faculty, women's studies was perceived as failing to meet the standards of a serious academic enterprise. Rather than recognizing the ingenuity of an interdisciplinary intellectual project that managed to survive without sustained university support, CSPAD penalized women's studies for its "deviation" from traditional disciplines. In addition, some administrators and faculty argued that women's studies was no longer necessary now that women had attained greater social, political, and economic equality.

In 1997, the newly appointed program director, Harriet Davidson, working with Barry Qualls, the new associate dean for the humanities, pushed to complete the line transfers, begin hiring the shared-line faculty, and launch the new MA program. Committed to enhancing diversity and recruiting faculty who could contribute to the new global curriculum, women's studies hired women of color in all four faculty searches. New faculty members helped energize the curriculum at the undergraduate and graduate levels, and new courses were introduced emphasizing feminisms in South Asia (1998) and Africa (2000); race, ethnicities, and nationalism (2002); and human rights (2003).

In 1998, women's studies faculty leveraged FAS interest in the creation of a PhD program into support for the creation of a department with additional faculty lines. Dean Foley was persuaded that departmentalization would resolve the program's anomalous status in the university by giving it a recognizable structure and faculty. After several years of intensive effort by women's studies faculty and administrators, the university authorized the creation of a department of women's and gender studies, and the university president and board of governors approved the creation of the PhD program in 2001. The line transfers begun in the mid-1990s continued at a glacial pace and were completed only in 2005 on the condition that the department trade 1.5 of the promised new faculty lines as compensation for the remaining line transfers. Coinciding with departmentalization, continuing fiscal crises in New Jersey mandated repeated cutbacks in higher education. As a consequence, "new" resources between 2002 and 2005 barely sufficed to restore the department's operating budget to its 2000 level. The department has, however, received small funding increments from the Graduate School, linked to its success in recruiting outstanding students of color to the PhD program. Of the twenty-six students participating in the doctoral program, half are women of color.

The establishment of a department granting bachelor's, master's and doctoral degrees has been a thirty-year process at Rutgers University, subject to uneven development and recurrent interruption, initiated, sustained, and led by dedicated faculty, often working without compensation for the arduous labor required to invent and institutionalize interdisciplinary women's studies. At each stage of this process, faculty innovators have been confronted by questions, at times hostile, about the integrity and value of this interdisciplinary field of study, opposition to a form of knowledge that challenges fundamental assumptions, biases, and omissions in traditional disciplines, and more material forms of opposition manifested in the denial of resources, status, and recognition to the field of women's studies. Despite such formidable obstacles, feminist faculty have succeeded in creating a department that offers a comprehensive range of undergraduate and graduate degrees and attracts thousands of students to its courses each year, contributing to the creation of new generations of social-change activists.

The Center for American Women and Politics (CAWP)

Suffrage leader, cofounder of New Jersey's League of Women Voters, advocate for women's higher education, and one of the first women to serve as a trustee of Rutgers University, Florence Peshine Eagleton (1870–1953) bequeathed more than $1,000,000 to establish the Wells Phillips Eagleton and Florence Peshine Eagleton Foundation at Rutgers. Her bequest stipulated that the funds be used to endow an institute to provide education in practical politics for "young women and men" and to foster responsible, problem-solving leadership in civic and governmental affairs. Founded in 1956, the Eagleton Institute of Politics quickly established a reputation for excellence in the study of American politics, with a specialization in state politics and the politics of state legislatures. Fourteen years later, an advisory committee appointed by Don Herzberg, the first director of the Eagleton Institute, endorsed Herzberg's plan to include funding for a Center for the American Woman and Politics (CAWP) in a grant proposal, which the Ford Foundation funded, providing a two-year grant of

$50,000 to launch the first center in the nation established to study women's political participation.

Under the direction of Ruth B. Mandel, CAWP built an international reputation for its pathbreaking research, which investigates the characteristics and progress of women candidates and officeholders and the significance of women's presence in public life. In the early years CAWP research focused on identifying and describing women who sought and held elective office. Because governments at most levels did not (and in many cases still do not) maintain data about officeholders by sex, CAWP developed the National Information Bank on Women in Public Office. Both on its Web site and in print CAWP provides comprehensive historical and current data about women in elective office, women candidates and officeholders at the federal, statewide and state legislative levels, women appointed to presidential cabinets, the gender gap, and many other topics. The Center's Election Watch materials, available during presidential, congressional, and major statewide elections, track numbers, records, and patterns for women candidates. CAWP has also launched a series of pioneering studies to identify ways to bring more women into public office, and, with support from the Revson and Ford foundations, CAWP initiated a series of studies to assess the impact of women in public office.

While research is a central part of CAWP's mission, the center goes beyond studying women's status and prospects in American politics. Through work with women elected officials, potential candidates for public office, and students, CAWP has created programs to redress the underrepresentation of women in public office, increase the impact of women officeholders, and help make political women's leadership more effective. CAWP has designed programs to encourage women to seek both elective and appointive offices in New Jersey and across the nation. CAWP has also launched initiatives specifically aimed at increasing the number of women of color in elective offices in the United States. With the support of a $1 million grant from the W. K. Kellogg Foundation, CAWP designed National Education for Women's Leadership (NEW Leadership) not only to encourage college women to partic-ipate in politics but also to equip them with the knowledge and skill to pur-sue careers in politics. Organized as a summer residential institute, NEW Leadership provides women college students with an immersion program in practical politics involving sustained interaction with women elected offi-cials, party activists, political operatives, and legislative staff. Over the past decade CAWP has created the NEW Leadership Development Network to train other universities across the nation to offer comparable programs, enabling college women to learn about the challenges of running for political office and the equally demanding challenges of serving in public office. Since the pro-gram's creation in 1991, more than one thousand young women from thirty states have participated in NEW Leadership, nearly half of them women of color.

Although CAWP's research and program initiatives have been supported primarily by successful grant writing and fund-raising, being a unit of the Eagleton Institute has afforded CAWP both tangible and intangible advantages. Moreover, in the mid-1990s when one of the most prestigious universities in the United States tried to recruit CAWP to its campus, Rutgers responded with an offer of much-needed resources, including staff support, operating funds, and two faculty lines. Hiring faculty on these lines has proven to be very difficult, however. University rules do not allow faculty to be tenured in research centers, bureaus, and institutes. Thus CAWP must "partner" with a discipline-based department to hire faculty. Although the political science department, whose feminist faculty launched the first women and politics PhD program in the world in the late 1980s, might be considered a natural partner, hiring additional scholars with specializations in women and politics research has not been among the department's priorities. Despite urging from the FAS dean's office, the women and politics scholars within the department, and an external review committee, political science has been reluctant to participate in joint searches. Although the recent creation of the department of women's and gender studies opened the possibility for an alternative hiring partner, this opening coincided with period of fiscal crisis in New Jersey. Indeed, the $88 million cut in state funding that Rutgers suffered in 2006 necessitated staff cuts.

The Institute for Research on Women (IRW)

The idea for the Institute for Research on Women originated with faculty and administrators who had dual objectives: to develop women's studies as a new interdisciplinary field and to improve women's status within the university and within society. The Women's Caucus, a group of administrators formed on the New Brunswick campus in the early 1970s, generated the first administrative visions for the IRW. Feminist faculty members launched parallel discussions, and in 1974 Nancy Bazin, English professor and coordinator of women's studies at Rutgers College, volunteered to organize the Women's Studies Institute, which sought to increase opportunities for women in all areas of women's studies by encouraging New Brunswick units of the university to provide graduate and undergraduate offerings in all appropriate departments. From its earliest days, the institute also sought to be as widely inclusive as possible. According to the 1975 bylaws, institute membership included "all members of the faculty, who hold the rank of instructor and above in the New Brunswick area, and who teach or are actively engaged in research in the area of women's studies." In addition, "other interested persons could apply for associate membership."

Success in securing external funds has been key to IRW's growth. IRW directors secured grants from the Rockefeller Foundation, the New Jersey Department of Higher Education, the Ford Foundation, the National Endowment for the Humanities, and the American Council of Learned Societies to support major conferences on cutting-edge topics such as gender and diaspora, gender and disability, race/gender/ethnicity, and the meanings of feminism in contemporary politics, as well as summer institutes for high school teachers, fellowships for visiting scholars, and publications to disseminate the scholarship supported by the IRW. IRW directors also worked with the Institute for Women's Leadership (IWL) to secure increased financial support from Rutgers.

When the university's strategic plan, "A New Vision for Excellence," identified gender studies as one of twelve university-wide "areas of excellence" in 1996, the IRW initiated a series of discussions with the IWL about strategies to convert this university recognition into programmatic resources. The inclusion of gender studies as an area of excellence within the strategic plan was itself the result of intensive effort by the IWL to increase the visibility of the centers and institutes focused on women's lives. When the university created Strategic Resource and Opportunity Analysis (SROA) funds to strengthen the identified areas of excellence, a university-wide Gender Studies Committee worked for more than a year to develop an SROA proposal that included funding for the IRW/IWL Interdisciplinary Seminar among its priorities. The Gender Studies proposal identified twenty priorities for funding in the university's capital campaign with estimated costs of $16 million (including endowed chairs). Although the university allocated $3 million in seed money to help the twelve designated areas of excellence launch their fund-raising efforts, it did not distribute these funds equitably among the areas of excellence. Instead the university established a "competitive process" mediated by a committee of PII professors, who chose to award only $100,000 to the Gender Studies Committee to initiate its priorities. Thus the committee had to make very difficult choices, ultimately deciding to support several initiatives, including $20,000 to pilot a "long sought research seminar that builds in a public lecture series." This SROA funding was the first step in the "institutionalization" of the annual IWL/IRW interdisciplinary seminar. Piloted with university funds for two years and continued with Ford Foundation funding for two years, the IRW/IWL seminar was made "permanent" after a great deal of behind-the-scenes negotiating when the FAS dean and the vice president for academic affairs pledged full funding. This pledge of permanent funding was short-lived, however, and support for the IRW seminar was dramatically curtailed in the 2006 budget cutbacks.

Despite its continuing struggle for financial support, the IRW seminar brings together Rutgers professors and graduate students, visiting scholars, and other interested members of the community to develop research in areas of importance to historically underrepresented groups. Two multiyear evaluations of the seminar have included diversity among the signal accomplishments of the seminar. The dimensions of diversity that the seminar has fostered are themselves multiple: participants of diverse races, ethnicities, and national origin are included in each seminar cohort; participants are drawn from a wide array of disciplines and interdisciplinary fields; the methodologies employed in analyzing thematic material are remarkably diverse; and the faculty and graduate students participating each year are drawn from a diverse range of schools and colleges from Rutgers-Camden, Rutgers-Newark, and Rutgers-New Brunswick. A growing number of faculty and participants are women of color.

Seminar participants are not the only ones to benefit from the scholarship fostered by the IRW seminar. It serves as a springboard for colloquia and conferences, and research launched within the seminar is often presented to wider audiences; many such initiatives have culminated in the publication of books. The IRW also routinely hosts visiting scholars, working with the American Association of University Women International Fellowship Program and the International Institute for Education and the Fulbright Commission, as well as with the governments of other nations to bring a diverse group of international scholars to campus. Through these diverse initiatives, the IRW/IWL seminar has been and continues to be an important mechanism for intellectual community building. The IRW/IWL seminar helps to preserve and promote excellence in women's and gender studies research and teaching. It also provides vital support for faculty and graduate student research while fostering friendships and forging professional connections among faculty and graduate students from diverse departments, schools, and campuses across Rutgers, providing a model of a diverse and inclusive university community.

The Center for Women's Global Leadership (Global Center)

Since its creation in 1984, the Laurie New Jersey Chair in Women's Studies at Douglass College has provided a means to bring outstanding feminist scholars and activists to Rutgers to teach and share their work with students and faculty. Internationally renowned feminist theorist and activist Charlotte Bunch was recruited to the Laurie New Jersey Chair in 1987. At the time Bunch was beginning to investigate the possibilities of framing women's issues, particularly violence against women, as human rights issues. Her work provided the impetus for the creation of the Center for Women's Global Leadership.

The Global Center was officially founded as a project of Douglass College in 1989 with the mission of developing and facilitating women's leadership for women's human rights and social justice worldwide. During its first fifteen years, the Center for Women's Global Leadership has made significant contributions to global feminist activism and policy making in the area of human rights, initiating and shaping the global movement for women's rights as human rights. The center has trained a generation of women leaders from all regions of the globe to use the human rights framework to achieve strategic objectives. It has engaged in campaigns, tribunals, networking, and strategic planning around the United Nations world conferences on women, human rights, population, and against racism, xenophobia, and related forms of intolerance, helping to set the agenda for global women's activism. The Global Center has been consulted by many UN agencies and other international actors on a wide array of women's rights issues.

Since its creation, the Global Center has won international recognition for its strategic contributions to theoretical debates and practical policy recommendations concerning some of the most pressing issues facing women and men in the contemporary period, including human rights violations, globalization and its impact on women's lives, economic migration, trafficking, militarization and war, and the complex effects of racism, ethnocentrism, and nationalism upon contemporary social relations. The Global Center has been at the forefront of international debates concerning the rise of various forms of religious and ethnic fundamentalism(s) that threaten women's rights; the perceived conflict between cultural diversity and the universality of human rights, which is often manifested in challenges to the human rights of women; growing global inequities linked to globalization that have further marginalized poor women and displaced many young men; an escalation of racist and sexist violence; and an increase in wars, conflicts, and terrorism that target civilians—increasingly women and children—and the resulting need to bring more women to the negotiating tables in peacekeeping and global policy making.

Within Rutgers, the Global Center has also made important contributions to diversity, expanding students' awareness of and knowledge about global issues, international policies, and transnational activism. The Global Center has created an archive of historic materials related to transnational feminist theory and practice, which students use for research purposes. In a June 2003 report by Rutgers University Libraries, the center's archive was characterized as "one of the most significant collections pertaining to international activism and women's rights worldwide."

Each year, the Global Center organizes public lectures, panel discussions, and international consultations featuring distinguished women leaders. These campus events afford students, staff, faculty, and members of the larger Rutgers community opportunities to hear and interact with internationally renowned women. The center has worked closely with the IWL Leadership Scholars Program, the Rutgers Women's Center based at Douglass, and with students on all the campuses, to develop "16 Days of Activism against Gender Based Violence" activities at Rutgers as part of the annual Global Campaign that was originated at the center in 1991. The center has also partnered with the women's and gender studies department in developing the innovative Douglass Human Rights House, the first such living-learning house in the country.

Since its creation, however, the Global Center has struggled with insufficient institutional support from Rutgers. Rather than increasing with the growth of the Global Center, the minimal level of institutional support for the Global Center was cut during successive periods of budgetary retrenchment from $23,000 to $20,000 per year. To supplement the meager support provided by the university, Bunch undertook external fund-raising. The first major support for the Global Center came from the Ford Foundation in the form of a planning grant for $50,000 to support the first International Planning Meeting. The Ford Foundation has been a major funder for the Global Center since its inception with total grants reaching over $4 million to support programs and general operations. The MacArthur Foundation, the Open Society Institute, the Moriah Fund, UNIFEM, the Rausing Trust, the Sister Fund, and the Shaler Adams Foundation have also provided vital support for the center. In addition to raising more than $10 million in external funds, the center has also sought seed money from a variety of university sources over this period and has secured $462,000 in university matching funds for several research initiatives. Despite repeated efforts, the center has not succeeded in securing university lines for key professional staff positions, however, and has had to raise external funds to cover staff salaries. Over time it becomes ever more difficult to persuade external funders to cover salaries for positions such as associate director and administrative assistant because foundations expect the university to cover these positions as a sign of its institutional commitment to the center and its work. Thus the Global Center finds itself in the unenviable position of having to work even harder at external fund-raising to maintain the status quo. Moreover, the lack of permanent staff lines continues to hamper the center's growth, making it difficult for it to respond adequately to new opportunities or to assume additional responsibilities, especially within the university, no matter how attractive and important they may be.

The Institute for Women's Leadership (IWL)

The growth and success of the Women's Studies, CAWP, the IRW, and later the Global Center, brought national and international prominence to Douglass College and to Rutgers. This recognition brought both opportunities and challenges. The heads of the various units, including Ruth B. Mandel, Carol Smith, Cora Kaplan, Alice Kessler-Harris, and Charlotte Bunch, began meeting regularly in the late 1980s to explore possibilities for the future and to work collaboratively to address challenges. Convened by Mary S. Hartman, then dean of Douglass College, this group brainstormed a vision for women's education that would build on established success and address the next great challenge for women—advancing to leadership and decision-making positions in all arenas. This brainstorming gave rise to the creation of the Institute for Women's Leadership, a Rutgers consortium of academic units and research centers and institutes on women.

Conceived as a means both to amplify the voices and trumpet the accomplishments of its constitutive units, as well as to create a new synergy to address leadership issues and to further women's leadership, the IWL was envisioned as a collaborative endeavor to preserve and enhance the units through greater program coordination, strategic fund-raising, and appropriate resource sharing. Capitalizing on the successes of Women's Studies, CAWP, the IRW, and the Global Center in fostering women's leadership at local, state, national, and global levels, the IWL adopted the advancement of women's leadership in education, politics, the workplace, and the world as a unifying theme. Officially launched in 1991, the IWL board of directors, which now encompasses the directors and associate directors of the constitutive units including the dean and associate dean of Douglass College, is organized on the basis of equality. Programmatic decisions are made and priorities are set by consensus. Information sharing, networking, and strategic planning to address challenges within Rutgers and in the larger world outside the university remain central aspects of board meetings.

The collaborative programs undertaken by the IWL are rich and various, linked by a commitment to explore and elaborate a distinctively feminist conception of leadership. In addition to the IRW/IWL seminar, IWL collaborated with CAWP in launching Ready to Run, an annual training program for New Jersey women seeking election to public office. With women's and gender studies, IWL cosponsors the Leadership Scholars Program, which offers undergraduate women a two-year interdisciplinary experience and certificate program combining course work, internships, and social action projects designed to cultivate leadership capacities. The IWL/CWW Senior Leadership Program for Professional Women provides training and networking opportunities for twenty-four corporate and professional women annually. The WINGS (Women Investing in and Guiding Students) mentoring program, also jointly sponsored by IWL and CWW, pairs undergraduate students with senior corporate women to provide career awareness and preparation for success in work. Working with the Division on Women of the New Jersey Department of Community Affairs, IWL has published *NJ Women Count*, a series of reports on the status of women in the state. IWL board members conducted interviews with women leaders of distinction from around the globe and published their findings in *Talking Leadership: Conversations with Powerful Women* (Rutgers University Press, 1999). In addition, the IWL raised funds to create the Wittenborn Scholars Residence, which provides accommodation for visiting scholars, and to build the Ruth Dill Johnson Crockett Building, which houses the IWL administrative offices and the department of women's and gender studies. Over the past fifteen years, IWL has secured more than $4 million in grants from foundations, individuals, and corporations. The IWL has also been vocal and effective in urging successive university administrations to take women's issues seriously.

A number of factors have been critical to IWL's successes, many of them tied to the unique talents of its founding director, Mary Hartman. In addition, its creativity and resilience stem from the intellectual resources and political skill brought to IWL board meetings and decision making by the enormously talented unit directors, who are themselves outstanding feminist scholars and activists with extensive state, national, international, and philanthropic networks.

Center for Women and Work (CWW)

The Center for Women and Work grew from an idea of Dorothy Sue Cobble, a professor of labor studies, women's studies, and history at Rutgers. Keenly attuned to changes in employment and work practices in the current era of globalization, Cobble had been active in the national movement to make higher education more accessible to low-income and union workers. During her early years at Rutgers, she helped create residential institutes on campus to provide educational opportunities to low-income and union women, and she envisioned the center as a mechanism to build upon and enhance these forms of university outreach and assistance.

The CWW was launched officially in 1993 at the School of Management and Labor Relations. It was dedicated to advancing the needs of working women, both in the United States and internationally, through the development of relevant research, education, and public policy. From the start, the CWW was designed to offer a variety of programs including conferences, symposia, residential institutes, and noncredit educational programs open to the public. The center's mission also included consultation services to individual organizations on current issues affecting women and employment.

CWW's support from the university has been limited. the labor studies and employment relations department provided the initial support, which included office space and partial release time (one course) for Professor Cobble to direct the center. During the first three years, the dean of the School of Management and Labor Relations contributed $2,000–$3,000 annually, and the bulk of the center's operating funds were generated through programming fees, approximately $10,000 each of the first two years. Despite its small budget and staff, the CWW developed an active program and research agenda. Working closely with the Institute for Women's Leadership, CWW produced "Boxed In and Breaking Out: New Jersey Women and Work in the 1990's," the second report of the NJ Women Count series. Also in partnership

with the IWL, the CWW created a four-part lecture series on women's employment issues at Merrill Lynch. Other CWW programs included a policy
roundtable for women leaders in business, labor, government, and academia
and several lectures by visiting scholars and policy makers.

Although at one time the center stood on the brink of closure for lack of
funds, it has been reinvigorated by the entrepreneurial leadership of previous
director Barbara Lee and current director Eileen Appelbaum. CWW has
become the research arm of the New Jersey Council on Gender Parity in Labor
and Education and has secured multiple and diverse research grants. Current
CWW programs provide a wide range of interventions to enhance women's
equality in the workforce and identify "best practices" for use by organizations
to promote racial and gender diversity. The Online Learning Project for recent
welfare leavers—single working mothers with young children—employed in
New Jersey, for example, raises their technological literacy and workforce
skills, enabling participants to secure jobs that pay a living wage. Producing
impressive results, the project was quickly extended to larger numbers of New
Jersey workers employed in low-wage jobs, providing vital assistance not only
to women with family responsibilities but also to workers in rural areas and to
workers with disabilities. Ten states have now implemented the Online
Learning Project and ten more are in the process of implementing the
program. Attuned to the complex issues pertaining to the working poor, CWW
has devised creative strategies, such as the Workforce Development Program
for low-wage workers to help women find employment in skilled-craft
positions that pay union wages. CWW's workforce development efforts
include education and training programs for nontraditional occupations
(defined by the U.S. Department of Labor as any occupation where one gender
makes up 25 percent or less of those employed) for women incarcerated in
New Jersey's women's prison as well as for students in grades seven through
twelve across the state. The center has also launched various initiatives with
women in the corporate sector, providing mentoring and capacity-building
programs to help corporate women break through the glass ceiling.

The origin and growth of the CWW has depended on creative collaboration with women faculty members, the development of powerful allies outside
the university, and assertive fund-raising. The center's success is a testament
to the personal commitment and persistence of faculty and staff, who often
work against established university systems, priorities, and traditions to make
changes that benefit women.

The Challenges of Incomplete Institutionalization

CAWP, the Global Center, CWW, IRW, and the IWL itself were launched by
enterprising faculty who devoted their energies to significant fund-raising

activities to support feminist research and social change. These centers and institutes, like Douglass College itself, were created by women leaders who devised innovative strategies to educate and enhance the power of diverse populations of women. As an academic department, women's and gender studies has achieved a greater degree of university support than its partner units in the IWL, but this support too reflects thirty-five years of strategic intervention by a small number of faculty who pressed the university for institutional resources.

The IWL and its constitutive units continue to struggle with incomplete institutionalization, a paradoxical combination of strength derived from entrepreneurial innovations that have won national and international renown and fragility stemming from lack of university resources and respect within the institution. In general, faculty members within the IWL units have achieved the greatest successes in areas in which they have the greatest autonomy: curriculum development, research, teaching, and policy initiatives based on grant support and leadership development programs funded by external support. The tangible results of these successes are numerous: the development and growth of women's studies as a comprehensive degree-granting department; the creation of five distinguished centers and institutes producing pathbreaking research on women; the establishment of model programs that engage diverse student populations in innovative learning experiences; the creation and sustenance of the IWL/IRW Interdisciplinary Research Seminar, which weaves diverse faculty into a supportive and stimulating intellectual community; projects to enhance the income of impoverished women that have been replicated across the nation; mobilization of transnational coalitions to achieve UN recognition of women's rights as human rights; innovative programs that attract new populations of women to campus to mentor students and to share leadership experiences; and programs that help corporate women devise strategies to break the glass ceiling. Moreover, grant-writing and fund-raising efforts that have raised millions of dollars in external funding for feminist projects constitute unparalleled success.

The IWL has also succeeded in creating a structural vehicle to support and link the intellectual work of the units. This structure is exemplary in its ability to work collaboratively, share staff, and relate to a wide variety of constituencies. The consortium is a recognized entity, internally and externally, that works to increase visibility and funding for leadership education. As such, the consortium enables units to speak and act collectively. In addition, it is widely perceived as a space of feminist solidarity, creative synergy, and brainstorming to identify innovative solutions for complex institutional and strategic problems. The physical proximity of the units, made possible by the two buildings of the Women's Scholarship and Leadership

Complex on Ryders Lane, has been a major factor in this community-building success. The IWL and its constitutive units have forged collaborative efforts that sustain creative feminist scholarship and teaching and help sustain the psyches of individual feminist faculty members when they feel besieged by male-dominant institutional norms and practices. Collectively, they have been a key force in putting diversity—gender, race, ethnicity, nationality, sexuality, disability—on the agenda at Rutgers and have won national and international recognition for their pathbreaking efforts in this domain. Through such collaborative efforts, the IWL has helped feminist scholars at Rutgers find ways around obstacles, push against established and shifting boundaries, and refuse to accept institutional constraints linked to raced and gendered practices. By carving out a space in which feminist inquiry is valued and vindicated, the IWL and its constitutive units have found ways to replenish the psychic and physical energy of feminist activists on campus and give them the strength to engage the transformative struggle through periods of success and through periods of retrenchment.

The histories of these innovative institutions demonstrate that faculty initiatives cannot succeed without university assistance. Faculty members do not control allocations of office space, access to buildings, or power to initiate capital campaigns. They have power to hire only when deans provide necessary lines, salaries, authorizations, and budgets for searches. For all these reasons, faculty initiatives cannot succeed without some measure of institutional support and key interventions by senior administrators, who can divert critical resources to faculty initiatives.

Since the 1970s, feminist faculty members seeking to transform the university have worked with key feminist administrators, men and women, who have been willing to expend their political capital to advance feminist transformative ends. But these feminist faculty members and administrators have faced administrative structures and standard operating procedures that have worked against feminist initiatives. Despite the arduous efforts of trans-formative agents, incomplete institutionalization stems from college and university priorities that fail to take gender and racial diversity seriously, male-dominated committees restricted to PII professors who too often know little and care less about interdisciplinary feminist scholarship, and adminis-trators and faculty who pay lip service to equal opportunity while remaining suspicious of scholars who contest the boundaries of traditional scholarship and cautious in their investment of resources in race and gender initiatives.

Recruitment and retention of diverse faculty have been serious problems at Rutgers, problems that interdisciplinary feminist units have few resources to address. Although feminist faculty members and administrators have worked to create a hospitable environment and transform education to include women and diverse populations, there is much that they do not control. Joint-hires that give decision power to discipline-based departments have thwarted multiple efforts to hire diverse scholars. Tenure and promotion guidelines that make no consideration for the time-consuming mentoring and advising that an increasingly diverse student population requires can work against women and minority faculty upon whom these tasks dispropor-tionately fall. Efforts to include token diversity on college and university committees within an institution in which scholars of color are dramatically underrepresented impose disproportionate service burdens on faculty of color, another factor unconsidered in tenure and promotion cases. The "invisible labor" invested in efforts to create and sustain innovative interdisciplinary initiatives is not widely acknowledged or valued by the institution. In addition, race and gender bias has generated impressive efforts to retain eminent white male scholars, while eminent women and minority faculty have not been given comparable counter-offers.

Given the power, jurisdiction, and number of traditional white-male administrators and the ways bureaucracies operate to maintain the status quo, it is remarkable that feminist scholars, working individually and collectively, have made the institutional inroads documented in this chapter. But the reliance of the IWL and its constitutive units upon external fund-raising raises important questions about self-help strategies. Preoccupied with the demands of fund-raising and sorely lacking in institutional support, the IWL and its constitutive units continue to operate under severe constraints. Their national and international acclaim has continued to coexist with what is, at best, the university's grappling with multiple priorities and, at worst, indiffer-ence and neglect. Without built-in structures, systems, processes, and resources to protect and promote progress, faculty members who work to sup-port educational excellence through racial and gender equity are dependent upon the individual interests and priorities of a few key university leaders. The current Rutgers administration, for example, has articulated a commitment to diversity issues and taken initial steps to recruit scholars of color, even as it has further constricted the autonomy of Douglass College. How and whether these commitments and changes will be permanently incorporated into the workings of Rutgers is a critical question. A recurrent theme in interviews with unit directors and activist faculty is whether these vibrant but still fragile ini-tiatives will continue to survive as the generation of founders begins to retire. In an era of transnational backlash and university austerity, whether hard-won feminist gains can be maintained over time remains a pressing concern.

NOTES

I. This analysis of the changing composition of Rutgers's student population is based
    upon the Student Unit Record Enrollment (SURE) Reports generated by the Rutgers

Office of Institutional Research. Faculty data was also provided by the Office of Institutional Research, based upon Rutgers's annual reports to the Higher Education General Information Survey (HEGIS), which was later renamed Integrated Postsecondary Education Data System (IPEDS), and upon a new database created by University Human Resources in 1990. The Rutgers Office of Institutional Research cannot provide demographic data for students or faculty prior to 1975–1976.

2. Professor II (PII) rank was initially created to address problems of salary compression among full professors with long years of service at Rutgers. With the move to attain Research I status, PII was gradually transformed to recognize outstanding scholarly accomplishment. Appointment of a scholar to PII rank is initiated by academic departments and requires a complete career review, including external evaluation of scholarly work by a dozen international experts in the scholar's field.

REFERENCES

Acker, Joan. 1992. "Gendered Institutions: From Sex Roles to Gendered Institutions." *Contemporary Sociology* 21:565–569.

Douglass, Mabel Smith. 1929. "The Early History of New Jersey College for Women: Personal Recollections by Dean Douglass." *Quair*, 37.

Duerst-Lahti, Paula, and Rita M. Kelly. 1995. *Gender Power, Leadership and Governance.* Ann Arbor: University of Michigan Press.

Faculty of Arts and Sciences Gender Equity Committee. 2001. "A Study of Gender Equity in the Faculty of Arts and Sciences, Rutgers University-New Brunswick." October.

Hall R., and B. Sandler. 1982. *The Classroom Climate: A Chilly One for Women?* Washington, DC: American Association of Colleges.

———. 1984. *Out of the Classroom: A Chilly Campus Climate for Women?* Washington, DC: American Association of Colleges.

———. 1986. *The Campus Climate Revisited: Chilly for Women Faculty, Administrators and Graduate Students.* Washington, DC: American Association of Colleges.

Hornig, Lilli. 2003. "Current Status of Women in Research Universities." In *Equal Rites, Unequal Outcomes: Women in American Research Universities,* ed. Lilli Hornig. New York: Kluwer Academic/Plenum Publishers.

Memorandum on the Status of Faculty Women at Rutgers, Newark. 1971. November.

Office of Affirmative Action and Employment Research. 1982. "Affirmative Action Work Force Analysis of Regular Faculty and Part-Time Faculty: A Comparison of AY 1982–83 with AY 1981–82." December.

———. 1989. "Work Force Analysis of Regular Faculty and Part-Time Faculty, 1989–90." November.

Sandler, Bernice. 1992. *Success and Survival Strategies for Women Faculty Members.* Washington, DC: Association of American Colleges.

Showalter, Elaine. 1993. "Only the Conception: Becoming a Feminist Critic." *Douglass Alumnae Bulletin* (Summer).

8

Agents of Change

Faculty Leadership in Initiating and Sustaining Diversity at the University of Arizona

JENI HART, LINDY BRIGHAM, MARY K. GOOD,
BARBARA J. MILLS, AND JANICE MONK

In the late 1990s, the collective action of several women faculty members in the School of Science at the Massachusetts Institute of Technology (MIT) initiated a study that found gender-based disparities in salary, office and laboratory space, awards, resources, committee assignments, named chairs, teaching obligations, and retention. With the support of their dean and president, these women made recommendations aimed at ensuring equity for senior women faculty, improving the professional lives of junior women faculty, and increasing the number of women faculty (Massachusetts Institute of Technology 1999). Their study and MIT's quick, positive response received wide national attention; other institutions, among them the University of Arizona (UA), were inspired to investigate inequities on their own campuses (National Academy of Sciences 2004).

UA's parallel study—known as the Millennium Project—was a collaboration between the president of the Association for Women Faculty (AWF) and the chair of the Commission on the Status of Women (CSW). Although the university administration did not initiate the project, it did provide funding; "The Millennium Project Report: Phase I: Faculty" was released in October 2001 (Cress 2001; Cress et al. 2001). That study's goals were to measure the campus climate for faculty women and faculty of color, and its findings identified multiple changes that would enhance academic excellence. A subsequent study focusing on university staff members and their experiences of campus climate, "The Millennium Project: Phase II: Staff," was released in October 2002 (Johnsrud et al. 2002).

While there has been significant research on campus climates (National Academy of Sciences 2004), researchers have rarely investigated the impact of such studies or explored efforts to pursue recommended changes. In this chapter, we report on an exploratory case study that addresses how faculty leadership at UA implemented, fostered, and sustained diversity initiatives. The study drew on a conceptual framework developed by Huberman and Miles (1984), who presented findings from a comparative case study about the implementation of K–12 school improvements. Their goal was "to show just what happened in the course of these school improvement efforts, to explain why it happened, and to suggest the implications for changes . . . elsewhere" (vi). Following that imperative, our study asked: (1) How did UA implement the Millennium Project recommendations? (2) Why did it choose those approaches? (3) What are its implications for improving the campus climate? Our central focus was on who implemented the changes and how faculty and administration worked together.

In January 2002 the university president and the faculty cochairs organized a university-wide Millennium Report Oversight Committee (MROC), which had a five-year mandate to oversee implementation of the project's recommendations. Our study looked at the work of this committee as it reached the middle period of its mandate as well as related faculty-led MROC committees that were established at most of UA's fifteen colleges. We also studied MROC's three subcommittee task forces, which focused, respectively, on diverse, fair, and hospitable communities.

The University of Arizona

UA prides itself on its reputation as a research university with a high level of research productivity. Many of its programs are ranked among the nation's top ten. At the time of our study, UA had a student population of more than 37,000, 77 percent of them undergraduates. It employed more than 14,000 people, including 1,540 instructional faculty members (defined as "regular tenured and tenure-track instructional faculty, permanent lecturers") and 841 other faculty members (defined as "adjunct, emeritus, clinical, research, and visiting faculty; non-tenure-track instructors, and non-permanent lecturers," including librarians) (University of Arizona 2003–2004). The administration had 276 employees categorized as executive or other administrators, department heads, and academic directors, and 2,384 employees classified as academic professionals: this constitutes a remarkably diverse group, some of whose work encompasses traditional faculty functions (such as research), others whose primary roles are managerial or administrative.

UA's fifteen colleges and its other administrative and professional units are governed by the Arizona Board of Regents (ABOR), a state-level board of appointed officials responsible for overseeing all three universities in Arizona's public higher-education system (Arizona Board of Regents 2003). At the local level it was led by President Peter Likins (also on ABOR), with various functions managed by a team of vice presidents, the provost, and several vice provosts. Faculty and professional staff shared in university decision making through councils, a faculty senate, and advisory committees.

Faculty- and University-Initiated Diversity Efforts

One response to the Millennium Report has been the increased number of diversity-focused organizations. Although several were active for many years before the report's release, their structure and collaborations changed considerably after it was issued.

Millennium Report Oversight Committee. As discussed, MROC was established in 2002 to monitor implementation of the report's recommendations. President Likins appointed its first members with advice from the original Millennium Project chairs. New members were subsequently invited by existing MROC members, with the list of participants submitted to President Likins for endorsement.

At the time of our study, MROC had twenty-four regular and five ex officio members led by a chair and two cochairs. Leadership was gender- and minority-diverse. Members were divided into three task forces paralleling emphases in the Millennium Report: the "diverse" subcommittee focused on diversity in recruitment and retention; "fair" addressed equitable hiring, compensation, and workloads; and "hospitable" dealt with campus climate. Each was cochaired by two or more faculty members. Together, these task force chairs and the MROC chair and cochairs formed the MROC executive committee, which prioritized yearly initiatives and met with a very supportive president and provost at least once per semester.

Diversity Coalition. After the Millennium Project, the President's Council on Diversity was reconfigured and renamed. As the Diversity Coalition, it was designed to ensure communication among groups with diversity interests and give central administration a clear view of campuswide concerns. Bringing together members of MROC along with representatives of all other faculty, staff, and administrative groups involved in diversity work, the coalition was chaired by Edith Auslander, vice president and special assistant to the president, who was also a former member of ABOR and an active member of Tucson's Hispanic community. Other members included the president of the Association of Women Faculty; the chair of the Commission on the Status of Women; the heads of the president's advisory committees on American Indian, African American, Hispanic, Asian American, and community outreach; the chair of the Committee of Eleven, an elected faculty committee; a representative from the Medical School's GRACE Project, a study that paralleled the Millennium Report and explored the climate for gender equity in the college of medicine; and a representative of a group known as Faculty Women of Color. They shared information monthly with involved staff and administrators and reported on staff and student diversity efforts.

The Association for Women Faculty. Founded by women faculty members in 1982 to support and advance women's position at the university, AWF has long actively addressed issues such as salary equity, child and family care, and other women's concerns. Founding member Myra Dinnerstein, who was the director of UA's Women's Studies Program, wanted to institutionalize the program academically and believed that a complementary grassroots activist group could support women faculty in general. Over time, participation has waxed and waned, although certain issues, such as salary equity, have galvanized involvement. The degree to which upper-level administrators have been open to working with the group has also influenced membership (Hart 2002).

College-Level MROCs. After the Millennium Project, the deans of each of UA's fifteen colleges were encouraged to develop college-level MROCs; and about half did establish formal committees. To facilitate communication, the college MROC chairs attended best-practice and information-sharing meetings with the university MROC, and several college MROC members were incorporated into university MROC task forces. This overlap in membership was both an asset and a detriment: although it enhanced collaboration and consistency, it also required some faculty members, especially women of color, to devote a tremendous amount of time to these volunteer activities. To bring more faculty members into leadership positions, the university MROC executive committee has since extended task-force invitations to a broader demographic of faculty.

Gathering and Analyzing the Information

Data collection involved five components:

1. From the groups involved in the original study for the Millennium Report we interviewed faculty for four focus groups representing the following fields of study: agriculture, biological sciences, social and behavioral sciences, and education. We also held discussion groups with current AWF board members.
2. Regarding groups arising after the report, we interviewed the entire university-based MROC committee and all members of the Diversity Coalition.
3. For the academic years 2003 and 2004, we analyzed each college MROC's annual report to the provost detailing its goals, objectives, and progress to date. (We excluded the College of Medicine from this ranking because its faculty was engaged in the GRACE Project.)
4. We selected two colleges with differing histories of involvement in campus climate change—the College of Science (COS) and the College of Social and Behavioral Sciences (SBS)—and interviewed college MROC members using the semistructured protocols and demographic surveys.
5. For academic year 2004, we analyzed pertinent sections of college deans' and center directors' annual reports to the provost.

For this case study, we analyzed transcripts and field notes from focus groups, discussion groups, individual interviews, and documents, employing a constant comparative approach to discern patterns and themes in the data (Merriam 1998; Strauss and Corbin 1990). We further analyzed these patterns and themes, looking for divergence and convergence. Trustworthiness was assured through triangulation of data sources and saturation of categories (Patton 1990; Lincoln and Guba 1986). To manage the data throughout the analysis process, we used NVivo, a qualitative computer software package.

As previously stated, this study draws on the work of Huberman and Miles (1984), who found that the school improvement efforts they investigated fell into four categories: highly successful, relatively successful, relatively unsuccessful, or highly unsuccessful. The efforts of the various task forces and groups in our study mirrored those categories. Faculty initiatives for change were analyzed at the level of each individual college-specific MROCs, through the reports submitted to the university provost. However, when analyzing the data for each focus group (MROC, Diversity Coalition, and AWF), one overall measure of success did not emerge. We analyzed separately the findings from the faculty primarily housed in the Colleges of Science and Social and Behavioral Sciences who had participated in the original Millennium Project study and again in the current Agents of Change study. This analysis found patterns and themes that described the campus climate at two distinct points in time. Further, focus group interviews with the Social and Behavioral Sciences MROC and College of Science MROC members (including an individual interview with the chair of the COS MROC) were analyzed to uncover what happened in each of these colleges related to faculty change initiatives. These analyses aimed to explore the effectiveness of MROC initiatives as perceived by those participating in change efforts and by those whose lives may have been influenced by them. Finally, we analyzed the most recent annual reports submitted by college deans to the university provost to capture a glimpse of the current college-related attitudes and activities around diversity.

MROC

HIGHLY SUCCESSFUL. First, participants saw the organization's longevity (it was established in 2001) as a measure of success. Second, they saw concrete evidence of achievement. In the words of one participant, "[I]f success is determined by consciousness raising, then I think that . . . we can say that that has been achieved—the . . . fact that we are in . . . the diversity resource office, that there are staff members here, that there was the Diversity Day." Third, the task force organized successfully around the specific issues of cluster hiring and subtle discrimination.

RELATIVELY SUCCESSFUL. Participants identified other successes but tempered their evaluations with some degree of hesitancy. For example, one member said that although MROC crafted specific climate-change strategies for colleges and programs, those ideas were implemented university-wide, so success was uneven. Another example of relative success involves the term "diversity" itself: "Diversity is very visible, and people say it all the time. It may be an empty phrase in a lot of their mouths, but it is said. It is recognized. People do pay obeisance to it . . . which is better than nothing. . . . It's nowhere near everything, but it is something. I think that this committee had a lot to do with it."

RELATIVELY UNSUCCESSFUL. Participants resoundingly expressed the sense that MROC was a fairly invisible group on campus, which made it difficult to achieve institution-wide success. Several members also felt frustrated by lack of leadership, particularly the provost's, on issues of diversity. One member even felt that participants were beginning to lose energy and passion for the work: "I think that has been one of the underlying problems of implementing things because it has been not only the administration that doesn't see the value of implementing some of these things or understand the significance or the process of implementing these; . . . the people [involved] are part of the oversight too."

HIGHLY UNSUCCESSFUL. There was palpable frustration in the room during the MROC focus group interview, even when stories of success were shared. One faculty member felt strongly that all efforts to enhance UA's campus climate and diversity had been highly unsuccessful, that there had been no change in attitude, and that lack of resources was an inadequate excuse: "It's very easy to say, "Oh, we have no money; now we can't do this fancy thing." . . . [But] it's a change in attitude that has not happened."

Diversity Coalition

RELATIVELY SUCCESSFUL. Members of the Diversity Coalition were pessimistic about the degree of success achieved by their initiatives; none reported a high degree of success, although one more optimistic member did cite improved recruitment and retention guidelines as relatively successful.

RELATIVELY UNSUCCESSFUL. The very existence of the coalition suggested that the initiative was not entirely unsuccessful. Yet many participants thought its reason for being had yet to be realized. While the coalition was intended to bring together individuals from different campus constituencies to advise the president on matters of diversity, members felt that they had little say: "There is an intersection between the Diversity Coalition and decision making but not at crucial points of decision making. [One member] is at the decision-making table but not the [whole] Diversity Coalition. When budgets and other main issues at the university get decided, the 'diversity' gets left out or lost because no one is there to hammer home the issues."

HIGHLY UNSUCCESSFUL. Members described a "sense of doing something" but not of affecting real change. Meeting and discussing issues of diversity did not improve the campus climate, and members of the coalition felt as if they hadn't yet moved toward real action.

The Association for Women Faculty

HIGHLY SUCCESSFUL. Women in the AWF focus group celebrated their successful fight for campus policies that stop the tenure clock or allow parents to negotiate alternative work duties when children are born or adopted. Another identified success was the comprehensive salary study that AWF helped to conduct in the early 1980s, which resulted in significant salary adjustments based on gender gaps in pay. In both cases, AWF earned a reputation for its ability to achieve specific successes and enjoyed wide-ranging support among women faculty. Participants also identified less tangible measures of success: "I walked into [the] fall AWF reception, probably in '89, . . . and there were probably seventy-five women in the house. And I came home and said to my husband, 'Oh my God, there are women on this campus!' I had been here seven years, and I had seen one. And here were seventy-five all in one room. [I found] out that there was a lifeboat out there that has got people in it [and] whether there were ever issues addressed, to some extent, did not matter."

Moreover, the organization's longevity (at the time of study, it was twenty-three years old) reminds administrators and the campus community that AWF still has work to do and will not fade away: "There is some fear factor, perhaps [between] the provost and president, associated with when AWF comes to town, I think, . . . which is a good thing."

RELATIVELY SUCCESSFUL. Some AWF studies and related efforts, however, were only partially successful. One AWF member observed, "I have to say, I don't think the salary remedies over the last twelve years or more are at all as good as what they did in . . . '85, '86, '87."

One policy in particular, the sick-child policy,, had only relative success. The AWF was instrumental in originally developing this policy for faculty, which provided low-cost child care for children who were sick and could not attend school or other child care programs. But after several years the Department of Human Resources modified it, leading to ongoing negotiations among the department, the president, the provost, and AWF. Although in the end the policy was not radically altered, the fact that it was modified at all made participants feel that had been only relatively successful.

RELATIVELY UNSUCCESSFUL. For decades, campus child care has been the most important initiative on AWF's agenda. Despite apparent headway, however, the organization has never fully achieved a victory: "So we got [an outside child-care program expert to examine the situation]; she was doing a good job, . . . and somehow Human Resources decided that what she was doing was not important to them and that they would reassign her to other duties, and then things just fell to pieces."

More generally, members sensed that women faculty involved with AWF still operated at cross-purposes: "I was hoping that in AWF, we can have more of a discussion that is across the disciplines, because I find that . . . there are unique cultures in each college with a completely different idea of the universe. . . . We are not helping with the dialogue with how to better do what we are supposed to be doing. We are not all agreeing with what we are supposed to be doing."

HIGHLY UNSUCCESSFUL. AW, alone among the organizations we studied, considered the very definition of success that permeates university discourse to be highly unsuccessful: "Whose standards are we using? Who gets to define those standards? . . . I don't see any discussion of the definitions having changed. . . . I do not see a real frank discussion about it."

In institutional terms, the definition of success is based exclusively on quantitative measures such as resources and research. Less tangible qualitative measures, such as diversity or respect, are not rewarded or seen as successes: "You wouldn't go to the state legislature and say, 'I need a ten-million-dollar salary package because there's just not enough respect at Arizona!' You go because Georgia Tech hired four chemists. You say, 'Boy, if you'd just given me a forty-million-dollar building, I would have had four more chemists.' . . . But, fundamentally, it comes down to respect: who gives respect, who gets respect. More often than not, we are losing people because of a respect issue."

In the end, where the AWF has been highly unsuccessful is in trying to broaden and legitimate a definition of success that includes the voices of women and other underrepresented groups, diversity, and respect.

College-Level MROCs

HIGHLY SUCCESSFUL. We categorized as highly successful the MROC committees from the university library and from the colleges of Agriculture and Life Sciences; Humanities; Science; and Social and Behavioral Sciences. Each used recommendations from the original Millennium Report and adapted them according to the nuances of their disciplinary fields. Agriculture and Life Sciences, Humanities, and Science all gathered additional data and research and made specific suggestions to recruit more diverse faculty, create equity in salaries and workload, and provide mentoring and support for any scholars who were members of historically underrepresented groups (e.g., faculty of color, women faculty). The College of Science even proposed a departmental emphasis on creating diversity initiatives. Both the College of Agriculture and Life Sciences and the library provided time lines for implementing recommendations and mentioned ongoing data collection efforts.

RELATIVELY SUCCESSFUL. The colleges of Education and Law were less specific about how to achieve the goals of the original climate study but did create reports detailing the efforts necessary to address particular inequities. Faculty members took the initiative to educate themselves on issues related to diversity and attended several seminars to become better informed on issues such as subtle discrimination. Although they saw themselves as change agents, they also said that administration was ultimately responsible for instituting new policies. They could identify what needed to be done, but rarely claimed any responsibility for implementing those changes.

Two other colleges were also only relatively successful. The Graduate College had a genuine desire to foster interdisciplinarity, but because it did not provide a tenure home for faculty, its powers were limited. Although the College of Nursing focused in detail on the lack of diversity among its students and faculty, the Millennium Report did not deal specifically with student diversity, making Nursing's report only relatively successful according to the parameters of this study.

RELATIVELY UNSUCCESSFUL. The College of Fine Arts and the Mel and Enid Zuckerman Arizona College of Public Health (MEZACOPH) were both categorized as relatively unsuccessful. Each convened on more than one occasion to discuss the original study and possible responses, but both also saw their colleges as diversity success stories with little need for change. Both colleges claimed they had been unrepresented in the original report's findings, but neither provided concrete evidence to support this claim. According to MEZACOPH, recruiting members for its college-level MROC required "pleading" and "strong-arm tactics," which suggests that diversity issues were not faculty priorities. However, as discuss in greater detail later, the structure and nature of the MEZACOPH in particular may make the MROC model less likely to "fit" for this college and may be why strong-arm tactics were deemed necessary to get buy-in from its faculty.

HIGHLY UNSUCCESSFUL. Those MROCs categorized as highly unsuccessful met only once or twice after the original report was disseminated. Membership consisted of only a few faculty members who were strongly persuaded by their deans to participate. The committees created no progress reports or goals, and the colleges of Architecture and Landscape Architecture, Engineering and Mines, and Pharmacy as well as the Eller College of Management did not submit MROC reports to the provost in 2003 or 2004.

Following Up

Focus Group Interviews

The women in the follow-up focus groups overwhelmingly confirmed the salience of gender in their faculty lives. They identified some climate improvements since the release of the Millennium Report but also said that some things were getting worse. They continued to be concerned about the lack of mentoring and support, ambiguity in the promotion and tenure processes, the problem of being overextended and overcommitted, and the need for stronger leadership among department chairs and deans. It appears, then, that UA's climate for diversity did not change dramatically in the four years since the report's release. To elucidate the findings, comparisons were drawn from data from the Millennium Report (2000) and data gathered for the 2005 study on which this chapter is based.

Leadership was a significant consideration:

> The Dean doesn't get it. . . . He doesn't really feel and understand what women go through. . . . I think that because he has a wife, an aunt, and a mother who were in home economics, he feels somehow that he "gets" me, when I don't feel that he really does. (Agriculture and Biological Sciences focus group, 2005)
>
> You know what came back in my tenure evaluation from the outside reviewers? It . . . was put into the letter that the dean sent to me, saying that no one at the junior level should have ever been "allowed" to do the kind of service that I did as a junior faculty member. And my response was "Allowed?" It was assigned [by my chair,] and I couldn't say no. (Agriculture and Biological Sciences focus group, 2000)

In every focus group, women shared stories of positive experiences and healthy, supportive climates, including some evidence of improvement over time. But there were also stories of frustration, particularly among those who had been at UA for a long time. Even though they often believed the university had taken advantage of their loyalty, they felt a sense of responsibility about improving the campus culture and climate.

> In my case, that is what is keeping me. . . . They don't know what to do with someone who is 100 percent teaching. There is no model for that even though we give lip service to that. It has never happened. So I think when my daughter graduates, which is this year, I am just going to have . . . to put my foot on the gas and really blaze the trail. But you know, it's tiring. (Agriculture and Biological Sciences focus group, 2005)
>
> That's the only way that things change: slowly, slowly; by being there and being who you are biologically as well as disciplinarily. You slowly, slowly change the system, and I guess I don't have any great illusions that

I'm going to do that myself, but I do feel that . . . played a part in why I was hired and so I consider it as part of the work that I do. (Agriculture and Biological Sciences focus group, 2000)

The faculty members we interviewed felt that their college-level MROCs had been able to make some impact on climate, but their sense of success was tempered. Interestingly, each MROC under study seemed to admire the work of the other MROC under study.

Perhaps when there is a good connection between Social and Behavioral Science MROC and the Dean's Office [we will be more effective]. I get a sense that that works well through the College of Science. I get a sense that there is good communication there. (Social and Behavioral Science MROC focus group)

It's hard to keep optimism up. We've got so far to go. Look at [the Social and Behavioral Science MROC] . . . on the march to achieving equity; here, we've just got the conversation going. (Science MROC focus group)

Each MROC had a lesson to learn from the other, yet each also had a particular set of influential circumstances. For instance, Science has a very supportive dean, who told us:

I didn't want the committee to consist entirely of people whom department heads routinely nominate for this sort of work. Because I thought, if it was going to do anything, you also wanted a mix. You wanted also some people who are not necessarily women . . . or minorities, and I also wanted department heads to nominate people who . . . carried some weight within their departments.

The Science MROC focused on encouraging individual departments to apply for funding to conduct research that addresses pipeline issues in ways that speak to scientists. The committee chair explained:

If you want scientists to actually do something different, you have to convince them that there really is something that needs to be done. And I thought that the way to do that is to have the science departments themselves do their own information gathering; . . . to give them a certain amount of leeway as to exactly which area had to be related to diversity but within that framework. . . . Then we went to the provost and the dean [and] got some money.

Another member concurred:

We're trying to create an environment of interest and knowledge, getting people to care. I don't think people are actively sexist or racist, but there's a culture of resignation that nothing will change. Our efforts are to find sparks of interest; we're trying to make things not imposed from above. We did ask for money, too. It's a small amount of money, but there have been some successes.

Nonetheless, although there have been tangible outcomes from this MROC's work, the women who participated in the science-based focus groups did not notice a markedly different climate; and members of the Science MROC articulated some similar challenges and frustrations:

> The frustration is to see that people are interested in change, but now we are confronted by these [diversity] issues on a daily basis. I'm not necessarily feeling like we're having an effect.
>
> It is taking up time. I'm getting put on lots of committees because of my active involvement; I'm the "token white male."
>
> I'm running out of energy, and people are busy. Our best bet for sustaining is producing more active, interested, involved people. We need to get a number of people interested and educated.

According to members of the Social and Behavioral Science MROC, participation helped them feel part of something larger.

> You learn more than you would in your home unit: diversity, salary equity, lots of talk about salaries in the college. So, one of the things that happens in this committee is that I learn about and know what is going on, be represented by all of my colleagues and we can exchange information that gives us all a better understanding of what SBS is in the colleges.

One member of the current SBS college-level MROC also served on the university MROC. Moreover, a college administrator attends meetings and actively participates as an ad hoc member, which has added a sense of realism and university advocacy to the endeavor.

> A department head here is also on this committee ... so that when they're at a head's and director's meeting and they say [the college] MROC supports this, it was very hard for the heads and directors to argue with what [we] had said. So it was really effective; and without that, it would have been very difficult to get the heads to agree to a number of somewhat controversial aspects.

Committee members also highlighted other successes—for example, creating a template for a consistent performance review process and initiating the Salary Equity Project. Nevertheless, members also dealt with frustrations:

> I'm not sure we are successful. I think that we are successful ... in terms of being advisory, having a voice that is listened to within [the

college]. We have been unsuccessful when we set out to try to make an initiative that requires funding and when we grow beyond [college] funding. That has been unsuccessful.

Annual Report Data from Colleges and Centers, 2004

UA requires annual reports on goals and objectives from each college dean, associate dean, or center director. For academic year 2004, fourteen deans and directors submitted reports to the provost. Reports from the colleges of Medicine and Engineering and Mines were unavailable at the time of our data analysis. For reasons already discussed, we had previously excluded the College of Medicine from this study, but the College of Engineering and Mines, with one of the lowest percentages of female tenure-track faculty at UA, has also faced national challenges with regard to faculty diversity issues (Nelson and Rogers 2005). Thus, its absence was disconcerting, particularly because it also failed to submit MROC reports.

The author of each report was asked to reflect on her or his unit's progress in cultural inclusiveness and diversity. In every case, authors relied on numbers as a way to demonstrate diversity. Some units felt they were making significant progress with regard to numbers of women; however, each indicated that increasing diversity continued to be a goal. (It is interesting to note that the College of Architecture reported numbers of women and people of color together, rather than as separate categories, making it difficult to discern its demographics.) Units generally spoke of enhancing diversity through recruitment; only the colleges of Humanities, Law, and Architecture addressed retention and promotion issues for underrepresented populations.

Five reports specifically mentioned the work of their college-based MROCs. Only one, the College of Law, mentioned campuswide diversity efforts and the university MROC, but only as a means of recognizing two women faculty members who were involved. The reports also highlighted specific strategies and programs to address diversity in their units:

- Grant-funded initiatives to increase numbers of minorities (College of Pharmacy)
- Outreach with Native American communities and Mexico (colleges of Education and Public Health)
- Scholarships, postdoctoral, endowed, and visiting scholar opportunities for underrepresented populations (colleges of Humanities, Fine Arts, Public Health)
- Curricular and research initiatives with a distinct multicultural focus (colleges of Education, Public Health, Fine Arts, Law)
- Bilingual services and support (College of Public Health, UA South)

- Research development fund for research to support faculty (predominantly women and underrepresented minorities) who have heavy teaching and service (College of Humanities)
- Hosting local conferences highlighting underrepresented populations in keynote and other predominate roles (College of Nursing)

Conclusions

First, it important to understand who participated in these faculty-led change initiatives at the University of Arizona in order to capture the complexities of what happened. Although demographic data of those faculty involved in drafting the college-based MROC annual reports were not recorded for this study (except for the colleges of Science and Social and Behavioral Sciences, which were recorded through their involvement in focus groups), demographic data for those participating in other focus groups were recorded. From these data, we learned that most of the faculty involved in the change initiatives were tenured. In addition, most of the change agents participating were women. And on a campus where less than 20 percent of the faculty members self-identify as people of color, nearly one-third of the faculty members involved in focus groups for this study self-identified as people of color.

Second, the conceptual framework used in this study further enhanced the understanding of what happened. Huberman and Miles (1984) considered success when analyzing the innovation and change at twelve schools based upon stable, institutionalized widespread use that has had a positive impact on climate. They also discussed the highly unsuccessful measure as based in part on indifference among administrators and teachers. When adapting this conceptual framework to understand what has happened at the University of Arizona related to implementing the recommendations of a campus climate study, the results were mixed. Our findings in this study were uneven not only among individual colleges and MROCs but also within individual faculty-led organizations. Overall, our research suggests that faculty in some colleges have worked hard to create processes and recommendations based upon a model that reinforces the nature of faculty work. This professionalized activism (Hart 2005) demonstrated that activities like funding, collecting, and analyzing college-specific data (for example, research), attending and presenting professional development sessions and workshops on issues of diversity (for example, teaching), and meeting as a committee to consider the climate in each college (for example, service) were very much a part of the way some faculty engaged in change initiatives related to the campus climate study.

The extent to which particular faculty members and particular colleges participated varied across the university, ranging from some colleges in which faculty engaged in multiple professionalized activist strategies and events to others who did not engage at all in professionalized activism or any other sort of initiative. Further, despite the intent of the Millennium Project and subsequent change initiatives, administrative leaders tended to focus on diversity as an issue of numbers. Thinking about diversity as structural, or solely based upon numbers, seeks to reinforce the incomplete nature of what diversity can and should be (White 2005).

Most of the faculty involved in these initiatives had tenure. At a research university such as UA, junior faculty members are usually protected from service activities so that they can focus on their research, despite the potential benefits of service for creating a sense of belonging and self-worth (Boice 2000) and for facilitating networking and mentoring. In addition, committee service rarely counts in the promotion, tenure, and review processes, and active faculty members are often considered agitators and troublemakers (Theodore 1986). Those without the security of tenure (including those not on the tenure track) are therefore less likely to engage in change initiatives. At the same time, faculty climate issues are particularly salient for activists, and faculty issues related to tenure are particularly pronounced.

Most participants were women and people of color. In a documented climate (as evidenced in the climate study that precipitated the change initiatives under investigation) where women and faculty of color experience inequities, including subtle and less-subtle forms of harassment, these particular faculty members were among the most active in trying to improve the overall experience for themselves and their colleagues. As UA's campus-climate study made clear, both groups felt burdened with and unrewarded for service. Yet they continued to champion the service work involved in the diversity initiatives highlighted in the current study. This finding clearly supports work done by Bird et al. (2004), Baez (2000), and Turner and Thompson (1993), which suggests that women and faculty members of color were often drawn to academic "institutional housekeeping" (Bird et al. 2004, 194), a purposeful term intended to reclaim the significance of housekeeping (that is, service work) as legitimate and meaningful. Further, when the work of faculty members is examined at the college level, the situation is similar. The MEZACOPH is an example where the faculty members involved in the college MROC had been less successful. High proportions of the appointments in this college are supported only by grant funds, not tenured or on the tenure track. This vulnerability may lend itself to a lack of initiative, motivation, and availability by its faculty. Complicating the situation further is that those in public health, by the very nature of their chosen discipline, are interested in community outreach and activism, which makes them likely candidates to be involved in diversity initiatives. Yet when one looks at the structure of academic work within public health, it is notable that the reliance on soft money and numbers of non-tenure-track faculty does little to support activist academics who are interested in working on social change initiatives on their own campus. While it is not surprising that based upon the analysis of the MROC reports the more vulnerable faculty in the MEZACOPH did not participate, participation by other underrepresented (and therefore, vulnerable) populations became less intuitive. Many of the colleges and units that were the most feminized at UA were also the same colleges that developed stronger plans and had started to implement recommendations at the college-level. The data that emerged from the MROC reports from the library and the colleges of Humanities and Social and Behavioral Sciences were good examples of this. Moreover, even those colleges that had been identified as less successful in their change efforts at least made an attempt to think about the issues identified in the campus-climate study and created a college-based MROC. Other colleges chose not to participate in these change initiatives at all, nor did they submit the requested annual MROC reports. Among the colleges that did not submit MROC reports were the less feminized College of Engineering and Mines, where less than 10 percent of the faculty members were women. Thus, in the college where women and faculty of color were least visible, the efforts of faculty were the least evident—perhaps because there were limited numbers of underrepresented faculty in this college to conduct the institutional housekeeping (Bird et al. 2004).

In addition, many who participated expressed frustration about institutional leaders' (particularly the provost's) lack of interest in change efforts. Their stories were often discouraging, with the underlying lesson that change is slow. Participants frequently felt that working against the power structure, rather than with it, was sometimes necessary to build a more hospitable and equitable environment.

Implications

Our findings have several implications. First, the nature of faculty-led initiatives is complex. Who participates and how they participate vary widely. Gender, race, ethnicity, discipline, academic rank, and ideas of success are further complications. For instance, the number of non-tenure-track faculty members continues to grow. Given the clustering of women in these positions nationally and the degree to which they have become a significant portion of the instructional workforce in academe (which undoubtedly has an influence on the numbers of faculty of color as well), it is critical that faculty-led change initiatives must consider these faculty members as they work to transform institutions. Studies like Agents for Change and the others highlighted in this book indicate, however, that this growing cadre of faculty is often forgotten or ignored in the important work in which faculty change agents are engaging.

Second, some of the people we interviewed felt overwhelming discouragement yet remained committed to improving UA's campus climate. They were interested in social justice, the value of diversity in education, and the institution itself. Institutional leaders should capitalize on these loyal and dedicated faculty members and legitimately reward their work. Further, the faculty members involved already have strong institutional loyalty, and the university should think very seriously about how leaders can work with faculty activists to maintain that loyalty. Faculty change agents who have been involved in climate work for years will become disenfranchised if institutions donít respond to the dedication and service they provide. This ultimately means that institutional housekeeping must be institutionalized and valorized, not marginalized. Faculty and university leaders must reclaim service as a vital part of institutional transformation and academic excellence (Bennett 1998; Bird et al. 2004).

Finally, if domination and patriarchy are part of the organization and operation of the academy (hooks 1993), we must create a new model that includes diversity and respect and is not measured solely according a specious conception of merit. Working with institutional leaders may improve the campus climate for diversity, but faculty activists must consider whether their strategies replicate the patriarchy or are expanding into a new and vibrant model of success that dismantles hierarchy and domination.

REFERENCES

Arizona Board of Regents (ABOR). 2003. "Leadership in Higher Education." http://www.abor.asu.edu/1_the_regents/reports_factbook/brochure.html (accessed March 9, 2005).

Baez, B. 2000. "Race-Related Service and Faculty of Color: Conceptualizing Critical Agency in Academe." *Higher Education* 39:363–391.

Bennett, J. B. 1998. *Collegial Professionalism: The Academy, Individualism, and the Common Good.* Phoenix, AZ: Oryx /American Council on Higher Education.

Bird, S., J. Litt, and Y. Wang. 2004. "Creating Status of Women Reports: Institutional House-keeping As Women's Work." *NWSA Journal* 16 (1):194–206.

Boice, R. 2000. *Advice for New Faculty Members: Nihil Nimus.* Boston: Allyn and Bacon.

Cress, C. 2001. "The Millennium Project: Report in Detail." Tucson: University of Arizona, Office of the President.

Cress, C., M. Dinnerstein, N. J. Miller, and J. Hart. 2001. "The Millennium Project: Summary Report." Tucson: University of Arizona, Office of the President.

Hart, J. 2002. "Activism among Feminist Academics: Professionalized Activism and Activist Professionals." PhD diss., University of Arizona.

———. 2005. "Activism among Feminist Academics: Professionalized Activism and Activist Professionals." *Advancing Women in Leadership.* http://www.advancing-women.com/awl/social_justice1/Hart.html (accessed June 7, 2005).

Hooks, B. 1993. "Keeping Close to Home: Class and Education." In *Working-Class Women in the Academy: Laborers in the Knowledge Factory,* ed. M. M. Tokarczyk and E. A. Fay, 99–111. Amherst: University of Massachusetts Press.

Huberman, A. M., and M. B. Miles. 1984. *Innovation Up Close.* New York: Plenum.

Johnsrud, L. K., D. C. Perreira, U. K. Miller, L. T. Inoshita, and J. L. Hart. 2002. "The Millennium Project: Phase II: Staff." Tucson: University of Arizona, Office of the President.

Lincoln, Y., and E. Guba. 1986). *Naturalistic Inquiry.* Newbury Park, CA: Sage.

Massachusetts Institute of Technology. 1999. "A Study on the Status of Women Faculty in Science at MIT." http://web.mit.edu/fnl/women/women.html (accessed January 27, 2000).

Merriam, S. B. 1998. *Qualitative Research and Case Study Application in Education.* San Francisco: Jossey-Bass.

National Academy of Sciences. 2004. "Gender Faculty Studies at Research 1 Institutions." http://www7.nationalacademies.org/cwse/gender_faculty_links.html (accessed July 30, 2004).

Nelson, D. J., and D. C. Rogers. 2005. "A National analysis of Diversity in Science and Engineering Faculties at Research Universities." http://cheminfo.chem.ou.edu/~djn/diversity/briefings/Diversity%20Report%20Final.pdf (accessed April 15, 2005).

Patton, M. Q. 1990. *Qualitative Evaluation and Research Methods.* Newbury Park, CA: Sage.

Strauss, A., and J. Corbin. 1990. *Basics of Qualitative Research: Grounded Theory Procedures and Techniques.* Newbury Park, CA: Sage.

Theodore, A. 1986. *The Campus Troublemakers: Academic Women in Protest.* Houston: Cap and Gown Press.

Turner, C. S. V., and R. J. Thompson. 1993. "Socializing Women Doctoral Students: Minority and Majority Experiences." *Review of Higher Education* 16 (3):355–370.

University of Arizona. 2003–4. "Decision and Planning Support." *UA Fact Book.,* http://daps.arizona.edu/daps/factbook/factbook.html (accessed March 9, 2005).

White, J. S. 2005. "Pipeline to Pathways: New Directions for Improving the Status of Women on Campus." *Liberal Education* (Winter). http://www.aacu.org/liberaleducation/le-wi05/le-wi05feature2.cfm (accessed May 27, 2005).

9

Designs for Diversity

The University of Miami's Caribbean Writers Summer Institute and Caribbean Literary Studies

PATRICIA JOAN SAUNDERS AND SANDRA POUCHET PAQUET

The University of Miami (UM) is the largest, most comprehensive private research university in the southeastern United States; it has a well-earned reputation for academic excellence and cultural diversity. Located in the heart of Miami-Dade County, an area challenged by a myriad of diversity and immigration issues, the university is the temporary home to close to 15,300 undergraduate and graduate students from every state and more than 140 nations. It is also employs more than 9,400 full-time faculty and staff. When you walk across the campus you cannot help but notice the diversity of students who enrich the space. The various bodies, accents, and languages one encounters on the campus and in the classrooms contribute to the social and intellectual vibrancy of this campus.

In its September 2007 Diversity Report, *Hispanic Business* magazine ranked three University of Miami graduate schools in its list of the top ten U.S. schools for Hispanic students. In celebration of this accomplishment, UM president Donna E. Shalala remarked, "This recognition by *Hispanic Business* magazine is clearly a testament to our institution's respect and encouragement for diversity," noting that "all of our schools are committed to reflecting our wonderful diverse community through its faculties, programs and students. This recognition proves we are succeeding on a national scale" (University of Miami news release, September 4, 2007).[1]

Part of the success of the university's commitment to diversity has to do with the efforts of faculty who have been working in various ways to increase racial and gender diversity on the campus. While success has been achieved in certain areas for Hispanic students, many faculty members continue to address challenges related to students of other racial groups. The Caribbean

Writers Summer Institute and Caribbean Literary Studies programs are two faculty-developed and faculty-operated strategies that aim to address the challenges of diversity as it relates to students from the English-speaking Caribbean. This is a story of the successes and challenges of innovative faculty members at the University of Miami as they try to extend the reach of their scholarship into the realm of activism.

The Study

Articles from the *Chronicle of Higher Education, Journal of Higher Education Columbus*, and *Journal of Blacks in Higher Education,* questionnaires, and video interviews suggest that academically based enrichment programs are extremely effective in the recruitment and retention of both faculty and students of color. In articles examining the value of affirmative action for providing all students with a diverse educational environment, researchers agree that, regardless of their cultural and class backgrounds, students benefit from being exposed to different worldviews and value systems. The debate about how American institutions of higher learning can best achieve this goal while also addressing ongoing race and gender inequities has yielded several very productive and insightful approaches tested at the University of Miami.

Efforts to recruit and retain both faculty and students of color in institutions of higher learning continue to focus on several key components. While it is clear that these components are intimately connected to one another, we wish to call attention to how these components affect faculty and students at different levels. Recent studies suggest that mentoring is a crucial element in retaining students of color (Payne 2002, 652–659). However, these same studies highlight the fact that faculty members of color fulfill a larger role as mentors than do their white counterparts, largely because there are fewer faculty members of color to fulfill roles as mentors and advisors to graduate and undergraduate students. In the final analysis, faculty members of color are overextended by the demands of their students, departments, and college or university in respect to this mentoring process. Without support and mentoring, however, studies show that graduate and undergraduate students of color are less likely to complete their education or continue on to obtain graduate degrees (Gregory 2001, 24–38; Smiles 2001, 10–11). In the face of limited time and resources, many universities and colleges are unable to retain both at the graduate and professorial levels the faculty and students of color that they manage to attract. Recently, faculty-led initiatives across institutional and disciplinary boundaries, have launched several collaborative projects that provide effective models for addressing issues of race and gender diversity on college campuses.

Although the Caribbean Writers Summer Institute (CWSI) and Caribbean Literary Studies (CLS) programs at the University of Miami were not designed as affirmative action initiatives, they have operated effectively toward this effort by providing structural support that people of color have been histori-cally denied in many institutional settings in the United States. In other words, programs such as CWSI provide opportunities for students of color that have historically been available for only the most privileged classes in the United States. We use the term "class" here because it is clear that this is one element of the affirmative action debate that has receded to the margins. White women, like other "minorities," have been excluded and denied access to institutional support systems. Moreover, the nexus of race, class, and gen-der in affirmative action needs to inform the findings, decisions, and prac-tices in institutions of higher learning. The fact that people of color make up a large percentage of those living at or below the poverty line in the United States suggests that equal access to opportunity needs to be understood not just in racial terms but in terms of class also. Enrichment programs, work-shops and summer institutes are just a few of the effective methods of prepar-ing graduate students to compete in their respective fields.

The Caribbean Writers Summer Institute: A Brief History, 1991–1996

When the Caribbean Writers Summer Institute was founded in 1991, the pri-mary aim was to provide an intellectual space for critical and creative dia-logue among Caribbean writers at all stages of their careers, wherever they might be domiciled. Lectures and public readings like those by Nobel Prize winner Derek Walcott, who read at the University of Miami in 1992 shortly after winning the prize, confirmed what many within the university commu-nity believed: the University of Miami was poised to become a significant cen-ter of activity for the study of Caribbean literature. The event was free and open to the public, and the public response was so overwhelming that the event was shifted to the Biltmore Hotel. It was televised, played, and replayed to audiences across the Caribbean.

The CWSI initiative, which was established in the year preceding Walcott's visit, was the brainchild of several faculty members, administrators, and community leaders who took it upon themselves to foster the growing interest in Caribbean literature and culture. The CWSI was initiated by Zack Bowen, then chair of English, and undertaken with the institutional support of then dean of Arts and Sciences Ross Murfin, the former provost, Louis Glaser, the former president, Tad Foote, and faculty like Marvin Dawkins, pro-fessor of sociology, who headed the former Caribbean, African, and African American Studies program at UM. The goal was to generate awareness of the Anglophone (African, Asian, and Creole) Caribbean's literary culture and, in the process, increase the profile of the Anglophone Caribbean within the department, the college, the institution, and the greater Miami region of

South Florida. In the region the Caribbean was largely understood to be Cuban and Puerto Rican, with no acknowledged debt to the African, Asian, and Native American base of most Caribbean societies, many of them well represented in the populations of Miami-Dade, Broward, and a host of major sites in the United States.

This was initially envisioned as an initiative in partnership with writers from the nation-states and territories of the Caribbean that would bring Caribbean writers in dialogue with each other and with the United States, in a rigorous, enriching, critical, and creative space for studying Caribbean literary culture and producing new work. The six-week residential program would take place at the University of Miami each summer for three consecutive summers. It was conceived as prelude to the development of a program for the study of Caribbean literature and culture at the University of Miami that would attract minority scholars and faculty and establish the university as the premier site for such studies in the United States in partnership with Caribbean institutions of higher learning. Funding was provided initially by the now defunct North-South Center at the University of Miami, the interest from a million-dollar gift from James Michener to the English department for the establishment of an MFA program with scholarships for Caribbean students, financial and staff support from the English department chaired by Zack Bowen, and financial and administrative support from Ross Murfin, the dean of Arts and Sciences, and Provost Glaser.

After an extremely successful first year (1991), in which participants from the Caribbean archipelago, Belize in Central America, Guyana in South America, the Bahamas, and the United States received scholarships and English graduate credit for a rigorous six-week residential program, the department hired Sandra Pouchet Paquet at the associate professor level with tenure in 1992. Professor Paquet, who was teaching at the University of Pennsylvania, was a leading Caribbean scholar, with considerable experience in study of Caribbean and African American literature and culture. She was hired to develop courses in Caribbean literature for the department at graduate and undergraduate levels, to teach and mentor, and to assume responsibility for directing the Caribbean Writers Summer Institute in August 1993. In addition, Robert Antoni, a prizewinning Caribbean novelist who had attended the 1991 CWSI, was hired to teach writing in the newly formed MA program in the English department. From 1993 through 1996, with the aid of English department staff and research assistants, a summer stipend, and later a course reduction, he facilitated the growth of the department's graduate and undergraduate programs in Caribbean literature and culture, as well as the expansion of the Caribbean Writers Summer Institute to include a workshop in drama as well as fiction and poetry, seminars for pre- and postdoctoral scholars in Caribbean Literature and Culture and a mini institute in translation.

The Caribbean Writers Institute prompted the engagement of Fred D'Aguiar, another prizewinning Caribbean writer, in part to foster the emerging cross-sections of interest between the fledgling MFA program, the department of English and the Institute. Sadly, both Robert Antoni and Fred D'Aguiar left the University of Miami after the CWSI was shelved without future prospects for financial support. The record testifies to the range, scope, and success of the Caribbean Writers Summer Institute in generating a supportive academic culture of learning and achievement for all participating writers and scholars, regardless of gender, race, and nationality, around a singular focus on Caribbean art and culture.

The faculty and professionals who were most eager to support the summer institute were from the fields of African American, African, and African studies; Caribbean studies; English; foreign languages and literatures; history; sociology; women's studies; the Richter Library; and the School of Education. This also includes students and professionals with similar interests and concerns at Miami-Dade College, Florida International University, and the Miami-Dade and Broward public libraries. In addition to support from faculty members in the United States, the greatest support and commitment to the CWSI came from faculty, and writers throughout the region, many of whom make up the literary and political foundations of research and scholarship in the United States and throughout the Caribbean region. After the successful CWSI program in 1991, the Department of English at the University of Miami was invited to join the Consortium of Caribbean Universities by the University of the West Indies. An outstanding community contributor to the success of the CWSI was Mitch Kaplan of Books & Books, Coral Gables and Miami Beach. He spared no effort in facilitating public readings and publicizing the activities of the CWSI. Significant support came from public radio station WLRN in the form of live interviews with resident and visiting writers, public announcements, and popular Caribbean radio host Mike Andrews.

Curricular Design

The CWSI six-week curriculum was designed to bring together established and beginning writers at various stages of their careers in a series of workshops under the direction of highly accomplished Caribbean writers. They would meet regularly to critique each other's work and be given time and facilities conducive to writing, networking, and informal exchange. They would have the opportunity to meet distinguished visiting Caribbean writers, hear them read, and discuss the aesthetics of Caribbean fiction and poetry. They would be expected to produce new work at the CWSI and give a public reading. These activities revolved around full access to Richter Library facilities and computer labs, and a rigorous program of workshops in fiction and poetry for the first three years. In the fourth year, postgraduate seminars were added and subsequently a workshop in drama, and a three-day translation institute. Visiting scholars and symposiums were added to the program, and scholars and writers attended readings, lectures, and symposiums together. Individual consultations with the workshop and seminar directors were inherent to the design.

Evaluating Signs of Progress

One of the most significant fringe benefits of the Caribbean Writers Summer Institute was a growing national recognition of the University of Miami as a center of activity for Caribbean Literary Studies. Subsequent to the loss of funding, several participants from the Caribbean Writers Summer Institute applied for admission to the University of Miami's English graduate programs. Students applied both to the creative writing program and to the master's and PhD programs, all with a declared interest in studying creative writing and Caribbean literature. Many of these students came from the Caribbean region and several of them were graduates of the University of the West Indies. With this increasing influx of graduate students and an increasing interest among undergraduate students, the number of graduate students of color grew steadily in the years following the CWSI, from two to eighteen excluding MA and MFAs.

The increase in graduate students of color in the English department and the continued interest among faculty and students created an environment of remarkable intellectual stimulation and support for scholarly and creative writing. As a result, despite the shelving of the CWSI, there was a very supportive intellectual environment for Caribbean studies, and out of this space emerged the Caribbean Literary Studies program. This program came out of a series of initiatives led by graduate students and faculty members.

Once funding was depleted, several students working with Professor Paquet sought to continue the work begun at the institute, but on a smaller, more local level within the University of Miami. Graduate students from the departments of English and foreign languages and literatures (Kathryn Morris and Lynn Ink, working with Sandra Pouchet Paquet as adviser and chair in English, and later Yvette Fuentes from foreign languages and literatures) conceptualized a conference titled "Contextualizing the Caribbean: Redefining Approaches in an Era of Globalization," which was held at UM in fall 2000. In the case of the Caribbean Literary Studies program, graduate students in English decided that they would like to organize a conference for spring 2000 and enlisted the assistance of Professor Paquet and the permission of the English department. Within a week of posting the call for papers on the University of Pennsylvania's Listserv in 1999, the graduate student conference organizers began receiving abstracts. They secured Professor Peter Hulme as a keynote speaker, and shortly after Professor Carole Boyce Davies also agreed to speak.

According to the graduate students, they had initially envisioned the conference as a graduate student conference. With encouragement from Sandra
Paquet, however, they decided that since the interest was clear and present,
they would accept abstracts from graduate students and faculty alike. The
response indicated that interest came primarily from PhDs already working in
the field. It is important to note that these graduate students took on this project on a completely voluntary basis; there was no compensation available for
the organization of this conference. This group of students sourced financial
support for the conference from a host of university offices and organizations.

This conference was one of the first student-led initiatives to take place
since the discontinuation of the Caribbean Writers Summer Institute. The success of these first conferences and the subsequent boost to student morale
resulted in the creation of a graduate research assistantship for Sandra Paquet
and Caribbean Literary Studies to pursue initiatives—among them the archiving of CWSI records and the creation of a Caribbean studies journal—that had
been on hold following Zack Bowen's resignation as chair,. By bringing the conference together primarily through their own resourcefulness, the students
effectively made a strong case for additional support for conferences, graduate
student stipends, and other institutional support for Caribbean studies.

From this conference, graduate students were then able to request and
secure "niche group" funding for continued conferences, reading groups, and
other events that eventually grew into what is now Caribbean Literary Studies.
With an emerging critical mass of about a dozen women of color in the departments of English and foreign languages and literatures, this growing group of
graduate students subsequently applied for funding from the Graduate Student Association and the Provost's Office in order to present conference
papers at the International Conference on Caribbean Literature hosted by
Melvin Rahming in Bermuda. As a condition of obtaining the fiscal support to
attend the conference, students were asked to present their papers to the University of Miami community. In an effort to enrich the intellectual culture in
the graduate program, students decided to present their papers over the
course of a semester as a brown bag series and invite other interested students and faculty to participate in the presentations discussions about
Caribbean literature.

It is clear, based on our research and the responses from former students
both at the University of Miami and at the CSWI, that the most integral part
of both programs and the links between them lies in the sustained intellectual culture begun during the CWSI and now continued through the
Caribbean Literary Studies program in the English department. In many ways,
then, CLS emerged as a more streamlined version of the CWSI by transforming
what the Institute offered into a more diffused curricular program at the
University of Miami. While CLS has done a great deal in the way of providing

a continued rigorous intellectual environment for scholars in the field of Caribbean literature both nationally and internationally, the continued dependence on department funding, limited niche group funds ($1,000 annually), and occasional support from the dean of Arts and Sciences ($5,000 per conference) threatens to erode the truly remarkable potential of the program.

The Ford Foundation grant from Rutgers University allowed us to conduct a more sustained study into the specific benefits of programs such as the CWSI for graduate students of color. The responses to the questionnaires confirmed what many studies show: that sustained intellectual support for minority research and scholarship is essential for increasing the numbers of women and people of color in institutions of higher learning. Interviews conducted with individuals who were students in the Caribbean Summer Writers Institute indicated that they invested time and effort in order to build an intellectual community both within the University of Miami and beyond. Many who were graduate students then and are now faculty members identified the need to empower themselves intellectually by being actively involved in reading groups, conferences, and other activities beyond their classroom experiences as a primary reason for their volunteer efforts.

When asked to respond to the question "How has your research and scholarship benefited from your affiliation with the CWSI," several responses suggest that the intellectual environment of the CWSI was instrumental to peoples' successes in their respective institutes:

> As a graduate student in Caribbean literature, and a beginning graduate student in fiction writing, to be able to spend six weeks in the company of Kamau Brathwaite and George was an incomparable privilege. To hear their reflections and experiences of the development of Caribbean literature, and to be taken seriously as a creative writer after a disappointing first year in my academic program, deepened my understanding of the field and its development. I have subsequently taught works by Brathwaite and Lamming, as well as works by memorable colleagues from that summer, Velma Pollard and Zee Edgell in particular. I also wrote papers in graduate school on the works of these writers. (Assistant professor at George Washington University, CWSI class of 1991)
>
> Being able to take a seminar with George Lamming was invaluable. He provided input on my own (and each student in the classes' personal research interests) enabling me to take my ideas further into a particular paper or thread of thought regarding (in my case) Creole culture. So I can say that my knowledge of Caribbean literature and culture expanded tremendously during the program because of the quality of the seminars offered and the considerable expertise of the teachers. Many prominent and up-and-coming Caribbean scholars also attended this

program. I have been able to use these contacts to further my research interests in Haitian literature and other Caribbean writing. (University of Miami PhD and researcher at the Historical Museum of Southern Florida, CWSI classes of 1995 and 1996)

My dissertation focused on representations of motherhood in works by Caribbean women writers. Although I had read some fiction independently, the CWSI provided me with the framework I needed to explore the topic in an informed and sustained manner. I took two formal courses, one on Caribbean women writers and an Introduction to Caribbean Literary Theory, and had access to a handful of experts in the field as well as a diverse group of colleagues with whom to discuss the materials. It was an invaluable experience. (Associate professor at University of Kansas, CWSI class of 1994)

I attended the CSWI as a creative writer, specifically a participant in the poetry workshop. Still, I engaged in many critically important academic conversations there, and connected and kept in touch with scholars who continue to be central to the field of Caribbean Literary Studies. It was at the CSWI that I decided I wanted to go to graduate school to study Caribbean literature. (University of Miami PhD and assistant professor at Colgate University, CWSI class of 1995)

When I arrived at the CWSI, I had an idea of what I my dissertation research would entail and why. However, the seminars I attended that summer challenged my thinking and ultimately my research agenda in ways that I could not have imagined. I was enrolled in Lamming's seminar on Caribbean nationalism and it was in this seminar that I began to think more critically about how Caribbean nationalism is shaped by gender and sexuality. The dissertation I wrote in the final analysis was shaped in large part by the endless dialogues and debates I had with my colleagues that summer. The paper I wrote in Lamming's course, ultimately became a pivotal chapter in my dissertation. There were also other valuable experiences for the faculty who gave their time and energies for very modest compensation. One internationally known writer, offered to return for airfare and accommodations. Another indicated that whatever the CWSI could afford by way of an honorarium was enough. The point is that many of the writers who participated did so because of the venture itself, anticipating that the CWSI would transform the field as we knew it. (University of Miami assistant professor, CWSI class of 1994)

For many of the established writers, participating in the CWSI was not simply a job, it was in many ways a reflection of their long-standing commitment to the field of Caribbean Literary Studies. Their commitment was most evident in the fact that many of the writers returned to the CWSI in a number of different capacities—as seminar leaders, as visiting writers, as lecturers, and even as students themselves. Although several of the participants from the Caribbean region were accomplished, published authors, they came to the institute because it offered them an opportunity to have dedicated time, exclusive time to work on their writing with other writers who, more often than not, were grappling with similar issues from their respective cultural and creative perspectives.

We had the opportunity to interview Velma Pollard, who attended the CWSI in the first year. Velma Pollard was already a very well established academic, holding the position of senior lecturer at the University of the West Indies, Mona, Jamaica, and had published a collection of poetry and another collection of prose essays prior to her arrival at the CWSI. Why would such a well-established scholar and creative writer apply to attend a summer institute? This is one of the first questions we asked her when we sat down to talk with her in Jamaica:

PS: When you arrived at the Caribbean Writers Summer Institute, what did you expect? Did you have a project in mind when you arrived in Miami? Or were you there to perfect your craft as a writer since you were already well published?

VP: When I arrived in Miami I had one sentence. I was a little afraid because I had never been to a writing workshop. I had a book of poetry and a book of prose already out on the market, but I had never been to a workshop. So, I wondered whether someone was going to try to teach me to write. So, I applied for the scholarship and got it. I knew I wanted space and time but I didn't know if I wanted to be taught. But when I arrived there, it was very open. What I found most valuable about the experience was putting your work out there and having people read it. You get the chance to have ten people read something you have written and talk about it. That is extraordinary, it is a chance you cannot get in any other situation as a writer. That was the best thing about it.

Although we had classes most of the morning, we had the afternoons to write and then we had readings in the evening. In the afternoon you could just write or you could actually sit and just talk to people about what you were doing. There was access to a computer room four nights a week, so I set out a schedule for myself to write two pages every day, for four days, so I had about eight to ten pages written at the end of each week. I had five weeks at the Institute, [and] by the end of the period I had fifty single-spaced pages. . . . When I returned to Jamaica I felt I wanted to keep up the momentum I had started at the Institute. Shortly after returning from the Institute I met with an editor from Longman publishers who asked what I was working on, and I showed her the work I had. She looked at it and said, send it to me as soon as it is finished. The workshop ended in July and by December I had a very good first draft of the novel. And you know, I have not written a novel since! I have never had that kind of time since. I don't think I never will.

PS: But you must have other things you are working on now, no more novels in the pipeline?

VP: I've been trying with another novel for a very long time, but it can't happen. You see if you don't have a place where nobody requires anything of you besides that you should write . . . that is just an extraordinary opportunity. The space, the time and the exchange . . . I am still in touch with several of the people I met in that workshop, in fact several of the writers from that workshop have published novels and I have written some critical reviews of their works.

During our conversation, Pollard highlighted several other valuable aspects of her time at the CWSI. However, I have reproduced this part of the conversation to stress the crucial contributions to the field of Caribbean literature. On the acknowledgments page of her novel, *Homestretch*, Pollard writes, "A fellowship to the University of Miami Summer Institute for Caribbean Creative Writing June–July 1991 gave me the time and stimulation to write the first hundred pages of this novel. I wish to thank Professor Zack Bowen, the organizer of that institute, and all the fine people with whom I interacted that summer."

We cannot for a minute underestimate the value of growing a body of literature and a field of study in the way that the Caribbean Writers Summer Institute does. Providing a space conducive to the exchange of ideas, experiences, and certainly worldviews, the CWSI can very easily lay claim to an impressive list of writers who either cut their teeth or further perfected their craft at the University of Miami. Among these writers are numerous Commonwealth Prize winners, Casa de las Americas Prize winners, and winners of countless other literary prizes.

What is all the more striking is the fact that, despite the shelving of the program almost ten years ago, there are writers who are still producing literary texts that they began working on during their time at the CWSI. Most recently, Funso Aiyejina, a Nigerian writer who lives and teaches in Trinidad and is the winner of the 2000 Best First Book Africa Region—Commonwealth Writers Prize, published his second collection of poetry, *I the Supreme and Other Poems* (Kraft Books Limited, Nigeria, 2004). In his acknowledgments he writes:

> I would also like to acknowledge the University of Miami for the award of a James Michener Fellowship, which made it possible for me to attend the Poetry Workshop of the Caribbean Summer Writers of 1994.

Many thanks to Sandra Pouchet-Paquet (Director of the Institute) and her team for providing such a conducive atmosphere for participants to tease out their dreams. I would like to thank Mervyn Morris, the Director of the Poetry Workshop, and the other participants in the fiction workshop and the seminars, and their directors, for bringing a sense of wholeness and diversity to the experience.

Funso Aiyejina's comments about the institute are supported by several other writers who participated in the workshop as well as by the Mervyn Morris, who directed the Poetry Workshop from 1992–1994. I had the opportunity to interview Mervyn Morris in Jamaica and was most interested in hearing what his perspective was as the person leading the workshops. His comments, like those of many others interviewed, confirmed the importance of a rigorous intellectual environment that allowed for the continuous exchange of ideas:

PS: Can you tell me a little bit about your first two years as the director of the Poetry Workshop at the Caribbean Writers Summer Institute? What did you want the participants to leave with by the end of the six-week period? Did you feel you accomplished what you set out to do at the end of the six weeks?

MM: The most important aspect of any workshop for me is for the students to leave with a sense of having gotten useful feedback on what they are working on. That, more than anything else, is important—but also that they leave being sure that they contributed usefully to other people's development.

The first year I was at CWSI was an absolute dream workshop. It had nothing to do with the powers of selection—I mean we did select the participants but it still seemed to me to be a series of happy accidents. I have never, before or since, had a workshop as remarkable as that. It practically ran itself; I just had to make sure that I was not in the way! People were so willing to talk—you try to create the right atmosphere and also it depends on what your particular attitude to workshopping is—there are very different ways of effectively running workshops. There are many very good workshops that are leader-centered; mine was not, emphatically not. The whole idea was to create an environment where we were all willing to contribute and all respectful of each others efforts and contributions. It really was remarkable, it was remarkably partly because of the different skills that were thrown together. I recall that Claudia Rankin was in that workshop and it was quite clear to me that apart from being a very, very, good writer, she also had a very analytical perspective. There were also several participants in the class who had a great deal of experience in running workshops whose agenda was to keep helping the workshop succeed. There were also people in the workshop who had been taxicab drivers by night and teaching and writing by day.

Digital Media Archive

The idea of establishing CWSI archives was always under consideration. The videocassettes are evidence of a conscious attempt to record what was happening at the summer institutes. The question was how to accomplish this. We had to consider the limited life of the video recordings themselves and how to ensure that the archive would be preserved, valued, and readily available to scholars and writers who wanted to access them. The initial task of documenting what we had required more time than I had, and the task fell to Kathryn Morris, a PhD candidate in our program, who volunteered to find the right solution and assume responsibility for making it happen. Working on a volunteer basis, she documented the video archive and, acting on my behalf, initiated contact with the Richter Library about how best to store the archive. We knew at that point that digitizing was an option but did not know how this might be accomplished without a budget. Archives and Special Collections steered her in the direction of Jeff Barry, associate professor and librarian, who was in charge of Digital Library Initiatives. He met with Kathryn Morris and me, and in the course of conversation plans were drawn up for the CWSI Digital Media Archive (originally scholar.library.miami.edu/cls, now as.miami.edu/cls) and what is now *Anthurium: a Caribbean Studies Journal* (scholar.library.miami.edu/anthurium).

Kathryn Morris tackled the project with great earnestness, working on a volunteer basis under the guidance of the Digital Media Lab. Her first efforts were so promising that Sandra Paquet was able to secure a graduate assistantship in 2001–2002 to bring the project to completion. The English department has maintained that initial commitment to the digital archive and extended it to include the journal *Anthurium,* which remains a collaborative project between Caribbean Literary Studies in the English department and the Digital Media Lab at Richter Library.

The digital archive, while chronicling the events that made up this unique intellectual endeavor, has also emerged as an invaluable teaching and learning tool for students and teachers across the Americas. Several faculty members have written the Caribbean Literary Studies Web page to comment that the digital archive has opened a new gateway for their students to understand the historical can cultural context out of which Caribbean literature emerges. The archive provides students preparing presentations or writing term papers on the novels of Caribbean writers with access to extensive dialogues and interviews with the more than half the writers in the field of Caribbean literature.

These interviews feature novelist, critics, and poets discussing the particular aspects of their craft as creative writers, their political perspectives, the intellectual histories that produced literary movements in the region, and the historical events and figures that fill the landscapes of their novels and poems. Most importantly, undergraduate students have a unique opportunity to interact with the living artists through their own words, ideas, and perspectives while they are also reading works produced by notables like George Lamming, Olive Senior, and Michael Dash. The archive includes a tremendous amount of historical data that exists in limited circulation in print format. For example, Lamming's reflections on the speech he delivered at the fortieth anniversary of the Barbados Workers Union gives viewers an intimate perspective on the particulars of traditions within the trade unions in Trinidad, Barbados, and Jamaica.

For students of Caribbean literature, political science, history, or cultural studies, Lamming's historical speech, "The Honourable Member," originally presented on August 29, 1981 (and reconceptualized at the CWSI in 1994), is one of the most detailed critiques of the Caribbean middle classes and their political ambitions and nationalist sentiments. Lamming's audience included trade unionists and elements from the private sector, government officials, and agencies and embassies throughout the region. As Lamming notes, his speech addresses "the locations of power within both within the island (Barbados) and within the region." Before he begins his speech, Lamming outlines his aims as a writer of speeches and novels:

> I try to do on a platform what in fact I do in novels. The themes of the speeches are not any different from the themes of the novels. I write a speech, but as a novelist it is a speech which has structure. It does not work, that is the speech, it does not work like the language of the novel; which is the point I am trying to make. The speeches are addressed to the mind. With the intention of making the collective mind of the crowd feel—if you can get them—to make the mind feel. That is really what I am trying to do. The speeches are given in what we would call a language of statements. But the statements given and structured in such a way that makes the mind feel. The novels, on the other hand, are directed to an area of feeling and with the specific intention of making the feeling think. But they are both about the same issues, the same concerns.[2]

For any student of Caribbean literature, this distinction is not simply a matter of craft. Lamming's comments highlight a long-standing tradition in the Caribbean region whereby the voices of the leading literary and cultural critics are also the voices of the fiction writers and poets. His commentary, then, offers important critical insight about the political and poetic processes involved in all writing to students who are currently engaged in the creative arts and cultural studies.

However, Lamming's speech does a great deal more as a pedagogical device for teachers in other disciplines beyond Caribbean literature. His speech gives students an astute perspective on the historical and economic environment that produced the Crown Colony system of government upon which the region's current parliamentary government is based. This perspective is rendered in a personal and intimately political context, however.

> This grandfather has distinguished himself as a cooper. He made and repaired every kind of wooden cask and tub you could imagine, and by this achievement of a technical skill, he also made himself and the artisan class he represents indispensable to the technical function of the plantation.
>
> But it was this grandfather who preached the absolute necessity of education. He perceived school as the only possible means of rescuing his offspring from the humiliations his ancestors have endured. The book, the lesson, pen, and ink: these were his images of redemption. And thatís why his son, the Honourable Member's father, born in 1914, was destined to be a teacher. The elementary school became their chapel, Harrison College their cathedral, and an English University, the Kingdom of Heaven. And behind this immense effort was an even greater sacrifice of courage of the will: the women who fathered many a household, nursed man and child without a wage, and have remained to this day the last surviving example of legalized slave-labour.
>
> Those indolent critics who treat the past as though it were an amputated limb to be buried and forgotten and who complain about my insistence on restoring it do not pay serious critical attention to the society they describe. For a large portion of those who rule our lives today from the executive, the judiciary and all corners of the bureaucracy are the products of that tutelage I have described, and profoundly shaped by that social experience which has made the Honourable Member who he is.
>
> If we follow, in greater detail, that honourable line of ancestry from the estate hand in the 1880s to the professional great-grandson in 1981, we shall not find a single dominant landlord, a powerful merchant banker, certainly no industrial capitalist or great ship owner. But it is precisely these categories of men and their representatives whom the Honourable Member and his class have to deal with in very complex negotiations on our behalf in the political and industrial centres of the world: from Tokyo to Toronto, London, Brussels, and New York. Our Honorable Member and his class, bright, ambitious and often patriotic men, assume these challenging tasks without any historical social experience ownership and control of the means of production in their own country: just functionaries who take care of other people's business. It makes for a certain fragility at the heart of all of their protestations against unfair terms of trade, or the subtle not subtle bullying by capitalist powers to

make us shape a foreign policy that may not be in the interest of our people.[3]

We have quoted Lamming here at great length because his comments in this speech, made in 1981, of the utmost importance to the intellectual work undertaken by the faculty and students engaged in the endeavor of the Caribbean Writers Summer Institute. The historical and political trajectory Lamming outlines is one shared by many of the writers and scholars who volunteered their time and energies each summer. These scholars, like the grandparents Lamming refers to, understood themselves to be involved in an important institutional endeavor aimed at developing another generation of thinkers, in a tradition similar to those who labored, albeit in technical skills and trades.

As someone who was a student in the audience when Lamming delivered this speech, I (Patricia Saunders) have repeatedly encouraged my own students in my Caribbean and world literature courses, both at Bowdoin College and at the University of Miami, to examine the links between the personal and the political in Caribbean intellectual histories. More importantly, through these archives students can begin to gain an appreciation for the interconnectedness between disciplinary areas like history, economics, political science, gender studies, and literature, all of which are eloquently represented in the Lamming passage. This interdisciplinary approach to literary studies has long been a vital part of postcolonial literatures, and Lamming's speech offers students a framework that represents these integral connections and shows how these interactions shape policies, political movements, and cultural values. As a teaching tool, these speeches are timeless because they offer students such an astute critical framework for understanding colonialism, democracy, and labor movements, not just in the Caribbean region but in all the parts of the world where there are members of the underclass struggling for their rights within systems of oppression.

Colleagues teaching in history and political science have commented that the CWSI digital archive brings historical events to life through the words and ideas of those who shaped the intellectual terrain of these movements across the Caribbean region. Once more, these archival materials are becoming all the more valuable as many of these intellectuals are nearing the end of their careers, and their lives. Antonio Benitez-Rojo, who participated in the CWSI on more than one occasion as a visiting writer and scholar, died on January 2, 2005. Another important voice in Caribbean literature, Felix Morriseau-Leroy, the Haitian poet, died in the summer of 1998. Sam Selvon, the award-winning writer from Trinidad died in April 1994, less than a year after he was a visiting writer at the Caribbean Writers Summer Institute. In addition to their substantial contributions in arts and letters, these writers have, through their participation in the CWSI, also gifted to a generation of students and teachers their insights and perspectives in their own words through this digital archive. They also model for our students what a commitment to the life of the mind and ideas meant for writers and scholars of their generation and how these writers sought to bridge the time gaps between themselves and the generation of scholars they are addressing at the CWSI.

Caribbean Literary Studies

CLS is clearly a successful program that has made numerous gains.

1. There have been faculty hires in the field of Caribbean literature and culture: Sandra Paquet, professor of English and formerly director of the CWSI in 1992, and Patricia Saunders, assistant professor of English in 2003.
2. The graduate curriculum now includes four different graduate courses in the field that are taught on a rotating basis. The undergraduate curriculum includes courses in Caribbean literature at every stage of the undergraduate program. On both graduate and undergraduate levels, these courses are fully enrolled.
3. Since 1992, the English department has graduated six PhDs exclusively in the field, and four PhDs in association with Irish studies, African American literature, and ethnic American literature. All of these are women; ethnically one is Irish American, one is Hawaiian Chinese, one is registered Seminole American, one is Bahamian, one Jamaican, and all the others are Caribbean American and black American.
4. In addition, there are six persons of color currently enrolled in the PhD program in the field, and one person of color in the MA program with a declared interest in the field. Another has just graduated from the MA program and has been urged to apply elsewhere for her PhD because her first two degrees are in English from the University of Miami. Statistics for the MFA program are not available, but broad contact with these students in the classroom suggests that the same pattern applies.
5. With growth in the number of graduate students in the field at UM, other positive developments became possible, among them an active interdisciplinary graduate student niche group in the field; graduate assistants dedicated to organizing international conferences, the institution of a free-access, peer-reviewed electronic journal, and the creation of a digital archive that documents the achievements of the CWSI, 1991–1996, and post-CWSI events organized by faculty and students under the Caribbean literary studies banner.

The XXII Annual West Indian Literature
Conference and *Anthurium*

In an effort to maintain institutional ties established with the University of the West Indies campuses, CLS hosted the sixteenth annual West Indian Literature Conference at the University of Miami. It had the support of President Foote, the college, and the English department, and graduate students were encouraged to participate in the organization of the conference and present papers. Part of the impetus for the fall 2000 conference was the students' desire to repeat this success and make this kind of conferences a regular occurrence. In 2003, CLS cohosted the XXII Annual West Indian Literature Conference, "Caribbean Currents: Navigating the Web and the Word," from March 20 to March 22, 2003. More than one hundred scholars attended and presented their work at this very successful conference. The conference featured many familiar faces from past Caribbean Writers Summer Institutes, but it also was a memorable occasion because it also included several students who were once CWSI students and were now faculty and scholars in their own right at universities across the United States and throughout the Caribbean region.

One of the most significant products that emerged out of the joint efforts of faculty, students and the administration at the University of Miami after the West Indian Literature conference was the online, peer-reviewed, journal *Anthurium* (scholar.library.miami.edu/anthurium/home.htm). It features creative writing and critical essays on Caribbean literature and culture, and its editorial staff includes faculty from universities in the United States, Canada, and throughout the Caribbean region.

Anthurium is well positioned to make unique contributions to the field of Caribbean Literary Studies. Its publication of Brathwaite's previously unpublished manuscript already marks a historical moment in its brief history. Moreover, *Anthurium* joins the ranks of a very few journals in the United States dedicated to publishing quality scholarship in Caribbean arts and letters. Submissions to the journal continue to arrive consistently from notable, well-established scholars in the field as well as from young scholars whose research will shore up the foundations of this field.

The joint efforts of the faculty and graduate students of the CWSI and CLS, and Jeff Barry and the Digital Media Lab at the University of Miami, have culminated in two digital projects that have transformed the way teachers and students of Caribbean literature and culture conduct their classes and their research. It is our hope that the continued support of the staff at the Otto Richter Library's Digital Media Lab will help to strengthen the impact that CLS can make on the field by bridging the technological gap between universities in the United States and those in Latin America and the Caribbean region. The online journal and the digital archive are resources that have the capacity to transform how we teach and what students can learn beyond the classroom. In effect these resources have the power to level the playing field by giving access to students and faculty who might otherwise not have the resources to participate in institutes such as the CWSI, or to attend conferences held at the University of Miami. More importantly, the caliber of scholarship published in the journal is a testament to the reputation of the Caribbean Literary Studies program at the University of Miami.

Preparing the Path for the Future of the Field

Over the last ten years, students who were involved in various stages of numerous CWSI and CLS programs and initiatives have successfully completed their PhDs in English at the University of Miami and have become well-respected faculty members at institutions all over the United States and the Caribbean. Their achievements are a testament to the effectiveness of academic programs like the Caribbean Writers Summer Institute and Caribbean Literary Studies at the University of Miami in the recruitment and retention of graduate students of color and in diversifying the curriculum. Key components are academic excellence, mentoring, and structural support that are the result of faculty and administrative initiatives. But perhaps the most important element in achieving academic excellence and diversity is the institutionalization of an international and area studies program that is able to capitalize on the accessibility of Caribbean diversity as a lived experience and as a field of study, a growing Caribbean Diaspora that is a model of difference and diversity, geographical proximity to the Caribbean region, building institutional and faculty ties with Caribbean institutions of higher learning, the establishment of a physical base for cultural and creative exchange and production, the cultivation of a community of shared experience that is identical with achievement in creative and academic spheres, and an ethos of inclusiveness and accommodation of difference, dialogue, and international exchange.

Lessons and Recommendations

Of course, the unnamed ingredients thus far are financial resources in the form of faculty, financial aid, institutional infrastructure, and an adequate budget. The challenge remains of how to endow this achievement at the University of Miami to ensure its continued success regardless of the vagaries of institutional budgets and academic rivalries for limited resources in a particular department or college. The University of Miami has a winning institutional model for achieving academic excellence and diversity within an area studies framework. The model began with the Caribbean Writers Summer Institute, which provided the ideal academic and cultural environment for a multipronged approach to achieving diversity in institutions of higher learning. If the restoration of the Caribbean Writers Summer Institute is to be achieved so that it can continue its valuable experiments in academic enrichment and diversity, it must be endowed with the necessary funding. Throughout the course of the CWSI and the subsequent programming and curricular initiatives by the Caribbean Literary Studies program, it has become increasingly clear that this kind of initiative cannot survive and prosper beyond the endurance limits of key faculty and administrators without the kind of institutionalization that an endowment provides.

It has long been understood that programs such as nursing, medicine, biology, and other "hard sciences" are engaged in strengthening the community beyond the university through research and scholarship. The tangible results of scholars' research in all of these areas certainly help to improve the quality of life with advances in science and technology. However, we cannot underestimate the tremendous contributions made in the humanities, particularly where research and scholarship serve to enhance creative expression while also producing knowledge and disseminating ideas through art, which expands our understanding and appreciation of diverse cultures and worldviews. The comparison between the humanities and the sciences is an important one, particularly when we begin to think about institutional funding for research, curricular development, and scholarship. The sciences have long been supported by external funding, endowments, private donations, and internal institutional funding; as we well know, however, the humanities have been one of the areas hardest hit in recent years by cuts in funding for the arts.

When we begin to think about the impact of limited resources across the board, there is a particular danger where programs whose research and scholarship address cultural, racial, and gender diversity are concerned. When there is limited funding for these programs, more often than not, as this chapter shows, faculty members and students of color take on the responsibility, through volunteering their time and energy in order to make up the shortfall of fiscal support. In the end, there are many successful programs, but these successes are short-lived and, more often than not, can also lead to shortened careers for faculty members of color who have exhausted their better energies in the trenches because they understand their work to have the same potential for achieving social justice and stability and advancing democratic values as the work done by doctors and nurses. The University of Miami has the potential to be both a leading science research university and a prominently positioned center for the study of Caribbean arts and letters. The reports on which this chapter is based show this to be the case already; the missing ingredient is the kind of funding that would make these achievements part of an enduring institute for Caribbean literary studies.

The success of the CWSI and the CLS is well noted and documented. Both programs are recognized nationally and internationally by scholars and artists. More importantly, the University of Miami should be aware that although this kind of programs may not benefit the University of Miami community immediately, the returns in the long run are more than worth the effort and support. Patricia Saunders's presence at the University of Miami is certainly one of these "unexpected outcomes" and a testament to these long-term investments. Ten years ago she attended the CWSI as a graduate student and knew then, as now, that the University of Miami was building a truly phenomenal model of research and scholarship. Saunders observes,

> When I applied for the job at the University of Miami, I knew that I would be competing not just with scholars from all over the U.S. but largely with scholars who were all shaped by the CWSI, scholars I had encountered at conferences, seminars, scholars whose books I had both read and taught (and continue to teach here at UM). In other words, the CWSI is indeed benefiting the University of Miami community, as this report has shown in great detail. However, these contributions are not the traditional, immediate benefits we so commonly expect to find. The CWSI has educated a generation of scholars in Caribbean literature (many of whom are now encouraging their students to attend graduate school at the University of Miami), it has provided a space and intellectual environment for writers to produce novels, poetry and short stories that are the core of many courses at UM (and around the world) and it has firmly situated the University of Miami as a "hot spot" for Caribbean literature (as the readings by the Nobel Laureate, Derek Walcott, Edwidge Danticat, George Lamming and other countless award winning, world renowned writers suggests).

Recently, during a site visit, the team from the Institute for Women's Leadership (IWL), who funded our grant through a Ford Foundation–funded initiative, reaffirmed our sense that the University of Miami is sitting on a golden opportunity to distinguish itself from all other universities in the United States both because of its unique location in Miami (the gateway to the Caribbean and Latin America) and because of a hard-earned reputation as a site for rigorous research and scholarship in Caribbean literature. The comments, funding, and support offered by the Ford Foundation and the IWL have reopened and reinvigorated the debate about when and how the university can make its mark as a leading institution for research and scholarship in Caribbean culture. How then can we begin to attract the same kind of funding commitments to the humanities, and more specifically to Caribbean Studies at the University of Miami? Here are our recommendations:

- Formalize the Caribbean Literary Studies Program at the University of Miami with a budget, an equipped office, and staff. Currently, the program exists through its services to the intellectual community of the campus and its course offerings. Through the branding of the CLS program, the prestige of the works produced and the writers associated with the CWSI would become a formal part of the University of Miami's contribution to developing the field of Caribbean literature.

- Following on the previous recommendation to formalize the CLS program, the university would then be in a better position to begin the process of a national fund-raising campaign that might provide long-term funding in the form of an endowment supported by private donors as well as funding institutions such as the Ford Foundation, the National Endowment for the Humanities, and donors from the private sector.

- The CLS program should be allotted its own physical space at the University of Miami. As this chapter has shown, the faculty and students involved in the program are actively involved in several professional ventures (such as conference planning, electronic journal, and archiving projects). To date all of these activities and projects have been facilitated through sacrifices by faculty who give over their office space to accommodate the planning and delivery of these projects. In addition, physical space on the campus would increase the visibility of the program to potential donors and scholars to the University campus.

- Finally, and most importantly, we recommend that the University of Miami revisit the plans put forward to fund and support a national and international Caribbean Center for the Study of Caribbean Culture requested by the college in 2004. As this chapter shows, the integral components for such an endeavor are already in place and the University of Miami is ideally positioned culturally, geographically, and intellectually to undertake this important effort.

NOTES

1. The full text of the news release can be accessed at http://www6.miami.edu/UMH/CDA/ UMH_Main/1,1770,2593-1;57262-3,00.html.

2. The comments read during this 1994 meeting of the CWSI are from an original speech delivered on November 1982 in Grenada. Lamming, along with other writers, including Ngugi Was Thiongo, the Kenyan writer, later traveled to Carriacou where they addressed a smaller audience of teachers, community leaders, and members of the

New Jewel Movement. According to most sources, the original text of this speech no longer exists. Lamming is speaking from a transcribed version of the speech made on that occasion. . See Drayton and Andaiye 1992.

3. This passage, although originally presented at the 40th Annual Conference of the Barbados Workers Union on August 29, 1981, was transcribed from the CWSI Digital Media Archive where Lamming presented his historic speech, "The Honourable Member," as the first of a series of lectures during the Caribbean Writers Summer Institute in 1994.

REFERENCES

Gregory, Shelia T. 2001. "Black Faculty Women in the Academy: History, Status and Future." *Journal of Negro Education* 70 (3):24–138.

Drayton, Richard, and Karia Andaiye, eds. 1992. *Conversations: Essays, Addresses and Interviews 1953–1990.* Ann Arbor: University of Michigan Press.

Payne, Laura. 2002. Review of *Retaining African Americans in Higher Education: Challenging Paradigms for Retaining Students, Faculty and Administrators,* ed. Lee Jones. *Journal of Higher Education* 73 (5):652–659.

Smiles, Robin V. 2001. "Pursuing the Professorate." *Black Issues in Higher Education* (November 18, 20, 21):10–11.

PART FOUR

Administration–Faculty Collaborations for Diversity

10

Institutional Contexts for Faculty Leadership in Diversity

A University of California–Santa Barbara Case Study

JOSEPH CASTRO, SARAH FENSTERMAKER,
JOHN MOHR, AND DEBRA GUCKENHEIMER

In 1996 voters in California passed Proposition 209, a ballot initiative that disallowed more traditional forms of affirmative action at state-funded universities and colleges. A significant setback for progressives, it marked an initial decline in the diversity of incoming student cohorts (Anderson, 2002; Okong'o, 2006). Even so, the passage of Proposition 209 did not mark the end of affirmative action in California so much as the beginning of an era of programmatic initiatives to achieve greater inclusiveness for women and people of color through alternative means (Pusser, 2004; Douglass, 2007). Using the University of California–Santa Barbara (UCSB) as a case study, we examine how one university responded to the challenges of a shifting terrain for affirmative action policies and the experiences of faculty members with a new institutional context for change.

In this chapter, we first examine the changing political economy of higher education that helped determine the outcome of new policy initiatives on the UCSB campus. We also provide brief descriptions of some of the formal campus programs that constitute sites for faculty leadership in diversity. With that institutional context, and employing data from both qualitative interviews with faculty leaders and an online campus survey of the faculty, we explore four common themes. Our interest is in how faculty leaders define their own activities, including those involving diversifying the campus, how they came to be involved with change-making activities on the campus, their perception of the impact of these activities on policy outcomes, and the consequences of these activities for faculty careers and personal satisfaction. We then offer an analysis of significant interventions that helped contribute to innovative responses to the new post–affirmative action institutional milieu. The story is largely one of successes, as the campus moved to implement new initiatives to overcome the limits of Proposition 209 and brought about significant increases in student diversity. We conclude with a contemplation of some contradictions and costs—both personal and institutional—of faculty efforts at institutional change.

A Campus in Transition

With 20,000 students and 1,000 faculty members, over the last decade and a half the University of California–Santa Barbara has emerged as a leading Research I institution. It joined the elite Association of American Universities, garnered five Nobel Prizes in the nine years from 1998 to 2007, hosts nine national research centers, and was named by *Newsweek* as one of "America's hottest colleges" twice between 2002 and 2007. In the same time period the campus demographics shifted profoundly. Primarily known in the 1970s and 1980s as one of the "whitest" campuses in the UC system, UCSB has seen its proportion of underrepresented minority students climb steadily since the early 1990s to the point that the campus was recently singled out by the Quality Education for Minorities (QEM) Network as being one of the top ten research universities in the nation in the graduation of students of color at the baccalaureate and doctoral levels in the social, behavioral, and economic sciences. The QEM award recognized campus accomplishments in the five years after the passage of Proposition 209. If anything, we are doing even better today, as the number of new freshman of color has increased by about 32 percent since 2002. And, although the campus is smaller than most of the other UC schools, in fall 2006 UCSB admitted the largest number of Chicano/Latino freshman of any UC campus. Minority student enrollment now stands at 24 percent, with UCSB on the brink of a formal designation as a "Hispanic Serving Institution." All of this has occurred even as the university has had to adapt to the cessation of traditional affirmative action programs and as the competition for undergraduate enrollment has spiked sharply upward. Although the size of campus enrollment has changed little, the number of undergraduate applicants has more than doubled in the last decade (and nearly a third of undergraduate applicants in 2004 had a GPA of 4.0 or higher).

Although a great many factors contributed to changes of this magnitude, we are convinced that programs and policies put in place by UCSB administrators and faculty have been instrumental in bringing about the successful enrollment and retention of ever more students of color at UCSB. Recognizing success is different from explaining it, however. We know from our own experience and observation on a campus that values (and frequently valorizes) a "shared governance" model that faculty members have played an important role in bringing about this state of affairs, but there is a great deal more to investigate. Our qualitative interviews with faculty and our larger national online survey of faculties were motivated by a variety of questions: how do faculty actions come to accumulate over time to bring about genuine organizational change? What differences, if any, are there between faculty members who are simply good campus "citizens" and those that give themselves (and substantial time) over to the work of institutional change? What brings them to it, what sustains them, encourages or discourages them? Are there identifiable "careers" for faculty agents of organizational change? If so, do these careers have distinctive shapes, trajectories, or cycles that define them? We were also motivated by questions concerning the relationship between the broader organizational context in which faculty operate and the lives that they lead as change agents. Are there key institutions or institutional patterns inside the organization that facilitate or enable these faculty interventions? Is there a particular system of social organization or style of authority that promotes (or discourages) sorts of contributions?

One problem is the sheer complexity of institutional change surrounding diversity. Recruitment programs are intermixed with academic intervention schemes. Elementary schools are targeted along with every other kind of local school organization up to and including neighboring community colleges at Santa Barbara. Efforts to recruit a more diverse graduate student population have led to the development of partnerships with historically black colleges and universities (HBCUs) in Mississippi and Washington, DC. Campus climate is a key factor, as is campus reputation. Faculty hiring is a primary arena for intervention; so are grant submissions to the National Science Foundation (a central source of support for minority graduate students). Faculty attitudes about what counts as excellence, about the nature of social inequality, about how creative scholarship happens, about what leads to a productive intellectual atmosphere, and many more issues are tangled up in efforts to promote diversity and equity on the campus.

Another problem is that means and ends are loosely coupled. Rarely does an action lead to an immediately successful outcome. Far more often, the work of faculty leaders involves endless meetings that may not yield discernable results; writing applications for grants that may never be funded; arguing with colleagues over the meaning of "academic merit" while hiring and admissions committees continue to implement default selection principles; mentoring individual students whose sense of academic satisfaction may eventually translate into a more welcoming campus climate for students of color even as they recount ways in which the institution has failed them. Mixed in with a few programmatic successes are many individual failures and frustrations; indeed, it appears that the former are in some way fundamentally dependent upon the latter.

Our goal in the larger endeavor is to learn how faculty members understand and make sense of the current state of affirmative action and outreach policies and how they themselves come to be engaged in programs and policies that seek to promote greater diversity and equity in campus admissions, hiring, and retention practices. We are also keenly aware that none of this action happens outside of a complicated institutional context. In the next section we briefly describe some key examples of campus initiatives that provide opportunities for faculty activity that both shape the nature of faculty leadership in achieving diversity and set the stage for institutional change.

University of California–Santa Barbara Faculty-Led Campus Outreach Initiatives

Beginning in 1997, UCSB joined other UC campuses in significantly expanding its outreach (now referred to as academic preparation) efforts with K–12 schools and community colleges that serve large numbers of underrepresented students. These efforts are viewed by the UC system and by state political leaders as an essential tool to help increase student diversity in the aftermath of Proposition 209. Using an infusion of new funding generated by a rapidly growing state economy, UCSB and other UC campuses expanded outreach programs that had been in existence for more than thirty years (for example, the Early Academic Outreach program and Mathematics, Engineering and Science Achievement program) and developed several new programs.

Each of the UC campuses had some autonomy in designing outreach programs and allocating funds to these programs in order to meet regional needs. This autonomy was balanced by the need to adhere to a statewide framework for implementing and funding outreach programs that had been adopted by a systemwide task force (which had faculty involvement), approved by the UC Board of Regents and funded by the governor and state legislature.

The UCSB Chancellor's Outreach Advisory Board (COAB) was established in 1998 to help guide the campus's regional outreach efforts and serve as oversight for program allocations. COAB, which includes thirteen mostly senior faculty members and a vast array of staff "consultants" is the governing and policy board for outreach and provides advice to the chancellor and executive vice chancellor about outreach matters. With a broad charge by the chancellor to help stimulate new outreach initiatives on the campus, COAB designed and funded the Faculty Outreach Grants program (FOG) in 1999.

UCSB Faculty Outreach Grants Program

The FOG program, which is now administered by the UCSB Office of Academic Preparation, provides seed funding for new outreach initiatives designed by

UCSB faculty. Since it was established, FOG has allocated approximately $2.5 million in funds to more than thirty new faculty-led initiatives. The program has stimulated new faculty-led outreach efforts that serve underrepresented students and schools in the region. The programs have varied in size, scope, and lasting impact. Some programs have focused on a select group of underrepresented students within a school or several schools. Others have focused on all students within a particular school or schools. Many programs focus exclusively on working with students, while others include work with teachers, administrators, and families. The FOG program guidelines require that all faculty-led efforts serve the needs of the campus's "partnership" elementary and high schools (which have very large proportions of underrepresented students) and that these efforts seek to create a stronger college-going culture in these schools. These programs provide services to schools, churches, community centers, and the area's Indian reservation.

The FOG program has helped to bring faculty from different departments together around a common goal of preparing underrepresented students for higher education. Although state funds for these programs were reduced between 2001 and 2004 because of a decline in state tax revenues, UCSB allocates $150,000 of its own funds annually to sustain this successful program. Many of the new FOG program proposals come with matching support from schools, districts, or other academic units. UCSB faculty are also leading an effort to gain support from the UC Office of the President for a systemwide FOG program, which would provide matching funds for campus efforts that stimulate faculty involvement in new academic preparation programs. Following are five prominent examples of new faculty-led programs that were funded by the FOG program.

Kids in Nature. The Kids in Nature (KIN) program, established in 2001, was designed by faculty in the Department of Ecology, Evolution and Marine Biology to enrich the learning experiences of underrepresented and underserved youth in northern Santa Barbara County. KIN provides ninety mostly Latino and Native American fourth- and fifth-grade students in Santa Maria and Santa Ynez with a dynamic combination of hands-on, inquiry-based, classroom activities, interactive custom-designed computer simulations, and field trips to UCSB's Museum of Systematics and Ecology and to Sedgwick Reserve, one of seven Natural Reserve sites managed by UCSB. The activities focus on environmental science, botany, ecology, and habitat restoration. Students participate in habitat restorations at Sedgwick Reserve that engage them in authentic scientific and ecological experiences.

KIN provides students with opportunities to observe, engage in, and understand the importance of programs that preserve ecosystems, thus helping to develop an educated population able to make informed decisions about the future of the environment. KIN was funded solely by the FOG program in its early years but now also receives gifts from individuals and private entities such as the Santa Ynez Band of Chumash Indians, the Bella Vista Foundation, and the Shoreline Preservation Fund. It has also been nominated for a special award by the Governor's Office that honors model environmental education programs.

The Floating Lab. The Floating Lab was established in 2001 by faculty in the UCSB Marine Science Institute to provide students in grades six through eight with an educational research cruise experience in the ocean channel adjacent to the UCSB campus. Through the Floating Lab, students from our partnership schools and the nearby reservation of the Santa Ynez Band of Chumash Indians—including many who have never been to the beach, seen the ocean, or boarded a boat—are able to explore the Santa Barbara Channel. During the five-hour educational cruises, students and their teachers gain a rare and unparalleled glimpse into the complex and fascinating underwater world directly off the Santa Barbara coast.

The Floating Lab is funded through a partnership involving the U.S. National Oceanic and Atmospheric Agency and a local businessman who owns the high-speed catamaran that is used for the trips. UCSB has contributed more than $150,000 in funds from the FOG program to help outfit the boat with educational equipment and to cover some of the program's initial operating costs. Funds from federal research grants secured by UCSB faculty and from private donations have been used to help support the program, and more recently a number of individual gifts.

Project Excel. Project Excel is an academic preparation program that was designed by faculty in the English department, Gevirtz Graduate School of Education, and the Center for Black Studies. The program, begun in 2005, seeks to increase the number of African American, American Indian, and other underrepresented students in Santa Barbara–area schools and to strengthen the relationship between UCSB and these communities. Project Excel focuses attention on students and their families. It provides undergraduate student mentors for each program participant and a counselor to identify and help address the academic needs of the students. In addition, the program sponsors workshops that provide parents with resources to actively support the academic achievement of their students.

Project Excel was launched in 2005 with $55,000 in seed funding from UCSB, including $35,000 in FOG funding. The campus is actively supporting Project Excel's efforts to secure private funding to supplement the campus' contributions.

Robo-Challenge. Robo-Challenge is an academic preparation program designed by faculty in the College of Engineering that provides K–12 students from UCSB partnership schools with an opportunity to learn more about science and engineering while building robots. Students learn from UCSB faculty members and graduate and undergraduate engineering students about computer programming and mechanical design during the robot-building process. Robo-Challenge was established with funding from the UCSB FOG program in 2000 and has received additional outreach funds in subsequent years.

Summer Arts Institute. The Summer Arts Institute was an initiative designed by faculty members in the UCSB College of Creative Studies. It provides underrepresented students in Santa Barbara–area schools with an opportunity to expand their knowledge about the arts and to become better prepared for admission to a college or university. The five-week summer institute, which takes place at the UCSB College of Creative Studies, includes a focus on creative writing and journalism, photography, and painting and drawing. Students perform monologues and present stories and poems in the College's theater, go on field trips, and meet professional writers and artists.

While the Institute was open to underrepresented students in grades seven through ten throughout the local community, a special effort was made to recruit interested students who had also been served by Project Excel. This sharing of resources between FOG programs and other outreach efforts has enabled the campus to serve students more effectively. The Summer Arts Institute was the largest and most visible initiative of its kind that has been sponsored by the College of Creative Studies.

With that brief introduction to what sorts of outreach programs populate the campus, we turn to a description of the methods used to identify and survey faculty leaders.

The Data Sets

This chapter draws on a preliminary analysis of two data sets to address the questions surrounding the relationship between institutional contexts and faculty leadership in diversity. The first is a qualitative data set made up of thirty faculty members engaged in one or more specific domains of campus diversity work. The second is drawn from the UCSB portion of an eight-campus survey of faculties across the country.[1]

The UCSB Interviews

The qualitative interviews were conducted as a local campus project in its own right and as a way of developing relevant question areas for the larger survey previously described.[2] The sampling frame that we proposed was complex. Rather than relying on a convenience sample of faculty leaders in diversity efforts known to us, we made a decision to sample faculty systematically according to the types of projects they were engaged in or what we refer to as domains of faculty activity. We chose this approach for several reasons. Establishing specific sites or locales of diversity activism allowed us to create a systematic framework for identifying faculty diversity leaders. This provided us with a practical basis for establishing a controlled sampling frame. By choosing specific activity domains, we have been able to vary our research design parameters to maximize certain identifiable features of faculty leadership and commitment. Specifically, we selected our five research sites (out of a larger universe of possible candidates) in order to maximize several strategic goals. We sought to identify a variety of locales: those in which faculty have been key players and initiators; those that have had significant impacts (or significant potential impacts) on campus diversity; those that reflect the broad range of activities being pursued on campus (such as local/extra-local, campuswide/department specific, student/faculty, race/gender); those that strike us as being particularly innovative or distinctive; those that reflect a broad range of outcomes (successes as well as failures); those that may have some effect—positive or negative—on subsequent faculty participation. After much discussion we settled on five sites (at four initiative levels).

Campus level—local initiative. The Chancellor's Advisory Committee on the Status of Women is a long-standing campus administrative committee that each year identifies particular areas of investigation and recommendation directly to the Chancellor. The Chancellor's Outreach Advisory Board (COAB) includes thirteen mostly senior faculty members who act as the campus' governing and policy board for outreach programs. The board provides advice to the chancellor and executive vice chancellor on all outreach-related matters.

Campus level—extra-local initiative. The W. K. Kellogg Foundation–supported ENLACE (Engaging Latino Communities for Education) y Avance ("Get Ahead") Project is a regional outreach initiative aimed at increasing the number of Latino students who are academically prepared to enroll in higher education institutions. ENLACE y Avance is a partnership that proposes to collectively assess the needs of the local Latino community (see http://research.ucsb.edu/ccs/enlace/abstract.html.)

Academic department level—local initiative. The COAB-sponsored Faculty Outreach Grants program provides seed funding for new outreach initiatives led by UCSB faculty. Since 1999, more than $2 million in funding has been allocated for these projects.

Academic department level—extra-local initiative. There are currently four NSF-sponsored IGERT (graduate training grant) projects on campus; each has a formal obligation and commitment to encourage graduate student diversity.

We then identified all of the individuals who had ever officially participated in any of these five organizational arenas and used this to construct a list of interview subjects. Each of us has performed various official administrative roles on the campus: Castro was the campus affirmative action officer and directed campus K–16 outreach; Fenstermaker was founding chair of the Chancellor's Outreach Advisory Board and served as faculty chair of the Chancellor's "Post-209" Diversity Task Force; and Mohr was associate dean for the Graduate Division and directed the campus Alliance for Graduate Education Program (AGEP) program. As a result, we quickly realized that if we wanted to obtain impartial data we needed to employ surrogates to conduct the interviews. We hit upon the idea of teaching a graduate methods seminar that would focus on the topic of how to conduct research on diversity matters in a university setting. We titled the course "Researching Institutional Diversity" and team-taught the course in autumn 2005. Six graduate students (some from the sociology department, some from the Graduate School of Education) participated.

We began the course with theoretical issues. We sampled from the professional literature on modern universities and brought our own cumulative expertise on the politics of diversity in higher education into the classroom for discussion. We then worked with the students, who were assigned readings on the interview method, to devise an interview schedule for our project. This took several weeks and involved much iteration, since we wanted to be sure that the questions we posed to respondents would resonate with their experience, and we wanted to be sure that our student interviewers were comfortable with whatever paths the respondent drew them down. We then role-played the interviews with a video camera and finally divided the students into three teams of two and sent them into the field to conduct interviews. The thirty interviews were recorded, and most took about an hour and a half, although some ran longer. The student interviews provide the foundation for the results. For this preliminary analysis, we identified six interviews with faculty members drawn from campus locations consistent with our interest in the five domains of diversity activity described earlier, and who constituted a diverse group in age, level of activity, professional rank, and longevity on the campus.

The group was composed of three men and three women. Four are people of color (one Latino, one Filipino, one Haitian American, and one South Asian), and five are tenured. Three are from social science departments, one is from science, and two are from education. Each respondent is known to be someone who can be called upon for committee service related to diversity and equity. For this analysis, it is the commonality across respondents, and not their differences, that is our primary focus. Moreover, we cannot here unequivocally assert any particular relationships; we can only speculate about productive future paths to pursue. Thus the picture is incomplete and suggestive, but nevertheless it is an important first step in analysis.

Surveying the UCSB Faculty

After completing the thirty in-depth interviews with faculty chosen because of their high profile in change-making activities on campus, we shifted our attention to a second phase of the research concerned with the broader contours of faculty engagement on campus. We constructed a twenty- to thirty-minute online survey and invited the entire faculty to participate.[3] The survey was intended to assess how our colleagues conceive of their role in campus governance and to map the distribution of faculty participation in various types of activities across the university and the broader professional field. We had several goals. Although our primary interest was in gaining a better understanding of the causes, consequences, and contributions of faculty engagement in campus diversity efforts, we wanted to contextualize those activities in terms of the broader range of faculty participation in the life of the campus. To this end we asked faculty members to tell us about their experience across a wide range of campus functions, from academic planning and student conduct committees to faculty housing, campus parking, and academic senate meetings. We also sought to assess how active individual faculty had been across a broad swath of professional responsibilities, from sitting on graduate student committees, teaching classes, and serving as department chairs to working with national disciplinary associations, scientific academies, and other types of scholarly communities. We also used the survey as an opportunity to learn something about faculty attitudes toward the institution, asking questions such as whether respondents felt that the campus was devoting too little or too much attention to student diversity, campus climate, and pay equity matters for women and underrepresented faculty. Finally, we constructed separate sections of the survey that was administered only to respondents who, on the basis of their responses, were identifiable as particularly active in diversity matters or who had served in central campus administrative roles.

From the outset, our goal was to forge an analytic connection between our understanding of individual faculty motivations and institutional climate that encourages or deters faculty choices to participation. In this chapter, we use preliminary data from both survey and interview to illustrate four themes that emerged in preliminary interviews and that we believe will illuminate the connection between individuals and the institution. This connection is found in its more general form in sociological discourse as the relation between individual agency and social structure. Our interests in this study follow that of Philip Abrams (1972, 227) in his assertion of a "sociology of process," where "[s]ociety must be understood as a process constructed historically by individuals who are constructed historically by society." That idea is meaningful for our purposes as it points to the imperfect but nonetheless obvious relation between the constrained, self-interested, maneuvered choices of individual faculty and the changing character and practices of institutions over time. Four themes are explored in this analysis: understandings of "diversity work"; biography; respondent accounts of barriers to institutional participation; and visions of an institutional change. We believe each can provide insight into how faculty members understand their place in an institutional diversity effort, and together they can provide a road map for change. With these organizing themes, the data from both survey and interview hint at the relationship between individual action and institutional change.

Four Overarching Themes

Understandings of Diversity

Each interview respondent was asked explicitly about his or her definition of diversity in the context of the institution. Some emphasized issues of inequity more than others, with most clearly resistant to relegating diversity to the easy catchall of multiculturalism. For example, one woman of color said,

> How do I define diversity? Embracing cultures, modes of being, modes of thinking, modes of functioning, and exhibiting respect for a variety of perspectives. . . . It is not about, you know, let's celebrate Chicano dance and eating this Japanese food near the Multicultural Center. It has a strong political element in it and it takes courage to stand up for it, you know?

Another woman of color immediately offered a critique:

> I should say that I see diversity work as being antiracist work. I don't like the term [diversity], I feel it is overused . . . so I don't like it because I think I like the notion where you have a sense of power and equality embedded in it . . . I prefer "antiracist" work, because it's got an edge to it.

A senior white woman scientist came at it from an apparently different angle with an emphasis on tolerance:

> What I kinda want more than diversity is tolerance . . . I've had to spend my whole life going against expectations . . . I would like it if future generations didn't have to. Now, I'm working to get rid of that culture of expectations. You need lots of different kinds of people to be able to accept that they can all make different kinds of contributions.

Finally, one of the respondents immediately focused on difference as the central focus:

> "Diversity" is just a gloss for covering all kinds of difference and I'd like to think that it covers differences in class, differences in country of origin, differences in language, differences in sense of values, and then see if we can do something, not just celebrate . . . What are we going to do with difference? I don't want to pretend, but it sure would be nice if we could get people who are fundamentally different from one another to talk, to be clear, about how they're different.

Beyond abstract definitions of diversity, we also found fascinating the ways in which faculty made sense of their specific activities, and the nature of those activities in their larger worldviews:

> I think of my whole career in the sense of what I write about and what I teach and the professional service I do is about diversity. But there are two levels for me: the level where you are engaged in whatever it is that you are researching . . . really the scholarship part and then there's another level of you know, more administrative work, more systematic work . . . in you know, trying to bring in more students of color on campus and working toward retention.

Despite their uniform discomfort with the term "diversity," their responses to our question about what "diversity work" they were engaged in gave us a sense of how faculty members grant more or less value to their various activities. Some see valuable work in the day-to-day service in specific programs and committees; others view value primarily in pushing for systemic change in infrastructures and policies directed to diversity. Some locate their primary activities at the department level, some the campus committee, some within the classroom. This suggests that faculty may sometimes judge themselves as unengaged if they are not participating at a level or location they judge to be valuable. What "counts" with faculty—for themselves and others—as institutional change agents sheds light on the institution/faculty leader connection for change:

> I think I am doing very little at the moment that is explicitly antiracist. . . . But certainly I try to make my classes friendly for students of color and for all sorts of students who may not have a certain sense of . . . entitlement, is all I can call it. . . . It's part of your everyday life, you're dealing with it all the time.

Our senior woman scientist might not have "counted" the following activity when she described diversity (or "tolerance") work, but it obviously figured in her account of what she felt was important:

> Inevitably, on both kinds of committees, the first list of candidates will never include a woman . . . I say, "Well, wait a minute. How come there

aren't any women on this list?" And then they'll go, "Well, who could it
be?" And you go, "How about so and so?" And they say, "Oh, yeah, so
and so. She's really good. Put her on the list."

One difference we see hinted at in these preliminary data is something
we will explore in future work: the way in which discourses about diversity
vary by discipline. At the same time, we will also be alert to the ways in which
participation in diversity activities by faculty from across disciplinary
divisions creates a common vocabulary and sensibility about what should be
involved in the work of institutional change.

Biography

Interview respondents were asked to tell their "stories" of how they came to
be involved in diversity-related activities, how their experiences mattered to
their choices, and how their activities have changed over time. Of course, as
a managed sort of self-presentation, such stories inevitably privilege some bits
of information over others. Thus, their value comes not just from the "facts"
of the matter but also from selected content of the narrative. These stories
combine elements of the underlying motivations for professional activities
that carry little extrinsic reward and of the continuing satisfactions that reside
in the experience of diversity work.

As one might expect, some of our colleagues marked the beginning of
their consciousness about diversity because they were "onlys" within the
academy. One of our respondents was at one time the only black woman working full-time within academia in Great Britain; another was for many years the
only woman in her department. Another recalls a childhood of discrimination
and denied opportunity in a Texas border town that motivated a lifetime of
political activism. Another spent his time in college as a community outreach
worker, serving neglected urban populations. Especially for the faculty of
color, experiences with racism and tokenism propel them to activism:

> So I was part of the black community in England. My mother taught in
> . . . a South Asian area of London. And so basically I knew what racism
> is and was and so . . . Also in 1960 was Sharpsville, and in 1970; 1970 was
> the tenth anniversary of Sharpsville, which was the massacre of people
> in South Africa. And that had a huge effect on me. And so I came to
> know about race and racism and then I went to university and then it
> was clear you had to get involved, you know, in antiracist issues.

We found some suggestion that past experience becomes the lens
through which all institutional efforts are viewed; certainly earlier political
lessons are likely to affect one's expectations later:

> And I'm thinking about the outreach work that I started a long time ago
> [community organizing in college] where things were much more

aggrieved, people there were starving. . . a process that was much more difficult, much more urgent. Much more urgent than what outreach and diversity on this campus are about.

And from our respondent who now works on educational issues directly:

I think school brutalizes people. . . . I think school falls short, for people, including me. So that's what I brought to my graduate study.

The survey data provide a much wider angle on motivations for diversity work. Respondents who were identified as active participants in diversity-related endeavors were asked an additional question to rate the importance of various factors in drawing them into and sustaining their commitment to these endeavors. Among factors cited as being the most important motivators was the sense that this work was "morally important" and that it was "intrinsically satisfying." Least important as a motivator was the promise of material or professional rewards for their efforts. Respondents differed quite a bit among themselves in their patterns of response to these questions, however. Underrepresented minority (URM) faculty were more likely than other respondents to identify a larger number of these motivations as being important to them (the URM variable was significant in nine out of the thirteen models). This is also true to a lesser degree among those faculty who were distinctive for being particularly active, as measured by their reported levels of participation in a wide range of activities. In other words, those faculty members who are most actively engaged in diversity activities are also the most likely to find affinity with a broad range of motivational factors.

More specifically, those faculty members with the most marginalized identities in the academy—women, people of color, and scholars who identified as lesbian, gay, bisexual, or transgender (LGBT)—were significantly more likely to identify with statements such as "Having experienced being marginalized myself, I empathize with underrepresented and other marginalized students" and "Earlier in my life, I was helped by programs such as the ones I am involved in."[4] Interestingly, full professors were significantly less likely to identify with these motivating factors, perhaps a reflection of the fact that this population of change agents includes more senior scholars who entered the academy at a time when little support or mentoring was available. Disciplinary differences were also apparent. Social science faculty members were significantly more likely than other scholars to identify their participation "in social/political movements earlier in my life that have led me to be motivated in the ways that I am." In contrast, engineering faculty members were significantly less likely to identify with more the personalized motivations such as "giving back" after having been helped in their own lives by programs or by mentors. Faculty members in the sciences were significantly less likely than other scholars to associate this work with any kind of professional or material rewards, perhaps because they are more tightly connected to a system of professional rewards that are orthogonal to these types of endeavors.

Barriers to Individual Participation

While respondent understandings of diversity figured centrally in the interviews, they rarely stood alone or apart from observations about the institutional climate in which the work was done. For some, this meant understanding their participation to run against the grain of expectations about scholarly work. For others, diversity-related work represented a responsibility that fell to them because so few others were engaged with it. For example, our senior woman scientist explained:

> So, as a board member [of a UC institute], I was automatically put on the diversity committee, so it kind of made me mad, because I should think they would also want my opinion on scientific programs, but anyway, I'm always put on the diversity committee and everybody on the diversity committee, except for the head of the institute, were either women or minority persons.

Here is highlighted the perennial complaint of the underrepresented academic: the sort of service demanded from women and faculty of color is essential to the workings of the institution, yet at an individual level little credit and less respect are granted for such service. The respondent goes on:

> This is like one of my biggest pet peeves, it's like now that they've got a few women and minorities it's like, well, we'll just wash our hands of this diversity thing, and it's gonna be their problem.

For our untenured respondent, the tension between his activities related to diversity and his understanding of scholarly expectations was quite explicitly felt and expressed:

> It's not like I can think of my scholarly work without thinking about it [work on K–12 outreach]. So, I've got a couple of, one project with college admissions, which I think would be super-interesting that would be completed next year. But that's next year, and in the meantime, it just looks like I'm there screwing around. . . . I mean you get the questions: "What's out, what have you sent out?" You know, if I'm in here meeting with students for an entire day I'll get a look. I've been told I've been meeting with too many students.

This young academic is worth quoting at some length, since, more than the "veterans" we spoke with, he was not reticent when talking about the contradictions or the satisfactions:

> For me it's hard, because I don't need an incentive to do it. It's its own incentive. I find it terrifically fulfilling. . . . But for people, especially

younger faculty, the pressure is tremendous, way more than I ever
realized when I was in grad school. The pressure is tremendous to
become a scholar in the model of the scholars who are already here. . . .
There is not a lot of existing institutional space to do it [diversity work],
and, it only gets recognized, it only gets valued as something that is in
addition to the stuff you're supposed to be doing.

The "senior" version of this familiar complaint is burnout. In our
interviews we found evidence that the committed individuals are deeply
affected by repeated (and seemingly failed) efforts to make change. As the
following quote exemplifies, even as those experienced in diversity work know
that the struggle must be a protracted one, they nevertheless register the
exhaustion that follows repeated attempts to make a difference:

I remember that first year I tried to go to a few donors to get some
funding to expand that project and I couldn't get people to respond at
that time. And I just laughed five years ago when everybody was waiv-
ing the outreach banner. And it's like some of us have tried, you know?

The survey data convey a clear picture across faculty leadership of this
"mixed bag" of satisfactions and ambivalences. We asked those respondents
who were identified as being more active in diversity-related activities
whether they felt supported by their department for their work in this
domain, and the answer was not encouraging. Only 13 percent of the respondents reported feeling supported to any degree, while fully two-thirds of the
respondents disagreed with the statement "I believe that my department
acknowledges and is supportive of my diversity and equity related efforts."
Although women faculty members tended to feel more supported then their
male colleagues, the difference was not statistically significant.

The matter is more complex than this, however. We also asked two
seemingly contradictory questions. We asked whether the respondents agreed
or disagreed with the statement "I believe my diversity/equity related activities
have impeded my success as an academic." Immediately after that we turned
around and asked them whether they agreed or disagreed with the statement
"I believe my diversity/equity related activities have enhanced my success as
an academic." The responses of underrepresented minority faculty members
were instructive. Fully 62 percent of them agreed that their participation in
diversity initiatives had impeded their academic careers. But when asked
whether the work had enhanced their academic careers, 27 percent answered
affirmatively (compared to only 14 percent among the non-URM faculty). This
contradictory response was also borne out in the regression analyses where
the variable for URM faculty was significant in both models, suggesting that
faculty members of color both feel more empowered and more encumbered

by their participation in diversity initiatives.[5] Here again, disciplinary differences are apparent. Engineering faculty members were significantly less likely than their colleagues elsewhere on the campus to believe that their diversity activities had no negative impacts on the academic careers, while faculty in the sciences were significantly more likely to assert that their participation in these activities has not helped their academic careers.

Visions of Institutional Change

When we asked our respondents how they think about progress made by the institution, their answers combine to suggest how change in the academic world works. Further, and by extension, we get a sense of how these faculty members envision an institution truly committed to diversity. For example, from our eldest respondent, we hear:

> Well, it is the whole philosophy of what the university is about. We're not here to educate everybody. We're here to educate the elite. Those who are a three-point something or other. Or who get certain GREs . . . Now to me outreach should be such that it makes every kid eligible to go to the university . . . That's a different mindset than what we've got which is not everybody can go.

This suggests that faculty efforts are highly constrained by a philosophy of education that contradicts those very efforts. How, we might ask, will success be defined under these conditions?

A faculty member of color in the social sciences described his vision of what real organizational change would be:

> What I'm talking about is a much more ongoing relationship where people kind of ebb and flow as part of the infrastructure . . . because . . . it's one thing to get students here for the BA; it's another to get them at the larger levels of professionalization. So I can't tell you what works, but I can tell you what would really make things feel better and that is creating a different kind of culture. It's not climate. We've got climate. It's a systemic reorganization of the way in which institutions flow into one another. It's a question of will too. . . . Does the UC have the will to transform in a much more radical way those relationships across institutions?

One view that was hinted at was the idea that administrators are disingenuous about real change, and interested in a numbers game only:

> Sometimes I think [institutional diversity efforts] are just a matter of numbers. It's more of a public relations matter, than a sort of deeply held ethical matter. It's a social justice matter.

Recent Institutional Changes

We close with a description of some of the recent institutional changes and programmatic initiatives that have resulted from UCSB faculty engagement in diversity work. These changes represent long-term intensive work on the part of those committed to diversity and foreshadow future efforts to diversify.

In early 2005, the University of California system made two significant institutional changes that reflect strong support for faculty work on diversity issues. First, the systemwide Academic Council approved a major change to the Academic Personnel Manual, which includes all policies relating to appointment and promotion of faculty throughout the UC system, to take into account faculty engagement in diversity activities during reviews for promotion. In addition, for the first time, evidence of efforts to maintain and increase diversity will be taken into account when deans and department chairs are evaluated. While this is a systemwide change, UCSB faculty, including the principal investigators for this project, played a leadership role in planning a systemwide Faculty Outreach Conference in late 2003 that provided a critical and timely momentum needed to get the policy change proposed and adopted, becoming effective in July, 2006.[6]

Another major systemwide institutional change was the adoption in January 2005 by the UC Board of Regents of a statement reaffirming the importance of work with P-16 students and schools in California. This public statement, which acknowledged the UC system's history as a land grant institution, forcefully articulated the vital role that UC students, faculty, and staff must play in providing more educational opportunities for the most disadvantaged students in the state:

> The University affirms that a fundamental part of its mission is to engage in efforts to promote the academic achievement and success of all students, including students who, because they are educationally disadvantaged and underrepresented, they need additional assistance. . . .
> The Regents of the University of California request that the President, in collaboration with the Governor, the Legislature, the other segments of California public education, and business and community leaders, develop and implement a plan for meaningful, consistent, and long-term funding of the UC academic preparation and educational partnerships infrastructure and communicate the importance of these collaborative efforts to the Governor and the Legislature.

The statement was strongly supported by key faculty at UCSB and the other UC campuses.

At the local level, UCSB has experienced some unique successes in its efforts to further diversify students, faculty, and staff. UCSB was one of only three universities on the West Coast to receive the QEM award referred to earlier in the chapter; the others are UCLA and UC Berkeley. Along with Howard University, UCSB is the smallest institution in terms of student enroll-ment of those honored. The award recognized the diversity of enrollments between 1996 and 2002. Since that time, the number of new freshman of color has increased by about 30 percent. This change has been fueled by a recent surge in Chicano/Latino undergraduates enrolling at UCSB. For the academic year 2007–2008 UCSB admitted the largest number of freshmen from underrepresented groups of any UC campus.

There also appears to be new institutional momentum within the UC system to increase the diversity of its graduate students and faculty. Along with other UC campuses, UCSB recently received a $10 million Alliance for Graduate Education Program grant from the National Science Foundation, which aims to increase the number of women and students of color at the graduate level. In 2005 UCSB joined other UC campuses and Stanford University, Cal Tech, and the University of Southern California to create the California University Pipeline Project. The goal of this project is to create a formal network of research universities in California to share information and work on joint projects that increase the diversity of graduate students and faculty. UCSB also combined with UCLA and UC Berkeley in the receipt of a new three-year $900,000 NSF grant titled the University of California Diversity Initiative for Graduate Study in the Social Sciences (UC-DIGSS) intended to promote greater graduate diversity in the social sciences.

Conclusion: Contradictions and Ambivalences

In all of these successes, UCSB faculty members have played key, even vital, roles. For understandable reasons, the faculty members interviewed for this project focused most of their comments on the experience of the long strug-gle to increase diversity. Yet there is mounting evidence that their actions are making a significant difference in changing institutional structures and practices in ways that support, rather than inhibit, efforts to recruit students and faculty of color.

Throughout the interviews we got a strong sense that the story here is one of contradictions, both for the institutions and for the individuals who seek change in them. For institutions, an increasingly perplexing problem is how to achieve a difficult secondary set of goals about which there is deep resistance, in order to fulfill a primary mission. Specifically, the University of California, a public land grant institution with a long history of service to the larger community, must reconfigure itself to address the charge to educate an increasingly diverse population of California's citizens and attract the highest-quality faculty to remain competitive in research. Thus, at each turn, fulfilling the primary mission necessitates diversifying faculty and student bodies. Particularly for some active faculty members, that contradiction is manifested in efforts to push and pull the institution to diversify. Such efforts produce great intrinsic satisfactions but also carry great costs in energy, reputation, and even future opportunity. This results, we believe, in a disconnect between the progress institutions may in fact make, which is all but missed by those who have taken responsibility for making change day-to-day. In our interviews, we get a sense a discouragement and even cynicism about the potential for meaningful, lasting change. We believe this perception sits side-by-side with very real evidence of significant change in how the institution proceeds regarding student and faculty diversity. It appears that the diversity glass is indeed half-empty and half-full, and it is this difference in perception that does more to discourage faculty diversity leaders than anything else.

> And I think we did some good, you know. And I can talk about this project more specifically, you know, about its shortcomings and why I'm not doing it anymore—we just don't have the number of black faculty. It's just too much.

This is exactly the kind of "success" that may be overlooked by faculty members who carry with them the accumulated fatigue of long-term struggles. As one faculty member said upon being notified of the Quality Education for Minorities award given to UCSB in early 2005:

> How do you accept an award you're kind of embarrassed to receive? We have so far to go.

Each institutional advance requires so much effort at so many levels and is so shot through with political machinations that the demands on individual commitment may simply be too great. Our own future research into faculty diversity leaders will address the question of how new generations of faculty will find enough satisfaction in the navigation of such treacherous institutional waters to make the journey at all.

NOTES

A preliminary version of this chapter appears in "Reaffirming Action: Designs for Diversity in Higher Education" (Rutgers University Institute for Women's Leadership, 2006). We gratefully acknowledge the help of our colleagues at the Rutgers University Institute for Women's Leadership, Paolo Gardinalli of the Benton Survey Research Center at UCSB, and the participants in our graduate seminar, "Researching Institutional Diversity." Thanks also to our UCSB faculty colleagues who graciously agreed to be interviewed and all our survey respondents. We also thank UCSB Admissions Director Christine Van Giesen and the UCSB Office of Academic Preparation. Funds for this research were provided by the Ford Foundation, the Rutgers University Institute for Women's Leadership, and the UC–Santa Barbara Academic Senate.

1. During the 2006–2007 academic year, the faculties at the Santa Barbara and Irvine campuses of the University of California, Clark-Atlanta University, the University of Maryland, the University of Missouri, Rutgers University, Smith College, and the University of Vermont were surveyed. Data reported in the current chapter are drawn from just the UC–Santa Barbara faculty survey. Three additional campuses were planned for survey during the 2007–2008 academic year.

2. We believe that this way of employing data at various points in the research process allows us to overcome some of the limitations of each data set: the qualitative material informs the construction of the survey, the survey takes the findings well beyond the confines of a few individuals, and the interviews shed light on the survey findings and ultimately on any additional interviews that are conducted.

3. With just over 1,000 faculty members on our campus, we received 263 responses to the online survey, for a response rate of close to 25 percent.

4. Results reported here are derived from multivariate (OLS) regression models (run in SAS version 9.1) in which dependent variables reflected respondents' subjective response to this question: "The following are factors that faculty frequently cite as being important in encouraging involvement. Please indicate just how important each motivator is for you." Respondents were given an option of ranking each of thirteen factors as being "Not a factor," "A small factor," "A moderately important factor," "An important factor," or "A very important factor." Predictor variables included a range of demographic measures (gender, race, sexuality, father's education, number of years since completion of highest degree, and whether the respondent was born in the United States) as well as a number of academic factors (academic rank, whether the respondent held a joint appointment in more than one academic department, academic discipline, and a constructed variable that assessed how active the respondent was in campus governance activities). All variables discussed in the text as being significant are statistically significant coefficients with a p value of .05 or less. Adjusted R-squares ranged from a high of .40 for models predicting responses to the statement "Having experienced being marginalized myself, I empathize with under-represented and other marginalized students" and the statement "Earlier in my life, I was helped by programs such as the ones I am involved in," to a low of .05 for the model predicting responses to the statement "Other people in my life were important in drawing me into these activities."

5. Again, results reported here are from OLS regressions in which respondents' subjective assessment of the costs and benefits of their participation in diversity initiatives was compared to a battery of predictor variables.

6. On our campus and a few others within the UC academic personnel system, conversations are beginning that may result in an expectation that all faculty members will engage in some effort to recruit and/or retain underrepresented students and faculty or work toward improving the campus climate for minorities and women.

REFERENCES

Abrams, Philip. 1972. *Historical Sociology*. Ithaca, NY: Cornell University Press.
Anderson, James. 2002. "Historical Perspectives." In *The Racial Crisis in American Higher Education*, ed. Phillip G. Altbach, 3–21. Albany: State University of New York Press.

Douglas, John. 2007. *The Conditions for Admission: Access, Equity, and the Social Contract of Public Universities.* Stanford, CA: Stanford University Press.

Okong'o, Edwin. 2006. "Prop. 209 Puts UC at Competitive Disadvantage, Says Officials." *Diverse Issues in Higher Education* 23 (20):1.

Pusser, Brian. 2004. *Burning Down the House: Politics, Governance, and Affirmative Action at the University of California.* Albany: State University of New York Press.

11

A Ripple Effect

The Influence of a Faculty Women's Caucus on Diversity and Equity at the University of Vermont

PEG BOYLE SINGLE AND DANNIELLE JOY DAVIS

In 1992, a small group of female faculty members representing fields in the humanities and social sciences sat around a small round table in one of the women's offices at the University of Vermont (UVM). The latest faculty demographics report had just been circulated. To the surprise of none, the number of both white women faculty members and faculty who were members of minority groups were severely underrepresented. Their discussion centered on what to do about it and how to organize themselves.

More than a decade later, their actions continue to have an influence on this small public research university in the Northeast. Some of the members of the Faculty Women's Caucus have changed, but their mission has remained the same: to identify where institutional policies or practices negatively influence equity and diversity, and to do something about it. Their actions have influenced the development of a campuswide faculty mentoring program, the composition of reappointment, promotion, and tenure (RPT) committees, and the offering of RPT workshops, practices around recruitment, retention, the availability of multiyear contracts for lecturers, and the equalization of faculty compensation. Recently, with the support of the Faculty Women's Caucus, a Diversity Faculty Caucus has been established. The ripple effect from the Faculty Women's Caucus continues to widen and to influence many, if not all, parts of faculty life at UVM.

This chapter documents the history of the Faculty Women's Caucus and the influences of its work. While issues of diversity and equity have been fought on the national stage, the stories of small groups of committed faculty members have not received enough coverage. This chapter addresses the deficiency of the documentation and heralds the University of Vermont Faculty Women's Caucus.

Like most research universities, UVM is a primarily white institution (PWI). And like most PWIs, UVM has an overrepresentation of Anglo faculty members and male faculty members. Along with the zeitgeist toward diversity in higher education, UVM has engaged in efforts to bring greater diversity to the university. While diversity and equity efforts occur throughout the university, these efforts are primarily housed within the President's Commission on Diversity and Inclusion, the Provost's Office of Multicultural Affairs, and the Diversity and Equity Unit. There are three additional commissions focusing on diversity: the President's Commission on Racial Diversity, the President's Commission on the Status of Women, and the President's Commission on Lesbian, Gay, Bisexual and Transgendered Equity.

For issues regarding race and ethnic diversity, UVM uses the acronym ALANA, which stands for African Americans, Latinos/as, Asian Americans and Native Americans. Diversity efforts are being conducted within the context of Vermont being one of the whitest states in the nation. In 2005, 95.9 percent of the Vermont population was classified as white not Hispanic compared with 66.9 percent of the U.S. population (United States Census Bureau 2007). UVM is housed within the most diverse county in the state, with 93.9 percent of the population being white not Hispanic (United States Census Bureau 2007), largely because of the employees recruited by the university. UVM often needs to engage in recruitment efforts outside the state to bring race and ethnic diversity to its student body, staff, and faculty.

As current (Single) and past (Davis) members of the UVM community, we began exploring the role of the Faculty Women's Caucus indirectly. One of us is the newly appointed director of the Faculty Mentoring Program and both of us are educational researchers who focus on the field of mentoring. We jointly applied for a grant to conduct an evaluation of the UVM Faculty Mentoring Program. This grant was submitted to the Rutgers University's Institute for Women's Leadership Reaffirming Action Grant Program, which was funded by the Ford Foundation.

To strengthen our grant application, we were encouraged to examine the role of faculty activism at UVM. This was not a difficult task, as we already knew that the Faculty Women's Caucus was responsible for the development of the Faculty Mentoring Program. As we dug more deeply, we found a much broader and deeper story about the ability of a small group of committed faculty members to help their institution become more equitable.

As we examined this story by interviewing some members of the Faculty Women's Caucus and through documentation review, the influence of the Faculty Women's Caucus became increasingly clear. These intertwining stories are common within the lives of feminists and women. The good works of a few dedicated individuals resonate within individual lives, groups, and institutions.

The Faculty Women's Caucus

The UVM Faculty Women's Caucus was initiated to be an informal caucus within the Faculty Senate. It has no budget. Nor does it have administrative support or resources. In spite of this, it has made regular and incremental changes at the institution.

Every year, the university institutional research office presents the annual demographics of the faculty members. Based on examination of this data and their knowledge of some of the challenges facing white female and minority faculty members, members of the Faculty Women's Caucus informally began offering workshops on the RPT process. These informal workshops were targeted toward those faculty members who research reported at that time as less likely to be in the kinds of informal networks that would provide them with information about the RPT process (Boice 1993). At UVM, the RPT process is referred to as the Green Sheet Process, in reference to the original forms, which were copied on light green paper.

One of the current members of the Faculty Women's Caucus got involved with the caucus through these events. The following quote illustrates how the workshops influenced her:

> I think the most important thing that they have done is with the Green Sheet Process. . . . [The Faculty Women's Caucus] provided a network and alternative senior faculty for junior faculty to consult with. . . . There's a lot of evidence that women faculty and faculty of color have this sort of imposter syndrome, that's a very hard thing to overcome. And really the faculty women's caucus, in doing these Green Sheet panels, really helped us to . . . overcome that, . . . (to) see ourselves as viable candidates for tenure, demystified the process, and communicated the message that the institution was a very fair place. So it really kind of reduced anxiety tremendously.

Today this member of the Faculty Women's Caucus is a full professor and an educational leader in her college.

In 1992, the institutional research office issued its first annual report on the demographics of faculty members. The percentages of women and minority faculty members were low. At that time, mentoring programs for faculty members were gaining interest and popularity as a mechanism for supporting female and minority scholars (Boice 1990; Boyle and Boice 1998; Ragins and Cotton 1991). The Faculty Women's Caucus decided to sponsor a faculty mentoring program by collaborating with the Women's Center. After the exchange of a number of memos, the Women's Center decided it did not have the funding to sponsor a mentoring group for female and minority faculty members.

The next course of action was to bring up the development of a faculty mentoring program through the Faculty Senate. One of the members of the

Faculty Women's Caucus was nominated to serve on the Executive Committee of the Faculty Senate. In that role, she introduced the idea of a mentoring program. Consequently, an ad hoc committee was established to research and explore the possibility of supporting a faculty mentoring program.

The ad hoc committee was made up of a second member of the original group of Faculty Women's Caucus members. The two other committee members were a faculty member who would later become provost and a faculty member who would become the chairperson of a humanities department. After writing and revising a draft program, the program was presented to the Faculty Senate. It was passed and implemented by the Provost's Office.

An additional member of the growing Faculty Women's Caucus was charged with pulling together and building the program. The original director of the University of Vermont Faculty Mentoring Program was given a one-course buyout to conduct a campuswide faculty mentoring program. Because of time constraints and based on the original charge of the program, she focused her energies on recruiting the new faculty members least likely to fall into informal but infinitely valuable networks within the university. She paid special attention to contacting the new female and minority faculty members and encouraged them to participate. Not surprisingly, many members of the Faculty Women's Caucus served as mentors to the new hires. For five years, until her retirement in 2004, the director of the Faculty Mentoring Program served in this capacity. During her tenure, the Green Sheet Workshops continued as a collaboration between the Faculty Women's Caucus and the Faculty Mentoring Program.

The Faculty Women's Caucus also sought to influence university policy regarding issues of multiculturalism and compensation for lecturers. One of the most prominent of the actions taken by the Faculty Women's Caucus occurred in 1996 (Warhol 1998). The student body at that time raised concerns about racism and the lack of diversity on the UVM campus and staged a series of protests. The president and provost at that time failed to address issues of racism on the campus, and the Faculty Women's Caucus called for a censure of the president and provost at a Faculty Senate meeting. The censure failed by a slim margin, but it helped to bring additional attention to these issues.

While the caucus was and is composed mainly of tenure-line faculty members, the caucus is open to lecturers. In the early to mid-1990s, the situation of lecturers came up regularly at the informal meetings of the caucus. At the time, lecturers were offered one-semester or one-year contracts and often received their contracts in the month of two before the academic year began. The Faculty Women's Caucus took up this issue because working conditions of the lecturers could be "framed as a feminist issue" (Warhol 1998, 223). This was the case because women were and still are overrepresented in lecturer and part-time teaching positions.

In order to influence university policy, the caucus had one of its members nominated and voted into the role of vice-chair for the Faculty Senate. From this platform, the vice-chair formed an ad hoc senate committee to review the issue. When a proposal to offer contracts to the lecturers was presented on the floor of the senate, the lecturers, who were voting members of the senate, came out in numbers to endorse the proposal. The proposal also had strong support from the chairpersons who oversaw departments that were dependent on lecturers to teach their undergraduate courses. Robyn Warhol, in an article on this situation, speculates that the chairs were very supportive of the lecturer's plight because many of them had close personal relationships with lecturers: "Was it a coincidence that each of those chairs but one happened also to be married to a lecturer? Or that the one who was not married to a lecturer had been herself a "faculty wife" and lecturer at UVM for many years?" (1998, 228).

The result was "qualified" even with strong faculty support. The administration resisted accepting the proposal until the proposal was changed so that "the possibility, rather than the certainty, of a contract" could be offered to the qualified lecturers (Kent 1998, 231). As this example demonstrates, not all the proposals put forth by the Faculty Women's Caucus were fully implemented. Still, these efforts had a ripple effect on the working conditions of lecturers. When the full-time faculty unionized and ratified its first contract in 2003, lecturers were included as members of the bargaining unit

The Faculty Women's Caucus also worked within the current system to get a more diverse perspective on important committees. As mentioned earlier, the caucus has nominated and then generated support for feminist candidates on university-wide committees and the Faculty Senate. Some of what may be the most important and influential committees on campus are the collegewide and university-wide standards committees. These committees review the dossiers of faculty members up for reappointment or tenure and offer recommendations to the dean or provost, respectively. Based on the import of these committees, the Faculty Women's Caucus began to make sure that a woman was on each of these committees who was well versed in the inherent discrimination in many of the evaluation measures of the university.

The result of having feminists on these committees was that they were informed about the institutional and academic practices that disadvantage women and minority faculty members and about how the accepted metrics for teaching and scholarship reflect this disadvantage. Research has repeatedly shown that regardless of teaching effectiveness, women received lower student evaluations (Basow 2000). Research has shown that different types of scholarship were rated higher or lower based on historical artifacts of field information or the sex of the scholar, and not on academic quality (Moody 2004; Wenneras and Wold 1997).

The first course of action was to identify women who were qualified to serve and then to campaign for their appointment. What caucus members soon found out was that they were coming up against a long-held institutional tradition that had been a holdover from earlier times. For example, a woman who was the mother of a young child was nominated to the campuswide Standards Committee. The committee met on Monday nights, as it had done for decades. It always had, it always would. Initially, changing the meeting to a more family-friendly time was not an option. The first woman decided to decline membership in the committee rather than cut into the time she spent with her family. The next year, another woman was nominated to and selected for the campuswide committee. This woman, too, had a young child. She, too, was told that the campuswide committee always met on Monday evenings. Always had, always would. Never before had this practice been questioned. She discussed the situation with the Faculty Women's Caucus, which sent a letter to the chair of the campuswide Standards Committee. The chairman received the letter and the recommendation well. As a result, the committee now meets during regular work hours. The chairman went on to be an associate vice president at the university.

The Faculty Women's Caucus has focused on changing the institutional culture and practices, where needed, to broaden the appeal of the university for all of its faculty members. Sometimes the work was done within the system; sometimes alternative routes were taken. The actions were swift, well chosen, and targeted. While these changes were being effected, the leaders who were the recipients of letters from the Faculty Women's Caucus reacted in various ways. Through the process, these leaders were exposed to issues pertaining to women and minority faculty members. As they moved up the ranks of the university, becoming deans, provosts, or associate vice presidents, they took these instances and lessons with them. As the influence of a ripple effect is unpredictable, so too is the influence of any activity that changes the way things are done.

The UVM Faculty Mentoring Program

As faculty members struggle with challenging workloads, we continue to be amazed at the willingness with which senior faculty members volunteer to serve as mentors. Traditionally, this has not been recognized as part of their service commitment. It does not bring in additional grant money and rarely will it end up in a collaborative published work. Senior faculty members volunteer for many reasons. Some have said they want to be mentors because they had received outstanding mentoring that greatly influenced their careers. Others note that they did not have the type of mentoring they had hoped for and wanted to spare new faculty members from that situation.

The senior faculty members serving as mentors are passing along what they have learned. They are providing support and insight into the workings of the university. They are reading papers and reviewing Green Sheet submissions. While these individual acts of support too often go unheralded, they provide the impetus for helping to support new faculty members and changing the way things are done at a small public university. These formal networks are particularly advantageous for the underrepresented scholars, whether women in science, mathematics, and engineering or minority scholars in all fields, who traditionally were left out of informal networks. With each meeting, these mentoring partnerships move the university toward greater community, diversity, multiculturalism, sexual pluralism, and gender equity.

The UVM Faculty Mentoring Program came directly out of activism on the part of the Faculty Women's Caucus. A member of the caucus became the founding director and set up a governance structure that continues to serve the program well. In addition, she kept the focus of the program on the original goal—to support the retention of women and minority faculty members. When she retired, there was some question about whether the program would continue. After a lapse of a semester, there was a call for nominations for a new director, and a series of interviews of internal candidates took place. The current director, one of the authors of this chapter, built on the strong foundation she inherited with the program and infused the initiative with some research-based features and procedures to broaden the reach and the efficacy of the effort. The program's expansion was made possible by funding beyond the one-course buyout offered to the previous director.

As both authors and educational researchers, we developed an extensive evaluation for the Faculty Mentoring Program. The evaluation focused on examining the protégés' experiences with the mentoring program.

Governance

The founding director of the Faculty Mentoring Program purposefully sought to situate the program as being cosponsored by the Faculty Senate and the Provost's Office. The Faculty Senate was the means by which the Faculty Mentoring Program was originated. The Provost's Office provided the course buyout, and later the salary, to support the directors.

This situation is advantageous for various reasons. The Faculty Senate is the voice of the faculty of the University of Vermont. This strong affiliation lends credence and support to the program. The cosponsorship by the Faculty Senate provides support and faculty input into the implementation of the Faculty Mentoring Program. The support of the Provost's Office is advantageous for obvious financial reasons. In addition, it supports the provost's focus on providing centralized faculty development. By situating the program within both of these strong leadership units, the program is both supported and protected. It allows the program to focus on its role of supporting faculty members and staying clear of any political zeitgeist blowing through the university.

In addition, the founding director recruited a Mentoring Advisory Group. This group is composed of faculty members across the university. Many have been at the institution for numerous years and thus provide invaluable feedback when matching protégés with mentors. A few are new and therefore can inform the group on the experiences of junior faculty. This advisory group provides advice and direction to the director not only in matching but also in deciding ways to develop programming to meet the strategic goals of the university and support the current group of new hires and faculty members. The president of the Faculty Senate is a sitting member of the Mentoring Advisory Group.

Demonstrating the Need for Faculty Mentoring

Early in the faculty mentoring movement questions were often raised about the necessity for faculty mentoring programs. Now, prospective faculty members ask about mentoring programs and professional development opportunities while they are visiting and being interviewed at campuses. Once tenure-track faculty members were the overwhelming majority of academics; now, various types of contingent faculty fill the needs of the university. As the times have changed, so has our knowledge about the efficacy of mentoring programs.

The Faculty Mentoring Program at UVM is open to all new faculty members and instructional staff. This includes not only tenure-track assistant professors but also research, extension, library, and clinical assistant professors. (For a detailed description of the UVM Faculty Mentoring Program and the research that influenced the implementation, see Single forthcoming.)

The Faculty Mentoring Program at UVM begins with matching. While it may seem intuitive to match mentors and protégés in the same departments, research suggests otherwise. In an early study of faculty mentoring programs, cross-department pairs had higher satisfaction ratings than pairs within departments (Boyle and Boice 1998). Apparently, the protégés appreciated being able to talk with someone outside their departments who would not be voting on them and who could serve as an impartial support. As a result, UVM's Faculty Mentoring Program pairs new hires with mentors outside their departments wherever possible. This does not undermine any mentoring that occurs, and should occur, within the department. Rather, the program advocates a multiple-mentor model. This model advocates the premise that new hires on today's campuses need to have an array of mentors to succeed: someone outside your department and college and someone inside.

The matching process only marks the beginning phase of the mentoring program. No longer can mentoring programs justify matching protégés with mentors and leaving them alone until the year-end survey needs to be completed. The knowledge base of the mentoring program literature has gone well beyond that. Now, not only is training for mentors, but training for protégés has become an important part of any structured mentoring program (Kasprisin, Single, Single, Muller, and Ferrier forthcoming).

A newer and increasingly popular feature of mentoring programs is the notion of coaching. Coaching emails are monthly messages sent to all participants in the Faculty Mentoring Program in the form of "Faculty Development Tips and UVM Trivia." These short, concise messages provide a link for recipients or mentoring pairs who want to gain additional information about the topic under discussion. Topics range from advocating the use of a "regular writing routine" (Single 2007, 167) to information about the upcoming free jazz concerts being performed by the students in the music department.

Coaching messages serve multiple purposes. First, they provide incentives for the mentors and protégés to stay in contact (Boice 1992). If the email exchanges have lagged, the coaching prompts provide an opportunity to start up the exchanges again. Second, the coaching messages provide educational material to the participants and help broaden the scope of their interactions. Third, they allow the program coordinator to stay in contact with the mentors and the protégés. Keeping the lines of communication open allows the program coordinator to consult, to troubleshoot, and to rematch, as needed and as resources allow (Single and Muller 2001).

In addition to training and coaching, community building or group mentoring is an important part of any mentoring program. Group meetings encourage participants to develop a sense of affiliation with the whole organization and are often identified as the "best part" of a mentoring program (Boyle and Boice 1998). These group meetings allow for peer mentoring and increased opportunities for networking and information exchange (Chesler, Single, and Mikic 2003). These group-mentoring opportunities are one-time sessions focused on issues of importance to the faculty members. A series of what we are calling Group Discussions are being offered that address issues such as "Time Management and Scholarly Productivity," "Faculty Governance at UVM: The Role of the Faculty Senate," and "Time Management and Teaching Effectiveness." Not surprisingly, we recruited heavily from the Mentoring Advisory Board for senior faculty members who would be willing to present.

In advertising the event to the members of the Faculty Mentoring Program, we made our intentions explicit. We wrote, "While these groups are topic-focused, they will also provide an excuse for us to get out of our departments and to meet colleagues in other departments." In addition, we kept these group discussions very informal. By focusing on keeping the group discussions informal, we also sent the message that we did not want these events to be another "to do" on the long list of responsibilities of new hires. As a result, the following message was prominently placed on the flyer promoting the group discussions:

> We will be keeping these groups very informal, so if you need to arrive late or leave early, please don't let that stop you from attending. These are family-friendly workshops. You are welcome to bring your children; however, there may be times when it would be appropriate to take your child or children out in the hallway. Similarly, if you need to keep your cell phone on, please do, and if you have to take a call, please step outside.

Mentoring as Faculty Activism: Qualitative Data and Analysis

While the popularity of faculty mentoring programs has increased on campuses, and many of these programs assess the outcomes and satisfaction associated with participation, little is known about what goes on within the faculty mentoring dyads. We conceptualized this relationship as an outgrowth of faculty activism. That is, through seemingly normal and everyday activities, faculty members can make a difference in the lives and careers of their junior colleagues and can change the campus community for the better. Our research addresses some of the holes in the research literature about what occurs within faculty mentoring pairs.

We sampled eleven mentoring pairs and interviewed the protégés in these pairs about what occurs within the mentoring relationship. Junior faculty participants of the study included three women and eight men, of whom three were identified as racial minorities. Two of the men and one woman interviewed were from other countries. With the exception of one female participant, all were tenure-track faculty. While some junior faculty members were recent graduates of doctoral programs, others held previous experience as faculty members at other institutions. The academic fields represented included the life/hard sciences, social sciences, and humanities. Participant level of engagement with the program ranged from high to minimal involvement.

We asked the protégés to identify why they participated in the Faculty Mentoring Program, amidst busy schedules. We identified the information that they discussed and the benefits they perceived they had received from the experiences. We focused not only on the aspects of the Faculty Mentoring Program that facilitated mentoring but probed further and identified the tasks, behaviors, materials, and experiences shared by the faculty mentors in supporting their faculty protégés. To identify the ways that faculty members engaged in activism daily, we focused particularly on the mentoring pairs that were successful. We paid particular attention to the way they conduct their work and to their ability to impart highly effective mentoring strategies on other mentors, as well as mentoring program developers. Toward the end of the protégés' first year on campus, Dannielle Joy Davis conducted interviews with paired participants of the Faculty Mentoring Program.

Our findings are organized to address the following research questions:

What are faculty members doing to transform their institutions for the purpose of achieving racial and gender equity?

Who are these faculty members and why do they do this work?

What have been some of the outcomes of their efforts?

Which environments encourage or discourage faculty engagement?

Particular focus is placed upon the experiences of marginalized faculty or those most likely to experience isolation, such as women and racial minorities.

Actions Taken by Faculty Members to Achieve Racial And Gender Equity

The majority of protégés were inactive in terms of promoting racial and gender equity. When asked about campus climate, junior faculty members perceived UVM as possessing a welcoming environment for underrepresented groups, particularly sexual minorities. Yet these statements were countered with their observations of the low numbers of racial minorities within the campus community. An activist approach toward racial equity was exhibited by only one protégé, who explained how a senior faculty member suggested two candidates for an open faculty position. Both were white women, who were interviewed. The senior person was impressed, but the protégé was not, as neither candidate was a person of color. Following the interviews he expressed disappointment with his colleague, noting the discrepancy between department and institutional goals toward diversity and lack of recruitment and consideration for qualified racial minorities.

This finding is not surprising, as it would be unusual, and perhaps unwise, for new faculty members to take on roles of faculty activism in their first year. From a socialization standpoint, they would do well to observe the mores and practices of the university before they begin efforts to assist in organizational change.

Faculty Activists and Their Nonactive Peers

The majority of junior faculty members did not report participation in activist activity; two of the protégés described activities that we would label as activism. The first protégé had a history of involvement on issues related to women and minorities via committee work and as a former campus administrator. Interest in advocacy for these groups derived from the faculty member's concern regarding lack of parity for underrepresented minorities at institutional and national levels. It is not surprising that a first-year hire who engaged in this type of activism already had experience at a previous institution.

The second non-tenure-track faculty member incorporated service learning into the classroom and was active within the local community. This lecturer incorporated her focus on teaching with a push for service learning that was occurring on the university. As a result, she had the opportunity to merge her teaching with issues of diversity. Other junior faculty members reported no activist activity. One noted discomfort engaging in activism because of potential political ramifications, yet her discomfort was mitigated by some observations she made about her senior colleagues:

> I see people who are vocal and outspoken getting tenure, getting promotions, but I can't feel comfortable with that myself. My next-door neighbor is a radical Marxist, communist activist. A senior faculty member here ... is a major union activist and an agitator who was marching and protesting with the tent city protestors. She just got promoted to full professor. People who I would expect to have some sort of retribution or reprisals have not, which is why I think I'm probably just paranoid.

Other faculty members also expressed concern regarding activism and often expressed negative viewpoints on getting "involved in politics." The majority of protégés did not share details about their rationale for holding such perspectives, and they cannot be blamed for these hesitations. From an institutional standpoint, we may be better off shielding our new faculty members with activist tendencies until they have obtained some type of job security. Furthermore, with the standards for tenure at UVM changing rapidly with a new president and almost all new deans, there is greater uncertainly around the amount, type, and quality of scholarship that are acceptable to receive tenure.

Work Environments That Encourage and Discourage Faculty Engagement

The experiences of protégés in mentoring programs suggest a connection between a junior faculty member's professional relationship with those within his/her department, faculty engagement, and involvement in the Faculty Mentoring Program. Those with the strongest departmental ties utilized the mentoring program the least, while the majority with weaker ties tended to actively utilize the program and its resources.

All participants had one or more colleagues, in addition to their mentor, who they could go to for advice outside of the department and institution. These external mentors included former chairs at previous institutions, dissertation advisors, and former professors. One faculty member noted how additional mentoring relationships were developed via committee work and networking with others in his academic field. Junior faculty reported regular interaction with these external mentors and their role in continued occupational development and transition to their new university environment.

Outcomes of Efforts

The outcomes of efforts to integrate new faculty, including women and racial minorities, into the university community are demonstrated via each protégé's understanding of the reappointment, promotion, and tenure process, perception of how fair and transparent the RPT process is at UVM, and overall satisfaction with the faculty mentoring program. The majority of novices rated their understanding of the reappointment, promotion and tenure process a 5 out of 7, with 7 being the highest score. Many noted the importance of the Green Sheets workshop to their familiarity with the process; this is the workshop that had been cosponsored by the Faculty Women's Caucus and the Faculty Mentoring Program.

Regarding the expressed fairness and transparency of the RPT process, protégés rating the process high for fairness noted how program-related workshops on RPT contributed to this belief. On the other hand, those reporting low scores stated concern for not personally knowing anyone who had recently gone through the process to go to for advice. One man observed, "I have a . . . pragmatic view of power and what happens sort of behind the scenes. . . . That makes [me very] cautious and not quite trusting of the RPT process here" (personal interview, October 15, 2005).

All of the protégés expressed satisfaction with the faculty mentoring program, reporting high scores of 6 to 7. Protégés particularly highlighted the importance of having a faculty mentor available, the usefulness of the program workshops, and the program director's periodic emails.

Differences in frequency of contact with mentors varied based upon gender, national origin, and race. The three women all met with their mentors three or more times during the year, with the minority woman meeting with her mentor the most, at once per month. Among the men, foreign-born males reported more frequent contact with their mentors than did American-born males, reporting meeting once per month. This suggests that groups prone to marginalization (women and those who are foreign born) utilized mentoring more than other junior faculty members. Junior faculty members, both white American men, reported meeting with their mentors less than twice during the academic year. Although these faculty members did not perceive a need for mentorship and elected not to interact with their mentors regularly, one, ironically, operated within a negative departmental microclimate. The other depended upon the guidance of senior colleagues rather than his assigned mentor.

Most of the time that participants spent with their mentors focused upon discussion of teaching, research, or balancing the two to yield increased productivity in scholarship. These reports reflect the previous research of Boice (1992), which suggests that less productive junior faculty spend too much time on teaching at the expense of their writing and scholarship; the "Quick Starters" moderated their teaching preparation, leveling out the amount of time spent on teaching over the full week, which allowed them to engage in regular writing and scholarship, again, leveled out throughout the full workweek.

Conclusions

This early evaluation of the Faculty Mentoring Program suggests its efficacy. We were particularly pleased that new hires who were traditionally isolated or unconnected in academe seemed to make good use of mentoring arrangements by meeting with their mentors often. While some new faculty members witness their senior faculty mentors being involved in faculty and community activism, they reported no large involvements on their own part, which could be a result of new hires' challenging workloads at UVM. It may also be attributed to their concerns that getting involved in activist activities too early in their careers may disrupt chances for tenure, either by taking up too much time now or by experiencing retribution later. The third reason may be that they don't yet know the organizational structure well enough to get involved in activist activities. In the meantime, they are observing and learning about the organization before they begin engaging in organizational change activities.

The George Washington Henderson Fellowship Program

The George Washington Henderson Fellowship Program was not directly influenced by the actions of the Faculty Women's Caucus. Rather, the ripple effect of the Faculty Women's Caucus through the Faculty Mentoring Program and the Ford Foundation grant from Rutgers University influenced the development and implementation of this fellowship program. The timing was auspicious. Around the time we received the this grant, the Henderson Fellowship Program had received a letter from the Center for Equal Opportunity threatening a law suit if UVM continued sponsoring a targeted fellowship program. Advice from other grant recipients and from Rutgers University's counsel proved to be very helpful. This advice helped us modify the fellowship program so that it was not a targeted program but still met the program goals.

Although Vermont was the first state to have its constitution outlaw slavery (in 1777, the year it became a republic in its own right), racism continued to severely hamper the opportunities of its African American citizens. The George Washington Henderson Fellowship honors one of the first African American students to graduate from the University of Vermont. George Washington Henderson was born a slave in Virginia in 1850. He traveled to Vermont by becoming the manservant of a Vermont infantry officer who had been in Virginia during the Civil War. After Mr. Henderson moved to Vermont, he graduated from the University of Vermont as the valedictorian and was the first African American initiated into Phi Beta Kappa at UVM. Afterward, he earned a master of arts degree from the University of Vermont and, in 1883, a bachelor of divinity from Yale Divinity School. As an educator and minister, he went on to become the university pastor and the chairperson of the theology department at Straight University in New Orleans. Straight University, renamed Dillard University, is a historically black college and sister institution to the University of Vermont. In 1896, UVM bestowed on the Reverend George Washington Henderson an honorary degree of doctor of divinity (Ledoux).

Later historical documents disputed the claim that George Washington Henderson was the first African American to graduate from UVM (that distinction goes to Andrew Harris, class of 1838 (Weaver 2004)), but UVM continues to honor him through its George Washington Henderson Fellowship Program.

Prior to being renamed the Henderson Fellowship Program, the program at UVM was called the Citibank Fellowship, later the New England Board of Higher Education (NEBHE) Fellowship. In the early 1990s, UVM received a grant from the Citibank Corporation to fund an annual dissertation fellowship. Soon afterward, UVM joined the NEBHE Fellowship Program. The NEBHE program was supported via a grant from the Pew Charitable Trust and funded the vast majority of the fellowship stipends (70 to 80 percent of the costs). Later the stipends were funded by the GE Foundation. These fellowships focused on bringing minority predoctoral graduate students to the New England areas with the goal of diversifying the faculty ranks in the humanities and social sciences throughout the region. Through the NEBHE program, UVM sponsored forty fellows, two of whom are currently working at the University of Vermont. The majority of the fellows were sponsored within the department of the College of Arts and Sciences, with one in business, seven in education, and one cosponsored by arts and sciences and the education college. In 2002–03, the external funding monies dried up and UVM assumed funding of this fellowship program. During the same year, UVM changed the name to the George Washington Henderson Fellowship Program.

At this time, Peg Single was having lunch with the university's vice provost of multiculturalism to discuss the future of a Henderson Fellow she was mentoring. Over lunch, many ideas about how to strengthen the program and transform it into a faculty recruitment initiative were discussed. As a result, the director for the Henderson Fellowship Program position was funded in autumn 2004 and a dedicated person was able to manage the fellowship program so that it aligned with UVM's strategic goals of diversifying the faculty.

That same fall, the University of Vermont received a letter from the Center for Equal Opportunity. The signatory, Roger Clegg, was well-known for his activities in attacking programs that supported affirmative action and diversity.

The letter threatened a lawsuit if the targeted nature of the Henderson Fellowship Program was not changed. The university received this letter in the midst of conducting an assessment of the efficacy of the program and a review of effective programs for supporting scholars of color. The letter also arrived just prior to the Ford Foundation grantee meeting held at Rutgers University the summer of 2005. Through talking with others and the presentation of information from Rutgers's general counsel, we were able to develop a fellowship program that worked within the constraints of the current legal environment to support the university's strategic goal of diversifying its curriculum and faculty ranks.

Our first move was to revise the program's mission to set the stage for developing an effective faculty recruitment program. The mission is "to honor the memory of one of the first African American students to graduate from the University of Vermont by sponsoring predoctoral and postdoctoral fellowships to support scholars who can diversify UVM's curriculum and address issues of multiculturalism throughout the UVM campus community." Next we linked the sponsoring of Henderson Fellows to future hiring opportunities. In the past, the selection of fellows was based on the applicant pool. Now, we would identify departments, colleges, and units who would cosponsor fellows and actively recruit in these areas. Institutions of higher education have complete control over their curriculum. One of UVM's needs was to recruit faculty members who could include issues pertinent to U.S. racial and ethnic minorities in their curriculum regardless of the field. Thus we delineated criteria for the fellowship to include the statement: "Candidates who have a demonstrated commitment to the incorporation of racial or ethnic diversity studies into their research or teaching are encouraged to apply." Even with this phrase, we did receive a number of applications that defined diversity more broadly to include teaching issues of white privilege or social class. While these topics are of importance, they do not represent areas where there is a university need. Just as an electrical engineer will not suffice when one is recruiting for a mechanical engineering position, neither will a person who is well versed in class issues suffice when one is recruiting for a position addressing issues of U.S. race or ethnic diversity.

The fellowships are only offered in areas where there is a strong alliance with the departments. The person chosen for the fellowship is someone they would be committed to support as a future faculty hire. The departments also provide office space and computer support. A senior member of the department mentors the fellow, and the department provides a research and travel stipend. In addition, the fellow has the opportunity to co-teach one course during the first semester on campus and one course per semester thereafter.

While the departments provide strong support, so does the central program. Many fellowship programs bring fellows to campus and leave the socialization process to the departments. All too often, departments are not well versed in issues of socialization and enculturation to the academy; nor are they adept at faculty development or issues of faculty diversity. The Henderson Fellowship Program provides writing workshops and academic professional development to the fellows. Not only is this a time to transmit information, it is an opportunity for a cohort effect. As a result, the fellows have the opportunity to support one another through various means, whether attending each others' talks on campus, providing feedback on papers, or celebrating a birthday at a local brew pub.

This program was influenced indirectly by the Faculty Women's Caucus and directly through the receipt of the Reaffirming Action grant funded by the Ford Foundation. As this program moves forward, we hope to continue to expand the initiative. We also envision this program having its own ripple effect. That is, the current fellows will enjoy the support provided to them, realize its unique nature in the life of most universities, and advocate or support such programs as they build and develop their academic careers through becoming senior faculty members and administrators.

Faculty activism is at the heart of most, if not all, major changes to the higher education system. While working on issues of diversity was once relegated to the margins, now most, if not all, institutions have some sort of diversity statement. The programs once run by small groups of committed faculty members may now be institutionalized programs. Typically, small groups of committed faculty members, such as the UVM Women's Faculty Caucus, or social entrepreneurs committed to addressing racism and sexism in faculty hiring, such as JoAnn Moody, implement new programs. After their efficacy is demonstrated, the institutions are more willing to embrace and fund these programs. As this happens, we hope that the roots of these activities will not be forgotten or lost. As the academy changes so must our avenues for activism. As Margaret Mead once noted, "a small group of thoughtful committed citizens can change the world," but there may be times when the change comes from without and other times when the change comes from within.

Acknowledgments

This project was supported in part by a grant from the Mary Jean Simpson Fund of the University of Vermont, which is administered by the UVM Women's Center.

REFERENCES

Basow, S. A. 2000. "Best and Worst Professors: Gender Patterns in Students' Choices." *Sex Roles* 43:407–410.

Boice, R. 1990. "Mentoring New Faculty: A Program for Implementation." *Journal of Staff, Program and Organization Development* 8 (3):143–152.

————. 1992. *The New Faculty Member.* San Francisco: Jossey-Bass.

————. 1993. "New Faculty Involvement for Women and Minorities." *Research in Higher Education* 34 (3):291–341.

Boyle, P., and R. Boice. 1998. "Systematic Mentoring for New Faculty Teachers and Graduate Teaching Assistants." *Innovative Higher Education* 22 (3):157–179. http://www.uvm.edu/~pbsingle/pdf/1998Boyle.pdf (accessed October 122, 2003).

Chesler, N., P. B. Single, and B. Mikic. 2003. "On Belay: Peer-Mentoring and Adventure Education for Women Faculty in Engineering." *Journal of Engineering Education* 92:257–262. www.uvm.edu/~pbsingle/pdf/2003Single2002.pdf (accessed October 2003).

Kasprisin, C. A., P. B. Single, R. M. Single, C. B. Muller, and J. L. Ferrier. Forthcoming. "Improved Mentor Satisfaction: Emphasizing Protégé Training for Adult-Age Mentoring Dyads." *Mentoring and Tutoring* 16.

Kent, B. 1998. "Response to Robyn R. Warhol." *Profession,* 229–234.

Ledoux, T. George Washington Henderson (1850–1936). http://vermontcivilwar.org/units/8/henderson.php (accessed October 17, 2006).

Moody, J. 2004. *Faculty Diversity: Problems and Solutions.* New York: Routledge Press.

Ragins, B. R., and J. L. Cotton. 1991. "Easier Said Than Done: Gender Differences in Perceived Barriers to Gaining a Mentor." *Human Relations* 42:1–22.

Single, P. B. Forthcoming. *Demystifying the Writing Process: A Guide for Doctoral Students.* Sterling, VA: Stylus Publishing.

Single, P. B. Forthcoming. "A Campuswide Faculty Mentoring Program: Putting Research into Practice." In *The Handbook of Successful Faculty Mentoring Programs,* ed. C. Mullen. Norwood, MA: Christopher-Gordon Publishers.

Single, P. B., and C. B. Muller. 2001. "When Email and Mentoring Unite: The Implementation of a Nationwide Electronic Mentoring Program." In *Creating Mentoring and Coaching Programs,* ed. L. K. Stromei, 107–122. Alexandria, VA: American Society for Training and Development. http://www.uvm.edu/~pbsingle/pdf/ 2001Single.pdf (accessed October 22, 2003).

United States Census Bureau. 2007. State and County Quickfacts. http://quickfacts.census.gov/qfd/states/50000.html (accessed October 17, 2007).

Warhol, R. R. 1998. "How We Got Contracts for Lecturers at the University of Vermont: A Tale of (Qualified) Success." *Profession,* 223–229.

Weaver, T. 2004. "Breaking News from 1838."*Vermont Quarterly* 64 (Summer).

Wenneras, C., and A. Wold. 1997. "Nepotism and Sexism in Peer-Review." *Nature* 387: 341–343. http://www.eb.tuebingen.mpg.de/women/papers/nepotism.html (accessed March 322, 2005).

12

Linking Mobilization to Institutional Power

The Faculty-Led Diversity Initiative at Columbia University

EMMA FREUDENBERGER, JEAN E. HOWARD,
EDDIE JAUREGUI, AND SUSAN STURM

In 2004 a diverse group of motivated faculty members conceived an initiative that would yield sustainable, lasting change in the area of diversity at Columbia University. Their work led to the creation of a vice-provostial position dedicated to diversifying the university's faculty and administration and heralded an unprecedented period of cultural change within the institution. Supported by an initial $15,000,000 commitment, the initiative has stimulated innovation across the College of Arts and Sciences and the university's professional schools and has mushroomed to involve change agents within the faculty, the student body, and the academic and administrative staff. In this chapter we will briefly outline the origins and history of this mobilization effort and, more importantly, will attempt to outline the theory of institutional change that continues to guide the effort. While the initiative's successes have been due to many factors, including the canny deployment of data, the cultivation of a strong leadership network, and an orientation toward concrete program building, they have above all depended on finding how to implement faculty ideas and mobilize faculty energies in ways that have the greatest impact on key decision makers within the university—chairs, deans, vice presidents, the provost, and the president. In short, this is a story about how faculty mobilization, a source of power in itself, can be effectively linked to other sites of power within the institution to promote progressive change.

The authors undertook the writing of this chapter as part of a broader effort to build self-reflection into the diversity initiative. Two of the four writers—Jean E. Howard and Susan Sturm—have been important architects of the Columbia diversity initiative. Much of the history described here involves their own efforts, and they cannot claim to be impartial observers. In an effort to introduce a critical lens on the initiative, however, two other researchers have been engaged in the process of documenting and analyzing the diversity initiative. Eddie Jauregui and Emma Freudenberger, law students enrolled in a field research seminar who were not involved in the work of the initiative, joined the study team and reviewed the extensive documentary record of meetings, reports, and email exchanges concerning the initiative. They also interviewed many of the major players who have been involved in the initiative and played an important role in narrating the story, validating or refuting Jean Howard and Susan Sturm's interpretation of events and framing the analysis.

Origins

In 2004 the core group of faculty leaders spearheaded a mobilization effort; the effort emerged in part through a sense of urgency about the lack of diversity in key parts of the university and in part from analyzing the limits of previous reform efforts. The two senior faculty members who convened the group—Susan Sturm from the law school as cochair and Alice Kessler-Harris from the history department as its most senior faculty member—had been involved in the University Senate's Commission on the Status of Women, which in 2001 produced an important report, "The Advancement of Women through the Academic Ranks of the Columbia University Graduate School of Arts and Sciences: Where are the Leaks in the Pipeline?" (familiarly known as "The Pipeline Report"). The data in this report revealed that except in a few places in the humanities, women and faculty members from underrepresented minorities were not present on the faculty in numbers commensurate with their availability in the key pools from which Columbia hires. In addition, the overwhelming majority of external senior hires without competitive searches (target-of-opportunity appointments) went to men. For example, in the decade covered by the 2001 Pipeline Report, eleven of eleven target-of-opportunity hires in natural science departments had been filled by male scholars. In an institution heavily dependent on renewing the faculty through senior appointments, this fact showed why the process of demographic change had been slow.

When the Commission attempted to use the report to promote institutional change, however, Commission members found few institutional leaders ready to address its challenges. While the Commission could usefully pinpoint problems, it was not positioned to transform information into action. It became clear to Professors Sturm and Kessler-Harris that data alone was insufficient to generate an institutional commitment to changing race and gender demographics at Columbia. Consequently, they convened a working group of influential faculty members with a track record of commitment to gender and racial inclusion. This group evolved a new strategy that seized on the opportunity presented by the appointment of Lee Bollinger as the new president of Columbia. He had defended the University of Michigan's affirmative action program before the Supreme Court in *Gratz v. Bollinger*, and his public commitment to diversity resonated with the goals of the core faculty group.

After a process of discussion that lasted a number of months, the core group decided to ask the president and the provost to create an administrative position, but one to be held by a distinguished faculty member and not by a career diversity officer, dedicated to overseeing a university diversity initiative aimed at increasing the diversity of the faculty and the upper administration. The group making this request had itself a great deal of institutional credibility. Included were, among others, the past and present chairs of history, the chair of psychology, the chair of anthropology, the head of the Institute for Research on Women and Gender, the head of the Institute for Research on African-American Studies, the most senior woman in the biology department, the cochair of the Commission on the Status of Women, and one prominent legal scholar well known for his work on law and sexuality and critical race theory. The initial composition of the group proved crucial. As one faculty member put it:

> They knew us all. Everybody on the committee had a reputation for probity and working with the institution and for being sensible but everybody had a reputation for being tough. . . . I'm sure when we walked in they said, "Oh, I see, these are the most senior women on campus and they are united . . . whoops."

By assembling individuals with strong academic credentials as well as a history of institutional leadership across many domains, the core group leveraged the legitimacy of key individuals for a collective enterprise. It also established the precedent, so important for subsequent efforts, that faculty would lead the way in determining the shape and content of the initiative.

Armed with the data from the Pipeline Report, the group met several times with the president and provost, who, after some initial skepticism, assented to the creation of a new university post, a vice provost for diversity initiatives, and to the appointment of Jean Howard, the person nominated by the faculty group, to be the first holder of this office. They also agreed to create a Presidential Advisory Committee on Diversity Initiatives composed of distinguished faculty members who would help the new vice provost in structuring and defining the work of the office, establishing priorities, and keeping key administrators focused on how to transform ideas into programs and policies. In creating the position, the faculty group argued that the vice provost should have an all-university purview and so should report directly to the provost and regularly to the president; that it should be located, physically, within Low Library, the key administrative hub at Columbia; that it should have an ongoing claim to the data-gathering capacities of the Office for Institutional Research; and that it would be supported by an executive assistant and draw as needed on the support of the University Counsel, the Office for Equal Opportunity and Affirmative Action, and other administrative units such as the Office of Human Resources.

Equally important was the choice of Jean Howard as the first person to hold the post. Howard had been a faculty member at Columbia for nearly twenty years. A noted scholar of Renaissance literature, she had been graduate director in her department, head of the Institute for Research on Women and Gender, and chair of the Commission on the Status of Women when it produced the Pipeline Report. She was known and trusted by the faculty, was familiar with the workings of the institution, and had a track record of accomplishment as an administrator as well as a deep commitment to the creation of a more inclusive academic community. In securing her agreement to hold the position for a three-year term, the group established the precedent that the office would be held by a respected faculty member nominated through a faculty process.

The group spent some time attempting to find the right language to name its initiative. The group considered different possibilities and settled on the language of "diversity" mainly because that language has gained ascendance as a result of the Supreme Court's decision in the Michigan affirmative action cases. In practice, the term took on different meaning in different situations, depending on the nature of the problem at hand. "Diversity" would encompass, certainly, women and people of color, but initiatives aimed at removing barriers to their participation in university life often had positive impact on other groups as well. Search and hiring initiatives focused on advancing gender and racial diversity in fields of persistent underrepresentation. When attention turned to the question of full participation in academic life and opportunities for advancement, the initiative's work also took into account and benefited other groups that had experienced marginalization or barriers to participation. The diversity provost was, for example, to address concerns pertaining to sexual orientation and disability. Intellectual and disciplinary diversity became important as part of opening up the discussion about what excellence means within different fields.

No one was satisfied with the language of diversity as an adequate goal or vision for the initiative. The inadequacy of the language reflected the complexity of the problem and the lack of a clear consensus about the justification for a goal about which many agreed. The project of trying to create a normative commitment by finding just the right definition for the term seemed elusive and ultimately futile. The group came to see that language alone would not answer the question of how to define diversity or why diversity mattered. There was no universal or right answer to the question of nomenclature. Different language worked in different communities. This point was vividly illustrated by differences among other diversity provosts in the language each used to describe a shared goal. Diversity, equity, inclusiveness, and multiculturalism were each offered as the preferred language. Some change agents embraced "equity" over "diversity," which was described as having too much baggage and being associated with race rather than with gender. Others disagreed with this view, arguing that "equity" had its own baggage. The humanities understood the concept of diversity, but this idea had not been integrated as much into the sciences. Different language worked in different communities; for this reason it deemed impossible to come up with a single, universal terminology. "Diversity" must be continually embedded in practice, challenged, and redefined contextually.

Building the Infrastructure

Once she assumed the office in September 2004, Jean Howard moved swiftly to appoint the Presidential Diversity Committee, composed jointly of those who had formed the core group that led to her appointment and others who represented key constituencies such as science faculty and faculty concerned with the study of race and ethnicity. Members were chosen with an eye to their institutional prominence, their experience with and often their research interests in issues of diversity, and their administrative sophistication. When the committee was first seated, it included a female member of the National Academy of Sciences, a member of the Brown University Board of Trustees, a past university vice president, three law professors, a trustee of Smith College, and three faculty members in leadership positions in Columbia's Institute for Research on Women and Gender, its Institute for Research in African-American Studies, and its Center for the Study of Race and Ethnicity. Each member of the group had his or her own informal network of faculty connections, so the body was able to extend its reach deep into many quarters of the Arts and Sciences and Law faculties, the two schools most involved in the proposal to create the office. This group, which meets three to four times each semester, has remained an essential advisory body for the office from its inception.

In year two, a second advisory board, the Professional Schools Diversity Council, was constituted. It was composed of faculty and administrators from each of Columbia's professional schools including Law, Business, Social Work, Architecture, Journalism, Medicine, Public Health, Dentistry, and Nursing. This board has overseen initiatives unique to the professional schools as well as increasingly cooperated with the Arts and Sciences Advisory Committee to coauthor pan-university initiatives in areas such as work-life enhancements and the creation of faculty development and mentoring programs.

In addition, Vice Provost Howard, not being a scientist but aware of the special need to increase the percentage of women and underrepresented minorities on the science faculties at Columbia and to build pipelines to encourage their entrance into these disciplines, appointed an Ad Hoc Committee on Diversity in Science and Engineering chaired by a distinguished member of the psychology faculty, Norma Graham. As a happy coincidence, the fall that Howard was appointed also coincided with Columbia's receipt of an NSF ADVANCE grant of $4.2 million to promote the advancement of women in fields connected to Columbia's Earth Institute and the Lamont-Doherty Earth Observatory. From the beginning the vice provost and the leaders of the ADVANCE grant worked in partnership with Norma Graham's committee to institute innovative programs and policies that would realize the goals of the ADVANCE grant and that would be generalizable, with appropriate modifications, across the institution. These have included such things as the administration of a climate survey, the development of a lecture series on the Science of Diversity, focus groups for graduate students in the science departments, and targeted support for women scholars in the form of workshop leadership awards and research productivity grants.

These three committees have provided the primary vehicles for formal ongoing faculty input into the work of the vice provost's office. At times they have initiated major projects, such as planning training sessions for search committees on how to do inclusive searches; at other times they have requested information from other university offices, advised the vice provost on how to respond to particular problems, presented the case for change to other members of the administration on behalf of diversity initiatives, been part of vetting committees assessing potential faculty recruitments, and taken an active role in a number of public events and programs including faculty development workshops, colloquia on research related to diversity topics, and meetings with funding agencies and potential donors. They have been, in short, policy-making, advisory, and persuasive entities. They have given the office a reach into the faculty that the vice provost alone could never have achieved, and they have kept her accountable at all times to faculty concerns and priorities. Composed of distinguished members of the faculty, they have given the work of the office legitimacy.

In addition to these faculty committees, the office has been supported by an executive assistant, Andrea Thomas, and has worked in tandem with the Office of Institutional Research in the production of data ranging from salary equity reports to analyses concerning underrepresentation. The work of the office has at various times also been supported by Public Affairs, Development, the President's Special Events staff, the General Counsel's Office, Human Resources, and the Office of Equal Opportunity and Affirmative Action, each of which has played a leading role in bringing particular projects to completion. Human Resources, for example, worked closely with the office to prepare data for our Child Care Self-Evaluation; Special Events has helped the vice provost stage diversity-related lectures and conferences; Development has helped the office approach foundations for support for diversity initiatives; Public Affairs has publicized events and successes; and the General Counsel's Office has vetted all of the office's programs to be sure they meet legal standards. The office has, in short, carefully made use of the many kinds of expertise to be found across a range of university offices and has worked collaboratively with those offices to build programs that would be deeply embedded in the university's infrastructure.

At the same time, in order to be sure that the importance Columbia places on diversity is a central part of key university conversations, the vice provost has been a member of a number of standing university committees including the Provost's Committee on Housing, the Provost's Council of Deans, the Academic Review Committee for the Arts and Sciences, the Council of Chairs in Arts and Sciences, and the all-university Commission on the Status of Women. Informally, the vice provost meets regularly with faculty and with chairs and deans throughout the university who come to her with problems or with ideas for initiatives that would further the university's diversity mission. The office, as was intended by its faculty designers, is meant to be a physical and symbolic hub, a place to which ideas flow from many quarters of the university and from which a number of initiatives are undertaken, often in cooperation with a range of other university offices and decision makers, whether the head of Human Resources or the dean of the Columbia School of Public Health.

Facets of the Initiative

So what has the office done? The problem facing a brand-new office was that there was no blueprint for how to implement change. And, of course, there was widespread skepticism about how fundamentally the university meant to alter the ways it operates in order to create a more inclusive faculty and foster a campus climate that values diversity as a means to achieving excellence. Since searches are the mechanism by which university faculty and administrators reproduce and renew themselves, thoughtfully reexamining the hiring process was identified by the Diversity Committee as the most important task it faced. The question it asked was: what would have to change to get more women and underrepresented minorities into recruitment pools and then into faculty and administrative positions?

Search Practices

Nothing is more important for the intellectual vitality of a university than the rigor and creativity with which searches are undertaken. They are the means by which the university expresses its commitment to excellence and diversity.

Too often, however, searches are passive and routinized activities. Ads are posted; dossiers arrive; committees use certain often unarticulated criteria to winnow files. To produce better diversity outcomes, every aspect of the process—from where ads are placed to how recruiting visits are structured—had to be examined. A subcommittee of the larger advisory committee took on the task of deciding how best to engage faculty, especially search committee chairs, in a conversation about inclusive hiring practices. Drawing on a model developed at the University of Michigan, the subcommittee urged that search and department chairs in each division of the College of Arts and Sciences (and later in all of the professional schools as well) should be invited to dinner meetings at which they would hear three brief presentations. One would deal with data on the racial and gender demographics of that division over the last fifteen years. The second would deal with all the barriers that prevent more inclusive recruitment and hiring. A third would detail the best practices that might help overcome those barriers and produce a more diverse pool of candidates and, eventually, a more diverse faculty. These presentations, all of which would be made by faculty members from the division under discussion, would be followed by an extended question and answer period.

As of the fall of 2007, these search and hiring dinners, as they have come to be known, had been extended across the entire university. Crucial to their success are, first, the fact that they are led by faculty members from the departments under discussion; these faculty members have credibility in their intellectual communities and understand the particular problems facing, for example, an engineering faculty in the recruitment of minority candidates. Second, it has been important that the presentations are data- and research-driven. As one of our interviewees said, "In dealing with scientists not only is the data element crucial but the visual element is crucial. They want the graphs and the charts and the arrow bars and that's what prompts discussion, not a very eloquent report." We found this sentiment to be frequently reiterated. When departments and divisions could see graphic pictures of how they had or had not changed over the course of the last fifteen years in their recruitment of women and underrepresented minorities, and when they could compare their profiles to the hiring profiles of peer institutions and national-availability pool data, those were the situations in which the will to change was generated. Third, to be successful these dinner meetings must provide concrete tools to help faculty members change their practices. Over time, those doing the presentations developed an array of materials to disseminate: standard evaluation instruments to rate candidates on agreed-upon criteria; suggestions for new places to announce openings that might attract diverse candidates; sheets outlining best practices for conducting searches and recruitment visits; names and locations of nearby child care facilities, many affiliated with Columbia; lists of the benefits the university makes available to new faculty; even a sheet outlining the key benefits of living in New York City. Aimed at changing the way the university community thinks about searches, these search and hiring dinners, while labor-intensive, have been one of the key tools the office has used to encourage new ways of doing the daily business of university life.

The Hiring Initiative

At the same time, the Presidential Advisory Committee felt that the university needed to make a public commitment of new money in order to signal the sincerity of its intention to create a more inclusive institution and to jump-start the process of changing the demographics in Arts and Sciences, the symbolic heart of the university. Consequently, the committee worked with the vice provost to prepare a request to submit to the president, the provost and the trustees for $15,000,000 to be used for hiring outstanding candidates who would further the university's diversity goals through their teaching, research, and mentoring activities or if they were members of groups underrepresented in particular areas of the university. Positions were to be fully funded by the vice provost for five years.

The money was granted by the president in spring of 2005 and began to be used in academic year 2005–06. Several factors have proven central to the success of this initiative. First, nominations for these target-of-opportunity positions must come from departments and fully meet departmental criteria for excellence in research and teaching. Second, departments must commit future resources to obtain a line. After the initial five years of central support, going forward the lines are funded from departmental budgets as other faculty retire or leave the institution. In short, the departments must want and value the candidates they propose and not merely regard them as "freebies." Third, departments must compete for the lines, and not all proposals are accepted; priority is given to the intellectual excellence of the candidate and his or her potential impact across disciplines and academic units, as well as the ways in which he or she would centrally support the diversity mission of the university. The result has been that those who have received such appointments have been intellectually outstanding and have been avidly wooed by the hiring departments, resulting in a very high percentage of successful recruitments.

Both of these initiatives were decided upon in the first year of the vice provost's term, and they have been ongoing since that time. Last spring the first results of these efforts became visible. Underrepresented minorities made up 11 percent of the faculty hired in 2005 and 26.5 percent in 2006. Women made up 34 percent of those hired in 2005 and 38 percent in 2006. We believe these increases are due to a combination of more inclusive search practices and targeted recruitment efforts. One year is too short a time to determine trends, but we are pleased with these outcomes.

Outreach

The third priority of the Diversity Committee in the first year was a series of public events that would focus attention on diversity issues and would be seen to have the endorsement of the president and provost. That year, and in every subsequent year, the vice provost's office has arranged at least two such events strategically designed to highlight issues of crucial importance to the diversity effort. In the first year, for example, in cooperation with ADVANCE, Shirley Tilghman, the first woman president of Princeton, was invited to Columbia to talk about how to build the pipeline of women choosing careers in academic science. In a rousing address that drew national attention, President Tilghman made, among other things, an impassioned plea for the importance of university-supported child care to help young parents, especially but not only women scientists, as they advanced from graduate students to postdocs and then to career scientists. Part of her address constitutes the introduction to the comprehensive report on child care that was subsequently developed by the Office of the Vice Provost for Diversity Initiatives as part of the creation of a more robust set of work-life supports at Columbia. Other lecturers have included Charles Vest, the former president of MIT, Ruth Simmons, the president of Brown University, and George Chauncey, professor of history at Yale University, who spoke about the struggle for gay, lesbian, bisexual, and transgendered rights. These events provide ways of educating the Columbia community about key diversity issues and also put pressure on our institution to match the advances being made at comparable institutions.

The Professional Schools Diversity Fund

In the second year of its existence, the Office of the Vice Provost for Diversity Initiatives took on two major new initiatives. The first had to do with spreading the work begun in year one into the professional schools, and the second had to do with addressing a series of work-life issues that impacted both the recruitment and the retention of the increasingly diverse faculty Columbia hoped to attract. In regard to the professional schools, a second advisory council was formed, as detailed earlier in this chapter, and it began to discuss how to adapt the search and hiring practices dinners to the culture of the professional schools. With some modifications, the model is now being used in most of those schools; presentations have been made to faculty in Law, Business, Dentistry, Public Health, Social Work, and Engineering.

To create incentives for more robust diversity recruitment, the president, at the request of the Professional Schools Diversity Council, granted $2,000,000 to be spread over three years to enable schools to receive three kinds of financial support for their diversity efforts. They could request a short-term fellowship to underwrite recruitment visits stretching from two days to two weeks for a faculty candidate whose hiring would support the diversity goals of the university, or they could request a long-term (one-semester) visit for the same purposes. In addition, departments could nominate candidates for research fellowships of up to $25,000. These support the research agenda of new recruits or of untenured faculty who have the strong backing of their departments and have demonstrated the potential for long-term academic appointments. To date, five short-term visits have been authorized and fourteen research fellowships have been awarded. Though the amounts of money are relatively small (short-term visits typically are funded in amounts ranging from $3,000 to $10,000), they encourage departments to consider diversity candidates for long-term appointments, and they ask departments to focus on the development for tenure of those diverse faculty members they have already successfully recruited.

Work-Life Initiatives

After year one, the Diversity Committee felt that attention to hiring and recruitment needed to be supplemented by equal attention to retention, both in terms of improving the work-life supports that would enable all new faculty members, including especially women and underrepresented minorities, to thrive at Columbia, and in terms of improving faculty development issues across the board. Attention was devoted to three initiatives. The first was child care. There was a perceived lack of child care programs in the Columbia vicinity, and when programs could be found, the price of such care was often prohibitive. This was seen as a serious barrier to the recruitment of young faculty, and of particular importance to young women in the sciences whose long hours in the lab made proximate child care a major desideratum.

Working collaboratively with the Commission on the Status of Women, the vice provost hired Bright Horizons Consultancy Group to do an analysis of Columbia's child care policies and programs, the demand for such services among student, staff, and faculty, and the availability of child care in the vicinity of Columbia's Morningside Heights and medical campuses. Completed in spring of 2006, this comprehensive report was then considered by a small faculty working group that winnowed its recommendations and produced an action plan with seven major recommendations, five of which the president and provost in fall of 2006 accepted for immediate implementation. These included the hiring of an associate provost to oversee all work-life programs, including child care; the expansion of two of Columbia's affiliated child care centers to accommodate spots for infants and one-year-olds, the age groups for which demand is high and capacity low; the affiliation of four more area child care centers with the university to further expand capacity to accommodate infants and toddlers; the creation of a back-up care program for staff, faculty, postdocs, and PhD students; and the formulation of a university policy statement on the importance of supporting the work-life needs of employees. Deferred for consideration next year were a recommendation for an on-site child care center and for a plan to subsidize child care costs.

Two years in the making, the child care initiative is expected to have a major impact on recruiting faculty with young children and on the retention of those who have families while on staff. Interestingly, survey data indicated that older members of the faculty were nearly as likely to support the university's spending money on child care services as were younger faculty, indicating how widespread is the perception that such services are essential for the long-term health of the faculty and its hiring ambitions. As with many of the initiatives undertaken by the Office of the Provost for Diversity, this one began with the intention of meeting the needs of women and underrepresented minorities but, in actuality, identified a need experienced by many other faculty members as well. Targeted efforts can thus lead to wide-scale change and be the catalyst for much-needed institutional innovation.

A second initiative involved the "dual-career problem." Members of the science faculty early on pointed out that 62 percent of married female scientists have partners who hold PhDs in science. Hiring such a woman often means finding a good academic position for her partner. While the dual-career issue may be especially pressing for women scientists, it is not unique to them. Chairs throughout the university have said that the problem of placing partners is one of the main barriers to successful recruitments. Consequently, the Office of the Vice Provost appointed a committee to consider the dual-career problem at Columbia, to investigate what others schools are doing to solve it, and to make recommendations. Learning from other institutions, the committee recommended that Columbia follow Cornell in creating a dual-career office that would assist dual-career couples making the transition to New York City. Partners of recruited faculty seeking nonfaculty appointments within Columbia would be referred to a professional located in Human Resources for advice about possibilities for staff and administrative posts. For those seeking faculty employment the committee recommended following the lead of Stanford University and appointing a faculty "broker" whose job would be to arrange short-term appointments within Columbia for partners of recruited candidates. The broker would be a respected faculty member familiar with Columbia's schools and departments and would have resources that would enable him or her to arrange temporary appointments. The proposal is awaiting implementation.

At the same time, the vice provost began conversations with New York University and Yale University to set up an area academic job bank that would enable schools within a hundred-mile radius of New York City to cooperate in solving the dual-career problems that could not be resolved within any one institution. It was quickly discovered that there was already a national movement to create such regional job banks. HERCs (higher education recruitment consortia) exist in northern and southern California, in northern New England, and in New Jersey, and one is under development in upstate New York. The HERCs use a Web-based search engine that includes listings for all jobs at member schools, both faculty and staff positions. These postings are available at no charge to anyone seeking employment in higher education. The Web site prominently features a dual-career function whereby two people can specify what each needs by way of an appointment and the distance each is willing to travel. Email alerts inform both parties about any two posts that fit their specifications. In February 2007 the Metro New York and Southern Connecticut HERC launched with forty-three founding members. Based at Columbia, this new tool can not only help to solve dual-career problems; it also serves as an important resource for new graduates seeking regional employment, and it can be used to promote diversity outreach and to foster collaboration on a number of issues among member schools.

Faculty Development

In their third year of existence, the diversity committees and the vice provost extended their focus on retention to encompass faculty development efforts. Extensive interviews with untenured faculty members suggested that many are not adequately informed about tenure standards at Columbia or about how the tenure process works, that they sometimes receive little official feedback on their scholarship, research, and teaching from senior colleagues except at the moment of the tenure decision, and that they are not all included in the informal mentoring networks that faculty "naturally" establish with some of their junior colleagues. This is of particular concern for young faculty members who because of their race, ethnicity, or gender are in a minority in their immediate work environment. In addition, many untenured faculty are uncertain about what kind of university or department service is expected of an untenured faculty member and when they can say no to service requests. Others are never officially informed about parental leave or other policies that might be of assistance to them in their early years on the faculty. In some departments, untenured faculty members feel isolated from peers since there may be no other untenured faculty in their unit and because traditions of departmental autonomy militate against forming ties with junior faculty in other departments who might be sources of information and support in the pre-tenure years.

As a result, the Office of the Vice Provost, working with faculty advisory committees, has undertaken three new efforts. One is to prepare a report on the state of faculty development programs at Columbia and to survey what peer institutions are doing in this regard, especially in the area of faculty mentoring programs. Another is to begin to hold a series of meetings for untenured faculty in each school to discuss the tenure process. A third is to create occasions for untenured faculty to meet one another to create their own networks across fields and disciplines in order to combat the isolation some individuals may feel. Improving faculty development programs at Columbia is a long-term effort, but we have made a beginning.

Lessons Learned: Strategies for Connecting Mobilization to Institutional Power

The Columbia Diversity Initiative is still in its early stages. It has, however, produced dramatic results within a relatively short time. In its first three years, the diversity initiative has generated considerable financial and administrative support for faculty diversity and prompted the hiring of a significant number of new faculty women and people of color. It has motivated schools and departments to examine their search processes and outcomes. It has produced university-wide child care and partner-placement programs that will benefit all faculty hiring and reduce significant barriers to attracting diverse faculty. It has opened up conversations about gender and racial inclusiveness across the university. It has made diversity part of the university's capital campaign. It has produced ongoing activist and intellectual collaborations dealing with issues of diversity, bringing together faculty and administrators from different disciplinary perspectives. It has created a sense of hope and belief in the possibility for change among the many participants in its work.

In this section, we present our assessment of the principles that account for the diversity initiative's success thus far. We have identified three key strategies that we believe have been instrumental in producing meaningful change at Columbia and that could be applied in other institutional settings. First, the development of new kind of change agent, which we call organizational catalysts, plays a crucial role in connecting mobilization to power and in sustaining change. Second, the initiative shows the value of developing and communicating information so that it can mobilize effective action. Finally, we illustrate the importance of building change networks through distributing leadership as a strategy for sustaining change in universities with highly decentralized power structures.

Organizational Catalysts as Effective Change Agents

Achieving change within universities is like herding cats. Power is widely dispersed and decision making decentralized. Departments often lack information about each other and about central administrative priorities and initiatives; central administrators lack reliable information about departmental decisions and practices. Departments and disciplines do not regularly interact; they value different types of knowledge and communicate using different language and styles. In these situations, gender and racial underparticipation may not be noticed, and if it is noticed it may go unaddressed. It is often due to cultural and institutional patterns and practices that cut across these domains but are difficult to observe or change from any one location. Often there are no incentives or mechanisms to address problems that span many domains.

The vice provost for diversity initiatives offers a way of institutionalizing much-needed boundary-crossing efforts. It is an example of a role we call "organizational catalysts." This role involves individuals with knowledge, influence, and credibility in positions where they can mobilize change within complex structures such as modern research universities. Organizational catalysts occupy a position at the convergence of different domains and levels of activity. They have the mandate to connect information, ideas, and individuals and thereby solve problems and enable change. The diversity provost exemplifies this role as a conceptualizer, planner, coordinator, convener, and mobilizer of the institutional transformation process. She also reproduces this organizational catalyst role in many different locations within the university. This section explores the features of the role that seem crucial to its effectiveness.

INSTITUTIONAL POSITION: THE IMPORTANCE OF BOUNDARY-SPANNING. A key feature of the organizational catalyst role is its institutional location at the intersection of many different spheres of activity. The diversity provost works on the individual, group, and system levels. Her office draws authority from faculty participation but is located inside the university's central administrative structure. the vice provost is thus accountable to both the faculty and to the provost and president. She operates outside bureaucratic lines of authority but is strategically positioned within the provost's office, the administrative office bearing responsibility and authority for faculty. Her office is centrally located, but collaborates with many departments and schools. This position enables the diversity provost to draw together the diverse expertise and knowledge of people in different locations within the university to solve common problems and to equip them to bring the results of this work back into their day-to-day environment. This role thus creates a new space for innovation and problem solving that can improve mainstream practices within departments and schools. The university-wide initiative to help departments conduct more effective and inclusive searches is a good example.

At Columbia, the organizational catalyst's location in the provost's office affords her access to key points of power and knowledge within the university administration. Several design features of the vice provost's office facilitate the organizational catalyst's performance of this boundary-spanning function. The position does not itself have particular governance or organizational duties; it places the organizational catalyst at the table for important decisions affecting faculty. The vice provost has regular contact with people in very different positions throughout the university, from the provost to department chairs to faculty to the Office of Institutional Research to Human Resources. Her work brings her in contact with people struggling with similar issues in different departments. The office's dynamism is also sustained by involving multiple constituencies in its work, from high-level administrative to faculty, staff, and students committed to diversifying the university.

This boundary-spanning position enables the office to cut across the bureaucratic silos that typically constrain innovation. This position at the nodal point of multiple systems provides a vantage point for observing patterns and bringing that knowledge to bear on particular problems. The diversity provost's work as troubleshooter provides her with informal knowledge about the breakdowns or bottlenecks affecting women and people of color in particular departments. For example, a number of untenured faculty members who lack senior mentors in their departments have come to the vice provost for help. Many from the professional schools in particular have reported that they have never received information about the tenure process or tenure standards. These reports have led the vice provost to initiate faculty development programs focused in the first instance on getting every school to disseminate accurate and complete information about tenure to all untenured faculty. She learns about problems stemming from ineffective managers, dysfunctional systems, or simple lack of awareness and is in a position to intervene at the appropriate level within the university. This work produces cultural and institutional knowledge that organizational catalysts draw on in spotting patterns, analyzing dynamics, and enlisting participation of relevant actors. Her work over time and across different departments also provides information about overarching problems that require coordinated or centralized interventions. All over the university, for example, those in charge of searches have reported to the vice provost that the inability to place partners causes searches to fail and creates enormous frustration.

In addressing the problems brought to her attention, the vice provost can bring together the individuals from different institutional locations who otherwise would not connect and whose participation is necessary to address cross-cutting problems, such as lack of child care or partner-placement challenges. She can also focus this interaction on recurring problems and effective strategies for addressing them. This insider/outsider status enables the organizational catalyst to capitalize on the opportunities for change, to inject diversity considerations into ongoing decision making and long-term planning, and to bring together the mix of people needed to produce concrete results.

LEVERAGING LEGITIMACY. As an organizational catalyst, the diversity provost occupies a hybrid role, one that requires knowledge, legitimacy, and social capital to get powerful people to the table, include relevant constituencies in decisions, and allow the diversity initiative to influence their practices. Organizational catalysts must also be able to instill hope and trust in groups that have become skeptical about the possibility of change. The legitimacy of diversity as a goal must itself be continually reestablished as part of the change process, often by a spokesperson with sufficient credibility and status to be taken seriously. The role requires a person of sufficient knowledge, expertise, skill, and gravitas to work effectively with a wide range of constituencies.

The background and qualifications possessed by the role's occupants play a critical role in equipping them to perform the position's multiple functions. It was crucial to the initial mobilizing group to appoint a highly respected academic with strong scholarly values, administrative ability, and a demonstrated commitment to advancing women and people of color. The formal attributes of the position—title, level, reporting lines, staff, and resources— also play a role in defining its stature and influence. The credibility of the office was enhanced by Jean Howard's position as a senior member of the faculty, with the title of vice provost reporting directly to the provost and president. Her ability to marshal substantial financial support ($15 million) for the diversity hiring initiative further underscored the significance of the diversity initiative and the vice-provost's gravitas as a player in university decision making. The position's status and institutional support also play a signaling function; they communicate a view of the office's significance to the community within which it operates.

The diversity provost's continuing legitimacy depends on her ability to keep diversity on the agenda and to get things done. The success of the hiring initiative in its first year, for example, motivated more departments to work closely with the diversity office to identify and recruit outstanding candidates. The creation of the HERC has given departments hope that they will get genuine help with their dual-career problems. The working group and vice provost maintain a focus on intellectual and empirical rigor in all of their proposals or recommendations. As one faculty member put it, scientists (and most people) are "people who are used to having their minds changed by data." The vice provost's office based its presentations and proposals on current research from peer-reviewed articles and peer institutions. Many of those interviewed also linked the office's legitimacy to its ability to cut through red tape and solve problems that affect faculty generally as part of the process of advancing the participation of women and people of color. Howard has commented that if you can solve a "smaller problem" for a chair or other faculty member, you open up a line of communication that makes them amenable to your message.

"Columbia has a [reputation] where everyone thinks it doesn't work," said one faculty member. When people see concrete results, they sit up and take notice.

ORGANIZING WORK AROUND PROJECTS AND PROBLEM SOLVING. The work of the diversity provost depends upon the willing participation of busy people who already spend considerable time in meetings. It also depends on the capacity to sustain a focus on diversity in many different arenas and to cut through bureaucratic barriers to produce effective outcomes. A project orientation has proven helpful in meeting both of these requirements. The diversity provost provides an overarching conceptual framework for the diversity initiative, one that connects an understanding of the culturally and institutionally rooted dimensions of the problem to programmatic intervention, system design, and institutional change. This conceptual orientation prompts actors to think about their efforts in relation to each other and to larger goals and analyses. The office defines projects that respond to identified problems in order to achieve specified and measurable results.

The diversity provost thus organizes work around solving the problems that pose barriers to diversifying the faculty. Many barriers to diversity also affect a department's effectiveness in other core areas, including recruitment, hiring, promotion, retention, faculty mentoring, and interdisciplinary collaboration. The diversity initiative reveals how gender and racial equity connect to core institutional concerns and at the same time preserves diversity as a distinct analytical and normative category. This strategy explicitly links diversity goals to the broader normative frame of advancing academic inquiry and achievement. It encourages exploration of how advancing women and people of color can improve the quality and dynamism of the overall academic enterprise. For example, the emphasis on improving searches was in part motivated by a desire to bring more women and underrepresented minorities into our recruitment pools, but it has infused the recruitment process more generally with energy, rigor, and creativity. A problem orientation enables the diversity work to address core faculty concerns. It focuses energy on addressing underlying institutional limitations that must be remedied to achieve diversity but that benefit a much broader constituency. Often, gender and racial inclusion cannot occur without changing governance structures generally, which in turn benefits the overall institution. As Jean Howard has put it, "Everything that is good for the faculty in general can come from the diversity effort." What is good for the careers of women and faculty of color ends up improving the broader academic community.

The diversity provost's problem orientation also leads her to focus her efforts where the energy and momentum for change exist. These successes provide evidence that change can happen, which then provides a new basis for mobilizing hope and accountability in new locations. Success also puts pressure on other departments to follow suit. This project-oriented approach creates occasions and incentives for people in positions of responsibility to act and for people who care about diversity to press for change. It maintains the institution's focus on diversity as part of its core mission. The diversity provost thus keeps diversity issues on the front burner and puts together workable solutions, making it harder not to take action. As one faculty member has said, "Our job is to hold the institution's feet to the fire" and make sure that change gets institutionalized.

Organizational catalysts thus put issues affecting diversity and equity on the agenda. They help create multiple constituencies for change—constituencies who otherwise would not see their interests as overlapping. They frame issues so that faculty concerned about the quality of the graduate student experience and about faculty retention join with those concerned about the climate for women and people of color to push for change. They arrange meetings with high-level administrators so that they can hear the arguments from influential faculty members together with advocates for improving the institution's involvement of women and people of color. They use the evidence from the data to demonstrate the existence of the problem and construct a case for action. They use their social capital and that of others whom they have brought into the process to make it more costly to do nothing. Perhaps most importantly, the organizational catalysts help figure out what to do, and then they do the legwork to maintain the momentum so that these proposed changes actually occur.

REPRODUCING ORGANIZATIONAL CATALYSTS. The diversity provost is not the only organizational catalyst at Columbia. In fact, a crucial part of the Columbia strategy involves identifying individuals with the capacity to act as organizational catalysts within their own domain, then equipping them with the resources, access, and skills to perform this function. For example, in the School of Dentistry, Dennis Mitchell had been very effectively functioning as both a faculty member and associate dean in the Office of Diversity. He had markedly improved the dental school's track record in recruiting minority students. Because of his effectiveness in this role, the vice provost invited him to cochair the Professional Schools Diversity Council and to expand his purview to encompass faculty diversity initiatives. His knowledge of the medical sciences campus, which includes the schools of medicine, dentistry, nursing and public health, has enabled him to generate initiatives appropriate to those contexts and to translate initiatives developed for arts and sciences into the professional school environment. Other members of the Diversity Councils were also selected because of their promise as organizational catalysts within their own domains. The organizational catalyst role has been developed at the local level through newly created diversity positions, such as in the engineering school and the medical school. These individuals exercise everyday leadership at key pivot points that define access and participation. The architecture of the diversity initiative increases the number of these pivot points and decreases the risk of taking action. These structural innovations sustain the conditions permitting activism to flourish and leadership to emerge (Meyerson 2001; Katzenstein 1990).

Using Data to Mobilize Action

Data is crucial to an effective change process. Information can be used to signal that there is a problem, to document the problem, and to mobilize efforts to address the problem. However, experience has shown that information alone does not produce significant change. It must be connected to decision makers and leverage points for it to produce meaningful change and accountability. Information's potential to solve problems depends on its integration into a larger practice of institutional transformation.

The diversity initiative's use of information grew out of an understanding of key challenges that must be met for data to promote effective change. One challenge involved getting the right information, rather than information that the university collected only for compliance purposes. It was important to understand not only the extent of problems but also the reasons they persisted and the leverage points for change. A second challenge involved getting valid and reliable information. Studies relying on erroneous data would undermine the credibility of the office. Third, information had to be communicated in a form that would be persuasive to the relevant communities. This meant having the capacity to present information of different types and in different forms and through messengers who spoke the language of particular academic communities. Finally, effective use of information required communicating that information to those in a position to act at a point when it could actually influence decision making.

Three key strategies emerge from an analysis of the initiative's response to these information challenges: mobilizing different forms of knowledge, connecting knowledge to power and context, and overcoming barriers to effective data gathering.

MOBILIZING DIFFERENT FORMS OF KNOWLEDGE. Information gathering grows out of and informs the initiative's programmatic work. The diversity initiative develops the varied kinds of data needed to address particular problems and pursue programmatic goals, then develops varied forms of knowledge calibrated to addressing those concerns. The role of information in reforming search and hiring processes is illustrative. The provost's office now puts together data documenting recruitment, hiring, and promotion patterns within particular departments and schools. The office also gathers data on the pools from which particular departments recruit faculty, and comparability data with peer institutions. This kind of demographic data often initiates participation by faculty and administrators in a change process. Academics pay attention to quantitative data revealing patterns of underparticipation in particular departments, comparing those patterns to the pool from which departments actually recruit and providing comparability data with peer institutions. Indeed, this kind of information jump-started the diversity initiative itself; the president and provost did not realize the extent of underparticipation until they saw the Pipeline Report. This realization catalyzed an already sympathetic administration into taking action.

Understanding the scope of the problem is only the first step. Faculty and administrators often throw up their hands in frustration; they simply do not know why these patterns persist or, more importantly, what they can do to change them. The diversity initiative developed a strategy to bring the demographic data to the faculty's attention and simultaneously to respond to their "why" and "how" questions. The diversity provost first gathered the best available research on the dynamics producing underparticipation. This research included studies linking underparticipation to cognitive bias, informal professional networks, poorly structured search, recruitment, and hiring practices, and inadequate mentoring practices. As described earlier in the chapter, the provost's office, working in collaboration with Columbia's NSF ADVANCE project, also gathered information about best practices for addressing these problems. Building on the approach used by the University of Michigan STRIDE program, Jean Howard enlisted the efforts of highly respected faculty members within particular schools to put together presentations tailored to the culture of their departments (Stewart et al. 2006; Sturm 2006).

These dinners illustrate a more general approach of combining self-analysis, academic studies, and best-practices research to develop a comprehensive diagnosis and change strategy. The diversity provost often uses task forces chaired by faculty members with appropriate expertise to perform this information-gathering role. The search committee task force, chaired by a faculty member with expertise in university change initiatives, did so for search practices. The partner placement task force, chaired by a faculty member with expertise in gender and family law, conducted the research on dual-career hiring. When outside researchers were better equipped to conduct this research, as in the area of child care, Jean Howard arranged for a consultant to conduct the necessary study. In each case, the resulting information guided the development of programmatic responses. It also enlisted the support of key allies, mobilized constituencies for change, and provided powerful persuasive tools for taking action.

Informal and cultural information also plays a significant role in the change process. Jean Howard's role as a trusted faculty member gives her access to informal interactions with faculty from which line administrators might be shut out. Perhaps the most important kind of informal information involves identifying the movers and shakers within any particular department. Her success depends upon developing successful working relationships with those in a position to address specific kinds of problems in specific locations, and finding the right people to involve as partners. Sometimes the most obvious person, such as the one with the formal title, is not the person who has influence within his or her environment or who will actually get things done. Many of those interviewed commented on the importance of Jean Howard's skill in analyzing "who might be the people in different spaces of the university who were key."

CONNECTING KNOWLEDGE TO POWER AND CONTEXT. Information has its maximum impact when it flows to those in a position to take action, at a time when they must act, and in a form that they respect. The diversity initiative thus targets pivot points of decision making and key decision makers as focal points for information sharing. Data on search processes is, where possible, shared with active search committees and their chairs. Influential departments with open slots receive considerable attention. Meetings with department leaders are used as opportunities to communicate information, discuss goals, and establish time frames for taking action. Where possible, information about search processes automatically goes to committee chairs as part of the hiring process. They are required to report on the outcome of searches. This strategy builds information accountability into the doing of the work.

Form and context also figure into the initiative's information strategy. The office now calibrates the style of presentation to the culture and currency of particular disciplines and departments. Where possible, the diversity provost mobilizes groups with power and commitment to communicate information effectively and create accountability. This strategy is evident in the diversity dinners, where influential faculty members publicly present carefully researched information documenting problems and possible solutions and present them in the form most suited to their constituency. The diversity provost is continually leveraging the advisory committee members' intellectual, moral, and personal authority in the locations where they can have maximum impact.

OVERCOMING BARRIERS TO EFFECTIVE DATA GATHERING. The group mobilizing the diversity initiative recognized from the outset that long-term success required dramatic improvements in the capacity to generate reliable data in a timely fashion. One of their stated priorities in structuring the initiative was to design a process that would "assure that Columbia's data systems, as a matter of routine, gather, update, and make available usable information needed to identify, analyze, and act on the gender and racial demographics and dynamics of the university." Howard tackled this problem by connecting her office's data-gathering efforts with those of the Office of Institutional Research and the Office of Equal Opportunity and Affirmative Action. Her office acquired dedicated time from the Office of Institutional Research and worked with an analyst with specific expertise in the data systems the university uses. All three offices are now working together to streamline the data gathering process, avoid redundancy, and increase the availability of information about recruitment, selection, hiring, promotion, and retention. For example, working together, the vice provost, the head of the Office of Institutional Research and the head of the affirmative action office have begun systematic salary equity reports for all parts of the university.

The diversity provost now has the capability to respond to requests for information as they come in. These requests are both internally and externally generated; the office can respond to queries from department chairs and deans looking for information about their own departments or schools, and it can generate information identified as necessary from inside the initiative. The office has also learned how to use the process of assuring accuracy to mobilize action. For example, one department responded to her office's data about its hiring patterns with disbelief: "This can't be right." In response, Howard sent the department the name of every faculty member on the department's rosters for the last ten years so that any errors or omissions could be corrected. After checking the names, the department's leadership realized that the numbers were in fact accurate. At that point, the response mirrored that of the president when he learned about the Pipeline data: "Oh my God, it is right. Things are worse than I thought!"

Sustaining Change Networks through Distributing Leadership

Top-down strategies alone will not diversify faculties. Research has shown that underparticipation results from everyday interactions across the entire spectrum of faculty life, involving decision makers at every level of the university (Valian 1999; Etzkowitz et al. 2000). Universities are highly decentralized institutions; this fragmented authority structure limits the power of any one level or actor to achieve change (Sturm 2006). Sustained institutional change requires both bottom-up and top-down mobilization. The Columbia initiative has developed a strategy for achieving both by identifying and empowering formal and informal leaders who are part of larger networks and in a position to solve problems. The diversity provost's office uses central resources to strengthen the role of local leaders. It leverages its own committees and task forces to provide an infrastructure for the development of formal and informal diversity leadership distributed around the university. It works to sustain activism by enlisting existing networks, such as the institutes on gender and race, the Earth Institute's ADVANCE program, and the Commission on the Status of Women. An institute leader described the synergies resulting from this collaboration:

> I like to think our work feeds into Jean's work. Her work is definitely the umbrella to ours, and her work provides legitimacy for our work . . . the departments quickly realize that we know what Jean thinks, and what she wants. And so to get this new hire that they're trying to finagle they'll come to us usually to try to help them write the proposal to Jean.

One form of this network and leadership development involves finding unlikely allies among people in positions of power who are persuaded by the data and willing to harness their intellectual and social capital to the effort. So, for example, the chair of the economics department has become an important ally and supporter of the initiative through his work with the vice provost. He participated in the team that presented to various departments at diversity dinners. He played a critical role in the economics department's success in hiring women and has been a powerful spokesperson for diversity to other department chairs. The initiative's problem orientation has enabled the vice provost to enlist the leadership of faculty and administrators with more broadly defined concerns about improving faculty governance and achieving academic excellence.

The diversity office has also institutionalized informal leadership by including influential faculty on working committees with access to formal power and by placing them in leadership positions on diversity task forces and committees. This diversity work has made it easier for participating faculty members to assume an informal leadership role within their own departments and schools. Routine decisions become occasions for exercising situational leadership. In addition to building capacity and hope, the diversity initiative has multiplied the occasions when people can understand themselves as part of a larger phenomenon and act in accordance with this realization.

As we have already discussed in the section on organizational catalysts, the office has also fostered the creation of local diversity leadership—respected faculty members who are charged with formal responsibility for leading a diversity effort within their department or school. The vice provost's office operates as the "mother ship" creating and supporting homegrown satellite offices. This dynamic interaction between the local and the center helps sustain the momentum in each location. It also maintains involvement in the face of the inevitable obstacles and failures that could easily derail isolated efforts. Through distributing leadership, the diversity initiative helps create multiple constituencies for change.

Conclusion

The diversity provost role holds considerable promise as a strategy for developing organizational catalysts, connecting information to power, and mobilizing distributed leadership. Many universities have created new administrative positions with responsibilities similar to that of the vice provost for diversity initiatives at Columbia. Indeed, there is even a new national association of diversity provosts.

There are, however, risks attached to relying upon a permanent organizational position as a change strategy. First, there is the risk of role substitution: reliance on an institutional position in lieu of a institutional change process. Some institutions appear to have created a high-level position to spearhead a change process without supporting the institutional self-study, faculty mobilization, and strategic planning so crucial to the role's effectiveness. These initiatives may also fail to incorporate monitoring and external accountability into the role's operation.

Second, there is the risk of overcentralization. The position could foster the expectation that the responsibility for change lies primarily with this administrative official. The occupant of the role might also be tempted to use a top-down strategy relying on formal administrative authority and access to push through policy changes. This approach would undercut the development of shared responsibility for change and induce passivity by faculty and administrators whose active participation is necessary for cultural and systemic change. Overcentralization also encourages deference to administrative decisions and limits the capacity of faculty to hold the organizational catalyst accountable for her actions. Centralization of responsibility in a single individual also renders the change initiative vulnerable if the occupant of the position were to leave. The organizational catalyst role can be structured to minimize these risks by allocating responsibilities among different people, creating participatory oversight by groups in a position to evaluate the work of the office, and requiring ongoing public reporting on the office's activities and impact.

Finally, there is the risk of bureaucratization. Part of what makes the organizational catalyst role work is its fluidity and experimental character. The diversity provost at Columbia is constantly reinventing the office to respond to changes in the environment. If the position becomes too directly intertwined with the central administration, it risks losing its independence, its openness to adaptation, and, ultimately, its legitimacy. If the position's occupants become full-time administrators for too long, they might lose scholarly credibility and access to local knowledge and thus also lose the social capital so crucial to the role's effectiveness. Over time, the role could become routinized and divorced from a change process with adequate resources and connections to constituencies for change, and at worst, devolve into a symbolic or toothless position. An unlimited term in an administrative position may also blunt the sense of urgency and drive that occupants bring to the role. The relentless questioning of the status quo, which seems so crucial to the position's impact, may be difficult for one person to sustain over the long run, especially without a break. For this reason, the diversity provost's position at Columbia carries a three-year term limit.

The challenge is to define a long-term role that institutionalizes the experimental qualities of the organizational catalyst. The role's effectiveness depends upon cultivating the qualities that make organizational catalysts effective: professional legitimacy, insider/outsider status, operation at the intersection of multiple systems, evidence-based decision making, deep knowledge of relevant contexts, and external accountability. This essentially poses an institutional design problem. The position can be structured to build in collaboration with diverse constituencies. Checks against cooptation and bureaucratization can be achieved by establishing rotating and shared positions, which might also make it easier to recruit high-status faculty role for these roles. It is also important that these roles maintain independence from the central administration as well as accountability to constituencies committed to gender and racial equity, including peer institutions involved in similar work.

We cannot know now whether the dynamism currently evident in the Columbia diversity initiative will survive the test of time. We do know that we have learned enduring lessons about the importance of linking mobilization to power.

REFERENCES

Ely, Robin, and Debra Meyerson. 2000. "Theories of Gender in Organizations: A New Approach to Organizational Analysis and Change." *Research in Organizational Behavior* 22: 103.

Etzkowitz, H., C., M. Kemelgor, and B. Uzzi. 2000. *Athena Unbound: The Advancement of Women in Science and Technology.* New York: Cambridge University Press.

Fiske, S.T. 2004. "Intent and Ordinary Bias: Unintended Thought and Social Motivation Create Casual Prejudice." *Social Justice Research* 17 (2): 117–127.

Katzenstein, Mary Fainsod. 1990. "Feminism within American Institutions: Unobtrusive Mobilization in the 1980's." *Signs* 16: 27

Meyerson, Debra E. 2001. *Tempered Radicals: How People Use Difference to Inspire Change at Work.* Cambridge, MA: Harvard Business School Press.

Massachusetts Institute of Technology. 1999. A Study on the Status of Women Faculty in Science at MIT. http://web/mit/edu/fnl/women//women.html 10–11.

Stewart, Abigail J., Janet E. Malley, and Danielle La Vaque-Manty. 2007. "Faculty Recruitment: Mobilizing Science and Engineering Faculty." In *Transforming Science and*

Engineering: Advancing Academic Women, ed. Abigail J. Stewart, Janet E. Malley, and Danielle La Vaque-Manty.

Sturm, Susan. 2001. "Second Generation Employment Discrimination: A Structural Approach." *Columbia Law Review* 101: 458, 460.

———. 2006. "The Architecture of Inclusion: Advancing Workplace Equity in Higher Education." *Harvard Journal of Law and Gender* 29: 247.

———. 2007. "Gender Equity As Institutional Transformation: The Pivotal Role of "Organizational Catalysts." In *Transforming Science and Engineering: Advancing Academic Women*, ed. Abigail J. Stewart, Janet E. Malley, and Danielle La Vacque-Manty.

Trower, Cathy. 2004. "Advancing and Evaluating Impact." Paper presented at National Science Foundation ADVANCE National Conference, April 20. http:// www. advance.gatech.edu/2004conf/3a_trower.ppt.

Valian, V. 1999. *Why So Slow? The Advancement of Women*. Cambridge, Massachusetts: MIT Press.

AFTERWORD

Faculty as Change Agents Redux—Reflections on My Academic Life

MARY S. HARTMAN

When I entered South Side High School in Fort Wayne, Indiana, in 1955, I wanted to be a stewardess when I grew up. The same was true, I have discovered over the years, of lots of teenage girls of my generation. (This had nothing to do, believe me, with Freudian-tinged fantasies of sex and flying, but everything to do with young women's shared fantasies of escape in the 1950s.) By the time I entered a small liberal arts college in Pennsylvania four years later, I had changed my mind and decided to become a French teacher. In the middle of my junior year in college, I gave up that idea, too, largely because a fascination with European history had somehow taken hold of me.

It made a difference that one of my favorite professors, a man (I recall being taught by just two women in my undergraduate years, and none in graduate school), told me I ought to consider college-level teaching. He urged me to apply for a Woodrow Wilson Fellowship, which I did. Without it, I don't think I would have given myself permission to go to graduate school. But I got the fellowship, and took it to Columbia University. I might have applied to Princeton, where my then boyfriend—now husband of forty-plus years—ended up. But Princeton was not accepting women in those days.

My master's adviser at Columbia, Rudolph Binion, a superb European intellectual historian, was a fine and open-minded mentor to women students. That a bunch of us in his seminars later became historians of women was probably no accident, even though the now-huge field of women's history did not yet exist in the mid-1960s when we were there. It was disconcerting after that welcome experience to be told the next year by my new adviser, upon admission to the doctoral program where I specialized in European political history, that since we few women had been given places that rightfully belonged to men, we would be under special scrutiny. Truth to tell, I am more irritated by that admonition now than I was at the time, when my women friends and I took it for granted that we were all winging it in men's spaces. Besides, my adviser turned out to be a decent person. I will always be grateful for his help in getting me a job at Douglass, the women's college at Rutgers. Before I received the Douglass offer, however, I got a rejection letter from Rider College that caught my attention. Rider, I was informed by the department chair, was "looking for a man." I would like to say I was really upset about that letter, but I was not. I did, though, have the sense to save it.

My introduction to Douglass was mostly positive, similar in many ways to that reported by my friend and distinguished colleague on this project Cheryl Wall, who joined the Douglass English faculty a few years later. Like her, I welcomed the gift of so many women colleagues, without appreciating its rarity. True, I was brought up short early on when a male colleague teasingly inquired whether I had been recruited at the local Princeton A&P. I did not get the joke—a standing one among our male faculty then—that most women teaching at Douglass were "Princeton housewives." Rutgers College, the larger men's school (six thousand students versus two thousand at Douglass), meanwhile had very few women on its faculty in the 1960s. By 1973, although the university as a whole had 27 percent women faculty on three campuses, nearly half of those faculty members were at Douglass.

In my own case, the senior woman who mattered most to me was the formidable Margaret Judson, a great English constitutional scholar who had retired by the time I arrived but who made it her business to support the younger women. Margaret had chaired the department, served as acting dean of Douglass, and helped to crack the Rutgers College history department's monopoly on graduate teaching. She regularly took me to lunch in those early days and asked me hard questions about my work. I realized with a certain headiness that she was taking me seriously as a scholar, which enabled me to take *myself* more seriously. After I reported that I had passed my PhD orals, she insisted that I celebrate by joining the Berkshire Conference of Women Historians, a group founded in the late 1920s by women who taught mostly at women's colleges in the Northeast. Formally excluded from retreats at Lake Placid set up by male members of the American Historical Association, these women began holding annual spring retreats of their own. An uptight would-be professional, I first envisioned these gatherings as an anachronism, although I soon recognized the Berks as a lifeline—a critical mass of smart, sympathetic historians of all ages who gathered yearly to share their work, enjoy each other's company, help advance women in the academy, and go for walks in the woods.

Margaret, who had graduated from Mt. Holyoke in 1922 and had a PhD from Radcliffe, was a bit of a grande dame, and hated whiners. She was visibly annoyed by tales of sexism that we, her young recruits, animatedly shared en route to those spring meetings in the Berkshires in the early 1970s. Only rarely, usually over a Scotch, would she offer glimpses of her own challenges as a woman scholar. I recall one tale of a famous Harvard historian who, when Margaret knocked on his office door to request a reading list for her predoctoral orals, slammed the door in her face after he opened it, announcing he had nothing to do with women students. She also recounted more routine indignities. Although in the 1930s she was allowed to do research in the Harvard Law Library, she was told she had to use the back entrance. Our own tales of sexism paled next to hers, and we wanted to hear more. Once, though, when I invited her to share other horror stories, she looked at me with some exasperation and said, "Mary, it was the depression. I earned a PhD, and was lucky enough to have a job. Others weren't so lucky." That shut me up.

Aside from four women in history, the female colleagues I first got to know were in English and political science. This was because our three departments of fifteen to twenty each were all housed in a then new, ugly, six-story building, named for a beloved historian and world peace activist called Emily Hickman. We joked later that our interdisciplinary women's studies program was created in the elevators of Hickman Hall.

The late sixties and early seventies were heady times on campus, with successful demonstrations for admission of more black students and for a new Africana studies department, as well as regular antiwar demonstrations. After the Cambodian invasion in 1970, I recall hastily compiling a page-long history of Southeast Asia for our demonstrating students and cranking it out on our aging ditto machine in aromatic purple ink. In a more localized drama, the Rutgers College faculty voted almost unanimously to admit women in 1968 after Yale did so, thereby generating strong pressure on Douglass to admit men. Early in 1970, events came to a head in an exciting meeting in which the Douglass faculty voted ninety to thirty-two not only to remain single-sex but, with the blessing of our dean, to embrace what our charismatic leader Elaine Showalter—then a junior professor from the English department—later described as a "bold experiment in feminist education." The faculty endorsed courses in women's history, a day care center, a community center for women, new emphasis on women writers and artists, improved career counseling and sexual information, and sponsorship of research on women (Showalter 1993, 1). Although we did not realize it then, this crucial vote enabled Douglass to go on to become a preeminent site for the new scholarship on women, as well as home to half a dozen centers devoted to research, teaching, and outreach to understand women's lives and advance their leadership.

Inspired by this faculty activism, and acutely aware of the inattention to women's experience in my own field of history, I realized that my scholarly interests were shifting. A sympathetic department chair, warning that the tenure clock was ticking, urged me swiftly to take my dissertation, a political biography of a nineteenth-century French parliamentarian, and turn it into a book. Goodness knows I tried; but my heart was already in a new project.

I wanted to see what, if anything, could be learned about the hidden lives of ordinary middle-class English and French women in the nineteenth century by exploring the lives of a dozen or so women from that class about whom we fortuitously had plenty of information, each having been tried for murder.

My sense of the rising interest in women's history was confirmed in spring 1972, when I learned from friends at the annual Berkshire gathering about many others like me who were trying to reinvent themselves as historians of women. With my Douglass colleague Lois Banner, another young scholar who was herself already embarked on work that made her a prominent historian of American women, I summoned the courage to approach the president of the Berkshire Conference to propose that ours was the logical group to sponsor an entire conference on this new research field of women's history. After some deliberation at the business meeting, our idea was approved, and Lois and I were allocated five hundred dollars to organize what became the first Berkshire Conference on the History of Women, held at Douglass in March 1973. Attendance, at about four hundred, was well beyond what we hoped, and the papers we later published as *Clio's Consciousness Raised* (Harper and Row, 1974) featured several young historians who went on to become major figures in the field. The large Berkshire Conferences on the History of Women have since been held every two to three years—at women's colleges until the 1990s, when they began to draw several thousand people. Sites then shifted to larger institutions, including the University of North Carolina (1996) and, most recently, the University of Minnesota (2008). Happily, the smaller New England gatherings of seventy-five or so, now dubbed the "little Berks," carry on as well.

The single downside for me early on was slowed progress on my "tenure book." When the vote came up in 1974–75, my department and later the Douglass promotions committee, aware that my manuscript on the murder-esses was well along, readily supported me. The same did not hold for the New Brunswick–wide meeting of the four college departments, which voted in my favor, but barely, followed by a university-wide meeting of all the New Brunswick, Camden, and Newark history departments, which voted me down. Still, by spring 1975, at the ultimate "summit" committee meeting (I am not making up this parade of meetings), I finally had a book contract in hand, and tenure was recommended. A colleague from Rutgers College had confided meanwhile—"as a friend," he said—that he had voted against me because all the time I chose to put in on the Berks conference signaled to him that I was not that serious about doing real history.

More than thirty years later, in 2007, Cheryl Wall and I, as coprincipal investiga-tors on this research project on faculty-generated initiatives for race and gender equity, were prompted to share our own youthful experiences here as "faculty change agents." We wanted to see how our own careers might illumine or inform what we have learned in these pages from the faculty teams of our dozen institutional partners. Their own varied accounts of the state of racial and gender equity on their twenty-first-century campuses are snapshots of now familiar struggles: to diversify student and faculty bodies; to stress links between a diverse faculty and the generation of new knowledge (and new perspectives on old knowledge); to improve campus climates that are often inhospitable for persons seen as "different"; and to promote positive, lasting change through faculty-administrative collaborations. Good news and bad news emerged from this exercise.

The bad news first. When we met the faculty diversity leaders on the different teams here, we found that too many of them were (how to put this?) too much like us. For one thing, they looked too much like us: they were mostly women—white or African American—with just a handful of men and only a few persons of other racial and ethnic backgrounds. This did not bode well at a time when power at all levels in most of our institutions still resided with people who don't look like us (even though, happily, more of them than ever are now thinking like us on matters of diversity, which is a start).

Just as worrisome, these faculty leaders were, more often than not, our contemporaries. While there were a number of junior faculty members among them, most had begun their "diversity work" decades ago as junior faculty members, and they were still at it. They had followed similar trajectories, often assuming a disproportionate share of committee tasks in diversity-related areas, creating women's or black or ethnic studies programs that campus authorities were hardly clamoring for, working—often overtime and behind the scenes—to recruit or train underrepresented students and/or faculty members and, in due course, often "crossing over" into short- or longer-term administrative posts, albeit typically posts with far less prestige than duties. Like us, too, a fair number of these leaders were now either on the verge of retirement or at least thinking it over. One more thing. Contrary to what you may be imagining by now, these people struck us as uncommonly upbeat and positive. Their strongest concern, it turned out, was that too few younger faculty members were stepping up to take their places. Such cheerfulness about professional careers chockablock with unremunerated service was not bad news, exactly, but the repeated bafflement about the scarcity of young faculty willing to follow their lead struck even Pollyannas like Cheryl and me as odd.

I confess that my own first reaction was "What are they thinking?" But then it dawned on me that Cheryl Wall and I, too, fit their dominant cockeyed-optimist profile, and we knew where the profile came from. Most of us working on this project, after all, shared passions that had been generated decades before by the gains of the civil rights and women's rights movements. This fact is sobering, since those passions had their roots outside the academy, not inside it. Now, after nearly three decades of a nationwide conservative reaction, today's young scholars can hardly be expected to import such passions into the academy, nor can they be expected to display boundless appetites for volunteer labor with no clear payoffs, either in rewards for opening new fields of scholarly inquiry or in creating diverse faculty or student environments. Indeed, given relentless, stepped-up tenure pressures on young faculty members, it would be unconscionable to expect them to take risks with their professional futures that many of our own generation, when the pressures were less intense, were already rash to take. In fact, I am persuaded that one explanation for the upbeat attitudes of so many older faculty on this project is that we see ourselves to this day as "survivors" who might as easily have perished. It is our own expression of Margaret Judson's crisp retort to me: "Others were not so lucky."

So the challenges out there are real. The generation that has, against the odds, successfully led many diversity initiatives in the academy is approaching retirement, and the younger generations, under current conditions at any rate, cannot and should not throw themselves into racial and gender equity projects that remain underfunded, unsung, and marginalized. Schools that would pursue the still incomplete institutionalization of racial and gender equity, or even successfully defend themselves against the forces looking to undo gains already won, must recognize that they can no longer take faculty-generated diversity activity for granted. They need to adopt new approaches and new reward structures.

Having said this, I add that the good news out there is everywhere visible. Women faculty, faculty of color, and their white male allies have so far, to quote a 2007 study,

> transformed the curriculum, and become advocates for newly diverse student bodies. In varying degrees they have humanized overly rigid structures and institution-wide policies, changed institutional missions, expanded static visions and boundaries in traditional disciplines, and transformed scholarly research in every field. Their widespread challenges to the cultures of higher education have revealed that racism, sexism, and homophobia are matters not only of individual negative hostile attitudes but also of structures and practices related to both external and internal factors. (Maher and Thomson Tetrault 2007, 184).[1]

In this project alone, it was heartening to see how an outside focus on their faculty's activities from a project sponsored by a major foundation helped to raise the level of positive institutional awareness, action, and support. For example, the team at the University of Missouri reported that the spotlight on their work provided by the Ford grant helped lead to approval of departmental status for their women's and gender studies program, as well as draw additional grant support for their interactive theater troupe, which is now playing a key role in educating the community about challenges facing senior women faculty in the science fields. At Arizona, meanwhile, data gleaned from this project helped enable the team to secure a prestigious National Science Foundation ADVANCE grant to support women in the sciences. In addition, after a lapse of several years, the Caribbean Literary Studies Program at the University of Miami sponsored a revived summer faculty seminar, *Archeologies of Black Memory*, in 2007.

At Rutgers, a new administration was prompted to act after our faculty team demonstrated that while our student and faculty diversity profiles look good compared to our peers in the selective American Association of Universities, percentages of women faculty and faculty of color have actually either stalled or declined over the past thirty years, as have the percentages of African American and Latino/a students. President McCormick announced a major initiative in September 2007 to make New Jersey's state university more reflective, in both its student and faculty bodies, of the rich racial and ethnic mix in the state as a whole. Our project also led directly to the president's creating an annual awards ceremony honoring faculty engaged in race- and gender-equity efforts. With another partner on the grant, Columbia University, Rutgers will also be the site in 2008 of a major national summit on diversity in higher education.

The University of California at Santa Barbara, already the home of many model diversity programs, lauded the advantages of ties with faculty doing diversity work from other institutions and expressed the hope for longer-range faculty training programs for which the teams from the Rutgers IWL project might form a core group of consultants. The University of Maryland team at the Consortium on Race, Gender and Ethnicity reported that participation in the program helped ease the challenge of passing the torch of leadership to the next generation. At Smith, the college community is now engaged in implementing some of the recommendations presented in the Smith chapter of this book. And at Spelman, follow-up projects are being pursued, including new Diversity Dialogues that continue to expand an understanding of what intraracial diversity, highlighted in their study here, might mean.

Columbia University, as well, reports that working on the Ford project allowed the large working groups from the university's various diversity efforts to become, in the words of team member and English professor Jean Howard, "more self-conscious about the architecture of our joint efforts, and to pay more attention to the points where pressure might be applied to produce change or support individuals positioned to act as change agents." In sum, says Professor Howard, "the model of moving forward on specific diversity initiatives with the advice and support of faculty committees and faculty leadership, is alive and well at Columbia."

While welcoming this and more good news, I nonetheless conclude these remarks on a cautionary note. The studies of our twelve teams, while offering much to celebrate, make it clear that the achievements they describe remain fragile. The new curricula and centers and recruitment initiatives, fueled by faculty energies, now depend for their survival upon institutional leaders who recognize their value, even in times of budget constraint, and make them priorities. Top administrators must move these efforts forward by institution-alizing mechanisms that work, including systematic planning with faculty leaders, ongoing discussion about the advantages of diversity at all levels, financial incentives for recruitment, accommodations for the needs of fami-lies, and guarantees that faculty are rewarded not just for their individual con-tributions but for their participation in transforming institutions.[2] Our students, who are our future, deserve no less.

NOTES

1. Portions of this commentary have been adapted from a review I wrote for *SIGNS: A Journal of Culture and Society*, vol. 33, no.3 (Spring 2008): 739–742.
2. These items paraphrase the conclusions of Tetrault and Maher in their studies of Rut-gers, Newark, Stanford, and the University of Michigan.

REFERENCES

Maher, Frances A. and Mary Kay Thomson Tetrault. 2007. *Privilege and Diversity in the Acad-emy.* Oxford and New York: Routledge Press, 184.
Showalter, Elaine. 1993. "Only the Conception: Becoming a Feminist Critic." *The Douglass Alumnae Bulletin* (Summer): 1.

CONTRIBUTORS

MARTHA ACKELSBERG, professor of government and of the study of women and gender, Smith College.

BARBARA BALLIET, associate professor of women and gender studies, Rutgers University.

ALMA JEAN BILLINGSLEA-BROWN, associate professor of English, Spelman College.

JOSEPHINE BRADLEY, associate professor of African American/Africana women's studies, Clark Atlanta University.

LINDY BRIGHAM, coordinator of professional science master's degree program—applied biosciences, University of Arizona.

WINNIFRED R. BROWN-GLAUDE, assistant professor in the department of African American Studies at the College of New Jersey.

JOSEPH CASTRO, associate vice chancellor for student academic affairs, University of California–San Francisco.

DEBORAH COOK, associate professor of biological sciences, Clark Atlanta University.

DANNIELLE JOY DAVIS, assistant professor of educational leadership and policy studies, University of Texas at Arlington.

BONNIE THORNTON DILL, professor and chair of women's studies, University of Maryland.

SARAH FENSTERMAKER, professor of sociology, University of California–Santa Barbara.

EMMA FREUDENBERGER, doctoral student of Law, Columbia University.

GERTRUDE JAMES GONZALEZ DE ALLEN, assistant professor of philosophy, Spelman College.

MARY K. GOOD, doctoral student of anthropology, University of Arizona.

MARGARET GROGAN, professor of educational leadership, University of Missouri–Columbia.

DEBRA GUCKENHEIMER, doctoral student of sociology, University of California–Santa Barbara.

SHARON HARLEY, associate professor and acting chair of African American studies, University of Maryland.

JENI HART, assistant professor of educational leadership and policy analysis, University of Missouri–Columbia.

MARY S. HARTMAN, professor of history and director of the Institute for Women's Leadership, Rutgers University.

MARY HAWKESWORTH, professor and chair of women's and gender studies and senior scholar at the Center for American Women and Politics at Rutgers University of Politics, Rutgers University.

LISA HETFIELD, associate director, Institute for Women's Leadership, Rutgers University.

JEAN E. HOWARD, George Delacorte Professor in the Humanities and past vice provost for diversity initiatives, Columbia University.

EDDIE JAUREGUI, doctoral student of law, Columbia University.

JACKIE LITT, associate professor of women and gender studies, University of Missouri–Columbia.

DEIDRE MCDONALD, instructor, Division of Communication Arts, Clark Atlanta University.

AMY MCLAUGHLIN, assistant director, Consortium on Race, Gender and Ethnicity, University of Maryland.

NAOMI J. MILLER, director of institutional diversity and professor of English and of the Study of women and gender, Smith College.

BARBARA J. MILLS, professor of anthropology, University of Arizona.

JOHN MOHR, professor of sociology, University of California–Santa Barbara.

JANICE MONK, professor of geography and regional development, University of Arizona.

JENNIFER MORGAN, associate professor of social and cultural analysis, New York University.

SARAH NORTH, associate professor of computer and information science, Clark Atlanta University.

SANDRA POUCHET PAQUET, professor of English, University of Miami.

KATE QUEENEY, associate professor of chemistry, Smith College.

DEBORAH ROSENFELT, professor of women's studies, University of Maryland.

PATRICIA JOAN SAUNDERS, assistant professor of English, University of Miami.

PEG BOYLE SINGLE, research associate professor of education, University of Vermont.

SUSAN STURM, George M. Jaffin Professor of Law and Social Responsibility, Columbia University Law School.

SUSAN VAN DYNE, professor of the study of women and gender, Smith College.

CHERYL A. WALL, Board of Governors Professor of English, Rutgers University.

MARTHA S. WEST, professor of law, University of California–Davis.

ROGER WORTHINGTON, assistant to the deputy chancellor, chief diversity officer and associate professor of counseling psychology, University of Missouri–Columbia.

INDEX

AASD. *See* African American Studies Department (AASD) (UM)

Abrams, Philip, 218

academically based enrichment programs, 185

Academic Personnel Manual (UCSB), 226

activism, 9, 35, 105; ADW and, 49; at HBCUs, 109–116; leadership and, 271–272; mentoring as, 240–244; professionalized, 179–180; at UCSB, 221; Unity and, 74–75

administration involvement, 98

ADVANCE grant, 107–108, 109; for women STEM faculty at Columbia, 254

advocates, 100

ADW. *See* African Diaspora and the World, The (ADW)

affirmative action, 3–6, 185–186; *Gratz v. Bollinger* and, 251, 252; MIT and, 104; Proposition 209 and, 209–210; Rutgers and, 140, 141, 144, 145, 146; UC and, 120–121, 124, 126; UCSB and, 212, 217; UVM and, 245

"Affirmative Action Guidelines on Recruitment and Retention of Faculty" (UCOP), 127

African Americans, 44; on HBCU faculty, 108; at MU, 61, 106; at Rutgers, 141, 142; women, 29, 41–42, 114

African American Studies Department (AASD) (UM), 22–23, 26–27, 29, 30, 31

African Diaspora and the World, The (ADW) (Spelman), 10, 39, 40, 43, 48–53, 57; transnational diversity work and, 46

Afro-American Woman: Struggles and Images, The (Harley and Terborg-Penn), 29

Agents of Change study (UA), 170, 181

Aiyejina, Funso, 194–195

ALANA (African Americans, Latino/as, Asian Americans, and Native Americans) (UVM acronym), 232

Alexander-Snow, M., 34

Allen, Walter, 106

Alliance for Graduate Education Program (AGEP), 217, 227

American Apartheid (Massey and Denton), 5

American Association of University Professors (AAUP), 4

Andrews, Mike, 188

Anthurium: a Caribbean Studies Journal, 196, 201

antiwar demonstrations, 279

Antoni, Robert, 187–188

Appelbaum, Eileen, 161

Archaeologies of Black Memory (UMiami seminar), 283

Arizona Board of Regents (ABOR), 167

Asian Americans, 6; at Rutgers, 140, 141, 143

Asian studies, 39, 48, 55, 57

assimilation, 45

Association for the Study of the Worldwide African Diaspora (ASWAD), 53

Association for Women Faculty (AWF) (UA), 166, 169, 172–173

Association of American Universities (AAU), 137, 210

Atkinson, Richard, 119, 127, 128, 129, 132

Atlanta UNCF Mellon-Mays conference, 57

Atlanta University Center, 57, 107

attitude, 111

Auslander, Edith, 168

AWF. *See* Association for Women Faculty (AWF) (UA)

Baez, B., 27, 63, 180

Banks, W., 34

Banneker Scholarship Program for African Americans, 19, 29

Banner, Lois, 280

Bar Ilan University (Israel), 24

Barry, Jeff, 196, 201

Bazin, Nancy, 154

Benitez-Rojo, Antonio, 199

Bennett, Gwendolyn, 51

Berkshire Conference of Women Historians, 278, 280

Bernstein, Michael, 129

Bielby, William, 125–126

Binion, Rudolph, 277

Bird, S., 180

Birgeneau, Robert, 133

blackness, 44

black students, 61, 106

black women, 29; activism of, 114; difference and, 41–42. *See also* Spelman College